D0803555

How to Read the Bible

The publication of this book was
made possible by a gift from

The Krancer and Twing families

In loving memory of

Anne Oxler Krancer

How to Read the Bible

Marc Zvi Brettler

5766 • 2005
The Jewish Publication Society
Philadelphia

The Jewish Publication Society
2100 Arch Street, 2nd floor
Philadelphia, PA 19103

Composition by Pageworks
Design by Pageworks

Manufactured in the United States of America

05 06 07 08 09 10   10 9 8 7 6 5 4 3 2 1

Library of Congress Cataloging-in-Publication Data

Brettler, Marc Zvi.
How to read the Bible / Marc Zvi Brettler.— 1st ed.
p. cm.
Includes bibliographical references and index.
ISBN 10: 0-8276-0775-X
ISBN 13: 978-0-8276-0775-0
1. Bible. O.T.—Criticism, interpretation, etc. I. Title.
BS1171.3.B74 2005
221.6'1—dc22
2005009440

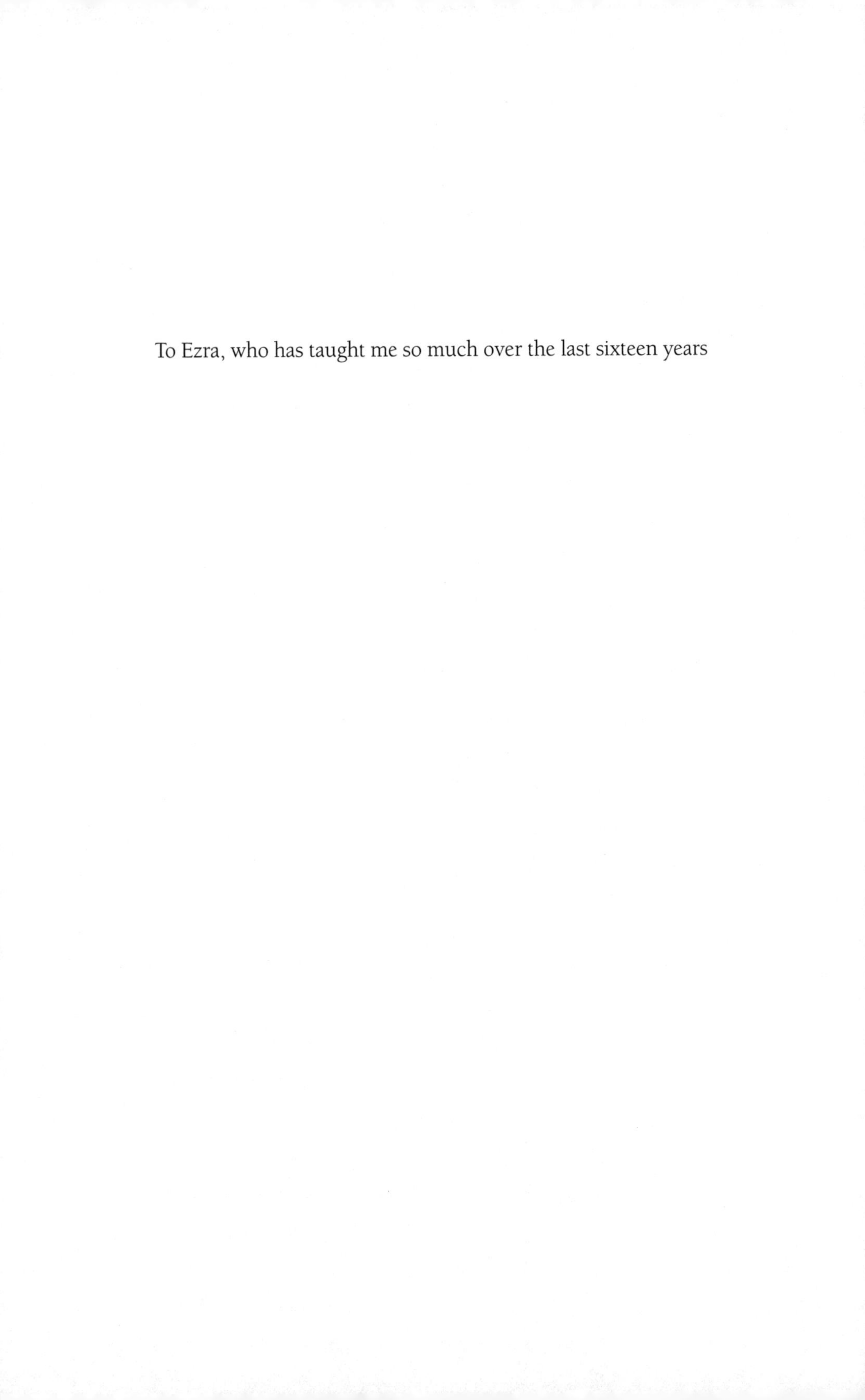

To Ezra, who has taught me so much over the last sixteen years

Contents

Preface

Several years ago, I mentioned to an acquaintance that I was writing a book called *How to Read the Bible*. He said: "What's so hard about reading the Hebrew Bible? You read it top to bottom, left to right." We had a good laugh after I pointed out that (1) Hebrew is read from right to left, and (2) my book was about reading the Bible, not reading Hebrew. As I then explained, this book is about the special "rules" for understanding texts from a different culture.

Indeed, this book is the product of many years of thought and writing. It is a response to the frustration that most people experience who read the Bible. To use the words of a biblical character, Daniel, the Bible is a "sealed book"—it arose in a culture whose values and conventions were fundamentally different from ours. Thus, the Bible today is either avoided as too strange, or else misread—taken as if it had been written yesterday or today.

In my two decades of teaching college students, and especially in ten years of teaching adults an introduction to the Bible through the Boston-area Me'ah Program, I have discovered that overcoming these obstacles is no easy challenge. Looking for articles to give to these intelligent adults who lack background in biblical studies, my colleagues and I have felt frustrated. Most essays on the Bible by scholars are too technical. Other books, written for the layperson, are wrong or simplistic, or they take a religious (typically Christian) perspective rather than an historical one.

This book attempts to fill the gap, to offer a Jewishly sensitive introduction to how to read biblical texts in their historical context. My hope is that the Bible might again become an open book for the Jewish community and other communities.

To keep this book accessible, I have added as few endnotes as possible and limited references to works found in English. (Such an arrangement unfortunately hides the fact that this book is based on a much wider body of knowledge, much of which is very technical.)

It is my pleasure to acknowledge the many people who have helped me along the way. Dr. Ellen Frankel, CEO and Editor-in-Chief of The Jewish Publication Society, has supported the idea of this book ever since I suggested it to her more than five years ago. She has served as an excellent and patient editor. Carol Hupping, JPS Publishing Director and COO, has done what she does best: making a book's author and all its editors look good. Janet Liss, Production Editor at the JPS, moved the book along with great care. Emily Law proofread the book meticulously and Robin Norman, production manager of the Jewish Publication Society, ensured that the typesetting, design, and cover production went smoothly. Rabbi David E. S. Stein, assisted by Rabbi David Mevorach Seidenberg, served as developmental editor and also copyedited the manuscript; together, they corrected many factual errors and helped me clarify what I was trying to say, making this book much more readable. Two undergraduate students at Brandeis University, Leora Koller-Fox and Jacob Merlin, double-checked all the biblical citations in the manuscript and offered helpful suggestions. Donald Kraus, Bible Editor of Oxford University Press, supervised the publication of two Bibles that I helped to edit, the third edition of the *New Oxford Annotated Bible* and *The Jewish Study Bible*; in the process, he taught me much about writing for an intelligent lay audience. Credit also goes to my students, especially those at Brandeis and Me'ah, who have constantly challenged me to express difficult and foreign concepts in a clear and concise fashion. They have embodied the truism that students are a professor's best teacher. In addition, the Theodore and Jane Norman Fund at Brandeis University has helped to defray the cost of preparing the manuscript; I am grateful for this contribution, as well as the many other ways that the University continues to support my work. Finally, I would like to thank the academic administrators of the Near Eastern and Judaic Studies Department at Brandeis, Anne Lawrence and Patricia Lucente, who offered help and encouragement at various stages of this project.

My teacher Nahum M. Sarna, ז״ל who broadened the biblical publications of The Jewish Publication Society, was not able to review a draft of this book, but the many things that he taught me are reflected on every page. He serves as a model teacher and scholar for me, both in the way he has performed each of those tasks and in the way he has seen them as intertwined.

When I quote the Bible, I mostly follow the New Jewish Publication Society (NJPS) translation. (Its translators completed their work in stages—*Torah* in 1962, *Prophets* in 1978, and *Writings* in 1982—revising it in 1985. The Jewish Publication Society further revised the translation in 1999.) This translation, published under the title *Tanakh* (a medieval Hebrew term for Bible), is the best idiomatic translation of the Hebrew Bible. It reflects very deep learning. Where I depart from the JPS translation and offer a rendering of my own, this is noted in the text.

Last and not least, I must mention my family. My mother was my first Hebrew teacher. My father was my first teacher of Jewish Studies and continues to take an active interest in my work, proofreading much of this manuscript. My wife, Monica, my daughter, Talya, and my son, Ezra, have all been supportive of my career. They have offered a wonderful environment in which I can continue to learn, teach, and write. It is appropriate that I dedicate this book to Ezra, named after the great sage who was "a scribe expert in the Torah of Moses" (Ezra 7:6; transl. adapted), and whom rabbinic tradition viewed as a second Moses.

Abbreviations

AB	Anchor Bible
ABD	*Anchor Bible Dictionary*. Ed. D.N. Freedman. 6 vols. Garden City: NY: Doubleday, 1992.
AnBib	Analecta biblica
ANET	*Ancient Near Eastern Texts Relating to the Old Testament*. Ed. J. B. Pritchard. Princeton, NJ: Princeton Univ. Press, 1954.
AnOr	Analecta Orientali
AOAT	Alter Orient und Altes Testament
BA	*Biblical Archaeologist*
BAR	*Biblical Archaeologist Reader*
BASOR	*Bulletin of the American Schools of Oriental Research*
B.C.E.	Before the Common Era
Bib	*Biblica*
BJRL	*Bulletin of the John Rylands Library of Manchester*
BJS	*Brown Judaic Studies*
BZAW	Beiheft zur Zeitschrift für die alttestamentliche Wissenschaft
CAD	*The Assyrian Dictionary of the Oriental Institute of the University of Chicago*. Chicago: Univ. of Chicago, 1956.
CBNT	Coniectanea biblica: New Testament Series
CBOT	Coniectanea biblica: Old Testament Series
CBQ	*Catholic Biblical Quarterly*
chap.	chapter
C.E.	Common Era
COS	*The Context of Scripture*. Ed. William W. Hallo. Leiden: Brill, 1997–2002.
DDD	*Dictionary of Deities and Demons in the Bible*. Ed. K. van der Toorn et al. Leiden: Brill, 1995.

DJD	Discoveries in the Judaean Desert
DtrH	The Deuteronomistic History (= Deuteronomy–2 Kings)
EJ	*Encylcopedia Judaica*
FOTL	Forms of the Old Testament Literature
HALOT	Koehler, L. et al. *The Hebrew and Aramaic Lexicon of the Old Testament*. Trans. M. E. J. Richardson. 4 vols. Leiden: Brill, 1994–99.
HAR	*Hebrew Annual Review*
HDR	Harvard Dissertations in Religion
HSM	Harvard Semitic Monographs
HTR	*Harvard Theological Review*
HUCA	*Hebrew Union College Annual*
ICC	International Critical Commentary
IEJ	*Israel Exploration Journal*
INT	*Interpretation*
JPS	Jewish Publication Society
JBL	*Journal of Biblical Literature*
JR	*Journal of Religion*
JSB	*The Jewish Study Bible*. Ed. Adele Berlin and Marc Zvi Brettler. New York: Oxford Univ. Press, 2004.
JSOT	*Journal for the Study of the Old Testament*
JSOTSup	Journal for the Study of the Old Testament: Supplement Series
NCBC	New Century Bible Commentary
NRSV	New Revised Standard Version
OBT	Overtures to Biblical Theology
OTL	Old Testament Library
OTS	*Oudtestamentlische Studiën*
RB	*Revue biblique*
SBL	Society of Biblical Literature
SBLDS	Society of Biblical Literature Dissertation Series
SBLMS	Society of Biblical Literature Monograph Series
SBT	Studies in Biblical Theology
ScrHier	*Scripta hierosolymitana*
SJOT	*Scandinavian Journal of the Old Testament*
TAPS	Transactions of the American Philosophical Society
VT	*Vetus Testamentum*
VTS	Vetus Testamentum Supplements
v., vv.	verse, verses
YNER	Yale Near Eastern Researches
ZAW	*Zeitschrift für die alttestamentliche Wissenschaft*

How to Read the Bible

1

Reading as a Jew and as a Scholar

If "reading" is the act of making sense of a text, then each of us reads differently. Further, we each have a different conception of what the Bible is. Not surprisingly, then, we each interpret biblical texts in our own way. Of the many approaches, we can describe as a "method" only those that are rigorous and systematic.

This book presents a method of reading the Bible. It is often called "the historical-critical approach." By highlighting this method, I do not mean that it is the only way to read the Bible. Indeed, many Jews have viewed with suspicion this way of reading, rejecting it in favor of other methods. Yet I commend this approach to readers because I have found it illuminating. When the Bible is viewed in the light of this method, we see the text as meaningful, engaging, and multifaceted.

Classical Interpretation

For much of the postbiblical period, readers of the Bible have all tended to follow the same method. They have seen the Bible as a cryptic yet perfect book, of fundamental relevance to its community of interpreters. They have assumed that much of the Bible, if not all of it, came (to some extent) from God. Hence the Bible is a privileged text that should be interpreted using special rules. That is, it should not be interpreted like regular, nonbiblical texts.[1]

This method developed during the late biblical period. As we shall see in a later chapter, one passage in the Book of Daniel explains an earlier prophecy of Jeremiah, which turned on the phrase "seventy years." Daniel interpreted this phrase to mean "seventy weeks of years," or 490 years. Normally, when an ancient Jew promised to return a borrowed ox in seventy days, it meant just that—seventy days. Yet Daniel could understand Jeremiah's "seventy" differently because the Book of Jeremiah is a biblical text, reflecting special, divine language.

Consider, too, the ancient Judean Desert community of Qumran, which thrived over a period of several centuries—from the second pre-Christian to the first post-Christian centuries. Their library—the part that is extant—is what we now call "The Dead Sea Scrolls." Like the author of Daniel, they believed in interpreting biblical books in a special way. Thus they kept a rich interpretive literature. For example, their Pesher Habakkuk, a type of commentary on the prophetic book of Habakkuk, held that their community's leader understood the true meaning of the book better than the prophet himself! The Pesher interpreted the text in relation to the interpreter's own period, more than half a millennium after Habakkuk lived.[2]

Classical rabbinic interpretation also shared these working assumptions. Even for the Torah's legal texts, it often subverted the plain sense of words for the sake of "harmonization." That is, when texts (from divergent places and times) appeared to contradict each other, it "reconciled" them so that they would agree. For example, a slave law in Exodus 21:6 suggests that in certain circumstances a Hebrew slave serves the master "in perpetuity" (*le-olam*). This contradicts Leviticus 25:40, which states that masters must release all such slaves on the jubilee year (every fiftieth year). However, according to the basic assumptions, God's word must be internally consistent. Therefore the rabbis insisted that the term "in perpetuity" in Exodus means "practically (but not literally) forever"—that is, until the jubilee year.[3] This type of interpretation is strange to the reader unused to classical Jewish (and to a large extent Christian) interpretation. But it is natural if we understand the Bible as a uniform, perfect, divine work, which may employ language in a cryptic fashion.

This is not to say that every traditional, premodern interpreter of the Bible took every word of the text according to all of these principles. Yet the few exceptions prove the rule. For example, Rabbi Abraham ibn Ezra (1089–1164) suggested that someone other than Moses wrote a small number of verses in the Torah. Yet even as that commentator made sure to inform his readers of that unorthodox view, he was careful to condemn it.[4] Likewise, Rabbi Samuel ben Meir (also known as "Rashbam"; 1080–1174) allowed that biblical language is not cryptic; rather, its words mean what they normally imply, even if this contradicts rabbinic tradition. Thus, he alone among the extant medieval Jewish exegetes did not find it necessary to "reconcile" Exodus 21:6 with Leviticus 25:40 (see above). However, this opinion survives in only a single medieval manuscript, and it has not appeared in most printed editions. This suggests that his approach stood at, or even beyond, the fringe of acceptable interpretation.

Only in the seventeenth century, with the rise of European rationalism, did scholars begin to question the unique, divine nature of the biblical text. Hobbes (in England) and Spinoza (in Holland) led the way. Consider the latter's magnificent *Theological-Political Tractate*,[5] with its chapter called simply "Of the Interpretation of Scripture." It replaces the earlier assumptions with a single premise that allows the Bible to be seen in a new manner: "I hold that the method of interpreting Scripture is no different from the method of interpreting nature, and is in fact in complete accord with it."[6] In a single sentence, Spinoza "deprivileges" the Bible. He renounces the traditional framework for biblical interpretation: The Bible is not cryptic. It no longer needs to be interpreted as a seamless whole. It is imperfect. In places it may be of historical interest only, no longer relevant to contemporary believers. In most senses, it is a book like any other.

The Historical-Critical Method

It would take two more centuries before the new working assumptions gained acceptance among Europe's rationalist intellectual elite. But once this happened, the historical-critical method took hold.[7]

What is the historical-critical method? "Historical" refers to the view that the main context for interpretation is the place and time in which the text was composed. "Critical" simply means reading the text independently of religious norms or interpretive traditions—as opposed to accepting them uncritically.[8] (In this context, it does *not* imply a judgmental or faultfinding approach, which is another meaning of the word "critical.") A main component of this approach is source criticism, also called "Higher Criticism" (which distinguishes it from the effort to establish the correct reading of the transmitted text, known as "Lower Criticism"). It seeks to identify and isolate the original sources of the biblical text as it has come down to us.

The new method crystallized in the late nineteenth and early twentieth centuries, developing into a school of interpretation. The most influential person of this school was the German scholar Julius Wellhausen, based on his magisterial work of 1878 (translated into English as *Prolegomena to the History of Ancient Israel*).[9] Indeed, it was mainly in Germany that the historical-critical movement took root, specifically in the theology departments of Protestant universities. For doctrinal reasons, Catholic scholars hardly participated in these developments until after the Vatican II pronouncements in 1965.

The Reaction Among Jews

The Jewish world, too, largely remained aloof. While a few Jewish contemporaries of Wellhausen favored his approach, others wrote polemics against him, trying to undermine his reconstruction of the text's history.[10] These scholars continued to advocate the rabbinic mode of reading, suggesting that what Wellhausen and his colleagues saw as textual contradictions are really not contradictions at all.

The most notable attack on the historical-critical perspective came from a renowned scholar of rabbinics, Solomon Schechter. At a 1903 banquet, he offered an address titled "Higher-Criticism—Higher Anti-Semitism."[11] He equated Wellhausen's approach with "professional and imperial anti-Semitism," calling it an "intellectual persecution" of Judaism.[12] Schechter's essay had an immense impact on the Jewish attitude toward the Bible. Its influence seems to explain why until the present generation many professional Jewish biblical scholars have been less engaged in historical-critical study than their non-Jewish counterparts.

Schechter actually offered a fair critique of Higher Criticism as it was practiced in Germany in the late nineteenth and the early twentieth centuries. Like nearly all Christians of the time, its proponents believed in the moral superiority of Christianity to Judaism, and they used their scholarly works to illustrate this. Wellhausen, for example, likened Judaism in late antiquity to a dead tree. He applied that image vigorously, describing the late biblical book of Chronicles thus: "Like ivy it overspreads the dead trunk with extraneous life, blending old and new in a strange combination. . . . [I]n the process it is twisted and perverted."[13] As painful as such sentiments are for Jews, they neither diminish the brilliance of much of his *Prolegomena*, nor negate the correctness of its basic methodology.

Beyond the Early Biases

Schechter had warned that the historical-critical method "is seeking to destroy, denying all our claims to the past, and leaving us without hope for the future."[14] In fact, however, the method itself is religiously neutral—neither discrediting Judaism nor promoting Christianity. Indeed, by the final decades of the twentieth century, many professional scholars, including Jews, had adopted the historical-critical method without attacking the Hebrew Bible or Judaism. These works illustrate that historical-critical methods are not by definition anti-Semitic.[15]

I would go even further. I insist not only that the historical-critical method is neutral, but also that it can be religiously constructive—even for Jews. The last two decades have seen a remarkable resurgence in interest in ethnic and religious roots among many Americans, including American Jews. Publishers have produced an unprecedented number of books on Jewish texts, such as Barry Holtz's *Back to the Sources*.[16] Serious adult Jewish education classes have reached new levels of success. Many Jews are going back to the Bible in a serious, more academic way, looking for what the Bible originally meant. They are exploring how its earlier meaning may bear on religious life as we might now live it. They do not wish to slavishly follow the norms of the Jewish past, but neither do they wish to ignore them. Such norms must first be understood before they can inform contemporary beliefs and practices.

About This Book

The purpose of this book is to show the value of reading the Bible in a historical-critical manner. This perspective greatly enriches the text, and allows us to recover a vibrant civilization over two millennia old. Understanding the Bible in its original context allows us to understand ourselves. For then we can see where our secular civilization accords with ancient Israelite perspectives, and where it has diverged from them. It also allows us to see where Judaism has (or has not) developed beyond biblical religion. Finally, the historical-critical method lets us appreciate the Bible as an interesting text that speaks in multiple voices on profound issues. Only with the help of the historical-critical method can these different voices be fully heard and appreciated.

In presenting my case, my first task is to explain this book's title, *How to Read the Bible*. Thus the following chapter defines what I mean by "the Bible," and then the third chapter explains what I mean by "reading." By exploring the act of reading, it attempts to show that reading in its fullest sense is far from simple. The subsequent chapters each focus on a specific biblical text or genre, highlighting how modern biblical scholarship makes sense of that text or genre. In an afterword, I discuss how the historical-critical method can help contemporary Jews relate to the Bible as a religious text in a more meaningful way.

All told, this book is *a Jewishly sensitive introduction to the historical-critical method*. Remarkably, it is the first such attempt.[17]

How to Read the Bible differs from the many so-called introductions to the Bible.[18] Most such works survey each book of the Bible, noting the critical problems presented by each, positing when each was written, and noting how modern historical-critical scholarship approaches each. Typically, they focus on isolating and removing what is secondary in each text. For example, they "root out" whatever appears in the book of the prophet Amos that he himself did not write. These works are often reference books, rather than true introductions.

In contrast, *How to Read the Bible* does not attempt to cover every biblical book. Instead, it surveys representative biblical texts from different genres, to illustrate how modern scholarship has taught us to "read" these texts. Its intended audience includes the curious adult who wants to read through sections of the Bible and appreciate them within a modern framework, and the college student in an introductory Bible course. It conveys the general principles of this unfamiliar methodology.[19] Such an introduction will enable the reader to understand more technical studies, encyclopedias, and commentaries on the Bible. Most significantly, it will prompt you to approach biblical texts with new kinds of questions, and to appreciate them in a new way.

2

What Is the Bible, Anyway?

The Bible can be an intimidating book. Its size alone is overwhelming—1574 pages in the Hebrew edition that is standard among Bible scholars (*Biblia Hebraica Stuttgartensia*), 1624 pages in The Jewish Publication Society's translation (see below), 2023 pages in the *JPS Hebrew-English Tanakh,* and 2181 pages in *The Jewish Study Bible* (including notes and essays). A significant amount of the biblical text is poetry, which is daunting to many, and certainly does not make for quick reading.

For such a book, an orientation would surely be helpful. This chapter covers the fundamentals: basic terminology for the Bible, its basic structure, and why such things matter. It also defines what I mean by "the Bible" for the purposes of this book.

Basic Terminology

The Name in English

The word "Bible" derives from the Greek *biblia*, meaning "books."[1] By its very name, "the Bible" refers to "*the* collection of books"—that is, the one that is deemed to be authoritative or canonical.

Different communities have different Bibles. For Christians, the Bible includes the New Testament; for Jews it does not. To distinguish it from the Christians' Bible, people have suggested a variety of names for the Jews' Bible (besides simply "the Bible"). Christians typically call it the Old Testament, where "testament" is an old way of referring to a contract ("covenant"). This name is based on a prophecy in Jeremiah that states: "See, a time is coming—declares the LORD—when I will make a *new covenant* with the House of Israel and the House of Judah. It will not be like the covenant I made with their fathers, when I took them by the hand to lead them out of the land of Egypt, a covenant which they broke, though I espoused them—declares the LORD" (31:31–32). Early Christian tradition understood this passage to refer to a new covenant, centered around Jesus, which replaces the old Mosaic one.[2] This led to the terms "New Testament" and "Old Testament"—in which "old" connotes obsolescence.[3]

Jews, however, view the original covenant as still operative. For this reason, Jews have tended to reject the term "Old Testament." Many simply call this body of literature "the Bible." For religious Jews, this name is by definition appropriate: these are "the books" that are authoritative for this group.

Academic scholars, meanwhile, generally prefer not to take sides in the debate as to which covenant with God is in force. Therefore, in scholarly circles, the more neutral terms "Hebrew Bible" or "Jewish Scripture(s)" have gained currency. Admittedly the first name is slightly imprecise, because some passages of the Bible are not in Hebrew but rather in Aramaic, a related Semitic language.[4]

Other Jewish Names: A Historical Review

In extant texts composed during the biblical period itself—which lasted more than a thousand years—no term at all appears for this set of books. The Bible was then still in formation as an authoritative collection. It received its title only after it came into being—signaling the start of the postbiblical period.

In the first century C.E., Josephus (the great Jewish historian who wrote in Greek) knew of the Bible.[5] He called it *ta hiera grammata* ("The Holy Writings").[6] He also called it *grammasi* ("that which is written")—often translated as "Scripture"[7] but better rendered uncapitalized, as "scripture."

In classical rabbinic literature, the two most common terms for the Bible were *mikra* (מִקְרָא, literally "that which is read or recited aloud") and *kitvei ha-kodesh* (כִּתְבֵי הַקֹּדֶשׁ, "the holy writings").[8] Sometimes, the rabbis referred to the Bible as *torah, nevi'im, u-khtuvim* (תּוֹרָה נְבִיאִים וּכְתוּבִים, "the Torah, the Prophets, and the Writings").[9]

In the Middle Ages, perhaps in the late first millennium C.E., scribes shortened *Torah, Nevi'im, u-Khtuvim* into the acronym תַּנַ״ךְ, which is pronounced *Tanakh*. Jews today still commonly use that name for their Bible. As the title of The Jewish Publication Society's 1985 one-volume translation, the Tanakh makes a point that other names ("the Bible," "Holy Scriptures," or even "Hebrew Bible") do not. Namely, it underscores that the translators rendered directly from the Hebrew (not from an ancient Greek version, like some Christians translations) *and* drew upon Jewish interpretive tradition.[10]

Making an issue out of what to call these texts might seem pedantic, but it is not. As we shall see, the "Hebrew Bible" and the "Old Testament" differ in more than name only. They comprise different numbers of books, which they place in a different order. (The ordering matters because it alters the context in which we understand the text; a book's meaning can shift depending upon which books we read before and after it.) More significantly, the term "Hebrew Bible" suggests a corpus that is self-standing, whereas the "Old Testament" does not. The meaning of many passages in the "Old Testament" changes when one views them as part of a larger whole that includes the New Testament.[11]

Name and Structure

As we have seen, the name *Tanakh* reflects a three-part ("tripartite") organization of the Bible; for Jews, this is the standard division of the Bible. The name of each of its parts, however, warrants some explanation. The name of the first part, as we have said, is *Torah*. Christians have often translated the term as "Law," but this is too restrictive; it misrepresents this collection of books, which features nonlegal elements such as narrative and poetry. (It also misrepresents Judaism, which is far more than a "religion of law.") Rather, *Torah* is a broad term that means "Instruction."

The name of the second part, *Nevi'im*, means "Prophets." However, many of its books are not actually prophetic works. Its first portion, often called the "Former Prophets," consists instead of narrative texts. They continue the story begun in the Torah. Although prophets play an important role in these narrative books, they dwell on far more than prophecies.

The name of the final part of the Bible, *Kethuvim* (sometimes transcribed as *Ketuvim*), means "Writings." Of course the rest of the Bible also consists of "writings." What therefore justifies giving the last set of books such a generic name? As we shall see in chapter 27, the answer is a matter of history. In this case, *Kethuvim* has come to serve as a catchall term. It is a miscellany. It contains such diverse works as Psalms (prayers), Chronicles (history), Daniel (prophecy), and Song of Songs (erotic poetry).

The chart shown on page 10 illustrates the typical arrangement of the books in Hebrew manuscripts and printed editions of the Bible (Tanakh).[12] It also illustrates how there are twenty-four books of the Bible according to Jewish tradition.

Torah	*Nevi'im*	*Kethuvim*
Genesis	Joshua[13]	Psalms
Exodus	Judges	Proverbs[15]
Leviticus	Samuel[14]	Job
Numbers	Kings	Song of Songs[16]
Deuteronomy	Isaiah[17]	Ruth
	Jeremiah	Lamentations
	Ezekiel	Ecclesiastes
	The Twelve Minor Prophets[18]	Esther
		Daniel
		Ezra-Nehemiah
		Chronicles[19]

Alternative Arrangements

Only in Jewish Bibles will you find the books grouped into three sections. This tripartite structure is found in all Hebrew manuscripts of the Bible. All contemporary Jewish translations follow its outline.

In antiquity, however, this arrangement was not the only one that Jews employed. In particular, the Jews who rendered the Bible into Greek (producing the translation known as the Septuagint more than 2100 years ago)[20] divided it into four sections: Torah; Historical Books; Wisdom and Poetic Books; and Prophetic Books.[21] This order is quite logical—it begins with Torah, the most basic text, followed by books about the past (Historical Books), the present (Wisdom and Poetic Books), and the future (Prophetic Books). This ordering scheme most likely originated in the land of Israel before being transmitted to the Greek-speaking Jewish community of Alexandria, Egypt, together with the Hebrew texts of the biblical books themselves.

The Christians' Old Testament

The early Christians came to adopt the order of the Septuagint for two main reasons. First, they spoke Greek (rather than Hebrew), so it was natural for them to rely on the Greek translation and adopt the Greek order. Second, that order—unlike some others—ended with the prophetic books. In the Christian canon (Old Testament + New Testament), this arrangement juxtaposed the

Prophets (which according to Christian tradition predict the arrival of Jesus as messiah) with the Gospels (which describe that arrival, fulfilling the prediction). Thus, while the Christians' Bible used an order of Old Testament books that predates the rise of Christianity, it did so because that order served Christian purposes well.

The scope of many Christians' Old Testament is larger than that of the Jews' Bible. The former includes not only the books listed above but also the Apocrypha (which is Greek for "hidden"). These are various Jewish Hellenistic writings that the Catholic, Orthodox, Coptic, and other Christian Churches have held to be authoritative and sacred, but of lesser status than the other books of the Bible (that is, they are "deuterocanonical"). These include books like 1 Maccabees (a historical text) and Sirach (which goes by many names—Ben Sirach, Wisdom of Ben Sirach, Sira, Ben Sira, etc.; a wisdom text similar to Proverbs). Catholic Bibles often print these books in a separate section called Apocrypha, even though they were originally part of the Old Testament canon.

The Protestant Church later rejected the Apocrypha as canonical. Regardless of how we view the Apocrypha, if we set them aside for the moment we get the following four-part Bible:

Torah	*Historical*	*Wisdom and Poetic*	*Prophetic*
Genesis	Joshua	Job	Isaiah
Exodus	Judges	Psalms	Jeremiah
Leviticus	Ruth[22]	Proverbs	Lamentations
Numbers	1 Samuel[23]	Ecclesiastes	Ezekiel
Deuteronomy	2 Samuel	Song of Solomon	Daniel
	1 Kings		The Twelve Minor Prophets[24]
	2 Kings		
	1 Chronicles		
	2 Chronicles		
	Ezra		
	Nehemiah		
	Esther		

This is the arrangement found in non-Jewish translations ranging from the King James (1611) to the New Revised Standard Version (1989) and beyond. Its reflects not only certain ancient Greek manuscripts but also the influential translation of the Bible into Latin by the early Church father Jerome (340–420 C.E.).

In addition, in a small number of cases, chapters of biblical books begin in slightly different places in Jewish Bibles in contrast to Christian Bibles; this is yet another way in which the Hebrew Bible differs from the Old Testament.[25]

My Definition of "the Bible"

This book is a Jewishly sensitive introduction to "the Bible." Thus in this book I always use that term to mean what others call "the Hebrew Bible."

I do not mean to imply that this definition is either the original or the best one. (Indeed, the fact that the current Jewish order differs from what is recorded in the Babylonian Talmud is a good reminder that the order was never set in stone.[26]) My use of the Jewish arrangement merely acknowledges that this is what Jews currently use in what they call the Bible.

3

The Art of Reading the Bible

Reading is a complicated, multifaceted process.[1] I am not referring to the technical aspect of sounding out words, what is called "decoding"—this is relatively simple, especially in Hebrew. Nor am I referring to resolving the types of ambiguities that exist in any dead, or literary, language. These ambiguities can be quite significant in translating the Bible. For example, should the first sentence of the Bible be rendered "In the beginning God created heaven and earth" or "In the beginning of God's creation of heaven and earth"? Should the root *q-n-'* (קנא) when describing God be translated "jealous" or "zealous"? Lack of punctuation in the earliest biblical texts raises additional reading problems: should I read Isaiah 40:3 as "A voice rings out: 'Make clear in the desert a road for the LORD!'" or as "A voice rings out in the desert 'Clear a road for the LORD!'"? As theologically significant as these issues may be for reading or translating the Hebrew Bible, they pale in comparison to the reading challenges caused by the fact that the Bible was written in an ancient society that had fundamentally different literary conventions from ours.

Especially if we know only one language, and live mostly in one society or social group, we may not be aware of the extent to which convention guides so much of what we do and how we behave. Conventions, however, by definition have particular meanings in particular groups. Anyone hitchhiking in Israel using the American hitchhiking sign, which is considered an obscene gesture there, will quickly appreciate the importance of convention.

Conventions combine with the meaning of words to determine how a text should be understood. Words alone do not determine meaning; we interpret them based on the context that they are in, namely their genre. The same words will be interpreted differently if they are found in a different genre or context. For example, the words "slow children" will be understood one way if they are found as part of a report dealing with special education in a school district, and another if they are found on a yellow, triangular street sign. The words are the same; their context, which determines their genre (school report vs. street sign), will ascertain whether they are descriptive of children with below-average IQs, or are prescriptive, telling the driver to slow down because a large number of children live in a neighborhood. The proper interpretation of the same two words differs based on their genre.

Reading and the Biblical Text

There are many ways of reading the Bible. My interest, however, is in reading the Bible like an ancient Israelite,[2] what is often called reading the Bible from a historical-critical perspective. As noted in chapter 1, "historical-critical" is an unfortunate term; much more than history is involved in this type of reading, and the term "critical" incorrectly suggests that the "critic" is interested in somehow dismantling the Bible or any faith-based commitment with the Bible at its core. This is not what I am attempting here. Instead, I am assuming that the Bible, like any ancient text, has been read differently in different periods, because readers read the Bible using their own conventions or rules. James Kugel, for example, has shown how readers in the early postbiblical period understood the Bible; their readings are often very strange from our perspective, because these interpreters lived two thousand years ago and worked within a religious and cultural system that is so different than ours.[3]

Whether a particular biblical interpretation is right or wrong in an absolute sense is usually impossible to say, because the validity of any reading depends on its time period and the conventions of that period. Everything depends on what rules the reader uses when reading the biblical text.

The Rules of the Game

Those who play the board game Monopoly® might know the official rules (printed on the box), but they might also be familiar with alternative sets of rules. Nowhere do the official rules suggest that $500 must be added to Free Parking after anyone lands on that space and collects the money, nor do the rules deal with the special cases of the player who rolls double ones or double sixes. Yet almost all Monopoly players have *conventions* that determine how these situations should be handed. What is crucial is that before the game starts, all participants agree on the rules governing that particular game; otherwise, chaos ensues.

Similarly, the way of reading suggested here—which emphasizes what the

Bible meant when it was written—is not intended to disparage other "rules" that might be used for reading the Bible. I do not mean to argue that these methods, whether based on certain religious or literary principles, are fundamentally wrong. Instead, this book develops, explores, explains, and justifies a different set of rules. In the afterword, I will argue that these rules do work for religious use—although for now this might seem unlikely, or even impossible.

The importance of proper rules or genre for understanding the Bible is most easily illustrated through the following examples. They presume, for illustrative purposes only, the existence of someone from a wholly different culture who is perfectly proficient in the English language, having mastered the grammar of English and an English dictionary. This individual (let me call her Marta) would be comparable to the modern scholar who has complete mastery of biblical word use and grammar (which incidentally is impossible). Marta will illustrate three situations that indicate how mastery of lexicon (word use) and grammar alone are insufficient for reading in the most comprehensive sense.

Let's imagine that Marta arrives at my house as I am reading some poetry. I happen to turn to a poem called "Subway," translated from Japanese. It begins: "Every day I step into a coffin / with strangers."[4] Reading even this first line, I sigh in pleasure—after all, I grew up in New York, and traveled on many trains during rush hour, unable to breathe, feeling like I was buried alive with strangers for an hour. Marta, however, has no comprehension of this experience, for at least two reasons. She has never experienced the subways. Just as significantly, she has never encountered poetry, and thinks that these initial eight words about entering coffins with strangers describe either a strange ritual or a kinky practice. Though she understands the words, by reading them literally, she misunderstands their meaning in this particular context.

Only after Marta learns about subways, and more importantly, about genre conventions—for instance, that literature presented in short lines is poetry, that poetry uses metaphors, and that metaphors should be interpreted in a particular way—will she understand those eight words. Reading that line of poetry thus extends far beyond a phonetic process, or even looking up each word in a dictionary.

Another scenario, from later in the day. Marta is looking over my shoulder as I sort the day's mail. I sort into two piles; one with notices (typically in red) such as "Urgent: Open Immediately," the other lacking such notices. But then I trash everything from the "Urgent: Open Immediately" pile. Marta is bewildered. She knows how to read, but nothing in her technical language preparation taught her about genres of mail. Had she learned that the words "Urgent: Open Immediately" (combined with other markers such as third class postage) typify a genre that we call "junk mail," then she would understand. But this lesson, which has to do with *social* aspects of reading and writing and how we as readers pick up on clues (what biblical scholars call "form-critical markers"), is typically only learned through experience within a particular social group.

For the final example, imagine that Marta watches as I read the *Sunday Boston Globe*. She clearly observes that the newspaper is comprised of various sections with different layouts, but doesn't know the significance of these differences. Specifically, she doesn't know that Doonesbury, printed on the first page of the comics, must be read differently than the first page of the first section. Though both sections contain the same words, even the same personal names, we know through experience that they convey different information or have different goals. The first page means to convey facts; the comics are intended to amuse. Marta, however, has no developed awareness of contexts and genres, how they might inform what something really means, or how it should be read, so she likely would use Doonesbury as a source for news in the same way that she uses the first page.

The Challenge of Reading like an Ancient Israelite

If Marta is smart, she will eventually figure these things out. She will learn based on experience what junk mail is, how to read the comics, even the nature of poetry. (Indeed, this is what each of us has learned to do.) It will take her awhile. Yet in learning to read (in this broad sense), Marta will have an advantage that we Bible readers never have: she has what linguists and anthropologists call "informants"—real, live people who can lead her down the right track. We have no informants from ancient Israel, so we must use other, less reliable criteria to determine whether we are reading the ancient texts correctly.[5]

When it comes to reading the biblical text within its original context, most people are hardly better than Marta. Those of us who have spent years reading biblical and other ancient Near Eastern texts, and trying to figure out their conventions, engage in a difficult and always somewhat speculative venture. There is no certain way of knowing that we have the convention right, other than the fact that it allows many texts to make sense, which is a partly subjective criterion. That begins to explain why this type of reading, which we call the historical-critical method, is so common in the university, but so rare outside of it. The historical-critical method makes two assumptions: that biblical society is discontinuous with our society, and that the Bible should be read according to its original social context, not anachronistically. The Bible must instead be understood only after its ancient conventions and genres are understood, but because there is so much discontinuity, this is a most difficult task.

Not only literary conventions are important. The Bible is the product of a particular society living at a particular time. Before we can begin exploring the issues of convention and genre, it is important to offer a schematic history of ancient Israel, so that biblical texts, genres, and conventions may be understood in this light. Accordingly, history is the subject of our next chapter.

4

A Brief History of Israel

This book attempts to understand the Bible as it was understood in the periods in which its books were first written and read, from approximately the twelfth century B.C.E. (the Song of Deborah in Judges 5) through the second century B.C.E. (the Book of Daniel).[1] Thus, we need to know some basic facts about history before exploring biblical texts.[2]

But we would run a strong risk of being misled if we simply opened a history book and believed everything we read there. Because of relatively recent reassessments in the field of history, some of the most popular and well-known histories of the biblical era are now obsolete. Consequently, we must first pause briefly to assess historians' assumptions and methods, taking note of the importance of point of view.

History as It Used to Be Told

Writing a history of the biblical era may sound like a simple venture, and until the latter part of the twentieth century, it was. Many books with the words *History of Israel* in their title were available, and they all more or less told the same story.[3] These works differed somewhat concerning the earliest history of Israel. However, from the period of David onward they were quite similar—typically paraphrasing the biblical story, removing the language of divine causality that is found throughout the Bible, and putting the biblical account within the context of ancient Near Eastern texts and cultures. Starting in the mid 1970s, this began to change.

Two main shifts happened that disturbed this consensus. In the first part of the twentieth century, a large number of cuneiform tablets were unearthed and published. Several scholars discovered in these tablets, especially those from the periphery of Mesopotamia, descriptions of various institutions that seemed to confirm details of the biblical account. For example, E. A. Speiser suggested that an institution existed at Nuzi, where a husband could adopt his wife as a sister, thereby explaining the so-called wife-sister stories in Genesis 12, 20, and 26. According to Speiser's reconstruction, a wife could be adopted as a sister as a special sign of affection.[4] Speiser was not alone; William Foxwell Albright, considered the dean of biblical scholarship and archaeology, outlined many correlations between the history that the Bible tells and what we might know about this history from external sources.[5] In general, the scholarly climate, at least in America, was that the Bible is to be trusted as a historical source until disproven by a reliable outside source.

Shifting the Burden of Proof

As scholars began to more carefully evaluate the evidence, however, this picture began to shatter. Two books published in the 1970s reflect this change in attitude: *The Historicity of the Patriarchal Narratives*, by Thomas Thompson,[6] and *Abraham in History and Tradition*, by John Van Seters.[7] These works and others showed that the many analogies brought between the so-called "Patriarchal Period" and the Bronze Age of the second pre-Christian millennium were specious. For example, scholars realized that Speiser was incorrect in reconstructing many institutions at Nuzi, including the adoption of a wife as sister—this was based on a misreading of cuneiform texts that was influenced by the Bible. Furthermore, they pointed out that the arguments brought by Speiser, Albright, and others were specious. That is, just because it has a second-millennium-B.C.E. parallel does not prove that a biblical passage is early or accurate, especially if it also has a (more recent) first millennium parallel—as most of them do. In other words, a number of scholars argued that these texts are not accurately reflecting the second millennium, but are projecting backward first millennium realities—and in some cases, coincidentally, these realities match the second millennium as well. Finally, the new scholars began to emphasize the anachronisms of Genesis. Earlier scholars had seen these anachronisms as exceptions, as a small number of adjustments that crept into the text as it was transmitted. Newer scholars, however, saw these as a fundamental part of the textual fabric, indicating that the text as a whole was not reliably reflecting a Bronze Age milieu.

The continued archaeological excavations and surveys, particularly those after the 1967 Six-Day War, also began to influence the way the Bible was seen as a historical source. In the early parts of the century, excavations were typically seen as confirming the Bible. When the evidence did not match the biblical description of a site, as in the destruction of Jericho by Joshua, scholars often said that the relevant layer (which once showed the destruction) has been eroded away.[8] When excavations did not show a level where destruction had taken place because of the biblically described conquest of a particular site, scholars would say that they dug at the wrong site, and that the name of a city had been applied to two different places in ancient and modern times. However, as the number of excavations increased, and the evidence was supplemented by large survey operations, it became clear that the archaeological record contradicted the story of Joshua's rapid, complete conquest of Canaan. As a result of archaeology, the Book of Joshua could no longer be seen as an accurate source for history.[9]

At the end of the twentieth century, the doubts that had developed on the basis of archaeological exploration of the "Patriarchal Period" and the conquest began to pervade certain groups of scholars, who suggested that similar doubts should exist for much of the Bible. A group of scholars centered in Copenhagen, often dubbed "the Copenhagen School," suggested that the Bible has little value as a historical source, and that ancient Israelite history should be written without recourse to the Bible. For example, they questioned the very existence of David. I call this attitude "creeping skepticism," where the doubts rightly shown for using the Bible as a source for reconstructing the earliest periods have crept into the interpretation of later periods as well.[10]

Although the Copenhagen School made biblical scholars aware of many of the theological biases that they held, they went too far. Several scholars have suggested that this school replaced the fundamentalism of previous generations, where the Bible was seen as historically true unless very strong evidence suggested otherwise, with a "negative fundamentalism," where the Bible must be viewed as false unless very strong evidence suggests otherwise. The debate around this issue has been divisive and often ugly.[11] Given the importance of this issue to Jewish identity and particularly to modern Israeli identity, it has often been tinged with accusations and manifestations of antisemitism and anti-Zionism.[12] Obviously, here is not the place to resolve in detail the argument about the usefulness of the Bible as a historical source. I would note, however, that the arguments of the more extreme scholars in this school are generally discounted, and a reasonable middle position would suggest that the Bible may be used, with significant caution, as a source for ancient history, just like any other ancient document.

The Bible's Limits as a Source for History

Two significant problems with using the Bible as a historical source must be acknowledged. The first is that it is fundamentally a theological document. Though it certainly relates many historical events, its authors were not primarily interested in the accurate depiction of the past. The past is almost always refracted through a theological lens, and often through a partisan political-ideological lens as well. These lenses are a fundamental part of biblical texts. Thus, it is not sufficient to simply take God out of the picture, and to rewrite biblical tests in terms of "normal" historical causality rather than divine causality.[13]

The Bible is not unique in this respect—in fact, it is typical of ancient Near Eastern historical writing as a whole. It would barely be an overstatement to point out that almost all these texts center on the divine realm as much as the human.[14] For example, according to the Mesha inscription, from Israel's Moabite neighbors to the east, Israel was able to subjugate Moab because "Kemosh [the Moabite high god] was angry at his land."[15] Yet, this has not caused all historians of the ancient Near East to avoid every use of such documents in writing ancient history. Sources must be used with care: modern historians must be aware of the deep biases of the authors of these sources, and whenever possible, various sources that refer to the same event must be studied together, since they are often mutually enlightening. But these sources should not simply be discarded.

The second problem of using the Bible as a source concerns the unusually complex transmission of the biblical text. Most sources for ancient Near Eastern history were unearthed in the last two centuries; they typically represent tablets or steles that were written soon after the events that they record. These ancient documents were usually not recopied extensively,[16] and were buried for two millennia or more before being uncovered. In contrast, the Bible was transmitted on papyrus and parchment in antiquity, and was changed as it was transmitted, at least in its earliest stages.[17] It is naïve to believe that we may recover the Bible's original text (what scholars call the "Urtext"), namely the text as penned by its original authors. The biblical texts found at Qumran among the Dead Sea Scrolls, and the evidence of ancient Bible translations—especially the Septuagint (the pre-Christian translation of the Bible into Greek)—suggest that even in antiquity, many different versions of the same text circulated. The multiple forms of texts in the Second Temple period confirms that we cannot, for example, assume that the text of Kings as we now have it is the same as the text of Kings when it was originally written.

This is a serious problem that is not unique to the Hebrew Bible. Almost all classical texts suffer from the same issue—we have relatively few papyri that have survived from antiquity, and even these are not autographs by the original authors. Most are medieval manuscripts. Especially in Classical Studies, the methods of textual reconstruction are well developed, allowing scholars to piece together the best text possible using the many texts and other kinds of evidence that are available to them. This discipline is as much an art as a science, yet there is a consensus that is helpful in reconstructing texts. Although scholars do not have the original works by an ancient Greek historian such as Herodotus or Thucydides, they recreate Greek history via the textual criticism of manuscripts that postdate the author by centuries. In the same careful way, we may reconstruct history using the Bible.

Though I am suggesting that theological and ideological biases, as well as issues of textual transmission, do not present insuperable problems, they are nevertheless serious impediments to writing a history of Israel. This means that a history of ancient Israel can never be written with finality. However, since historical background is useful for understanding many biblical texts, I have not given up on this venture. What follows is a basic history that, though tentative, will provide the readers with an essential picture.[18]

The Beginning of Israel

As noted above, scholars writing at the end of the twentieth century cast doubts on the biblical account of the beginning of Israel. This was true not only for what had been called the Patriarchal Period, but for the Conquest and the period of Judges as well. No outside confirmation exists for any aspect of the "Patriarchal Period," and thus, from a historical perspective, it is improper to speak of Abraham, Jacob, or Rachel as real figures, or as early Israelites or Jews. In addition, there is no Egyptian evidence for an extended sojourn of Israel in Egypt.[19] The fact that the Bible shows relatively little influence from Egypt also suggests that the biblical account of an extended sojourn there by hundreds of thousands of Israelites is not factual. Finally, as noted above, the account of the extensive conquest by all Israel given in Joshua does not match the archaeological record as we currently understand it.

Though various myths describe the origin of ancient Israel, none of these may be taken at face value by the historian. They represent later self-understandings of the nature of Israel, its constituent groups, it relations to its neighbors, and its connection to the land of Israel and its God.[20] (Israel is in no way unique here—most myths of origins have similar purposes, and may not be used in a simple-minded way by historians.) Therefore, especially when examining origins, it is important to use external rather than internal sources alone.

The first external reference to Israel is found on an Egyptian monumental stone dating from the time of the Egyptian pharaoh Merneptah. This document, called the Merneptah Stele by modern scholars, records events that probably transpired in 1207 B.C.E. In the middle of a list recording the Pharaoh's campaign against peoples in the area of the Mediterranean, it notes: "Israel is wasted; its seed is not."[21] Egyptian, like some other ancient languages, uses special signs (called "determinatives") before certain words to indicate what class of word they belong to. (This is helpful in reading hieroglyphics or cuneiform, which are not written alphabetically.) The sign before "Israel" refers to an ethnic group. Thus, this inscription suggests that a people called Israel lived at the Eastern Mediterranean coast in the very late thirteenth century B.C.E. The Egyptian claim to have obliterated this people is generally seen as hyperbolic, which is typical of such inscriptions.

Two Perspectives on Historical Periods

Conventionally, scholars divide history into periods, based on both internal and external factors. In the case of ancient Israel, they tend to use two types of periodization: an internal framework based on Israel's own political changes, and an external framework based on the regional powers into whose orbit Israel was absorbed. Given that external factors often influence internal factors, these two approaches at points reinforce each other.

Israel's History as Seen from the Outside

The earliest known external documentation of ancient Israel in 1207 B.C.E. coincides with weakness in the two major imperial powers of the time: Egypt and Mesopotamia. Though there were reasons internal to both empires for these developments, the arrival of the Sea Peoples (including the biblical Philistines), who wrecked havoc on the ancient Near Eastern sea coast, were also a factor in weakening these superpowers, especially Egypt. Other city-states around Israel may have begun to develop at this time, taking advantage of the power vacuum that had developed.

The early history of Israel also coincides with a major power shift from Egypt to Mesopotamia. By the end of the twelfth century, Egypt ceased controlling sections of Asia, though in the following centuries it would occasionally invade Israel and the surrounding areas.

The fate of Israel (in the north) and Judah (in the south) would change with the rise of the Mesopotamian powers. Mesopotamia often had two competing empires: Babylon to the south, and Assyria to the north. Neither was particularly powerful from the thirteenth through the early ninth centuries. This changed with the rise of the Assyrian dynasty, called the Calah kings after the new capital they established. These include Shalmaneser III (858–824), who campaigned against the Mediterranean city-states, and who defeated a coalition in which Ahab, the king of Northern Israel, played a leading role. Thus Israel became a vassal state of Assyria.

This relationship meant some loss of political autonomy, and an obligation to pay a sizable tribute to Assyria, which reasserted its claims during the reigns of the kings called the Sargonides (744–612). This dynasty was begun by the powerful Tiglath-Pileser III (744–727), called Pul in the Bible. Northern Israel rebelled against the Assyrians, and between 722 and 720, Samaria, the northern capital, was destroyed. In different sources, this is ascribed to either Shalmaneser V or Sargon II. The Assyrians were defeated by the Babylonians in 612, and the last remnants of the Assyrian army lost their final battle in 609.

Thus, by 612, Babylon had assumed the power formerly held by Assyria. The rise of Babylonian power had begun a decade earlier, with the Babylonian king Nabopolassar (625–615). The kingdom of Judah rebelled against the Babylonians; following earlier policy, it was given several chances to fall into line after it rebelled. In 597, a group of Judeans, including the king, was exiled to Babylon, while after a second rebellion in 586, the Temple in Jerusalem was destroyed, and more Judeans were exiled to Babylon.

Though the Babylonians took over the Assyrian empire, their behavior was not the same. The Babylonians seem to have been less cruel in war—at least their royal inscriptions brag less about bloody exploits. More significantly, they allowed exiled peoples to live together in their own communities in Babylon, forming ethnic neighborhoods in which earlier religious and cultural practices could and did flourish.[22] In contrast, the Assyrians had made forced population transfers, mixing together defeated peoples from various places so that their ethnic identities would disappear, leaving only an identity as Assyrians. This explains why northern Israel had soon disappeared after its destruction in 722–720, whereas the Judeans survived as an ethnic and religious group.

In 539 the Babylonian Empire fell to the Persians. The final Babylonian king, Nabonidus, instituted certain religious reforms that alienated the powerful priests of Marduk the Babylonian high god; these priests viewed the Persian king, Cyrus, as their savior and allowed him to conquer Babylon. They expected the conquering king to allow the proper worship to be restored; following the typical tolerance shown by conquerors to their vassals, this indeed happened. The Persians established a satrapy (a Persian administrative unit) called Yehud in the area of Judea, and allowed the Judeans to return there in 538.

The Persian control of the land of Israel ended in 332 B.C.E. with the conquest of Israel by Alexander the Great. Though Greek culture had been important earlier, a more significant type of Hellenization began at this time. It typically was not forced, but represented the desires of particular people and social classes to adopt the prestigious and attractive customs of the Greeks—much like their ancestors adopted Assyrian, Babylonian, and Persian customs. The vast empire of Alexander fell apart upon his death, and was divided among his generals. Israel had the great misfortune of falling on the border between the Ptolemies, who ruled from Egypt, and the Seleucids, who ruled from Syria; it was first under the rule of the Ptolemies, then of the Seleucids. With the exception of Antiochus IV (175–164), these kings were generally tolerant of Judaism and Jewish practices. The reasons why Antiochus IV promulgated certain decrees against the practice of Judaism in 167, and converted the Jerusalem temple into a Temple for Zeus, are obscure. These decrees were reversed in 164 by the successful Maccabean revolt. Greek control of the land of Israel ended in 63 B.C.E., with the Roman conquest. The Romans would ultimately destroy the Second Temple in 70 C.E., following a Jewish revolt, but this brings us beyond the biblical period.

Thus, in terms of external influences on Israel, the biblical period can thus be divided into the following periods: the pre-Assyrian period, the Assyrian period (mid-ninth century–612), the Babylonian period (612–539), the Persian period (539–332), and the Greek period (332–63). This periodization is not trivial, since the political fate of Israel would often be determined by the political practices of the powerful kingdom under whose orbit they fell, and Israel would often be influenced by the religious practices of their overlords.

Israel's History as Seen from the Inside

The internal periodization is somewhat different. Given that we know that a monarchy developed in ancient Israel, it is customary to refer to the period that preceded the monarchy as the premonarchic period. Given major problems in the use of both Joshua and Judges as historical sources, it is wise not to further divide this period into the period of the conquest and the period of the judges.

(However, it is likely that the monarchy did develop from some sort of judge or chieftain structure.) The period of the early monarchy is obscure because it is not attested in non-Israelite contemporaneous sources. The initial kings (Saul, but especially David and his son Solomon), according to the Bible, ruled over a united Israel. This period, which covers approximately 1000–922, is called the united monarchy. After this period, the tenuous union of the area north of Jerusalem, which I will call Northern Israel, with the area to the south, called Judah, dissolved. The Davidic monarchy continued in Judah, while in the north various other dynasties established themselves. From 922 until its demise in 722–720 (see above), the northern kingdom was typically the larger and more powerful one. This period from 922 to 722, when competing dynasties ruled over Judah and Northern Israel, is called the divided monarchy.

After 720, some kings from Judah were able to expand northward, capturing some of the land that had belonged to the Northern Kingdom. As noted above, in 597 and then in 586, following rebellions against Babylon, some Judeans were exiled to Babylon; in 586, the Babylonian army destroyed the (First) Temple in Jerusalem, the capital of Judea. Thus, the years between 597 and 586 usher in the exilic period.

The exile did not last long. In 538, the year following his conquest of Babylon, Cyrus allowed the Judeans to return home to Israel, then called the Persian province of Yehud—an event often referred to in modern times as *shivat tziyyon* (שִׁיבַת צִיּוֹן, "the return to Zion"). Thus, the exilic period began between 597 and 586 (depending on who was exiled when), and ended in 538, with Cyrus' proclamation. The period after 538 is thus referred to as the postexilic period.

Though the exilic period was short, it was crucial. It represented a crisis for all the major Israelite institutions that had developed, particularly the monarchy, which no longer had a land to rule, and the priesthood, which no longer had a temple at which to officiate. Prophecy, too, may have fundamentally changed, as some people wondered whether God would continue to speak to his people, Israel, outside of the land of Israel. Thus, various important changes and realignments of religion transpired in this period.

In sum, and in the broadest strokes, we may speak of the exilic period as a watershed period, preceded by the preexilic period and followed by the postexilic period. Monarchy was a crucial institution of the preexilic period, where we may speak of the premonarchic period, the united monarchy, and then the divided monarchy.

Combining the Two Perspectives

Can we blend the internal and external periodization? Yes, by noting that the preexilic/premonarchic period was characterized by ascendancy of the Assyrians and then the Babylonians. Babylonian ascendancy continued through almost all of the exilic period, which ended one year after the Persian conquest of Babylon. The postexilic period was characterized by Persian and then Greek rule.

The chart below summarizes the periodization of ancient Israel from both an internal and external perspective:

CENTURIES (B.C.E.)							
CRUCIAL DATE		1000	922		586	538	
EXTERNAL							
	Egyptian domination			Assyrian domination	Babylonian domination	Persian domination	Greek domination
INTERNAL							
	Premonarchic	United monarchy	Divided monarchy		Exilic	Postexilic	

5

With Scissors and Paste

The Sources of Genesis

Primary Reading: Genesis 1–3.

Division of the Bible into Chapters

We are used to works of fiction and nonfiction being divided into chapters. Each chapter is supposed to be, in some sense, a self-enclosed unity. The divisions between chapters offer the ideal time to take a break—to reflect on the meaning as a whole of the unit you have just completed reading, a chance to get a drink or a snack, etc. Taking a break between Genesis 1 and 2 would seem natural for any of these purposes—but anyone who did this would be misreading the first unit of Genesis. That's because this chapter break is located in the wrong place.

The chapter numbers now found in Bibles are not integral to the text. Rather, they date from the thirteenth century C.E.[1] They first appeared in manuscripts of the Vulgate, the Latin translation of the Bible that the early Church father Jerome had written. By the mid-sixteenth century, Jewish editors introduced chapters into printed Hebrew Bibles as well. Thus, the chapter divisions are relatively recent, representing one particular understanding about how the Bible may be subdivided. The "standard" chapter divisions have no authority, especially for Jews, and they are best ignored.

Division of the Bible into Paragraphs

Torah scrolls divide the Pentateuch into the equivalent of paragraph units by placing white space between units.[2] These white spaces are of two types: short ones called *setumah* (סְתוּמָה, "closed"), where the next unit continues on the same line; and longer ones called *petuchah* (פְּתוּחָה, "open"), where the rest of the line is left open and the following unit continues only on the next line. This tradition of leaving spaces dates back at least to the Dead Sea Scrolls (mostly from the third century B.C.E. to the first century C.E.). However, the Dead Sea Scrolls do not always agree with the divisions found in contemporary Torah scrolls, which the great medieval Jewish scholar Maimonides (1135–1204) established on the basis of a highly accurate tenth-century biblical manuscript called the Aleppo Codex. In other words, spaces or paragraph divisions—which vary somewhat even among medieval Hebrew manuscripts and printed editions of the Bible—have never been entirely uniform. They do, however, represent a significant early interpretive tradition.

Unfortunately, these divisions are not reflected in English Bible translations. Rather, each translator has independently decided where units begin and end. The typesetters have set the type accordingly. Thus, for example, the paragraph breaks in the JPS translation represent the places where three committees working in the second part of the twentieth century felt new units should be demarcated. As with any translation, their decisions deserve consideration—but are not definitive.

Division of the Bible into Verses

Various rabbinic sources from the Mishnah (approximately 200 C.E.) attest to the division of the Bible into *pesukim* (פְּסוּקִים, literally "breaking points"), what we would call verses.[3] No early comprehensive list exists of where these breaking points were perceived to be. However, some evidence suggests that they were largely the same as the later divisions found in medieval Hebrew manuscripts, which indicate verse endings by a musical note (called a *silluk*—a vertical line) under the final word, as well as what looks like a colon (*sof pasuk*) after each verse. Thus, of the three divisions noted in manuscripts—chapters, paragraphs, and verses—the latter should be seen as the most ancient and authoritative. Yet, there are sometimes differences in how the same words are divided into verses in different biblical contexts; some medieval manuscripts reflect these differences in their verse counts. Given the variants that we find, the verse divisions should not be seen as fully authoritative. Occasionally, weighty evidence suggests that a unit of thought really ends midverse while the second part of that verse starts a new unit, or that a word at the end of one verse belongs at the beginning of the next, or vice versa.

Discerning the Bible's Literary Units

The foregoing conclusions concerning chapter, paragraph, and verse divisions have significant implications for how we read the Bible. We have to discover and use textual clues other than these "late" formal markings to decide where units begin and end. Thus, the Bible should be envisioned as a text punctuated only by word spaces[4]—with nothing to indicate sections, paragraphs, or even verses. Our first step when reading *all* biblical texts must be to subdivide that biblical text into these kinds of units.

An analogy illustrates this procedure and why it matters. Let's imagine that a typesetter made a mistake in laying out the type of a collection of poems, and printed them all as one long poem. Someone with modern or postmodern interests might enjoy reading the result as a unified work. But most of us would prefer to divide the long poem into separate poems. To do so, we would use stylistic and content-based criteria. If, for example, an E. E. Cummings poem followed an Emily Dickinson poem, this would be easy; in other cases, it would be more difficult.

The Bible should be treated like this imaginary poetry book. Even though our printed version shows chapters and verses, these should be ignored. It must be imagined as a single, continuous text. Furthermore, we must develop robust criteria for distinguishing the compositional units embedded in it. Otherwise, we might do the equivalent of reading the first two lines of a Cummings poem as the conclusion of the preceding Dickinson poem!

The criteria used for separating biblical sources are similar to those used to analyze poetry. We read carefully, attuned to changes in style and content, looking for contradictions between verses.

None of these criteria is airtight or *absolutely* objective. There is no consensus about how much variation a text may contain in order to be considered a unified work. Nor do scholars always agree on whether or not a larger text is self-contradictory. Thus in some cases we find real debate about where a unit begins and/or ends. In most cases, however, there is widespread agreement.

Genesis 1–3 as a Unit

Genesis 1–3 is inconsistent. It recounts several events twice—for example, the creation of humankind is narrated first in 1:26–28 and then in 2:7–23. These episodes cannot be seen as a general description of the creation of humankind in chapter 1, which is elaborated and filled in chapter 2, because these two accounts differ significantly in their detail. In chapter 1, on day six, first the land animals are created (vv. 24–25), and then man and woman are created simultaneously (vv. 26–28). In contrast, in chapter 2, first man is created (v. 7), then the animals are created (vv. 18–20), and only after these are found unsuitable to be man's partner (v. 20) is woman created (vv. 21–23). A single story, written by a single author, would not be self-contradictory in such a significant matter.

This might be the most significant difference between these stories, but once it is noted, other distinctions quickly become apparent. Each individual difference by itself might not be convincing, but cumulatively, they become compelling. Other differences include the fact that in Genesis 1 the deity is called God (**אֱלֹהִים**), whereas in much of chapters 2–3 the deity is called *YHWH Elohim* (**יְהוָה אֱלֹהִים**, "the LORD God").[5] The units use different words for crucial terms like "creation"—thus in 1:27, the first human is "created" (**ברא**, *b-r-'*), whereas in 2:7 the human is "formed" (**יצר**, *y-tz-r*). In fact, the word translated as "create" (**ברא**) is used a total of seven times in 1:1–2:3, but not at all in 2:4–3:24.

Additionally, the style of chapter 1 is unlike the style of most of chapters 2–3. Genesis 1 is highly structured into "days," each with a recurring set of formulas (e.g., "God said . . . it was so," "And God saw that this was good. And there was evening and there was morning, X day."). In contrast, most of chapters 2–3 is free flowing, with a much looser structure, and none of these formulaic phrases. This is connected to another distinction: the structure of chapter 1 portrays a powerful, majestic God, while the God of much of chapters 2–3—who "mov[es] about in the garden" (3:8), talks to people (3:9–11), and even tenderly clothes them (3:21)—has a fundamentally different nature. These two pictures of God are the work of different authors.

Giving the Text a Break

Where is the literary break between these two stories? In other words, where does the story that begins with Genesis 1:1 end? Verse 1:1 and the first half of 2:4, namely 2:4a, frame the story. The word pair "heaven . . . earth" (הַשָּׁמַיִם . . . הָאָרֶץ) as well as the verb "to create" (**ברא**) appear together in these two contexts only. This repetition forms a frame or envelope around the story. Genesis 2:4a, "Such is the story of heaven and earth when they were created," therefore concludes the first story.

This device—in which a phrase or several words indicate the limits of a unit—is called an "inclusio," and it is common in biblical writing. For example, the Tower of Babel story in Genesis 11 begins וַיְהִי כָל־הָאָרֶץ, "The whole earth was," and concludes עַל־פְּנֵי כָּל־הָאָרֶץ, "over the face of the whole earth" (v. 9; transl. adapted). Similarly, Psalm 8 begins and ends with the very same verse: "O LORD, our Lord, How majestic is Your name throughout the earth" (vv. 2, 10).

In general, the word *eileh* (אֵלֶּה, "such is") may be used either to point backward (as a conclusion) or to point forward (as an introduction). In this case, however, it cannot be an introduction for two reasons: (1) Its use of "heaven and earth" specifically refers back to Genesis 1:1 and other instances in that chapter, while this phrase is never found in 2:5–3:24; and (2) it uses the verb *b-r-'* (ברא, "to create"), which is characteristic of chapter 1 but absent in 2:5–3:24.

Genesis 2:4b, the second part of 2:4, thus introduces a new story, which continues past chapter 3. In fact, the vocabulary of 2:4 further suggests that it is composite; it is unlikely that a single author would refer to the created world first as "heaven and earth" (2:4a) and then as "earth and heaven" (2:4b). This explains why many Bibles, including the JPS translation, begin a new paragraph with 2:4b, breaking in the middle of a verse.

Two Stories and Their Relationship

Once the division between these two stories is determined at the middle of Genesis 2:4, a final difference between them jumps out—they are not both creation stories of the same type. The first story describes the creation of the world, in which people play a role alongside all else that is created. In contrast, the second creation story has people as its main focus, narrating the creation of parts of the world only to the extent that they are relevant to people. Thus 1:1–2:4a is an ancient Israelite story about the creation of the world, while 2:4b–3:24 is a different story, by a different Israelite author with different ideas, and its focus is the creation of humankind.

This analysis raises two issues: If Genesis 1:1–2:4a and 2:4b–3 are telling different stories, then why not read the second story as an elaboration of the first, thus reading chapters 1–3 as one long story? In addition, if we insist on reading them as two stories, is the model propounded here, of two stories being woven together, a plausible model for how literature was produced in the ancient world?

The possibility of reading Genesis 1–3 as a compositional unity is vitiated by the fundamental differences in vocabulary, style, and content between the two stories. While in theory, a story about the creation of humankind might come as an elaboration or culmination of a general creation story, in practice we could only claim that this were the case if the two largely agreed in content, style, and vocabulary. Given the significant differences in all of these areas, the stories should be separated, and viewed as written by different authors.

The second question, concerning the blending of the two stories together into a single story, highlights one of the main differences between much of ancient and modern writing—a difference that we must simply accept and get used to, or we will be like Marta (see chapter 3). In most modern societies, the name of the author is closely linked to the literary work he or she has produced; through copyright control, the author can protect that work. Ancient writing was quite different. Much writing in the ancient Near East was anonymous. Beyond that, there was no conception that a work must be copied over exactly. The copyist typically played a creative role in the transmission of texts, often adding to them. This may be seen most clearly in a variety of Mesopotamian texts, most especially the Gilgamesh epic, which expanded over time, and even incorporated large sections from other compositions.[6] It may also be seen in various Dead Sea Scroll manuscripts of the Torah as well.[7] In fact, in many ways the Bible is like modern texts that circulate on the Internet—their original author is often unknown, and many users who forward the texts revise them or add to them in significant ways. We must get used to this different notion of "text" as we approach the Bible.

Source Criticism of the Torah

The stories in Genesis 1:1–2:4a and 2:4b–3:24 should not be viewed as fragments that became incorporated into the Torah. Rather, they are each introductions to a much more extensive document, or "source," that may be found in the Torah. It is called "source criticism" when we use this type of analysis to divide the Torah text into earlier written documents that have been combined by editors or redactors. When applied to the Torah as a whole, it suggests that the Torah is comprised of four main sources—four originally separate, (more or less) complete documents—that have been woven together.[8] The date of these documents, called J, E, D, and P, has been the subject of much debate in recent biblical scholarship. The oldest document is most likely J, which was given this name since in Genesis it typically uses the four-letter name of God, *Yhwh* (יהוה), which some Christian translators have transcribed as "Jehovah." The JPS translation represents this name as "the Lord," while other translations use "the Eternal" or Yahweh or YHWH. Probably of Judean authorship, this source was written in the first half of the monarchic period. Next is E, the Elohist document, so named because it typically refers to God in Genesis using the term *Elohim*

(אֱלֹהִים, "God"). It may originate from the Northern kingdom, and is likely slightly later than J. E is relatively short, and unlike the J and P, it is unclear if it should be viewed as an originally separate document. P refers to the Priestly source, which also uses *Elohim* and other divine names (but not *YHWH*) in Genesis. This document is shaped by Priestly concerns, including order, purity, and assuring the divine presence among Israel. Its date has been an issue of great debate in biblical scholarship. Most likely, this source represents a school of thought that was active over a long period of time, both before and after the Babylonian exile of 586. The D source stands for Deuteronomy, the final book of the Torah. With the exception of parts of the final chapters, which contain a diversity of material, most of Deuteronomy features a special vocabulary and particular theological concerns—especially the proper worship of a single God in the proper way in the proper place (Jerusalem), where His "name" resides. Like P, D is not a totally unified composition from a single time and place, but represents a stream of tradition that is more or less coterminus with P. With the exception of the D source, which more or less has its own book, the Torah as it is now structured represents a careful combination of these sources.

Putting the Pieces Together

Given the apparent existence of individual sources, they must have been edited together, or "redacted," at some point. Most likely this occurred in stages. Scholars call the final editor R, for redactor. In this form, the work of the Priestly source has a particularly strong voice, and even introduces the Torah. (Gen. 1:1–2:4a is P; Gen. 2:4b ff. is J.) For this reason, some scholars equate R with the final voice of P.

Exactly why the sources were intertwined in this way is unclear. Exploring this issue really involves asking two questions: (1) Why were all of these sources retained, rather than just retaining the latest or most authoritative one? (2) Why were they combined in this odd way, rather than being left as complete documents that would be read side by side, much like the model of the four different and *separate* gospels, which introduce the Christian Bible or New Testament?

Since there is no direct evidence going back to the redaction of the Torah, these issues may be explored only in a most tentative fashion, with plausible rather than definitive answers. Probably the earlier documents had a certain prestige and authority in ancient Israel, and could not simply be discarded.[9] Additionally, the redaction of the Torah from a variety of sources most likely represents an attempt to enfranchise those groups who held those particular sources as authoritative. Certainly the Torah does not contain *all* of the early traditions of Israel. Yet, it does contain the traditions that the redactor felt were important for bringing together a core group of Israel (most likely during the Babylonian exile of 586–538 B.C.E.).

The mixing of these sources by intertwining them preserved a variety of sources and perspectives. (Various methods of intertwining were used—the preferred method was to interleave large blocks of material, as in the initial chapters of Genesis. However, when this would have caused narrative difficulties, as in the flood story or the plagues of Exodus, the sources were interwoven—several verses from one source, followed by several verses from the other.) More than one hundred years ago, the great American scholar G. F. Moore called attention to the second-century Christian scholar Tatian, who composed the Diatessaron.[10] This work is a harmony of the Gospels, where most of the four canonical gospels are combined into a single work, exactly the same way that scholars propose the four Torah strands of J, E, D, and P have been combined. This, along with other ancient examples, shows that even though the classical model posited by source criticism may seem strange to *us*, it reflects a way that people wrote literature in antiquity.[11]

The first step for reading the beginning of Genesis is complete. We know that the story that begins in 1:1 ends at 2:4a. This is a significant step, since it allows us, encourages us, or perhaps even forces us to read Genesis 1:1–2:4a apart from the story that follows. But this is only a technical, preliminary step to interpreting this material. The following chapter will address the meaning of each of these stories.

6

Creation vs. Creationism

Genesis 1–3 as Myth

Primary Reading: Genesis 1–3.

Genesis 1–3 as Science

Defining the boundaries between different biblical units, and thus understanding where one story ends and another begins, is a means toward an end, rather than an end in itself. The next stage, interpreting the story, or in this case, independently interpreting the two creation stories embedded in Genesis 1–3, is a more difficult and a more subjective task than determining that two stories have been combined. Interpretation depends on genre. Thus, as we begin to explore the meaning of these texts, we are no different than Marta (see "The Rules of the Game" in chapter 3), who is confronting the newspaper—and its comics section—for the first time.

We may even be worse off than Marta. We naturally make foreign stories fit the genre that they most resemble from our experience. The stories in Genesis 1–3 deal with creation—with the origin of the world, of vegetation, of human life, of the animals. At first blush, they look like science, a genre interested in answering basic questions about the *real* structure of the *real* world and its constituent features. If we subscribe to mainstream science, Genesis 1–3 looks like wrong, bad, or primitive science.

Particularly in America, many people understand the Bible to be science; in fact, they understand it to be more correct than mainstream scientific assertions, which are, after all, just theories. This book is not the place to explore in detail this position, often called "creationism" or even "creation science."[1] This movement has two primary problems: (1) it begins with an assertion, not explicit in the Bible itself, that the Bible must be understood as literally true—as science, natural history, or history; and (2) it ignores evidence within the Bible that biblical texts should not be read in the same way as modern scientific literature.

The first words of the Bible are: "When God began to create heaven and earth"; they are not: "This is a scientific treatment of the origin of the world." In general the Bible does not introduce works with genre labels; it does not explicitly mark the distinction between, for example, history and historical fiction. This is problematic for anyone who wants to interpret the Bible as an ancient Israelite, reading it as they did. Indeed, this is perhaps the biggest problem we confront in interpreting the Bible, since no section contains a library call number, telling us whether it belongs on the fiction or the nonfiction shelves. Nor may we automatically assume that the text, which is over two millennia old, may be read the same way as the contemporary genre that it is most similar to.

These observations have important implications for Genesis 1–3. They do not begin with a genre label "science," and there is no reason why we should presume that the author wanted them to be viewed as such. The difficult task of assigning their genre must follow an internal analysis of these texts, and must take into account ancient, rather than modern, ways of reading texts.[2]

Most people understand the goal of science as describing *the* way a particular phenomenon or object works or develops. In chapter 5, I raised problems about reading Genesis 1–3 as science, since it showed that this passage incorporates two mutually exclusive accounts of creation. Such contradictions are not acceptable in science; this suggests at the very least that the redactor who opted to combine these two stories did not understand them as *the* definitive, scientific account for how the world was created. The job of the scientist, like the modern historian, is to analyze competing theories, and on the basis of evidence to determine which *one* is correct.

Genesis 1–3 as Myth

The two creation stories incorporated into Genesis 1–3 should be understood as myths, not as science. "Myth" is an ambiguous term. Colloquially, it is often understood as wrong or bad science, as a fundamentally primitive and incorrect way of understanding the world that has no place in modern society. In fact, in everyday speech, the statement "That's a myth" is synonymous with "That's false."

The scholarly world, particularly within anthropology and classical studies, views myth—its significance and its interpretation—in a fundamentally different way. Though there are almost as many understandings of myth as scholars who explore this issue, there is a consensus that myth is an essential, and constructive, element of all cultures.

The classicist Walter Burkert, in *Structure and History in Greek Mythology and Ritual*, developed some of the most valuable insights concerning myth.[3] Most useful is Burkert's observation that "myth can be defined as a metaphor at tale level."[4] Let's imagine that Marta overheard someone say to a lover, "You are a rose." Marta would object, or might at the very least be bewildered, noting, "Your lover isn't green, doesn't have thorns, and is lacking a flower!" But metaphors, unlike nonfigurative language (e.g., "you are reading a book"), are neither right nor wrong.[5] Metaphors can be classified in other ways: helpful or unhelpful; original or standard; etc. Yet all metaphors are literally false—by definition. We can say the same about myths: they may be literally false, but like metaphors, they are true—often profoundly so—on a figurative level. Both metaphors and myths play an important role in society because of the limitations of nonfigurative language.

The more technical definition offered by Burkert of a myth is "a traditional tale with secondary, partial reference to something of collective importance."[6] Let us focus on the core of this definition: "something of collective importance." The job of the interpreter of myths is to discover how the myth is using mythological/metaphorical language to convey "something of collective importance." All of the typical tools of interpretation must be used to understand what this "something" is, and how the myth is constructed to develop its ideas about this something, or in the case of more complex myths, these "somethings."

Not only words and their individual meanings determine a literary work's interpretation. The way in which the words are patterned—their structure—is often as important in shaping meaning.[7] One question that helps us understand the structure of the first creation story of Genesis 1:1–2:4a is: Where does day one of creation begin? Various pieces of evidence suggest that it begins in verse 3, and that in terms of structure, there are six primary days of creation, which cover verses 3–31. At first, the idea that day one begins in verse 3, and not with verse 1, seems illogical, but every day of creation from day two onward begins with the formula: "God said, 'Let there be . . .'" (vv. 6, 9, 14, 20, 24). This suggests that the description of day one begins only in verse 3: "God said, 'Let there be light'; and there was light."

The significance of the preceding two verses and their place in the narrative become clearer in relation to the concluding verses, Genesis 2:1–4a. The intervening material, 1:3–31, is characterized by structure. Each day begins "God said, 'Let . . .'" The phrase "(And) God said" characterizes the initiation of creative activity, occurring in eight verses (3, 6, 9, 11, 14, 20, 24, 26). Surely this is the story that the psalmist is referring to when he states, "By the word of the LORD the heavens were made, by the breath of His mouth, all their host" (33:6). Six times after God creates "by the word," we read "it was so" (vv. 7, 9, 11, 15, 24, 30). Six times God sees that what He created was good (vv. 4, 10, 12, 18, 21, 25; with a modification of "very good" in v. 31).[8] Six times we have the refrain, "And there was evening and there was morning, day . . ." (vv. 5, 8, 13, 19, 23, 31; transl. adapted). All of these phrases are missing in both 1:1–3 and in 2:1–4a; the fact that those verses do not fit the pattern of the central creation story establishes them as "other," as not part of the actual story. Instead, they should be seen as an introduction and conclusion—or better, a prologue and an epilogue—to that story.

This prologue and epilogue are joined together not only through the elements that they lack, but also through the prominent use of alliteration that distinguishes these small units. The Bible opens alliteratively: *bereishit bara* (בְּרֵאשִׁית בָּרָא, "When . . . began to create"); the second verse describes the earth as *tohu va-vohu* (תֹהוּ וָבֹהוּ, "unformed and void") and mentions a *ruach merachefet* (רוּחַ מְרַחֶפֶת, "[divine] wind hovering"; transl. adapted). This attention to sound is echoed in verses 2:2–3, which seem to revel in the play among the repeating words *ha-shevi'i* (הַשְּׁבִיעִי, "seventh"), *shavat* (שבת, "to cease"), and *asah* (עשׂה, "to do"). Along with the phrase "create . . . heaven and earth" (found in 1:1 and echoed in 2:4a; see "Giving the Text a Break" in chapter 5), this alliteration helps to define 1:1–2:4a as a unit.

The Meaning of Genesis 1:1–2:4a

But what does this unit mean? The structural elements are not repeated for aesthetic purposes; rather, these repetitions encode a key message of this chapter: God is a highly organized, powerful creator. He says: It is so, it is good.[9] There are no ifs or buts—the world is completely responsive to His commands.

This aspect of the God of this creation story is further reflected in another aspect of the story's structure: the manner in which these six days of creation may be divided into two triads, where elements A, B, and C of each triad are connected.[10] The following diagram illustrates this structure:

<table>
<tr><td rowspan="2">Precreation</td><td>Day 1
Light</td><td>Day 2
Sky, water bodies</td><td>Day 3
Land, vegetation</td><td rowspan="2">Postcreation</td></tr>
<tr><td>Day 4
Luminaries</td><td>Day 5
Birds, fish</td><td>Day 6
Land animals</td></tr>
</table>

On day one God creates light,[11] and on day four, the luminaries; on day two God creates heavens and water, and on day four, its inhabitants, birds and fish; on day three God creates land and vegetation, and on day six, land animals, including humankind. The symmetry, which is striking, highlights the orderliness of creation. It is even present in the alliterative mirroring of the precreation (1:1–2) and postcreation (2:1–4a) story.

This emphasis on order is not surprising given that this is a Priestly story. The Priestly School in ancient Israel concerned itself with order and ordering, and how this reflects on God.[12] Such concerns may be seen, for example, in Leviticus 20:25–26, which deals with things that are being *b-d-l* (בדל, "set apart" or "separated"):

> *So you shall set apart* the clean beast from the unclean, the unclean bird from the clean. You shall not draw abomination upon yourselves through beast or bird or anything with which the ground is alive, which *I have set apart* for you to treat as unclean. You shall be holy to Me, for I the LORD am holy, and *I have set you apart* from other peoples to be Mine. (emphasis added)

That same verbal root is used five times in Genesis 1 (vv. 4, 6, 7, 14, 18).

The opposite of structure is chaos, and it is thus appropriate that 1:1–2 describe primeval chaos—a world that is "unformed and void," containing darkness and a mysterious wind. This story does not describe creation out of nothing (Latin: *creatio ex nihilo*). Primeval stuff already exists in verses 1–2, and the text shows no concern for how it originated. Rather, it is a myth about how God alone structured primordial matter into a highly organized world. Only upon its completion is this structure "very good." And only then can God "rest" (2:1–3).

Much of the activity of God throughout this story is described using the verb *bara* (ברא), typically translated "to create," a word used more than fifty times in the Bible. Unlike other creation words, however, it always has God as its subject. That is, so to speak, God may *bara* but humans can never *bara* (at least according to the attested evidence). This verb appears to be part of a small class of Hebrew words that are used in reference to God only, thereby suggesting that in certain respects, God is totally other.[13] Use of the verb *bara* accentuates God's majesty. It also fits the depiction of God elsewhere in this myth.

Language that sets God apart is unusually difficult to translate. In most cases, when biblical authors ascribed actions to God—like "to see," "to do," "to hear," "to fashion"—they used the same verb typically used for people: they modeled their understanding of God after their real-life experiences. Where the authors avoided depicting God through human analogy, they pointed to the incomparability of God—whom normal language cannot portray. Thus, Genesis 1:1 might (awkwardly) be translated: "In the beginning of God's creation (which is different from human creation, but "creation" is the closest English word to describe this action) of heaven and earth . . .."

Humankind in the Priestly Creation Story

Myths, like many other narrative genres, not only describe, but also prescribe. Few are neutral, and most make value judgments. Some of the value judgments made by the first creation story are obvious and have been noted already: the world is very good, and God is powerful and is heeded. The structure of our chart (above) might suggest that each of the boxed elements, representing what was created on each day, are of equal value. Is this so—or as a creation myth, does the text also establish value judgments concerning the most important or significant element(s) of creation?

This story highlights the creation of humankind. This is not surprising in a text written by people. The creation of humankind is the longest section, comprising verses 26–30. Only after people are created is the world "very good" (v. 31), rather than simply "good," as in all of the earlier days of creation. Only people "rule" and "master" (v. 28). Only for people is the act of creation expressed using the plural "Let us" (v. 26). And only with people does the text express itself in poetry (v. 27).

These last two points require further clarification. Let us look more closely at Genesis 1:26–27, which reads:

> And God said, "Let us make man in our image, after our likeness. They shall rule the fish of the sea, the birds of the sky, the cattle, the whole earth, and all the creeping things that creep on earth." And God created man in His image, in the image of God He created him; male and female He created them.

The meaning of the first person plural "us" and "our" has been the focus of great debate and polemic even in antiquity.[14] The suggestion that here God is speaking in the "royal we" is often propounded. However, this is unlikely, since such usage is otherwise unattested with verbs in the Bible.[15]

More likely, the text is implicitly portraying God in terms of a human king: God is talking to his royal counselors or cabinet.[16] Such imagery appears clearly in other biblical texts, such as Job 1–2, Isaiah 6, and especially 1 Kings 22:19: "I saw the LORD seated upon His throne, with all the host of heaven standing in attendance to the right and to the left of Him." The creation of people is so significant that this creative act alone demands that God consult his cabinet, comprised of angels or other heavenly figures. But as the next verse makes clear via a singular verb, consultation is their only role: God creates people without their assistance.

In several respects, the New Revised Standard Version (NRSV) translation better captures the essence of Genesis 1:27 than the JPS translation. The NRSV prints the verse indented, as poetry:

> So God created humankind in His image,
> In the image of God He created them;
> Male and female He created them.

Though a more thorough discussion of Hebrew poetry will wait until we study the more poetic texts such as prophecy and psalms (see "The Poetry of Isaiah" in chapter 17), this verse has obviously nonprosaic features: its division into distinct sections of roughly equal length, and its use of repetition (e.g., "God," "created," "image," "them") among its various lines. This poetic interlude in the middle of an otherwise prose passage heightens the significance of the creation of humankind.

In the Image of God

A close look at the Hebrew wording resolves the meaning of the phrase "image of God"[17] as well as whether it is "man" or "humankind" that is being created. Genesis 1:27 uses the word *ha-adam* (הָאָדָם). Generally this is a gender-neutral term, used to convey the meaning "humankind" as well as "a person" of either gender. The last part of the verse, "Male and female He created them," makes it clear that *ha-adam* refers to "humankind" rather than "man." (Largely under the influence of Genesis 2—which first describes the creation of a man, and then the creation of a woman—Gen. 1:27 has sometimes been understood as "God created man. . . ." But as we have seen, these are two separate creation stories, and Genesis 2 sheds no light on the meaning of *ha-adam* in 1:27, which is gender-neutral.)

The word *tzelem* (צֶלֶם, "image") elsewhere always refers to a physical representation. For example, the Book of Ezekiel uses *tzelem* when it refers to "men sculptured upon the walls, *figures* of Chaldeans drawn in vermilion" (23:14) or when it accuses Israel of fornicating with "phallic *images*" (16:17). The word often refers to idols (e.g., Num. 33:52; Ezek. 7:20; Amos 5:26; 2 Chron. 23:17).

It always signifies a concrete entity rather than an abstract one. This is not surprising since the Bible (in contrast to most medieval philosophical traditions, both Jewish and Christian) often depicts God in corporeal terms, as in Exodus 24:10: "and they saw the God of Israel: under His feet. . . ." Ezekiel, a priest whose writing shares many features with that of the Priestly school, describes God in highly corporeal terms in his initial vision (Eze. 1:26–28a):

> Above the expanse over their heads was the semblance of a throne, in appearance like sapphire; and on top, upon this semblance of a throne, there was the semblance of a human form. From what appeared as his loins up, I saw a gleam as of amber—what looked like a fire encased in a frame; and from what appeared as his loins down, I saw what looked like fire. There was a radiance all about him. Like the appearance of the bow which shines in the clouds on a day of rain, such was the appearance of the surrounding radiance. That was the appearance of the semblance of the Presence of the LORD.

God is here depicted as a physical being, who has an image in "the semblance of a human form." Furthermore, the gender of God cannot be distinguished, since from loins down, God is encased by fire. This may fit quite neatly the possible implications of Genesis 1:27: that humankind, created male and female, mimics God.[18]

However we interpret the creation of humankind, these creations are unlike any other. Various elements in Genesis 1:26–30 highlight the significance of humankind's being created in God's (physical) image, with male and female equal. The conclusion of this myth, however, describes the Sabbath in a manner that even surpasses humankind—only the Sabbath is "declared holy" (Gen. 2:3).[19] Holiness is especially important within the Priestly system, in which the Holy Sabbath plays a leading role (see especially Exod. 31:12–17). Thus, in offering these evaluations, the first creation story highlights the importance of both humankind and the Sabbath.

The Meaning of Genesis 2:4b–3:24

Critical biblical scholarship allows us—perhaps even forces us—to see Genesis 1:1–2:4a and 2:4b–3:24 as two distinct stories that should be interpreted separately. Of course we cannot easily forget the preceding story as we read the Garden of Eden story. However, it is even harder to put aside all that we already "know" about this story itself. No biblical story is more familiar in Western culture.

As it happens, the story as widely known has been filled out through various (Christian) interpretations. For example, nowhere does the text itself tell us what the forbidden fruit was. In early Christian tradition it was generally understood as an apple, whereas early Jewish tradition offered several opinions as to the fruit's identity, with the fig being the most popular—and contextually the most appropriate (see especially Gen. 3:7).[20]

Other dearly held views of this text are also not borne out by a close reading. Thus, we might believe that its main theme is the curse received by the woman (and all women), yet the word "curse" is absent in God's comments to her (Gen. 3:16), while it is present in God's statements both to the serpent (3:14) and to the man (3:17).[21] Moreover, the doctrines of the Fall of Man or original sin are nowhere to be found in this passage, though they appear in early Christian interpretation of the text.[22]

The Garden Story is about immortality lost and sexuality gained.[23] It begins from a simple premise: originally, people were immortal. In fact, the huge life spans recorded in the early chapters of Genesis are part of an effort to make a bridge between that original immortality and "normal" life spans. As immortal beings, they were asexual; in the Garden story God does not tell them to "be fertile and increase" as they were told in the first creation story (Gen. 1:28). Sexuality is discovered only after eating from the tree, when "they perceived that they were naked" (3:7). In fact, the divine command of 2:17 should not be understood as often translated—"for as soon as you eat of it, you shall die" (so the JPS translation)—but rather "for as soon as you eat of it, you shall become mortal." The connection between (procreative) sexuality and mortality is compelling and was well understood even in antiquity—if people were to be both sexually procreative and immortal, disastrous overpopulation would result.[24]

Many details within chapters 2–3 support this interpretation. The tree that is first forbidden is (literally) "the tree of knowledge of good and bad." Here *da-at* (דַּעַת, "knowledge") is being used in a sense that it often has in the Bible: intimate or sexual knowledge. "Good and bad" is being used here as a figure of speech called a "merism": two opposite terms are joined by the word "and"; the resulting figure means "everything" or "the ultimate."[25] (A merism is likewise used in Genesis 1:1, "heaven and earth," which there means the entire world.) The words "good and bad" have no moral connotation here.

Only after the primordial couple eat from the tree do they gain sexual awareness. Indeed, immediately after this story concludes, we read "Now the man knew his wife Eve, and she conceived and bore Cain" (Gen. 4:1). That is, eating from the tree of "knowledge" leads to a very specific type of "knowing." Nowhere in the text is this knowledge depicted as intellectual or ethical.

This reading also explains why the tree of life is mentioned only toward the end of the story (Gen. 3:22). Early in the story, people were immortal, so that tree offered no advantage, and thus was not mentioned. However, only after eating from the tree of ultimate "knowledge," becoming sexual, and becoming mortal, does the tree of life come into focus. Eating from this tree would allow people to become both immortal and sexual, creating an overpopulation problem. The first couple was expelled not as punishment, but so that they might not "take also from the tree of life and eat, and live forever!" (3:22).

The renaming of the woman as Eve, *chavvah* (חַוָּה, "progenitress"), "because she was the mother of all the living" (Gen. 3:20), happens only after eating from the tree. This too bolsters the "sexual" reading of this story—eating of the tree of ultimate "knowledge" turns the wife of Adam from *ha-ishah* (הָאִשָּׁה, "the woman") into a (potential) mother.

God's response to the woman after she eats from the tree is *not* a curse. The words "And to the woman He said, / 'I will make most severe / Your pangs in childbearing; / In pain shall you bear children. / Yet your urge shall be for your husband, / And he shall rule over you'" (Gen. 3:16) are a description of women's new state: procreative, with all the "pains" connected to procreation in the premodern world, including the natural pain of childbirth. This verse is not stating (as a harmonistic reading of Genesis 1–3 might imply) that before eating the fruit women gave birth painlessly, but now they would have labor pains. Furthermore, it notes that women will not do what most people do—try to avoid pain at all cost—because "your urge shall be for your husband, / And he shall rule over you." The meaning of this last section is ambiguous. The root *m-sh-l* (משל, "to rule") has a general sense, so that its use might suggest an overall hierarchy of male over female. However, the context of this verse suggests that it means merely that men will determine when couples engage in sexual intercourse.[26]

It is difficult to determine the attitude of this mythmaker toward the new state that he is describing.[27] Is he happy that a boring life as asexual immortals in Eden has been traded for a challenging, sexual life outside of Eden? Or does he miss immortality? Or is he being merely descriptive, noting how humankind moved from an earlier stage to its current one? The Bible (in contrast to much of Victorian and post-Victorian society) has a generally positive attitude toward human sexuality, as may be seen most clearly from the Song of Songs (see "Sex in the Song . . ." in chapter 25). In various places, it sees women in particular (in contrast to men) as very sexual beings (see especially Proverbs 1–9). Thus, it is quite reasonable within a biblical context to see Eve as a type of Pandora figure,[28] who is to be commended for bringing sex into this world.

Implications and Conclusions

Genesis 1:1–2:4a and 2:4b–3:24 are two separate stories, written by different authors using different styles. They are both myths—neither aims primarily at offering a scientific description of "the earth and everything upon it" (Neh. 9:6). They are metaphors on the story level, traditional tales dealing with issues of collective importance. As such, they are "creating" worlds.

The first story describes a very good world, which is highly structured and controlled by a most powerful God who in some ways is so dissimilar from humans that he even has his own word, *bara* (ברא), to express his creative activity.

The world of the second story is much more ambiguous. Its God, a master potter (Gen. 2:7),[29] is much more humanlike, walking and talking, even sewing (3:21). Also this world is unlike that in the previous story: it lacks the gender equality of the previous story, and it is not "very good."

Modern "critical" biblical scholarship fosters these observations by allowing the stories to be disengaged from each other, allowing each to be seen as an independent story, reflecting its author's perspectives. It understands them as constructive myths, which helped to frame the very essence of Israelite self-understanding, as well as their understanding of their relationship to their God, and to the world that they believed He had created.

7

The Ancestors as Heroes

Primary Reading: Genesis 12–50 (esp. chaps. 12, 20, 26, 37).

Patriarchal History?

The Book of Genesis is often divided into two parts: chapters 1–11, Universal Myth; and chapters 12–50, Patriarchal History. To the extent that names help us shape how we read units, these names (as well as these divisions) are both problematic.

The appellation "Universal Myth" is the less problematic of the two. By and large, the first eleven chapters of Genesis should be viewed as myths in the sense I described in chapter 6. They are stories dealing with issues of collective importance, and should not be seen as science, natural history, or history. Most of the stories deal with universal concerns. This is certainly the case for the initial stories, as I showed in chapter 6, but it is also true of most of the later stories. Genesis 10 is a long, segmented genealogy[1] that deals with the relationships among the earth's various peoples. Likewise, 11:1–9 contains the well-known Tower of Babel story, which ends: "and from there the LORD scattered them over the face of the whole earth"—it is hard to imagine a more universal story! This universal setting makes sense, since the first eleven chapters of Genesis may be read as a dialogue between "crime and punishment,"[2] or more specifically, as successive failed attempts by God to create an obedient humankind: the Eden generation disobeys, the flood generation disobeys, and finally the generation of the Tower of Babel disobeys. These failures justify the choosing of Abraham in chapter 12.[3]

Yet Abraham, or Abram, as he is first called, is not first introduced in Genesis 12. Rather, he is introduced in the genealogy in 11:26: "When Terah had lived 70 years, he begot Abram, Nahor, and Haran." In fact, one version of Abram's migration from Mesopotamia is preserved in verse 31: "Terah took his son Abram, his grandson Lot the son of Haran, and his daughter-in-law Sarai, the wife of his son Abram, and they set out together from Ur of the Chaldeans for the land of Canaan; but when they had come as far as Haran, they settled there." Thus 12:1, "The LORD said to Abram, 'Go forth from your native land and from your father's house to the land that I will show you,'" is not the beginning of a new story.

Furthermore, though much in chapters 1–11 is universal in outlook, not all of the material may be characterized that way. Genesis 2:1–3 describes the origin of the Shabbat, which is a uniquely Israelite institution, as "a sign for all time between Me and the people of Israel" (Exod. 31:17). Thus, this supposedly universal introduction includes elements of particularity—which is not surprising, given that Israelites wrote these stories for an Israelite audience.

The term "Patriarchal History" is doubly problematic as it is applied to chapters 12–50: they are neither "patriarchal" nor are they "history" in the commonly understood sense of the word. The Matriarchs play a major role in many of these stories.[4] In Genesis 27, it is Rebekah who makes sure that the right son (Jacob, not Esau) receives the blessing from Isaac. In 25:22, when she feels the two children struggling in her womb, she directly inquires of the LORD, and is answered directly (v. 23). Tamar in Genesis 38 is another strong woman, outsmarting her father-in-law, Judah. She is not condemned by the text; in fact Judah recognizes that "She is more right than I" (38:26), and she is rewarded with children. Her first born son, Perez, is the ancestor of David. She is even named in a blessing in Ruth 4:12: "may your house be like the house of Perez whom Tamar bore to Judah." Thus, although the Patriarchs outnumber the Matriarchs in terms of verses, and although the society depicted is by and large patriarchal (that is, the main locus of power is in the men),[5] this unit should not be called "*Patriarchal* History."

Meanwhile, "history" is notoriously hard to define. It is often understood as an account of what actually took place.[6] Such accounts can never be identical to the events themselves, yet we typically judge historians by how closely their account mirrors or maps those events—by what they add, omit, or twist. "History" in this sense hardly applies to the narratives in Genesis 12–50. There is no reason to believe that its authors were trying to relate exactly what happened, or even what they believed to be historically true. The stories were composed much later than the events they depict, for they reflect the background of that later period.[7] For these reasons, I avoid the term "Patriarchal History."

Role Models?

The stories of Genesis 12–50 are often understood to be presenting the ancestors as paradigmatic figures, as role models whose behavior should be emulated by the community. Probably this way of reading the stories is very old, for it is customary to view ancestors in this idealized fashion. However, these stories were likely not understood this way during the biblical period.

The biblical text corroborates this claim. It contains more than a hundred references to Abraham and Jacob outside of Genesis. (Isaac is hardly mentioned, just as he is hardly mentioned in Genesis.) For example, after Israel sins, Moses prays to God, asking him to remember Abraham, Isaac, and Jacob (see, e.g., Exod. 32:13; Deut. 9:27). However, never once does Moses tell the Israelites to remember the Patriarchs and to emulate their behavior. Even Isaiah 51:2, an exilic prophetic text that opens "Look back to Abraham your father / And to Sarah who brought you forth," does not continue by saying that you should follow their actions. Prophetic literature and Psalms offer many opportunities to encourage the people to emulate their ancestors, but this is *never done once,* implying that they were not viewed as role models in the biblical period.

In fact, a reading of the stories about the ancestors without the presumption that they are role models suggests that they have quite a few warts. This is clearest with Jacob, whose whole life is suffused with trickery. His brother, Esau, is quite correct when he remarks, "Was he, then, named Jacob that he might supplant me these two times? First he took away my birthright and now he has taken away my blessing!" (Gen. 27:36), punning on the connection between the words *bekhorah* (בְּכוֹרָה, "birthright") and *berakhah* (בְּרָכָה, "blessing"). The entire life story of Jacob could be read as a type of morality tale: trick others and you shall be tricked.[8] He tricks his brother, and then leads a life of being tricked by others, including his wife (31:19–32) and his children (chap. 37). This is a group of stories from which ancient Israelites might have learned about the dangers of trickery, as well as the divine concern bestowed on their ancestor named Israel or Jacob, but it does not illustrate a paradigm that should be emulated.

The same is true of Abraham. Nowhere does the text of Genesis or any other biblical text suggest that each Israelite should be prepared to sacrifice his child, as Abraham was in chapter 22. In fact, that story in its current form suggests that the purpose of this test was to reward Abraham by promising that his descendents would become numerous and conquer the land of Israel, thereby becoming a source of blessing for others (22:17–18).[9]

Several other actions performed by Abraham do not provide suitable models for emulation. For example, in Genesis 12, fairly early in the narrative when he and his wife are still called Abram and Sarai, Abram passes her off as his sister, so that he will not be killed (12:10–20). Sarai is taken into the royal harem (v. 15) as Pharaoh's wife (v. 19)! Abram is indeed saved, but at Sarai's expense. This is not paradigmatic, righteous behavior.

Many early postbiblical retellings of this story, written after the idea developed that the Patriarchs should be viewed as role models, respond to the moral problem that these stories present.[10] Jubilees, a pseudepigraphic work[11] from the second pre-Christian century, notes twice in retelling Genesis 12 that Sarai was taken "by force" (13:11–13). The great Hellenistic Jewish scholar Philo commented that Sarai "who in a foreign country was at the mercy of a licentious and cruel-hearted despot and had not one to protect her—for her husband was helpless . . ." (*On Abraham*, 94–95). In the Genesis Apocryphon, a greatly expanded retelling of Genesis in Aramaic found among the Dead Sea Scrolls (20:10) and in the medieval Midrash Tanchuma (*Lekh Lekhah* 5), Abram is depicted as weeping, rather than callously passing his wife off. In each of these retellings, Abraham's role is rewritten so that he is a victim of circumstances.

The Legends of the Jews, a compilation by Louis Ginzberg of rabbinic sources from the postbiblical period through the medieval period, shows a similar tendency. Drawing from a variety of postbiblical sources, this is how Ginzberg retells part of the story of Genesis 12:10–20:[12]

> On his journey from Canaan to Egypt, Abraham first observed the beauty of Sarah. Chaste as he was, he had never before looked at her, but now, when they were wading through a stream, he saw the reflection of her beauty in the water like the brilliance of the sun. Wherefore he spoke to her thus, "The Egyptians are very sensual, and I will put thee in a casket that no harm befall me on account of thee." At the Egyptian boundary, the tax collectors asked him about the contents of the casket, and Abraham told them he had barley in it. "No," they said, "it contains wheat." "Very well," replied Abraham, "I am prepared to pay the tax on wheat." The officers then hazarded the guess, "It contains pepper!" Abraham agreed to pay the tax on pepper, and when they charged him with concealing gold in the casket, he did not refuse to pay the tax on gold, and finally on precious stones. Seeing that he demurred to no charge, however high, the tax collectors, made thoroughly suspicious, insisted upon his unfastening the casket and letting them examine the contents. When it was forced open, the whole of Egypt was resplendent with the beauty of Sarah. In comparison with her, all other beauties were like apes compared with men. She excelled Eve herself. The servants of Pharaoh outbid one another in seeking to obtain possession of her, though they were of opinion that so radiant a beauty ought not to remain the property of a private individual. They reported the matter to the king, and Pharaoh sent a powerful armed force to bring Sarah to the palace, and so bewitched was he by her charms that those who had

> brought him the news of her coming into Egypt were loaded down with bountiful gifts.

This account (or more correctly combination of accounts) "cleans up" the image of Abraham. So do similar sources that insist, contrary to what the biblical text implies, that each time Pharaoh attempted to consummate the relationship, an angel protecting Sarai struck him.[13] (A much earlier retelling of the story by Josephus suggests: "But God thwarted his [Pharaoh's] criminal passion by an outbreak of disease and political disturbance."[14]) These various retellings, which embellish the biblical text, highlight for us the questionable behavior of the biblical Abraham, further suggesting that he, along with the other ancestors of Genesis, are not intended as role models.

The Ancestors as Symbols[15]

Given that Genesis was written over a long time period by different authors, we may not expect all of the ancestral stories to share the same goal. For example, in Genesis 14 Abram is presented as a great warrior,[16] an image that is not shared with the rest of Abraham material—this presents a single, particular view of Abraham in ancient Israel, which was preserved in the biblical text. Thus, the search for a single explanation for all of these ancestral stories is futile. In fact, it is likely that many of them were reworked as they were transmitted, and their original purpose or purposes were obscured in the process. However, in some cases, their goals remain visible.

Some of the stories in Genesis are symbolic, where the ancestor represents Israel as a whole, or a group within Israel. This is evident in the story we examined above, Genesis 12:10–20:

> There was a famine in the land, and Abram went down to Egypt to sojourn there, for the famine was severe in the land. As he was about to enter Egypt, he said to his wife Sarai, "I know what a beautiful woman you are. If the Egyptians see you, and think, 'She is his wife,' they will kill me and let you live. Please say that you are my sister, that it may go well with me because of you, and that I may remain alive thanks to you." When Abram entered Egypt, the Egyptians saw how very beautiful the woman was. Pharaoh's courtiers saw her and praised her to Pharaoh, and the woman was taken into Pharaoh's palace. And because of her, it went well with Abram; he acquired sheep, oxen, asses, male and female slaves, she-asses, and camels. But the Lord afflicted Pharaoh

> and his household with mighty plagues on account of Sarai, the wife of Abram. Pharaoh sent for Abram and said, "What is this you have done to me! Why did you not tell me that she was your wife? Why did you say, 'She is my sister,' so that I took her as my wife? Now, here is your wife; take her and begone!" And Pharaoh put men in charge of him, and they sent him off with his wife and all that he possessed.

This story has been the subject of much study because it is repeated again in Genesis, in chapters 20 (with Abraham and Sarah) and 26 (with Isaac and Rebekah).[17] The differences among the three versions are significant, and yield important information concerning how stories were told and retold in ancient Israel, and how variants of the same story might have developed over time. This comparison also highlights elements that are unique to each story.

Several features stick out in the Genesis 12 version: Abram, motivated by a famine, specifically goes to Egypt; through deceit he is enriched there; and he is eventually expelled. It is quite odd that despite Pharaoh's apparent anger at Abram, Abram gets to keep the various possessions that Pharaoh had given him.

When told in this outline form, it is evident that story is a "pre-telling" of the later story of Israel in Egypt. According to the Joseph story, Israel (the person and the nation) ends up in Egypt due to a famine. (Contrast this with Genesis 20, which is set in Gerar.) There the Israelites are ultimately enriched when they ask their Egyptian neighbors to "borrow" silver and gold objects and garments (Exod. 3:22; 11:2; 12:35). The Israelites are ultimately expelled (Exod. 12:31–32). The connection between Genesis 12:10–20 and the Exodus story is sealed by the word *nega'im* (נְגָעִים, "plagues") in Genesis 12:17 and again in Exodus 11:1 (of the plagues brought against Pharaoh).

The connections between these two stories were recognized in classical Jewish sources. Genesis Rabbah, an early rabbinic midrash (a type of Bible commentary), notes certain verbal similarities between our unit and later Torah texts: it introduces these observations by observing that "God said to Abraham our father, 'Go and prepare the path for your children'" (Genesis Rabbah 40:6). The medieval commentator Nachmanides, active in the thirteenth century, noted various thematic connections between these stories, and concludes by noting, "Absolutely everything that happened to the father happened to the children" (commentary on Gen. 12:10). For these scholars, history—or more precisely, certain elements of history—is cyclical,[18] and thus what happens once "helps" an event happen again. Modern biblical scholarship understands the same data differently—it assumes that an author prefigures later events by composing a story with the same elements but setting it at an earlier time. This highlights the importance of that later event. Here, the Exodus motif, one of the most central motifs of the entire Bible, is prefigured—this may be seen as a type of fulfillment of Deuteronomy 16:3, which enjoins that the Exodus should be recalled "as long as you live." Deuteronomy in particular does this by connecting various laws to the Exodus.[19] The centrality of the Exodus is also emphasized by placing it at the very beginning of the ancestral stories, in Genesis 12:10–20.

It is difficult to know how an ancient Israelite would have "read" Genesis 12:10–20, because, as is the case for biblical texts in general, it does not contain a genre label. We might distinguish various texts that present the past with such labels as "true history," "symbolic history," "historical fiction," or "light entertainment set in the past." Using various internal and external clues, we may sometimes surmise to which category a particular text belongs. In the case of Genesis 12:10–20, an overabundance of clues associating this passage with the Exodus would have suggested to the ancient Israelite that it is symbolic. Rather than depicting real events, it was meant to bolster the importance of the Exodus, and to support a view of providence that suggests a deity who protects his people—who goes down with them into exile, but also returns with them from there (see Gen. 46:4).

Genesis 12:10–20 is not unique as a symbolic text. Others may be identified by significant similarities between the text in Genesis and later texts or events, or when oddities in the text are best explained by observing that a story in Genesis is following the script of another story. These criteria are somewhat subjective, and isolating these symbolic stories can be difficult, especially because the Bible preserves for us only a small part of the traditions of ancient Israel. Other stories may quite possibly be symbolic, but we can no longer recognize what they are patterned after. For this reason we cannot say how many or what proportion of the ancestral stories in Genesis are symbolic.

The Joseph Story

In many ways, the Joseph story is different from many of the other stories in Genesis. Although there are a small number of inconsistencies within this story, such as whether Joseph was sold to the Midianites (37:28a, 36) or Ishmaelites (37:25–27, 28b), these are rather inconsequential when compared to contradictions in earlier sections of Genesis. Even chapter 38, the story of Judah and Tamar, which interrupts the flow of the Joseph story, is well integrated into the larger story through use of theme and vocabulary.[20] There is a sense of drama and deep interest in what we would call human psychology throughout the story. Genesis 37–50 incorporates a variety of traditions; it was not the work of a single author. However, it does not contain the usual sources found in Genesis

(J, E, P), and it contains many fewer contradictions than the previous part of the book. For these reasons, several scholars understand the story as a separate novella;[21] in any case, we may certainly speak of the Joseph *story*.

Several elements of the Joseph story are clearly symbolic. For example, a significant theme of this story is the conflict among the brothers (especially Joseph and Judah), which mirrors the conflicts of the divided monarchy (see "Israel's History as Seen from the Inside" in chapter 4). The story explains why Judah became the most important tribe among the children of Leah. In fact, much of the Joseph story can be understood as the narrative elaboration of an idea found in 1 Chronicles:

> (5:1) The sons of Reuben the first-born of Israel. He was the first-born; but when he defiled his father's bed, his birthright was given to the sons of Joseph son of Israel, so he is not reckoned as first-born in the genealogy; (2) though Judah became more powerful than his brothers and a leader came from him, yet the birthright belonged to Joseph.

In other words, the story describes the relationships among Reuben, Judah, and Joseph, which actually represent the later relationships among subgroups of Israel.

In genealogical lists, being firstborn often represents being the most powerful.[22] Thus, it is necessary to explain how this role moved from (the tribe of) Reuben to Judah. This is accomplished to some extent before the Joseph story begins, but is continued in the Joseph story. The beginning of Genesis 35:22 notes, "While Israel stayed in that land, Reuben went and lay with Bilhah, his father's concubine; and Israel found out"; according to 49:4, this disqualified Reuben from leadership. Similarly, the next two children, Simeon and Levi, are disqualified because they massacred a Canaanite city (chap. 34; see 49:5–7). Thus, before the Joseph story starts, Judah, the fourth-born son, is left as the dominant brother.[23]

This theme of who deserves the right of the firstborn is played out almost from the opening of the Joseph story. Reuben is unsuccessful in saving Joseph (Gen. 37:21–22, 29–30), while Judah's plan succeeds (vv. 26–27). The prominent role of Judah is then reflected in Genesis 38, which has as its focus Judah and his family. Later in the story, after the brothers have returned from Egypt while leaving Simeon behind as a hostage, Reuben offers to return to Egypt with Benjamin, but Jacob refuses (42:37–38). A few verses later, Judah makes a similar offer (38:8–14), and this time Jacob accedes to the offer. In both of these places, Judah plays the role of leader, of firstborn, instead of Reuben. The position that Judah's descendent King David will play is sanctioned through these details of the story, as well as others that place Judah in a position of leadership (see 44:16–34; 46:28). The Joseph story can also be viewed symbolically as a struggle between the house of Judah, representing the Davidic monarchy, and the house of Joseph, representing the northern kingdom. The story accurately reflects the fact that the northern kingdom ("Joseph") was much larger in area, and more powerful militarily, than Judah to the south.

However, reading the story as *only* a political allegory is erroneous. In antiquity, as in modern times, literary works were often written for more than one purpose. As already noted, the author or compiler of the Joseph story had an unusually strong dramatic sense, and was quite interested in human psychology. This may already be seen from the introduction to the story, which shows a keen interest in the various relationships between a father and sets of children from various wives. It notes details that are typically omitted in biblical stories, such as the age of the protagonist (Joseph is 17 years old, according to Gen. 37:2), and other mundane information, like Joseph spending his time with the concubine's children (v. 2). Thus, from its very beginning, the story sets up a problem—how will a young child, the son of the dead favored wife, fare, especially since he seems to be associating with the less powerful children?

Like many good stories, the introduction to the Joseph story leaves many questions unanswered. How are we to understand Joseph? Is he a spoiled brat who takes advantage of his situation as favored son, or is he naïve? What about Jacob? Why, for example, does he send Joseph out after his brothers (Gen. 37:13)—is he trying to teach Joseph a lesson, or is he oblivious to the dynamic among the brothers? Many more such questions are at the surface here, suggesting that it would be a simplification to read this story *only* as a political allegory.

An Obstacle Story?

In addition to looking at the meaning of individual stories, it is possible to see if they have been combined into a meaningful whole. The stories of Abraham's family may be read from beginning to end as a somewhat smooth narrative beginning with the promise of the land in Genesis 12, and ending with a recapitulation of that promise in the final chapter, in 50:24, by the dying Joseph: "I am about to die. God will surely take notice of you and bring you up from this land to the land that He promised on oath to Abraham, to Isaac, and to Jacob."

One scholar has suggested that much of the material in this large section may be read as an obstacle story. That is, it opens with the promise of land and progeny to Abraham and his descendents, and then in great detail, time after time, notes various obstacles that prevent this promise from being fulfilled.[24] The Abraham story, for example, may be outlined as follows: Abraham is given a grand promise with two main parts: land, and the progeny to fill it (Gen. 12:1–3). He successfully migrates to Canaan and walks throughout the land (12:4–9). Yet as soon as he has done so, he needs to leave due to famine; in the process, he is worried about being killed, and his wife, through whom he must bear progeny, is taken into Pharaoh's harem. Since he is childless, one might think that Lot, his nephew, would be his heir. However, when given the choice, Lot chooses not the land of Canaan but the plain of the Jordan (chap. 13). Lot is ultimately captured in war, and Abraham the warrior recovers him. In the process, King Melchizedek of Salem makes a generous offer to Abraham, who certainly could have attained some territory, but Abraham refuses (chap. 14). The covenant is renewed through a detailed ceremony (chap. 15). Since Sarai, Abram's wife, has not conceived, Sarai suggests that Abram take Hagar as a wife, so he might have an heir. No sooner does he do this then she conceives and is banished by Sarai to the wilderness, undermining the possibility that Abram's heir problem will be solved. The covenant is renewed and circumcision is mandated (chap. 17). (Genesis 18–19 is about Sodom, forming an interlude.) Sarah is taken by Abimelech of Gerar, again making us wonder how an heir to Abraham will be produced (chap. 20). Finally, the heir, Isaac, is born (21:1), so it is safe to banish Ishmael, the "backup heir" (chap. 21). No sooner does Isaac grow up a bit, than God asks Abraham: "Take your son, your only son, whom you love, Isaac, and offer him up . . ." (22:2); Abraham agrees, and is ready to kill his heir (chap. 22). Finally, Abraham makes a real estate transaction—but purchases only a cave for burial purposes (chap. 23).

By the time we get to Genesis 24, Abraham is elderly, has a single child to carry on the promise, and has no more of the land than a burial plot. Obstacle after obstacle has been put in his place—foreign kings who desire the wife who will produce the heir, banished children, almost sacrificed children, great wars, etc. This pattern can be seen as continuing throughout Genesis—it is especially evident in the fights that Jacob has with his twin Esau. Thus, it would seem quite appropriate to view Genesis 12–50 as one big obstacle story.

However, amid the various obstacles, the covenantal promise is repeated time and time again. The emphasis should not be on the obstacles, but on the constantly renewed promise. Even after the most difficult experiences, such as the binding of Isaac, the covenantal promise is renewed (Gen. 22:15–18). Even at the very end of the book, when the Israelites are in Egypt, with no immediate hope of returning to Israel, this promise is repeated: "God will surely take notice of you and bring you up from this land to the land that He promised on oath to

Abraham, to Isaac, and to Jacob" (50:24). In sum, the structure of Genesis 12–50 suggests that it should not be read as straightforward history, interested in the past for its own sake. Instead, this portion of the book functions as a myth of encouragement—it might seem impossible for the promise to be fulfilled, yet the promise is renewed time after time. It suggests that the fulfillment of the promise, the divine blessing, is right around the corner—a suggestion that would have been most welcome to readers of this text as a whole. Patterns in both individual stories, and in the stories as they have been combined, suggest that this material was not written in order to represent what actually happened, but rather, on the level of mythological material, to deal with such fundamental questions as: Why do we own this land? How should we react in the face of adversity?

8

Biblical Law

Codes and Collections

Primary Reading: Exodus 19–24.

The Nature of Biblical Law

Law should be the easiest genre to "read" and understand. We do not have an everyday acquaintance with prophecy, and historical texts play only a minor role in the contemporary United States, but we all encounter laws on a daily basis. Legal battles are often the subject of news headlines. We deal with laws when we are served with tickets for parking or traffic violations, when we buy houses or rent apartments, when we write our wills. Because law is a basic part of our lives, most Americans have some familiarity with the legal system and its underpinnings.

This familiarity, which on the surface makes biblical law easier to understand than other genres, is more of an impediment than a help. Though biblical law looks much like our own laws, in terms of its underpinnings and function it is fundamentally different.

The most significant difference between modern law and biblical law is its imputed author: Exodus claims that the origin of its laws is divine. The Decalogue (the "Ten Commandments")[1] is presented as unmediated revelation by God to all Israel; it is introduced by "God spoke all these words, saying . . ." (20:1). The laws that follow the Decalogue in 20:20[2]–23:19 are presented as God's revelation to Moses that Moses is supposed to relay to Israel, "The LORD said to Moses: Thus shall you say to the Israelites . . ." (20:19). Thus, all of the laws incorporated in chapters 19–24 are presented as divine law.

The structure of this portion of Exodus emphasizes that the laws it incorporates are God's laws by opening with a description of the revelation (chap. 19), which is followed by the Decalogue (20:1–14), which is followed by a description of the revelation (20:15–18), which is followed by a group of laws (20:19–23:33), which is followed by a final description of the revelation (chap. 24). This creates a double-decker sandwich, highlighting the significance of the law as divine revelation.

Revelation (chap. 19)
Decalogue (20:1–14)
Revelation (20:15–18)
Laws (20:19–23:33)
Revelation (chap. 24)

This structure corresponds to explicit statements about the divine origin of the law, which may seem like overkill. All of this may have been necessary, however, because this conception is one of the few in which the Bible was unique within its ancient Near Eastern context.[3] Elsewhere, it was not the deity but the king who established law and propagated legal collections. For example, the prologue to the famous Laws of Hammurabi[4] concludes: "When the god Marduk commanded me to provide just ways for the people of the land [in order to attain] appropriate behavior, I established truth and justice as the declaration of the land, I enhanced the well-being of the people. At that time: If a man accuses another man and charges him with homicide . . ."[5] The same idea is reinforced in the epilogue that follows the laws: "These are the just decisions which Hammurabi, the able king, has established . . ."[6] Still later, Hammurabi calls himself "king of justice, to whom the god Shimachu has granted [insight into] the truth. My pronouncements are choice . . ."[7]

Thus, in broadest strokes, the organization of Exodus 19–24 is similar to that of Hammurabi—they both have narrative material surrounding laws. However, in the law collection of Hammurabi, the surrounding material makes it clear that these laws originate from the human king, while God as King was understood to be the lawgiver in Israel.[8] This explains why, in contrast to surrounding societies, the Bible portrays kings as playing a relatively minor role in the creation of law, and according to some, even in the administration of justice.[9]

The fact that the Bible understands God to be the lawgiver also explains an oddity of the biblical law collections: the way in which they combine (what we would call) religious law and (what we would call) secular law, including criminal law and torts. For example, the Decalogue says both "You shall have no other gods besides Me" (Exod. 20:3) and "You shall not steal" (20:13). The law collection that follows in Exodus contains laws about goring oxen (21:28–32) as well as pilgrimage festivals (23:14–17). Such "religious laws" and "secular laws" are often mixed together in adjacent verses (e.g., 23:1–4).

Sometimes the Bible, in its structure, distinguishes between religious law—laws regulating how God should be worshipped—and interpersonal law. The Decalogue, for example, is divided into two sections: religious law, then interpersonal law. Yet, even here, a law that we would consider interpersonal, honoring one's parents, is given a religious justification: ". . . that you may long endure on the land that the LORD your God is assigning to you" (Exod. 20:12).[10] Exodus 22:20–23 is similar:

> You shall not wrong a stranger or oppress him, for you were strangers in the land of Egypt. You shall not ill-treat any widow or orphan. If you do mistreat them, I will heed their outcry as soon as they cry out to Me, and My anger shall blaze forth and I will put you to the sword, and your own wives shall become widows and your children orphans.

The notion that the biblical authors understood all law as divine law[11] shows up most clearly when comparing laws of adultery in the ancient Near East with those in the Bible. Adultery in the ancient Near East was typically treated as an offense against the wronged husband. In certain cases, the offended husband had a role in determining the punishment of his wife and her paramour—"he shall treat her as he wishes."[12] Though one biblical text seems to be familiar with this notion (Prov. 6:34–35, which is outside the Torah),[13] all biblical legal texts insist on absolute punishment—nothing is left up to the husband's discretion. This perspective is also found outside of legal texts; it may be seen, for example, in Joseph's answer to Potiphar's wife when she tries to seduce him: "How then could I do this most wicked thing, and sin before God?" (Gen. 39:9). Adultery here is not understood as a crime against the wronged husband, but as a "sin before God," who is understood to be the source of law.

The uniqueness of the Bible's conception explains why the Bible depicts revelation in such detail. It also accounts for an unusual number and diversity of sources that attempt to explain this event. All of these, in turn, help us see the underlying diversity of understandings of God, and of revelation itself, that existed within ancient Israel.[14] For example, most of the sources emphasize that Moses alone had close access to God, and that the process of revelation was dangerous, yet Exodus 24:9–11 notes: "Then Moses and Aaron, Nadab and Abihu, and seventy elders of Israel ascended; and they saw the God of Israel. . . . Yet He did not raise His hand against the leaders of the Israelites; they beheld God, and they ate and drank." Because the idea of divinely revealed law was so unique to ancient Israel, an unusually large number of diverse sources attempt to explain this event.[15]

The Decalogue

As noted earlier, the first set of laws contained within this corpus is the Decalogue, in Exodus 20:2–14. The usual name for this selection, "the Ten Commandments," is not attested in the Bible—and is inaccurate. The first statement in the Decalogue reads: "I the LORD am your God who brought you out of the land of Egypt, the house of bondage" (20:2); this is certainly not a commandment. The term "Decalogue," from the Greek *deca* (ten) *logos* (words), is superior. That Greek term is ancient—used in the Septuagint (the Greek translation of the Bible begun in Alexandria in the third pre-Christian century) to render *aseret ha-devarim* (עֲשֶׂרֶת הַדְּבָרִים; Exod. 34:28; Deut. 4:13, 10:4). The word *davar* (דָּבָר;), singular of *devarim* (דְּבָרִים), is one of the most common biblical nouns; typically it means "thing" or "word." (Given the importance of the Decalogue, its name in rabbinic tradition shifted slightly and not surprisingly to *aseret ha-dibrot* [עֲשֶׂרֶת הַדִּבְּרוֹת], which means specifically "the ten divine utterances.")

Both of the commonly used terms, Decalogue and the Ten Commandments, follow the tradition of Exodus and Deuteronomy in insisting that this text must be divided into ten sections. This most likely reflects a notion of ten as a number expressing perfection. Yet, the Decalogue comprises as many as thirteen separate statements:

1. (v. 2) I the LORD am your God who brought you out of the land of Egypt . . .
2. (v. 3) You shall have no other gods besides Me.
3. (v. 4) You shall not make for yourself a sculptured image . . .
4. (v. 5) You shall not bow down to them or serve them.
5. (v. 7) You shall not swear falsely by the name of the Lord your God . . .
6. (v. 8) Remember the sabbath day and keep it holy
7. (v. 12) Honor your father and your mother . . .
8. (v. 13) You shall not murder.
9. (v. 13) You shall not commit adultery.
10. (v. 13) You shall not steal.
11. (v. 13) You shall not bear false witness against your neighbor.
12. (v. 14) You shall not covet your neighbor's house.
13. (v. 14) You shall not covet your neighbor's wife . . .

Already the ancients knew of different traditions about how to group these thirteen pieces together to form "ten" statements.[16] Classical Jewish and

Christian understandings differed significantly.[17] For instance, Christians have normally taken them as "ten *commandments*," relegating verse 2, "I am the LORD" to an unnumbered introduction, while rabbinic tradition as a rule counts this as the first divine utterance. Thus, within Jewish contexts, the term Decalogue, which is more inclusive of all the verses, is the more appropriate term.

The Decalogue is the only collection of law that, according to biblical tradition, God revealed to *all* Israel without an intermediary. (Indeed, this helps to account for its significance within biblical and later religious traditions. In the Bible itself, it is not marked as the center of or source for all the other biblical laws, as sometimes claimed in Jewish tradition.) Critical biblical scholarship has attempted to produce an earlier proto-Decalogue, which is much shorter, and where the utterances tend to be similar in form and length to the group in v. 13: "You shall not murder. You shall not commit adultery. You shall not steal."[18] Such reconstructions are conjectural. Yet clearly the Decalogue existed in several forms in ancient Israel. The version in Deuteronomy 5 differs from that in Exodus 20 in both small and large ways.[19] For example, a totally different reason is given in Deuteronomy for why the Sabbath should be observed, and that text introduces the Sabbath injunction using a different verb, as may be seen from the following juxtaposition:

Exodus 20:8–11	*Deuteronomy 5:12–15*
Remember the sabbath day and keep it holy. Six days you shall labor and do all your work, but the seventh day is a sabbath of the LORD your God: you shall not do any work—you, your son or daughter, your male or female slave, or your cattle, or the stranger who is within your settlements. For in six days the LORD made heaven and earth and sea, and all that is in them, and He rested on the seventh day; therefore the LORD blessed the sabbath day and hallowed it.	Observe the sabbath day and keep it holy, as the LORD your God has commanded you. Six days you shall labor and do all your work, but the seventh day is a sabbath of the LORD your God; you shall not do any work—you, your son or your daughter, your male or female slave, your ox or your ass, or any of your cattle, or the stranger in your settlements, so that your male and female slave may rest as you do. Remember that you were a slave in the land of Egypt and the LORD your God freed you from there with a mighty hand and an outstretched arm; therefore the LORD your God has commanded you to observe the sabbath day.

On a more minor level, Exodus and Deuteronomy use different words, that likely have different nuances, for the prohibition against false testimony; Exod. 20:13 uses the noun *shaker* (שָׁקֶר, "false"), while Deuteronomy 5:17 uses *shav* (שָׁוְא, "vain"). In addition to the differences seen between Exodus and Deuteronomy, several biblical and early postbiblical sources quote the three short injunctions ("You shall not murder. You shall not commit adultery. You shall not steal") in a different order from the one preserved in both Exodus and Deuteronomy. For example, Jeremiah 7:9 asks rhetorically, "Will you steal and murder and commit adultery?" while ancient sources ranging from Philo to the Christians' New Testament (Rom. 13:9) know of the order "adultery . . . murder . . . steal."[20]

Though minor variations may exist in reasons given, in terms used, in syntax, or in the order of various injunctions, the basic injunctions are always the same. Are the differences then trivial? No, because they exist in the single biblical text that is supposed to contain *the unmediated word of God*. They teach us that the ancients did not transmit biblical texts like we transmit modern texts, using photocopiers and "cut-and-paste" word-processing programs. Rather, all biblical texts changed during their transmission. They were updated, expanded, and made to fit their broader context.[21] If this happened to the Decalogue—which is ascribed directly to God—then it certainly happened to other texts, which would have been even more fluid.[22] In any case, the many versions show that Exodus 20:2–14 cannot simply be seen as *the* words that God spoke on Sinai.

Another piece of evidence suggests that the Decalogue should not be upheld as *the* central biblical text. The Decalogue states why one should not bow down or serve other gods:

> For I the Lord your God am an impassioned God, visiting the guilt of the parents upon the children, upon the third and upon the fourth generations of those who reject Me, but showing kindness to the thousandth generation of those who love Me and keep My commandments (Exod. 20:5–6).

This notion of intergenerational punishment is expressed elsewhere in the Bible (see especially Exod. 34:6–7), and is illustrated, for example, when God "transfers" David's sin to the child of his adulterous affair with Bathsheba, and that child dies (2 Sam. 12:13–14).[23] Yet, this idea—unambiguously stated "by God" in the Decalogue—is disputed by other biblical sources, including Ezekiel 18, which states decisively: "the person who sins, only he shall die" (v. 4). Deuteronomy 7:9–10 is even more striking, quoting from this injunction in the Decalogue only to argue against it: "Know, therefore, that only the LORD your

God is God, the steadfast God who keeps His covenant faithfully to the thousandth generation of those who love Him and keep His commandments, but who instantly requites with destruction those who reject Him—never slow with those who reject Him, but requiting them instantly."[24] This polemic indicates that those who constituted biblical Israel did not all agree with the Decalogue's theology. In short, the Decalogue does not possess absolute authority, not even in the Bible itself.

There is a great deal that we do not know about the Decalogue. We cannot determine its original form, although we are sure that it is not currently in that form.[25] We cannot pinpoint when, where, and how it became viewed so centrally in Israel—quoted in various prophetic and other texts.[26] Nor can we easily discern its function (although we can rule it out as a collection of laws, since it contains no sanctions for violating particular norms). Despite these great uncertainties, it occupies a strikingly central position within Jewish, Christian, and indeed all of Western civilization.

The Covenant Collection

The legal collection that follows the Decalogue is often named the "Covenant Code."[27] Unlike the Decalogue, it appears in only one version. Furthermore, it is presented as mediated revelation that Moses is supposed to "set before" the Israelites (Exod. 21:1). It derives its name from Exodus 24:7, "Then he [Moses] took *sefer ha-berit* (סֵפֶר הַבְּרִית, "the record of the covenant") and read it aloud to the people. And they said, 'All that the LORD has spoken we will faithfully do!'" What the term "record of the covenant" refers to in this context is uncertain, but by convention biblical scholars use that name to describe all of the preceding laws found in Exodus 20:19–23:33.

An even better designation than "the Covenant Code" would be "the Covenant Collection." Codes are typically meant to be complete, and are organized for use by the courts. The material in Exodus 20:19–23:33 is neither. It contains, for example, no material on how individuals married or divorced, nor how shepherds fulfilled their obligations to flock owners (see Gen. 31:38–39), two areas of widespread concern in antiquity. Moreover, some parts, such as 22:17–19, are organized by punishment:

> You shall not tolerate a sorceress.
> Whoever lies with a beast shall be put to death.
> Whoever sacrifices to a god other than the Lord alone shall be proscribed.

(See also 21:15–17.) Such a system of organization would be cumbersome for lawyers and judges. In fact, because no Near Eastern culture appears to have had codes in the later Roman sense, it is best to speak in general of "collections."[28]

The diversity of materials found in Exodus 20:19–23:33 further suggest that it should not be read as a code. Most of the laws are couched in conditional terms: *ki* (כִּי, "If/When . . . then"). For example: "*If* a man seduces a virgin for whom the bride-price has not been paid, and lies with her, *then* he must make her his wife by payment of a bride-price. *If* her father refuses to give her to him, *then* he must still weigh out silver in accordance with the bride-price for virgins" (22:15–16, transl. adapted). This is called "casuistic" law. It is the main form of law known from the ancient Near East.[29] Other injunctions in this collection are couched in absolute terms, as in the Decalogue. One example of absolute (or "apodictic") law is "Whoever lies with a beast shall be put to death" (22:18). Apodictic law is hardly found in other ancient Near Eastern collections. The mixing of apodictic and casuistic law sets the Bible apart from other ancient Near Eastern legal texts.

At the same time, the Bible appears to share with other ancient Near Eastern law collections the character of not being a code intended for court use. Consider what appear to be impractical or impossible laws. For example, law 218 of Hammurabi reads:

> If a physician performs major surgery with a bronze lancet upon a member of the upper class and thus causes the person's death, or opens the temple of a person of the upper class and thus blinds that person's eye, they shall cut off his hand.[30]

In such a world, no physician would opt to serve the upper class. Laws 229–30 read:

> If a builder constructs a house for a man but does not make his work sound, and the house that he constructs collapses and causes the death of the householder, that builder shall be killed. If it should cause the death of the son of the householder, they shall kill a son of that builder.[31]

This law presents practical problems of a different type: What if a childless contractor kills the son of the householder?

Thus, although Hammurabi is longer, more comprehensive, and more logically ordered than the Covenant Collection—that is, although it looks more like a legal code—it too should be seen as a collection. Some of its laws may reflect the norms of the law courts in Hammurabi's period, but others, such as the laws just quoted, are most likely "theoretical law." Such laws express the ideals of a particular reformer within a society. Thus, law 218 expresses the notion that physicians are not supposed to harm their patients, even accidentally, while law 230 expresses the seriousness with which ancient contractors were supposed to work.

The Goring Ox

Unfortunately, we can no longer know which laws recorded in the Laws of Hammurabi were real, and which were ideal—there is no textual distinction between them. Nevertheless, all such laws may be examined to reveal how they reflect the norms (both real and ideal) of the legists who edited them. The same is true of biblical law. In the rest of this chapter I will attempt to tease out some norms that are woven into the Covenant Collection in Exodus. For the time being, I will narrow my focus to a single topic: a goring ox.

The passage in question is Exodus 21:28–32, which states:

> When an ox gores a man or a woman to death, the ox shall be stoned and its flesh shall not be eaten, but the owner of the ox is not to be punished. If, however, that ox has been in the habit of goring, and its owner, though warned, has failed to guard it, and it kills a man or a woman—the ox shall be stoned and its owner, too, shall be put to death. If ransom is laid upon him, he[32] must pay whatever is laid upon him to redeem his life. So, too, if it gores a minor, male or female, the owner shall be dealt with according to the same rule. But if the ox gores a slave, male or female, he shall pay thirty shekels of silver to the master, and the ox shall be stoned.

This law, or more properly, these laws, deal with the following four cases: (1) unexpected goring by an ox; (2) goring by a habitual gorer; (3) goring of a minor; (4) goring of a slave. Especially given that oxen do not typically gore people, the similarities in structure and even wording between the laws in Exodus and Hammurabi 250–52 are very striking. Hammurabi reads:

> (250) If an ox gores a man while it is passing through the street, that case has no basis for a claim. (251) If a man's ox is a known gorer, and the authorities of his city quarter notify him that it is a known gorer, but he does not blunt its horns or control his ox, and that ox gores to death a member of the upper class, he [the owner] shall give thirty shekels of silver. (252) If it is a man's slave [who is fatally gored], he shall give twenty shekels of silver.[33]

Though we are uncertain of the date of the Covenant Collection, it is certainly several centuries later than the eighteenth-century-B.C.E. Laws of Hammurabi. Although the "main copy" of these laws was inscribed on a basalt stele in Babylon, later removed to Elam (and now found at the Louvre), we know that the Laws of Hammurabi became part of the Mesopotamian scribal tradition, and were copied for several centuries.[34] Given the many similarities between the way this law is expressed in Exodus and Hammurabi, it is highly likely that the author of this section of the Covenant Collection knew the laws as they appeared in Hammurabi, perhaps via an intermediary source, and revised them to fit Israelite norms. Thus, although the similarities between the earlier Babylonian and later Israelite law are striking, the differences are even more telling. They can be analyzed to uncover the manner in which the Israelite legislator changed his source to convey different principles.[35]

Both collections deal with homicide caused by a person's benign animal. In modern terms, it is equivalent to a person driving a car that seemed to be in perfect running order but suddenly lost its brakes, so that the driver could not avoid hitting and killing a pedestrian. Given that not even negligence was involved, the owner of the ox is not held responsible in either ancient culture for the death. Yet, biblical law contains an additional provision absent from Hammurabi: "the ox shall be stoned and its flesh shall not be eaten." This is a significant economic loss for the owner of the ox—it would be the equivalent of insisting that the car that accidentally killed someone be brought to a "car cruncher" and flattened. The stoning of the ox most likely reflects a peculiarly Israelite idea, that the ox has perpetrated a boundary violation by committing a human homicide. As such, it became taboo, and it must be killed, and its owner is deprived of the normal benefit derived from a dead ox—its use as food.

Comparing the second case, the habitually goring ox, is even more instructive. For both ancient cultures, this is a case of negligence. In our culture, it is comparable to having your car fail an inspection because your brakes are faulty, being told not to drive anywhere without fixing them, and then driving away and killing a pedestrian because the brakes could not stop the car on time. Neither the action nor the choice of victim was premeditated, yet the killing could have been—and from the legislator's perspectives, should have been—anticipated. For this reason, Hammurabi does not consider the owner of the ox guilty of first degree murder (a capital crime) or even manslaughter, yet the guilty party must pay a monetary fine of thirty silver shekels, most likely the economic value of an upper-class individual at that time.

In contrast, the Covenant Collection notes that if this habitually goring ox kills "a man or a woman—the ox shall be stoned and its owner, too, shall be put to death. If ransom is laid upon him, he must pay whatever is laid upon him to redeem his life." The stoning of the ox is expected, following the norms developed in the preceding case. Yet, the law suggests that negligence which causes another person's death is so serious that the owner too deserves to be stoned. This conclusion is softened by allowing the owner to ransom himself, most likely by paying a fine to the family of the individual gored.[36] The initial suggestion that "its owner, too, shall be put to death" reflects a basic principle or postulate[37] of the Covenant Collection, and indeed of all of the biblical law collections: the fundamental value ascribed to human life. Thus, the person who accidentally and unintentionally but through negligence kills a human through an agent such as an ox, is deserving of death.

The subcase found in Exodus 21:31, "So, too, if it gores a minor, male or female, the owner shall be dealt with according to the same rule," is absent from Hammurabi. This too is significant. Many of the laws in Hammurabi are class conscious, distinguishing among three groups: the upper class, commoners, and slaves. For example, laws 196–99 read:

> If an upper-class person should blind the eye of another upper-class person, they shall blind his eye. If he should break the bone of another upper-class person, they shall break his bone. If he should blind the eye of a commoner or break the bone of a commoner, he shall weigh and deliver sixty shekels of silver. If he should blind the eye of the slave of an upper-class person, or break the bone of a slave of an upper-class person, he shall weigh and deliver one-half of his value [in silver].

Biblical legislators, including those who composed the Covenant Collection, accepted only part of this value system. As in Hammurabi, slaves are treated separately, since (in both cultures) the slave's owner must be compensated for the economic loss.[38] (For the status of slaves in the Covenant Collection, see Exodus 21:20–21.) However, nowhere do biblical laws distinguish between classes of nonslaves, as in the Mesopotamian distinction between upper class and commoner. In fact, the best explanation for Exodus 21:31, "So, too, if it gores a minor, male or female, the owner shall be dealt with according to the same rule," is that it is taking issue with the notion that (free) people should be treated differentially, based on their worth.

From the Goring Ox to Biblical "Law" in General

For reasons of space, I cannot treat here the many other laws contained in the Covenant Collection. (This book cannot substitute for a commentary, which explains each verse.) However, many of the above observations about the goring ox law do hold true for other laws in the Covenant Collection. That is, many of those laws may be ideal, many are revisions of earlier Mesopotamian laws, but they avoid the sharp class distinctions seen in Mesopotamia.

Moreover, many of our observations concerning the status of the Covenant Collection are equally true of law elsewhere in the Bible. Consider the other legal collections: the Holiness Collection of Leviticus 17–26 and the Deuteronomic Law Collection in Deuteronomy 12–26. None of these is organized like a law code; none is comprehensive. They all contain repetitions of the same laws. Some of their laws, many scholars believe, are ideal rather than real: the Jubilee year (Leviticus 25); the *cheirem* (חֵרֶם, "proscription" or "ban") of the Canaanites (Deut. 20:16–18); and others.[39] These features distinguish biblical law from law as we normally experience or understand it. Thus those "laws" may have functioned in ancient Israel differently than do today's laws as they apply to our own lives.

Furthermore, if we look at all of these law collections together, we see another reason to be cautious when we speak of biblical "law." As I will show in chapters 9 and 10, each of these collections comes from a different time period and reflects a different ideological perspective. (Although the date of the Covenant Collection is uncertain, it is likely the earliest of the three collections. In contrast to the others, it reflects a largely nonurban perspective.[40]) When dealing with the same issue, the three collections often differ significantly. For example, Exodus and Deuteronomy recognize that an Israelite may enslave another Israelite "forever" (21:5–6 and 15:16–18, respectively), whereas Leviticus insists that Israelite slaves must be released every fiftieth year, explaining that "they are My servants, whom I freed from the land of Egypt; they may not give themselves over into servitude" (25:42; cf. vv. 39–43). Another example: Exodus calls its fall festival "the festival of ingathering" and notes that it should be commemorated "at the end of the year" for an unspecified period (23:16). Deuteronomy knows the same festival as the feast of booths (*sukkot*), commemorated for seven days (16:13–15). Leviticus describes a feast of booths that begins in the seventh month, and it is concluded by a solemn gathering on the *eighth* day (23:33–36)!

Such differences among the various legal corpora are the norm rather than the exception. Nevertheless, certain postulates seem to stand behind all biblical laws. They include an attitude toward human life that makes capital punishment less frequent in the Bible than in Hammurabi's laws, and that shies away from vicarious punishment, that is, punishment for a crime committed by another family member.[41] Nevertheless, the internal differences in detail are large and frequent enough to warrant avoiding sentences that begin, "Biblical law suggests . . ."

9

"Incense Is Offensive to Me"

The Cult in Ancient Israel

Primary Reading: Leviticus 16.

Ritual Within the Bible

Religious ritual has an ambiguous place within modern life.[1] It is often critiqued as an archaic remnant of earlier practices, which should be replaced by more abstract forms of religion.[2]

This antipathy toward ritual is reflected in the work of many biblical scholars, especially those influenced by the work of the great German scholar Julius Wellhausen, who systematized much of biblical scholarship toward the end of the nineteenth century.[3] He viewed the history of biblical religion as a devolution, in which free expression of religion, reflected in the early sources, was gradually replaced—most especially in the Priestly Source—by fixed ritual. In this view, the prophets, some of whom are seen as hostile toward ritual, are viewed as the apex of biblical religion. It was not unusual, for example, for scholars to highlight the centrality of texts such as Isaiah 1:10–17:

> (10) Hear the word of the Lord, / You chieftains of Sodom; / Give ear to our God's instruction, / You folk of Gomorrah! / (11) "What need have I of all your sacrifices?" / Says the Lord. / "I am sated with burnt offerings of rams, / And suet of fatlings, / And blood of bulls; / And I have no delight / In lambs and he-goats. / (12) That you come to appear before Me— / Who asked that of you? / Trample My courts (13) no more; / Bringing oblations is futile, / Incense is offensive to Me. / New moon and sabbath, / Proclaiming of solemnities, / Assemblies with iniquity, / I cannot abide. / (14) Your new moons and fixed seasons / Fill Me with loathing; / They are become a burden to Me, / I cannot endure

> them. / (15) And when you lift up your hands, / I will turn My eyes away from you; / Though you pray at length, / I will not listen. / Your hands are stained with crime—(16) Wash yourselves clean; / Put your evil doings / Away from My sight. / Cease to do evil; / (17) Learn to do good. / Devote yourselves to justice; / Aid the wronged. / Uphold the rights of the orphan; / Defend the cause of the widow."

These verses are often understood as a blanket condemnation of ritual practices, especially those associated with the Jerusalem cult as prescribed in the Torah; ethical behavior is meant to replace ritual behavior. This unit from Isaiah will be examined in chapter 17 (see "Isaiah as a Typical Classical Prophet"); for now, it is sufficient to note that this negative view of ritual is exaggerated. The fact that the Bible is so rich in rituals certainly argues for their centrality. Indeed, this is confirmed by texts such as Isaiah 1:10–17, for only central practices would have been railed against so vociferously. Thus, developing a sympathetic understanding of ritual is crucial for understanding what biblical texts meant.

Ritual was a central part of all ancient Near Eastern religions. Many ritual texts covering a wide variety of situations have been discovered at Ugarit, a city near the Mediterranean coast of Syria, which has yielded a large number of texts from the fourteenth and thirteenth centuries.[4] These texts are extremely important given the geographical proximity of Ugarit to Israel, and although they predate biblical literature by several centuries, they show significant contiguities with the Bible. Ugaritic narrative texts highlight the significant role that ritual played in daily life there.[5] A similar picture is evident with Israel's immediate neighbors, where large numbers of ritual texts have been unearthed.[6] Thus, given the geographical and historical context of the Bible, the prominent role of ritual in it is expected.

I will focus here on the Temple ritual associated with Yom Kippur, the Day of Atonement. Since it was an unusual ritual even for the Bible, I will supplement its analysis with some general reflections on the place of ritual within Israelite life.

The Yom Kippur ritual is found in Leviticus 16. Actually, verses 1–28 outline two rituals that combine to form the larger ritual. The first ritual (which itself comprises several sub-rituals) transpires inside the sanctuary precincts (vv. 1–19, 27–28). The second ritual, involving the scapegoat, takes place outside the sanctuary (vv. 20–26). Verse 20 serves to integrate the two: "When he has finished purging the Shrine, the Tent of Meeting, and the altar, the live goat shall be brought forward." These rituals combine to assure that the desired results—the ritual cleansing of the sanctuary, and the purging of the people's sins—are accomplished.

The Day of Atonement Rituals: Background

Key Terms Used to Describe the Rituals

In contemporary Jewish practice, repentance is seen as the key feature of Yom Kippur, or the Day of Atonement. The liturgy of the day is replete with confessions, one of which has as its refrain "for all these, O God of forgiveness, forgive us, pardon us, grant us remission."[7] It is therefore natural to read the ritual described in Leviticus 16 in terms of this theme, as connected to repentance. Yet, a close reading of that biblical passage suggests otherwise: neither *teshuvah* (תְּשׁוּבָה, "repentance") nor the word from which it derives, *shuv* (שׁוּב, "to return"), are found anywhere in the chapter. Indeed, this root is first used in the Torah in the theological sense of "repent" or "return to God" only in Deuteronomy: "when you are in distress because all these things have befallen you and, in the end, *ve-shavta* (וְשַׁבְתָּ, 'you return') to the LORD your God and obey Him" (4:30). In fact, within the Torah, only in Deuteronomy does the concept of repentance play a central role. Given that Priestly texts and those from Deuteronomy represent the two great yet *different* streams of thought in the Bible, the fact that *shuv* is prominent in one and absent in the other is significant.

Rather than *shuv*, Priestly texts use the verb *kipper*. What then is the meaning of the root *k-p-r* (כפר) that is typically translated as "to atone"—and that is reflected in the day's name? Unfortunately, we have a rather incomplete knowledge of biblical Hebrew. As discussed in chapter 3, we lack what linguistic scholars call "informants," native speakers of a language who can tell researchers what a word or a grammatical structure means, or whether a particular locution is grammatical. Contemporary Hebrew is not a reliable source for understanding the biblical idiom; too much time has passed—the language has evolved meanwhile. Instead, we know what a particular biblical word means using the following three methods: (1) comparison with related (cognate) words in other Semitic languages; (2) consulting the ancient Bible translators (especially those of the Septuagint—the Greek translation most likely begun in the third pre-Christian century—because it is the oldest version and typically highly literal); and (3) inference from the literary context.

In the case of the root *k-p-r*, the first and third methods are the most helpful.[8] In Syriac, a dialect of Aramaic that is closely related to Hebrew, the root means "to wipe."[9] It was used of wiping hands or eyes. It was used metaphorically in the *Peshitta*, the Syriac translation of the Bible, in sentences like "Saul wiped out [i.e., did away with] the remnant of the Amalekites." The root is also well attested in Akkadian—a Semitic language of ancient Mesopotamia—which is more distantly related to Hebrew yet close enough to provide useful information. There too it had the sense of "to wipe off."[10] It was used, for example, of a person's feet, or of cleaning jewelry. Related to this use was "to purify," often via ritual (or magical) means, and referring to the purification of temples, countries, fields, and homes.

This latter sense of *k-p-r* fits several of its appearances in Leviticus 16. (Here I am applying method 3, above.) The core verse of our chapter uses the root *k-p-r* in this characteristic way: "Thus he shall *k-p-r* the Shrine[11] of the uncleanness and transgression of the Israelites, whatever their sins; and he shall do the same for the Tent of Meeting, which abides with them in the midst of their uncleanness" (v. 16). The root is used not in reference to people nor to an action performed by individuals (such as repentance); rather, two structures, "the Shrine" and "the Tent of Meeting," are "*k-p-r*-ed." In verse 20, the altar as well is "*k-p-r*-ed."[12] Several modern translations render these instances as "atone,"[13] but this seems at best opaque or unclear—how can one atone for the altar? Instead, the JPS translation's "purge" better reflects the underpinnings of the ritual outlined in this chapter, whose main theme is the purging or purification of the Sanctuary (or Temple).

Concept Behind the Inside Ritual

The Bible scholar Jacob Milgrom gives a compelling explanation of the first set of rituals, relating them to what he calls "The Priestly 'Picture of Dorian Gray.'"[14] The Sanctuary (the Priestly author's representation of the Jerusalem Temple) is like the painting in Oscar Wilde's story, which changes as a result of various human activities. Here the Priestly conception seems to assume that the Temple absorbs different types of impurities at different loci. For example, "wanton unrepented sin" pollutes certain parts of the Temple, including the Holy of Holies. The Temple absorbs such impurities, which build up as they are stored there. Thus the Temple must on occasion be ritually purified.

The buildup of these impurities is, from the Priestly perspective, a threat to national security. The priest Ezekiel evinces this concern in the first portion of the prophetic book that bears his name. Ezekiel prophesied in Babylon after being exiled there from Jerusalem in 597 B.C.E.[15] The first eleven chapters of his book portray "divine abandonment," a motif frequent in ancient Near Eastern—particularly Assyrian—literature.[16] According to Ezekiel, God—or more precisely, *kevod* YHWH (כְּבוֹד יהוה], "the Presence of the LORD")—exited the Temple. The Presence first left the platform of the Temple (10:18) and then "ascended from the midst of the city and stood on the hill east of the city" (11:23). This abandonment of the Temple by the divine Presence is what ultimately allowed it to be destroyed. Ezekiel also explains why God left: "And [God] said to me, 'Mortal, do you see what they are doing, the terrible abominations that the House of Israel is practicing here, to drive Me far from My Sanctuary?'" (8:6). Chapter 8 describes a wide range of "abominations" (improper acts), including worship of the sun (v. 16). These activities polluted the Temple, says Ezekiel, and caused God to abandon it. Similar thinking stands behind Leviticus 16 as well. Here the rituals are planned to purify the Temple from like pollutants, thereby assuring continued divine presence and blessing.

Physical Setting of the Inside Ritual

As background to the main ritual, it is important to remember that the Priestly Sanctuary—as depicted at the end of Exodus—has a three-part structure (see diagram):

- The general Temple area, which contains the main altar used for sacrifices; it may be entered by any person in a state of ritual purity.

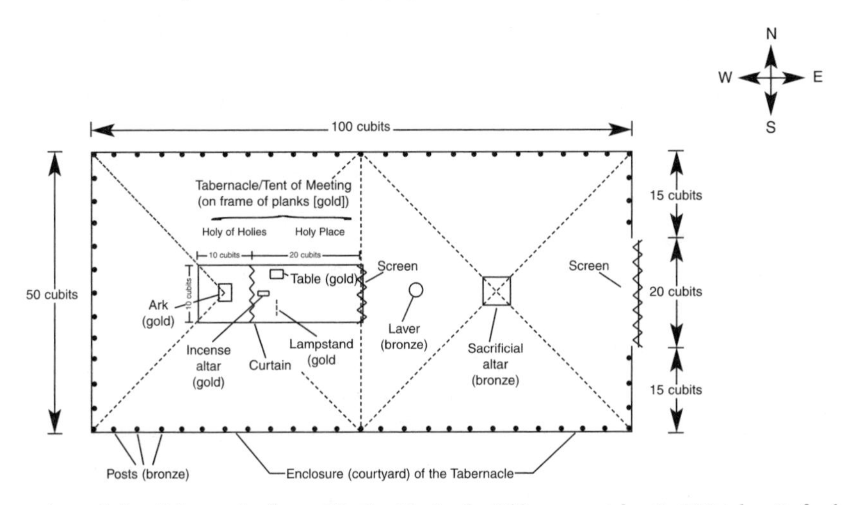

Illustration of the Tabernacle from *The Jewish Study Bible*, copyright © 2004 by Oxford University Press, Inc. Used by permission.

- *Ha-kodesh* (הַקֹּדֶשׁ, "the holy area"), typically translated as "Shrine" in the JPS translation, houses the lampstand, the table for the bread of display, and the altar of incense. Only (ritually pure) priests may enter this area.
- The Holy of Holies is behind this area. It may be entered only by the high priest—Aaron or future high priests descended from him—when purifying the Temple (Lev. 16:2–3). This area, according to Priestly tradition, contained the Ark, which was covered by a *kapporet* (כַּפֹּרֶת). Scholars debate the nature and translation of this word, and how it is related to the root *k-p-r;* the JPS translation renders it as "cover"; others render it as "mercy seat." According to Priestly accounts, a "curtain" separates the Holy of Holies from the Shrine.

The Inside Ritual

Leviticus 16:1–19 enumerates a set of rituals that share certain elements: sacrifice, blood, Sanctuary, and Aaron the high priest. This passage details a set of ordered activities that, if precisely performed, will purify the Temple, thereby guaranteeing the divine presence.

The beginning of the chapter connects the ritual to the enigmatic story concerning the deaths of Nadab and Abihu in Leviticus 10. (It is possible that in an earlier form of Leviticus, chap. 16 directly followed chap. 10.) These two chapters may relate to each other in a variety of ways. Nadab and Abihu have died in the Sanctuary, and thus it needs to be purged or cleaned. Perhaps, too, the deaths of these two sons of Aaron was caused by their improper entry into part of the Sanctuary, which would explain why chapter 16 outlines who may safely enter the innermost section of the Sanctuary, as well as when and how to do so. Verse 2 stresses the danger of entering the innermost part of the Temple ("into the Shrine behind the curtain, in front of the cover that is upon the ark"). It anticipates verses 12–13, which prescribe the manner in which Aaron may enter this area:

> (12) And he shall take a panful of glowing coals scooped from the altar before the LORD, and two handfuls of finely ground aromatic incense, and bring this behind the curtain. (13) He shall put the incense on the fire before the LORD, so that the cloud from the incense screens the cover that is over the Ark of the Pact, lest he die.

As elsewhere in the Bible, the assumption is that seeing God causes death (see, e.g., Judg. 13:22). The incense here acts as a smokescreen, preventing

Aaron (and his high-priest descendants) from seeing God's cloudlike manifestation in the Holy of Holies.

Leviticus 16:3–4 notes the preparation for the ritual. Aaron brings the requisite sacrificial animals (v. 3). He must be ritually pure and properly dressed in "work clothes." In addition, he brings three other animals on behalf of Israel (v. 5). Two of these are for a *chattat* (חַטָּאת); although the JPS translation and most others render this as "a sin offering," it is better translated "a purification offering," in other words, an offering that will purify or purge or cleanse a specific area of the Temple.[17]

The text continues with a description of the ritual itself: Aaron can only serve as a proper officiant if he (and his priestly family, for whom he seems to bear responsibility) is ritually pure, thus he must first offer his own purification offering (Lev. 16:6). Then he may begin to perform the main part of the ritual, determining which of the two he-goats will be used for the nation's purification offering (vv. 7–8). That offering is completed (v. 9), while the other he-goat is put on hold until the main ritual is completed (v. 10).

Leviticus 16:11 returns us to verse 6; it is not a new action, but a repetition of the previous taken action, with the additional note that this animal must be slaughtered. This is done in part because this slaughtering produced blood, which must be saved because it will be the central agent of the ritual that follows in verse 14. However, since that ritual will transpire in the Holy of Holies, "behind the curtain," it must be accomplished using incense, thereby producing a cloud so that the Divine Presence is not seen (vv. 12–13; see above, "Concept Behind the Inside Ritual"). While in the Holy of Holies, blood of two purification offerings is sprinkled: that of Aaron's purification offering bull (v. 14—see vv. 3, 11), and that of the nation's he-goat (v. 15—see v. 5). Like most rituals, in order to be effective, this one must be accomplished in a precise fashion; in this case, sprinkling the blood seven times, a number used frequently in the Bible to symbolize completeness.

The ultimate goal or result of these rituals is noted in Leviticus 16:16: "Thus he shall purge the Shrine of the uncleanness and transgression of the Israelites, whatever their sins; and he shall do the same for the Tent of Meeting, which abides with them in the midst of their uncleanness." This "purging" or ritual purification is accomplished through the use of animal blood, which for the Priestly authors is seen as a kind of "ritual detergent."[18] Exactly how and why blood functions in this way is unclear, though it is likely connected to the Priestly assertion that blood is to be identified as the *nefesh* (נֶפֶשׁ, "lifeforce") of the animal (17:10–14); perhaps in some sense it reanimates and thus purifies.

Leviticus 16:17 offers some additional background information, and verses

18–19 prescribe the final part of the purification ritual, purging the altar in the Holy section through a final blood ritual. The "horns of the altar" refer to quarter-circular protuberances like those found in various altars excavated in Israel. As may be seen from the different vocabulary used in verses 16 and 19, each act of purification accomplishes something slightly different, purifying parts of the structure from different types of sins. With verse 19, the main ritual is completed, and through the use of ritual detergent blood, the Temple or Sanctuary is restored to a state of ritual purity. It is again a "house" that will not repel God,[19] a place where He will want to reside.

The Outside Ritual

The function of the previous ritual was to purify various holy places and objects; the purpose of this scapegoat ritual is clarified in Leviticus 16:21: "Aaron shall lay both his hands upon the head of the live goat and confess over it all the iniquities and transgressions of the Israelites, whatever their sins, putting them on the head of the goat; and it shall be sent off to the wilderness through a designated man."

There may be some redundancy between this ritual and the previous offerings and blood ritual, or this may be seen as a totally different ritual, purging the Israelites of intentional sins, which may not have been covered by the previous set of rituals. At any rate, the goat is literally carrying off the sins of the people, removing them to an area outside of civilization, to "an inaccessible region" (Lev. 16:22). The actions of Aaron highlight the role of the goat. For other sacrifices, the person offering the animal is told to place one hand on the sacrifice (3:8, 13; 4:4, 29, 33) as an indication that this is his or her animal. Here, however, Aaron places both of his hands on the animal—a unique act within the Bible—through which he transfers the sins onto the animal.

The word "Azazel" appears four times in Leviticus 16 (vv. 8, 10 [twice], 26). It is etymologically difficult to explain, not fitting the three-letter pattern typical of Hebrew roots. Nor is context particularly helpful in clarifying its precise meaning. The Septuagint (the Greek translation of the Bible) understood it to mean "scapegoat," which is quite suitable for verses 8 and 10a, but less likely for 10b and 26. Some understand it to be a place-name. Alternatively, some understand Azazel to mean "for the elimination of divine anger."[20] This may be more satisfactory from a modern theological perspective, but is etymologically unlikely. The most likely explanation derives from the parallelism of verse 8, "one marked for the LORD and the other marked for Azazel," which supports the ancient tradition—found in a wide range of sources—that Azazel was the name of a demon.[21] This ritual would then be a remnant of an older prebiblical ritual, somewhat "Israelitized," propitiating a malevolent wilderness demon.

The definition of Azazel is likely an intractable problem. Nevertheless, it is clear that the ritual performed in Leviticus 16:20–22 complements the earlier ritual, supplementing the purification of the Temple with the purification of Israel through this rite of elimination.

The rest of this section is anticlimactic, tying together loose ends. Specifically, it deals with final actions of all of the participants in the rituals—Aaron, who purged the Temple (Lev. 16:23–25), the person who led the scapegoat (v. 26), and the person who burned the carcasses of the animals whose blood was used for purification (vv. 27–28). All of these people came into contact with either supercharged holiness, supercharged impurity, or both, and thus they require ritual purification before resuming normal life.

Reframing the Ritual

The language of the introduction to Leviticus 16 may suggest that it was a ritual to be performed as needed to purify the sanctuary: "The LORD said to Moses: "Tell your brother Aaron that he is not to come at will into the Shrine . . . Thus only shall Aaron enter the Shrine" (vv. 2–3). No particular time is specified for this ritual. One would expect it to be performed as needed—for example, after the pollution of the Temple through corpse contamination, as when Nadab and Abihu died in the Tabernacle (v. 1; see above, "The Inside Ritual").

For this reason, verses 29–34 may not be an original part of Leviticus 16. They further ritualize the purification ceremony by fixing when it should transpire: on the tenth day of the seventh month, what is called in Leviticus 23:27 *Yom Ha-kippurim*, the Day of Purgation (or Atonement). This addition supplements the rituals described earlier in Leviticus 16, which focus on the sanctuary and Aaron, with the requirement that "you shall practice self-denial; and you shall do no manner of work, neither the citizen nor the alien who resides among you. . . . It shall be a sabbath of complete rest for you, and you shall practice self-denial" (vv. 29–31), a requirement that is applicable to the broader community, not only to Aaron and his (priestly) family. This broader concern is typical of the work of the Holiness School, the group responsible for Leviticus 17–26, which has as its refrain "You shall be holy." This school tends to democratize the narrow priestly perspective seen elsewhere in Priestly literature.[22]

Apparently the author from the Holiness School believed that this type of ritual needed to be institutionalized at a particular time, on Yom Kippur, immediately preceding the festival of Sukkot. Biblical evidence suggests that Sukkot was *the* major fall festival. (Only in postbiblical times did Rosh Hashanah, the Jewish New Year celebrated on the first day of the seventh month, nine days before Yom Kippur and fourteen days before Sukkot, become central.) The dedication of Solomon's Temple was on Sukkot (1 Kings 8:2), and it is Sukkot that is celebrated with great fanfare during the early postexilic period (Neh. 8:13–18). The most appropriate time for an annual ritual "housecleaning" would be immediately preceding Sukkot.

But this is not the only logical occasion for such a ritual. Another major festival complex is in the spring, comprised of the one-day Pesach or Passover festival, followed by the seven-day Matzot, or Unleavened Bread, festival (Lev. 23:5–8).[23] Thus, it should not be surprising that a different tradition developed that would time this housecleaning then. Ezekiel 45:18–20 notes:

> (18) Thus said the Lord GOD: On the first day of the first month, you shall take a bull of the herd without blemish, and you shall cleanse the Sanctuary. (19) The priest shall take some of the blood of the purification offering and apply it to the doorposts of the Temple, to the four corners of the ledge of the altar, and to the doorposts of the gate of the inner court. (20) You shall do the same on the seventh day of the month to purge the Temple from uncleanness caused by unwitting or ignorant persons.

If both this and the Leviticus 16 ritual were performed, the Temple would be cleansed twice annually, helping to assure the presence of the Presence, with the attendant protection of all Israel.

Other Biblical Rituals

There is no such thing as the typical biblical ritual. Therefore the discussion of the structure and meaning of Leviticus 16 cannot be applied to all other rituals. However, we analyzed this example to show that rituals—even those involving lots of elements and lots of blood—are not meaningless prescribed actions. Rather, they are a series of activities that have meaning and serve particular functions.

Other rituals should be analyzed similarly. In some cases, their purpose is fairly transparent from the immediate biblical context alone. Consider the ritual in Deuteronomy 21:1–9 concerning expiation for a homicide when the murderer cannot be found. It uses blood to cleanse the land: "do not let guilt for the blood of the innocent remain among Your people Israel" (v. 8). With this in mind, it is relatively easy to understand much of the symbolism of the ritual.[24] However, many rituals do not detail their function so clearly. Their meaning remains more opaque without recourse to other types of analysis.[25]

Leviticus in particular is full of rituals. In contrast to many rituals found in other biblical books, these must be performed at the sanctuary. This is because Leviticus is a Priestly book, and the priests' lives centered on the Temple. There is a strong sense, often accomplished through repetition, that these rituals must be performed exactly as prescribed. This is mirrored in the highly repetitive sections of Exodus 25–31, 35–40, which detail the instructions for the Tabernacle and their fulfillment, and which culminate with:

> (39:42) Just as the Lord had commanded Moses, so the Israelites had done all the work. (43) And when Moses saw that they had performed all the tasks—as the Lord had commanded, so they had done—Moses blessed them.

From the perspective of the Priestly author, the rituals prescribed are divine commandments, and therefore it is crucial to follow their instructions exactly, insuring divine satisfaction, and thus human success. In the words of Exodus 25:8, "Let them make Me a sanctuary that I may dwell among them." This explains why such rituals play such a crucial role in ancient Israelite society, and in the societies of its neighbors.

Many of these passages lack an ethical or moral component, and we misunderstand (or "anachronize") them if we claim that such a component is implicit. We also misunderstand the function of ritual in the ancient world. The texts are quite clear: If the rituals are accomplished properly, if the blood is sprinkled the right number of times in the correct place, and the scapegoat bearing the sins is safely brought to the wilderness, then the Temple will be cleansed, and the people's sins will be annulled. No prayer, contrition, or repentance is necessary—the ritual *by itself*, if properly performed, assures the divine Presence and divine blessing.[26]

The belief that ritual prescriptions, if carefully followed, will maintain the divine Presence is a peculiarly Priestly view. It is easy to understand how this view might develop within a group that had the Temple and its rituals as their center. At the same time, as we shall see later, different groups had other views concerning what would lead to divine blessing.[27]

10

"In the Fortieth Year . . . Moses Addressed the Israelites"

Reading Deuteronomy

Primary Reading: Deuteronomy (esp. chaps. 1, 4, 5, 12, 31).

A Pious Fraud

Deuteronomy contains the longest introductory sentence of any biblical book:

> (1) These are the words that Moses addressed to all Israel on the other side of the Jordan—through the wilderness, in the Arabah near Suph, between Paran and Tophel, Laban, Hazeroth, and Di-zahab, (2) it is eleven days from Horeb to Kadesh-barnea by the Mount Seir route—(3) it was in the fortieth year, on the first day of the eleventh month, that Moses addressed the Israelites in accordance with the instructions that the LORD had given him for them, (4) after he had defeated Sihon king of the Amorites, who dwelt in Heshbon, and King Og of Bashan, who dwelt at Ashtaroth and Edrei, (5) on the other side of the Jordan, in the land of Moab, Moses undertook to expound this Teaching; he said: (transl. adapted).

The long list of details given here has a simple function: to legitimize the book as a whole. It is another way of saying: "I am authentic." There is a good reason that Deuteronomy in particular needs to be legitimated in this way so much of the book repeats narratives and legal material from earlier in the Torah. Deuteronomy 5, for example, recounts the Decalogue of Exodus 20. The second half of chapter 1 retells the story of the spies, found in Numbers 13–14. Its festival calendar in chapter 16 resembles the one found in Exodus 23:14–19. For good reason, the book is called in English Deuteronomy—from the Greek *deutero-nomos*, "second law"—and in rabbinic sources *mishnei torah*, "a repetition of the Torah." At first blush, that is precisely what the book is: Moses' repetition of selected earlier laws and narratives as his valedictory address.

The repetition, however, is far from exact. Even the Decalogue, which claims to be the words that the LORD spoke ("those and no more—to your whole congregation at the mountain"; Deut. 5:19), does not replicate exactly the words found in Exodus 20. Most especially in the Sabbath utterance, but not only there, the text of Deuteronomy deviates significantly from Exodus.[1] In fact, that utterance has been "Deuteronomized," that is, made to fit the theology and language of the book of Deuteronomy, which has no knowledge of the seven-day creation mentioned in Genesis 1 and Exodus 20, but is full of references to the Exodus, a major theme in Deuteronomy.[2]

The so-called spy story is also revised in a number of significant ways. For example, according to Numbers 13:2, it was God who initiated the sending of the scouts, while according to Deuteronomy 1:22–23, this was the people's idea, which Moses approved. According to Numbers 13:2, each tribe's chieftain was sent, while Deuteronomy 1:23 notes only that "one from each tribe" was sent. Many other differences may be cited.

Legal traditions are equally flexible. Though there are many similarities between the festival calendars in Exodus 23 and Deuteronomy 16, there are many differences as well. The similarities include a notice that there are only three pilgrimage festivals, incumbent upon males only. Exodus 23:17 reads, "Three times a year all your males shall appear before the Sovereign, the LORD," compared to Deuteronomy 16:16, "Three times a year—on the Feast of Unleavened Bread, on the Feast of Weeks, and on the Feast of Booths—all your males shall appear before the LORD your God in the place that He will choose." In both there is no mention of Rosh Hashanah (New Year) or Yom Kippur (the Day of Atonement), found in the Priestly calendar of Leviticus 23. The differences are also quite striking. For example, the fall festival is noted in quite brief terms in Exodus 23:16, "and the Feast of Ingathering at the end of the year, when you gather in the results of your work from the field." It is renamed, expanded, and changed quite significantly in Deuteronomy 16:

> (13) After the ingathering from your threshing floor and your vat, you shall hold the Feast of Booths for seven days. (14) You shall rejoice in your festival, with your son and daughter, your male and female slave, the Levite, the stranger, the fatherless, and the widow in your communities. (15) You shall hold a festival for the LORD

> your God seven days, in the place that the LORD will choose; for the LORD your God will bless all your crops and all your undertakings, and you shall have nothing but joy.

The name of the festival has been changed, it is celebrated for a prescribed time period, and it must be held "in the place that the LORD will choose," generally understood to be Jerusalem. Various elements of the underclass are mentioned as included, and divine blessing is explicitly mentioned as the reward for its celebration.

These changes of earlier narrative and legal material typify Deuteronomy[3] (and many more such examples could be cited).[4] They are all the more striking given that Deuteronomy notes: "You shall not add anything to what I command you or take anything away from it" (4:2), and "Be careful to observe only that which I enjoin upon you: neither add to it nor take away from it" (13:1). Yet it tampers with its sources extensively.[5]

These factors all suggest a special origin for Deuteronomy. Indeed, both traditional Jewish and modern critical scholarship have connected it to the book found, according to 2 Kings 22:8, in the Jerusalem Temple when King Josiah of Judah purified and renovated the Temple in 622 B.C.E.[6] As a result of reading this book, Josiah enacts several reforms (see 2 Kings 23) that resonate remarkably with the laws in Deuteronomy, especially the laws emphasized there concerning worshipping one God in a unified fashion in one Temple (in Jerusalem). According to the rabbinic perspective, Deuteronomy was hidden away by the apostate king Manasseh, who reigned two kings before Josiah. The critical position suggests instead that the book "discovered" in the Temple was the product of the scribes of Josiah's court, although it may incorporate still earlier works, perhaps of Northern Israelite origin. For this reason, the great biblical scholar Wilhelm Martin Lebrecht de Wette characterized the core or original text of Deuteronomy[7] as "a pious forgery."

Some contemporary scholars follow de Wette's opinion, suggesting that verses such as Deuteronomy 4:2 and 13:1 are inserted to cover up the nature of the book as a forgery. Others see these verses as typical ancient Near Eastern rhetoric, in which interpretation is depicted as a legitimate restatement of earlier traditions.[8] This idea extends beyond the biblical period; the great first-century-C.E. Jewish historian Josephus rewrites the Bible quite radically in his *Antiquities*, yet he too states (I.17): "The precise details of our Scripture records will, then, be set forth, each in its place as my narrative proceeds . . . neither adding nor omitting anything."[9]

Comparing Peaches and Nectarines

Comparison is an extremely useful tool for understanding biblical texts. It is generally acknowledged that the Covenant Collection of Exodus served as the basis for much of the Deuteronomic law collection, and was revised extensively.[10] The laws concerning the Hebrew slave in both collections will be compared here to see the defining characteristics of Deuteronomy. We will then be able to explore in greater detail when and why these might have developed.

The two laws are reproduced below.

Exodus 21	*Deuteronomy 15*
(2) When you acquire a Hebrew slave, he shall serve six years; in the seventh year he shall go free, without payment. (3) If he came single, he shall leave single; if he had a wife, his wife shall leave with him. (4) If his master gave him a wife, and she has borne him children, the wife and her children shall belong to the master, and he shall leave alone. (5) But if the slave declares, "I love my master, and my wife and children: I do not wish to go free," (6) his master shall take him before God. He shall be brought to the door or the doorpost, and his master shall pierce his ear with an awl; and he shall then remain his slave for life. (7) When a man sells his daughter as a slave, she shall not be freed as male slaves are. (8) If she proves to be displeasing to her master, who designated her for himself, he must let her be redeemed; he shall not have the right to sell her to outsiders, since he broke faith with her. (9) And if he designated her for his son, he shall deal with her as is the practice with free maidens.	(12) If a fellow Hebrew, man or woman, is sold to you, he shall serve you six years, and in the seventh year you shall set him free. (13) When you set him free, do not let him go empty-handed: (14) Furnish him out of the flock, threshing floor, and vat, with which the LORD your God has blessed you. (15) Bear in mind that you were slaves in the land of Egypt and the LORD your God redeemed you; therefore I enjoin this commandment upon you today. (16) But should he say to you, "I do not want to leave you"—for he loves you and your household and is happy with you—(17) you shall take an awl and put it through his ear into the door, and he shall become your slave in perpetuity. Do the same with your female slave. (18) When you do set him free, do not feel aggrieved; for in the six years he has given you double the service of a hired man. Moreover, the LORD your God will bless you in all you do.

r, he must not
her food, her
l rights. (11) If
ıree ways, she
ıyment.

in content and structure support the notion that these
ınected; in this case, that Deuteronomy knew and revised
visions are minor, and may be stylistic only, for example,
the slave's being "acquired" in Exodus, and being "sold to
Many, however, are quite major, including the way in
is discussed: she is in her own category in Exodus, while
treated the same as the male.

Several differences between these texts are especially important. Deuteronomy omits the subcases dealing with the slave's wife—perhaps it did not agree with the idea that a bought slave could be used to sire future slaves for the master, as Exodus 21:4 implies.[11] In fact, at the very place where that legislation was expected, Deuteronomy notes: "(13) When you set him free, do not let him go empty-handed: (14) Furnish him out of the flock, threshing floor, and vat, with which the LORD your God has blessed you. (15) Bear in mind that you were slaves in the land of Egypt and the LORD your God redeemed you; therefore I enjoin this commandment upon you today." This introduces two major themes of Deuteronomy: its humanitarianism, and the importance of the Exodus from Egypt—which is used as a motive clause in many laws.[12]

The subcase of the slave who wants to stay with his master appears in both books, with a significant change: the ritual of piercing the ear (not the earlobe!) with an awl in Exodus transpires "before God" (v. 6), while in Deuteronomy it takes place at "the [master's] door" (v. 17). Exodus allows God to be worshipped at a plurality of sanctuaries; in the words of Exodus 20:21: "Make for Me an altar of earth and sacrifice on it your burnt offerings and your sacrifices of well-being, your sheep and your oxen; in *every* place where I cause My name to be mentioned I will come to you and bless you." This fits with many traditions found in Genesis, where the ancestors built altars for God in a variety of places (see, e.g., 22:13; 46:1). In contrast, a cornerstone of Deuteronomy's theology is that God must properly be worshipped only in the *one* place that God has chosen for his name to dwell. This is not only the core theme of the first legal section in Deuteronomy (chap. 12), but also manifests in the subsequent revision of many earlier laws.[13] Thus, returning to the slave laws, it is now clear why Deuteronomy converts a ritual that was taking place at local sanctuaries into a private, home ritual: it does not want to trouble the slaveowner and slave to travel to Jerusalem to perform the rite.[14]

Deuteronomy has also changed the way in which the female slave is treated. Although the nature of the case in Exodus is not certain, it is likely to be that of a minor daughter who is sold into slavery by her father.[15] By omitting this case, and instead insisting twice (vv. 12, 17) that the female should be treated as the male, Deuteronomy is removing this possibility.

Finally, the end of Deuteronomy's text provides a motive for why the master should not feel bad when releasing a slave at the end of the seventh year—"for in the six years he has given you double the service of a hired man"—in other words, the slave was already a good buy, so do not be tempted to take further advantage of the situation. The argument to release the slave here is secular and logical rather than religious and symbolic.

This comparison brings into focus several fundamental features of Deuteronomy: its focus on centralization of worship, its humanitarianism, its betterment of the status of women, and its attempt to use secular logic to convince Israelites to follow divine law. Is there any social or historical set of events that can help explain these remarkably diverse changes?

Deuteronomy as a Treaty

Deuteronomy offers a final clue that might help understand its origin and meaning: its structure, which is unlike that of any other biblical book. Initially its format looks similar to Leviticus: both books are comprised predominantly of laws, and both have long passages toward the end that outline the results of following—and in much greater detail, abrogating—these laws (Leviticus 26; Deuteronomy 28). However, the two structures differ greatly as well: Leviticus begins with laws, whereas the main legal section of Deuteronomy begins in chapter 12. Furthermore, while these two books' laws overlap somewhat (especially the laws concerning permitted and prohibited animals in Leviticus 11 and Deuteronomy 14, the laws of keeping kosher, as they are called in postbiblical literature), their differences are far greater. (Partly for this reason, critical scholars have concluded that these books have different sources from different time periods, and more important, they arise from different social groups.)

On the crudest scale, then, Deuteronomy may be analyzed as Introduction (chaps. 1–11), Legal Core (12–26), and Conclusion (27–34[16]). This structure is similar to that of the Laws of Hammurabi, which is comprised of laws flanked by an introduction and conclusion. However, the contents and function of Hammurabi's introduction and conclusion are vastly different in content, goal, and vocabulary from that found in Deuteronomy, so it is unlikely they influenced this biblical text.

Half a century ago, George E. Mendenhall noted that Deuteronomy shared the structure of second-millennium-B.C.E. Hittite treaties.[17] The Hittites, who lived in part of the area of modern Turkey, were a major power of the second millennium, having subjugated a number of Near Eastern states. It entered into treaties with these states that cast the Hittite king as overlord (or "suzerain") and the vanquished state as vassal. As Mendenhall observed, these treaties had significant structural similarities to Deuteronomy, with both containing the following elements: preamble, historical prologue, treaty stipulations, provisions for deposit in the temple and periodic readings, witnesses, and curses and blessings. This suggested to Mendenhall that the early Israelites borrowed the covenant form from the Hittites.

In other words, Deuteronomy needs to be understood as a theologized treaty—in which God is the overlord and Israel is the vassal. Of course, some features of the Hittite treaties were modified; for example, rather than calling upon a variety of gods to witness the treaty, Deuteronomy calls upon heaven and earth (4:26; 32:1), but such adaptations do not negate the claim that Deuteronomy is the religious transformation of a political document. The fact that the word *berit* (בְּרִית) may be used both for a treaty between Israel and other nations, and as a technical term for the covenant between Israel and God, supports Mendenhall's idea.

Most biblical scholars accept the insight that Deuteronomy needs to be understood as a treaty. Since Mendenhall's article was published, however, a number of first-millennium Assyrian vassal treaties have also been published. Many now believe that the Esarhaddon treaties of the early seventh century (published in 1958) have closer and more direct connections to Deuteronomy than the earlier Hittite treaties.[18] In particular, the curses found in Deuteronomy 28 (but not in Leviticus 26) show striking similarities to the Vassal Treaties of Esarhaddon (abbreviated VTE). For example, Deuteronomy 28:23 reads: "The skies above your head shall be copper and the earth under you iron," and VTE 528–31 reads: "May they [the gods] make your ground like iron so that no one can plough [cut] it. Just as rain does not fall from a brazen heaven, so may rain and dew not come upon your fields and pastures."[19]

Judah was a vassal of Assyria for much of the seventh century. Although no vassal treaties between Judah and Assyria have been unearthed, it is likely that the type of language quoted above would have been used in treaties with Judah, and thus could have been borrowed from there for Deuteronomy.

This proposed context suggests a couple of conclusions. First, such treaties probably would have been known only among the more educated class or royal scribes, which means that this class may have been responsible for writing Deuteronomy. (The nature of the author[s] is often discussed in terms of the "Wisdom" influence on Deuteronomy.[20]) Second, if Deuteronomy is a religious appropriation of a political form, its point may be polemical: true allegiance belongs to the God of Israel—not to the Assyrian overlords and their gods.

In this connection, let us recall that Deuteronomy is often understood as the "book" discovered in the Temple in the late seventh century. As I said earlier, Judah was a vassal of Assyria for the preceding decades, during which some form of Deuteronomy might have been written. It may have even been meant to attack the type of Assyrian worship introduced in the early seventh century by King Manasseh, the great apostate king. By later in the seventh century, when Deuteronomy was "found," Judah was no longer a vassal of Assyria, which was busy fighting a losing series of wars against the ascendant Babylonians. It is easy to understand in this context why the book argues that God (rather than some Mesopotamian power) is the true overlord, and that the forms of worship introduced by Manasseh under Assyrian influence are offensive.[21]

For the Love of God

Understanding Deuteronomy as a theologized political treaty, in which the overlord is God and the vassal is Israel, affects how we understand the book as a whole, as well as some of its parts.[22] Certain elements of the book—such as the long historical prologue, the injunction concerning the reading of the book and its safekeeping (31:9–13, 26), and its interest in witnesses—are best understood within the broader treaty context.[23] More significantly, Assyrian treaties use certain words as technical terms (that is, they do not have their normal meanings); it is likely that Deuteronomy uses their Hebrew equivalents in the same way.

From the Jewish perspective, one of the most important sections of Deuteronomy is 6:4–9, which by early in the rabbinic period was recited as a prayer called the *Shema* after its first word (it begins: *shema yisrael,* "Hear, O Israel").[24] Before the discovery of the connection between Deuteronomy and Assyrian vassal treaties, the beginning of verse 5 was the subject of much discussion: "You shall love the LORD your God with all your heart and with all your soul and with all your might." How can such love be commanded?

The Vassal Treaties of Esarhaddon clarifies what this means. The main purpose of VTE is to assure the proper succession of Ashurbanipal, son of Esarhaddon, to the throne after the death of his father. (Rebellions by vassals were common after a king's death. Indeed, a rebellion had preceded the accession of Esarhaddon himself to the throne.) In this connection, one of the main stipulations of VTE is that the vassals must "love the crown prince designate Ashurbanipal."[25] In this context, it is quite clear that not emotional love, but obedience is being sought. William Moran, who first noted that this is the love that Deuteronomy as well is seeking, called it "covenantal love" and suggested that it is identical with loyalty and obedience.[26]

This has extremely important implications for how we should read Deuteronomy 6:5 and what follows. Most translations, including the JPS translation, put a period after verse 5, suggesting that love of God is separate from the injunctions that follow. Probably a better punctuation of this text would be:

> You shall love the LORD your God with all your heart and with all your soul and with all your might: Take to heart these instructions with which I charge you this day—impress them upon your children, recite them when you stay at home and when you are away, when you lie down and when you get up; bind them as a sign on your hand and let them serve as a symbol on your forehead; inscribe them on the doorposts of your house and on your gates.

In this reading, "love"—namely obedience and loyalty—is not important in itself, but matters to the extent that it is expressed through concrete actions: teaching children, reciting these words,[27] binding and inscribing them.[28] In the same way that human love can be fully shown only when emotion is expressed, love of God must be expressed through actions. Without understanding the treaty background of Deuteronomy, it is easy to miss this point, and to insist—as so many commentators and interpreters have—that Deuteronomy commands love as an emotion. The contextual, historical-critical reading of the book prevents this error.

Conclusion

Deuteronomy is a very special book. Almost any passage from it is recognizable instantly due to its characteristic vocabulary and distinctive phrases and rhythms.[29] Its ideas—especially the importance of worshipping *one* God in *one* fashion and in *one* place (e.g., "It has been clearly demonstrated to you that the LORD alone is God; there is none beside Him"; 4:35)[30]—also set it apart from the rest of the Torah. Although these ideas become central within Judaism, they were not expressed earlier in such clear, unequivocal terms. The origin and purpose of some of these ideas may remain unclear,[31] yet reading it as a response to a seventh-century vassal treaty imposed on Judah by the Assyrians helps to explain much of what makes Deuteronomy unique.

11

"The Walls Came Tumbling Down"

Reading Joshua

Primary Reading: Joshua (esp. chaps. 1–12, 21, 23–24).

A Challenging Book to Read

Joshua is a difficult book for us to read, for a number of reasons. First, its main theme is the conquest of the land of Israel. Few of us care to read stories of conquest, because war evokes great ambivalence. It isn't pretty. During the recounted battles, Israel practiced *cheirem* (חֵרֶם), a ban or proscription against conquered places—"exterminat[ing] everything in the city with the sword: man and woman, young and old, ox and sheep and ass" (6:21). Furthermore, almost half of the book is comprised of long (boring) lists. To complicate matters, it is extremely unlikely that the Book of Joshua represents what really happened. In the words of a recent commentator: "hardly any of the material it preserves is the sort that can be directly used for historical reconstruction."[1] Thus, the real question to ask about Joshua is: "Why would anyone have told the early history of Israel in this fashion?"

Joshua as History

As noted earlier, the present state of the evidence does not enable historians to reconstruct exactly how the people Israel came into being, and how they came to possess their land.[2] This much, however, is generally conceded:

- A people called Israel existed in the land by the end of the thirteenth century B.C.E. (see "The Beginning of Israel" in chapter 4);
- Someone conquered *some* of the cities that the Bible claims Joshua conquered;

- It is difficult to discern who conquered them (we know that the Sea People, including the Philistines, were also settling in the area at this time and taking over population centers);
- One reason that the conquerors' identity is obscure is because Israelite artifacts are practically the same as those of other local groups living at this time;
- Of the cities that according to Joshua were conquered in the period, archaeological evidence for many of those sites show no signs of conquest;
- This period meanwhile shows a remarkable upsurge of new settlement in the central hill or highland area of the country; and
- Egypt's longstanding political control over the area of Canaan had waned by this point.[3]

Significantly, the difficulty in distinguishing Israelite artifacts implies that Israel had not spent centuries enslaved in Egypt.

Archaeology is not fully objective—it interprets found artifacts, and thus some people may doubt a number of the points made above. We cannot always identify biblical places with certainty. Scholars debate which modern site corresponds to a biblical site, especially when the modern site with the same name as the biblical one does not corroborate the biblical evidence.[4] However, when determining correct place-names for sites, we should not begin with the assumption that the Bible is factual history, expecting the archaeological record to corroborate it. (Until recently, scholars made such an assumption—either explicitly or tacitly—all too often.)

The following question highlights the problems with the biblical account: What would the archaeological record look like if the Book of Joshua were factual? We would expect to find a complete destruction of the major Canaanite cities datable to the same time period. In addition, we would expect to find Canaanite material culture (pottery jugs, housing styles)[5] replaced by totally new styles, most likely with Egyptian motifs or styles, reflecting the origins of the conquering people.

However, such evidence eludes us even after a large number of excavations and surveys (mini-excavations). What have archaeologists found instead? Some evidence of destruction, but significantly more evidence for new settlement patterns at previously uninhabited sites in the highlands. This suggests to many that the main claim in Joshua—a complete and total conquest by Israel—is false; rather, many Israelites originated as Canaanites.[6] Archaeologists in general now doubt that the people Israel arose predominantly outside of the land of Israel.[7]

Embedded Clues in the Stories of Joshua

The Book of Joshua repeatedly paints a picture of a complete conquest of the entire land. This comes through clearly in two summary texts, one located in the middle of the book, and one toward the end. Each uses the word *kol* (כֹּל, "all, every, whole") repeatedly to highlight the theme that *all* was conquered according to *all* that God had promised. Thus the first passage reads:

> Joshua conquered the whole (כל) of this region: the hill country of Judah, all (כל) the Negeb, the whole (כל) land of Goshen, the Shephelah, the Arabah, and the hill country and coastal plain of Israel—everything from Mount Halak, which ascends to Seir, all the way to Baal-gad in the Valley of the Lebanon at the foot of Mount Hermon; and he captured all (כל) the kings there and executed them. . . . Apart from the Hivites who dwelt in Gibeon, not a single city made terms with the Israelites; all (כל) were taken in battle. . . . Thus Joshua conquered all the (כל) the country, according to all (כל) the LORD had promised Moses; and Joshua assigned it to Israel to share according to their tribal divisions. And the land had rest from war (Josh. 11:16–17, 19, 23; transl. adapted).

Similarly, the second summary passage reads:

> The LORD gave to Israel the whole (כל) country which He had sworn to their fathers that He would assign to them; they took possession of it and settled in it. The LORD gave them rest on all sides, according to all (כל) He had promised to their fathers on oath. Not one man of all (כל) their enemies withstood them; the LORD delivered all (כל) their enemies into their hands. Not one of all (כל) the good things which the LORD had promised to the House of Israel was lacking. Everything (כל) was fulfilled (Josh. 21:41–43; in some editions, vv. 43–45; transl. adapted).

Here the repetition of the word *kol* seems meaningful: it is like a bell rung over and over so as to sound a continuous thematic note. We call a repeated word that helps give structure and meaning to a literary unit a "leading word." (Bible scholars often use the German equivalent, *Leitwort.*) Leading words provide guidance to the reader; they are keys to a unit's meaning.

(Many contemporary translations—including that of JPS—seek to render the Hebrew's plain sense into normal English idiom. Their translation approach often does not precisely convey the repetition of leading words in the original language. Partly this is because normal English discourse avoids such repetitions as awkward or monotonous. More to the point, a given Hebrew word usually has more than one sense, and a plain-sense translation by nature chooses whichever English word best expresses its meaning in each context. A disadvantage of the idiomatic translation approach is that a biblical unit's theme may literally be lost in translation, as our two summary passages in Joshua illustrate.[8]

In contrast, other translation approaches are more sensitive to the text's use of a leading word. In particular, in their Bible translation, the two great twentieth-century German-Jewish thinkers Franz Rosenzweig and Martin Buber reflected such repetitions whenever possible by repeating the same German word.[9] A contemporary translator of the Bible into English, Everett Fox, is continuing to follow Buber and Rosenzweig's principles.[10])

In addition to the repetition of *kol,* other leading words in the text suggest a complete, total, and swift conquest. The miraculous and nearly instant conquest of Jericho—the first city attacked after crossing the Jordan (Josh. 6)—sets the stage for this idea. Later, when the Southern coalition is defeated (chap. 10), a sixfold repetition of "let none escape" (10:28, 30, 33, 37, 39, 40), reinforces the impression that the conquest was complete. A simultaneous description of six proscribed cities has the same effect (10:1, 28, 35, 37, 39, 40).[11] Chapter 12 also uses repetition for emphasis. The first part of that passage, about the conquest of Transjordan (the area east of the Jordan River), repeats the word *ve-ad* (וְעַד, "until" or "up to") six times, underscoring the all-encompassing nature of Israel's boundaries. The second part of that passage, concerning the conquest of the Northern coalition, is stylized and redundant. In enumerating the cities and kings captured, it says thirty-one times "the king of *X*: 1," where *X* is the name of one city after another. (This list is all the more remarkable because evidence dug up from the ruins of those city-states have shown that they did not have kings.) And in case the reader misses the point, the list concludes: "Total number of kings: 31."

In sum, through the strategic use of leading words, the predominant strand of Joshua highlights the claim that "the LORD gave to Israel the whole (כל) country which He had sworn to their fathers that He would assign to them" (Josh. 21:41).

Contradictory Assessments

A tale of swift and total victory, however, is not the only story that Joshua tells.[12] For instance, we also read: "Joshua waged war with all those kings over a long period" (11:18)—a sharp contrast to other passages' portrayal of a sort of ancient

Six-Day War. More important, immediately after chapter 12's summary of the completed conquest, we read:

> (13:1) Joshua was now old, advanced in years. The LORD said to him, "You have grown old, you are advanced in years; and very much of the land still remains to be taken possession of. (2) This is the territory that remains: all the districts of the Philistines and all those of the Geshurites, (3) from the Shihor, which is close to Egypt, to the territory of Ekron on the north, are accounted Canaanite, namely, those of the five lords of the Philistines—the Gazites, the Ashdodites, the Ashkelonites, the Gittites, and the Ekronites—and those of the Avvim (4) on the south; further, all the Canaanite country from Mearah of the Sidonians to Aphek at the Amorite border (5) and the land of the Gebalites, with the whole Valley of the Lebanon, from Baal-gad at the foot of Mount Hermon to Lebo-hamath on the east, (6) with all the inhabitants of the hill country from the Valley of the Lebanon to Misrephoth-maim, namely, all the Sidonians. I Myself will dispossess those nations for the Israelites; you have only to apportion their lands by lot among Israel, as I have commanded you."

As a glance at any Bible atlas indicates, this "land that remains" is substantial! In other words, this passage directly conflicts with the account given a few verses earlier.[13]

What are we to make of the fact that this book presents more than one idea concerning basic notions such as how the land was conquered and what its boundaries are? Like many other scholars, I conclude from its internal contradictions that the Book of Joshua is not the work of a single author. Rather, it is a composite book. Either it has gone through several stages of editing and redaction, or it was written by an author who (for some unknown reason) incorporated earlier sources—even though they did not agree with the author's point—or both.

Further evidence for the book's composite nature comes into view when we consider what critical scholars call the Deuteronomistic History.

The Deuteronomistic History

What is the relationship of the first several books of the Bible to each other? Scholars have grouped them in various ways.[14] The canon has joined the first five books together as the Torah or Pentateuch, literally "five books." This unit ends with the death of its main protagonist, Moses. Yet Moses is absent from Genesis, and one could argue that the theme of entry into the promised land—

which begins in Genesis 12—more accurately characterizes these books. This theme, however, is not fulfilled until Joshua. Thus many scholars, especially through the middle of the twentieth century, saw the first six books of the Bible, the Hexateuch (six books) as a literary unit. They believed that the Pentateuchal sources—collectively termed "JEPD"—spill over into Joshua (though not beyond), justifying the studying of these six books as a unit.

In 1943, the German biblical scholar Martin Noth proposed a new model.[15] Building on the work of others, he emphasized the fact that the books of Deuteronomy, Joshua, Judges, Samuel, and Kings share similar vocabulary and theology. Noth concluded that those books form a literary unit that he named the Deuteronomistic History (abbreviated "DtrH"). He suggested that this work, which incorporated earlier sources, was composed during the Babylonian exile.

With certain modifications, this hypothesis has gained wide assent.[16] Scholars have questioned Noth's claim that there was a single Deutero-nomistic "historian." Many now believe that there were two: one working during the reign of Josiah (late seventh century B.C.E.) and the other during the Babylonian exile (586–538), who may be distinguished on the basis of vocabulary and ideology.[17] Still others have suggested additional historians, seeing these historians' work as extending into the postexilic period.[18] Despite the many competing reconstructions of how the Deuteronomistic History arrived at its present form, a broad enough consensus exists that we can speak of Deuteronomy through Kings as a "collection."

Why we should consider Joshua a part of this collection is clear: it shares many features of Deuteronomy. For example, the establishment of altars on Mount Ebal and the curse ceremony performed there in Joshua 8:30–34 fulfill a ritual prescribed in Deuteronomy 17. In 8:29, the impaled corpse of the King of Ai is removed at sunset—this assumes Deuteronomy 21:23. Joshua takes for granted that the nations of Canaan need to be proscribed or killed—this institution is found in Deuteronomy only (20:16–18). A *sefer ha-torah* (סֵפֶר הַתּוֹרָה, "Book of the Torah") is mentioned twice in Joshua (1:8; 8:34); in the Torah, it is appears only in Deuteronomy (28:61; 29:20; 30:10). I could adduce further evidence that links Joshua not only to Deuteronomy, but also to Judges, Samuel, and Kings,[19] suggesting that the hypothesis of a Deuteronomistic History is quite robust.

The DtrH hypothesis is important for reading Joshua properly. It helps to explain significant contradictions in the text: these are the result of the complex evolution of the overall text. It also explains why the book is so inaccurate as a history of the premonarchical period: the book was not written until many centuries later.

Revising History

In antiquity, a storyteller typically related details about a past event because they were important, not because they were true.[20] The opening of the Book of Joshua illustrates this principle, while showing how a Deuteronomistic historian could revise earlier materials to keep them relevant for the (exilic) community:

> (1) After the death of Moses the servant of the LORD, the LORD said to Joshua son of Nun, Moses' attendant: (2) "My servant Moses is dead. Prepare to cross the Jordan, together with all this people, into the land that I am giving to the Israelites. (3) Every spot on which your foot treads I give to you, as I promised Moses. . . . (5) No one shall be able to resist you as long as you live. As I was with Moses, so I will be with you; I will not fail you or forsake you. (6) Be strong and resolute, for you shall apportion to this people the land that I swore to their fathers to assign to them. (7) But you must be very strong and resolute to observe faithfully all the Teaching that My servant Moses enjoined upon you. Do not deviate from it to the right or to the left, that you may be successful wherever you go. (8) Let not this Book of the Teaching cease from your lips, but recite it day and night, so that you may observe faithfully all that is written in it. Only then will you prosper in your undertakings and only then will you be successful. (9) I charge you: Be strong and resolute; do not be terrified or dismayed, for the LORD your God is with you wherever you go." (10) Joshua thereupon gave orders to the officials of the people: (11) "Go through the camp and charge the people thus: Get provisions ready, for in three days' time you are to cross the Jordan . . ."

This introduction to the book presents two interconnected problems: (1) It is unduly repetitive, especially in its use of the phrase "be strong and resolute"; and (2) It is confusing, moving from military matters to Torah study and back again. We can best account for these problems by assuming that most of verses 7–9 is a secondary addition.[21] The original text, as one would expect in this situation, dealt only with military strength; this was the context in which God told Joshua to "be strong and resolute"—words that fit the military sphere. However, such a charge meant little to the exilic audience living far from the land, and so an exilic editor modified the words (attributed to God!)[22] so that God told Joshua to be strong in relation to Torah study.

Internal evidence confirms this judgment. Editors who added material to a text often repeated a phrase before and after the insertion, forming a bridge of sorts. If the original text was A-B-C, to which X was added after B, the new text would often look like A-B-X-B-C. When B is repeated after the insertion, scholars call it a "resumptive repetition." It is a way of expressing "back to where we were."[23] The use of this device is quite obvious in Joshua 1. Here is the passage again, with the resumptive repetition marked in bold, and the intervening (secondary) verses in italics:

> (5) No one shall be able to resist you as long as you live. As I was with Moses, so I will be with you; I will not fail you or forsake you. (6) Be strong and resolute, for you shall apportion to this people the land that I swore to their fathers to assign to them. (7) **But you must be very strong and resolute** *to observe faithfully all the Teaching that My servant Moses enjoined upon you. Do not deviate from it to the right or to the left, that you may be successful wherever you go. (8) Let not this Book of the Teaching cease from your lips, but recite it day and night, so that you may observe faithfully all that is written in it. Only then will you prosper in your undertakings and only then will you be successful.* (9) **I charge you: Be strong and resolute**; do not be terrified or dismayed, for the LORD your God is with you wherever you go."

An exilic Deuteronomistic editor has added the material in italics and repeated the material in bold, updating the text to fit with norms that emphasize the importance of Torah study. Through such additions the biblical text was not allowed to atrophy, but was kept alive.

Origins

I have explained why a Deuteronomistic editor changed an earlier text. But why did those various early stories about the conquest arise in the first place? Critical scholarship recognizes many of them as a type known as "etiology," a word deriving from the Greek verb *aitia*, "to cause." An etiology explains something familiar by telling a story about its origin.[24] In the Book of Genesis, the story about Jacob/Israel fighting with the man/angel and getting wounded is an etiology. It gives meaning to the practice of not eating a particular part of livestock: "That is why the children of Israel to this day do not eat the thigh muscle that is on the socket of the hip, since Jacob's hip socket was wrenched at the thigh muscle" (32:33).

Etiologies also explain well-known names. Often they give a derivation that plays on words yet is false from a linguistic point of view (these are often called "folk etymologies"). Again in Genesis, the meaning of the name Edom is explained by a story in which Esau requests of his brother Jacob: "'Give me some of that *ha-adom ha-adom* ("red stuff") to gulp down, for I am famished'—which is why he was named Edom" (25:30). In both of these examples, the text uses the phrase *al ken* (עַל־כֵּן, "that is why" or "which is why").

Not all etiologies are marked with *al ken*. Stories as a whole can function etiologically, without giving an explicit signal to the reader. That the account in Joshua 7–8 of the conquest of Ai is etiological becomes clear once we know that city's actual history.

The name Ai means "heap" or "ruins," and archaeological evidence is quite definitive about it being an uninhabited ruin for well over a thousand years—roughly from 2400 B.C.E. until 1200 B.C.E.[25] Contrary to the biblical depiction, in Joshua's day Ai had no populace for him to overcome and kill off. This story therefore makes sense only as an etiological narrative. It told its audience why the city is called Ai, and what caused the destruction on this site that the Israelites now inhabited. The explanation: it was part of the great and miraculous conquest of the land, in which God fought for Israel as long as they observed God's commands. The story gave a national and moral meaning to the ruins.

Much of the rest of the Book of Joshua is etiological as well, explaining in a nonhistorical fashion how and when Israel conquered various sites. Etiologies of other sorts are mixed in, including the story of the Gibeonites: "Joshua made them hewers of wood and drawers of water—as they still are—for the community and for the altar of the LORD" (9:27).[26]

Contemporary readers may tend to downplay the value of such stories because they are nonscientific or ahistorical. However, etiologies were extremely important in antiquity.[27] Nevertheless, it would be a mistake to understand all of Joshua as etiological. Like most ancient literature, Joshua is complex, coming from a variety of time periods and social circles. It serves a variety of purposes.

Concluding on a Different Note

The biblical authors had little interest in the past for its own sake. Typically they retold or fashioned stories about the past for didactic, theological, or political reasons. Thus, it is significant that Joshua does not end when we reach the summary in 21:41–43 (quoted above), which ends, " Not one of all the good things which the LORD had promised to the House of Israel was lacking. Everything was fulfilled." This would have been an ideal ending for the book if it were concerned only with land-tenure and justifying the later Israelite's possession of the land. But Joshua is about more than that. In the book's final form, its last three chapters proceed to make its main point. They focus, in different ways, on obedience to God.

This theme is most explicit in Joshua 23, which concludes:

> (12) For should you turn away and attach yourselves to the remnant of those nations—to those that are left among you—and intermarry with them, you joining them and they joining you, (13) know for certain that the LORD your God will not continue to drive these nations out before you; they shall become a snare and a trap for you, a scourge to your sides and thorns in your eyes, until you perish from this good land that the LORD your God has given you. (14) "I [Joshua] am now going the way of all the earth. Acknowledge with all your heart and soul that not one of the good things that the LORD your God promised you has failed to happen; they have all come true for you, not a single one has failed. (15) But just as every good thing that the LORD your God promised you has been fulfilled for you, so the LORD can bring upon you every evil thing until He has wiped you off this good land that the LORD your God has given you. (16) If you break the covenant that the LORD your God enjoined upon you, and go and serve other gods and bow down to them, then the LORD's anger will burn against you, and you shall quickly perish from the good land that He has given you."

These verses, like the rest of the chapter, are bursting with Deuteronomistic terminology.[28] Here the promise of the land is conditional. The final chapter again displays these features. There a historical reprise emphasizes God's salvation of Israel from the time of Abraham until the entry into the land (24:3–13). Immediately following that passage, however, is one in which Joshua gives the nation a choice as to which god they want to follow (vv. 14–15). And that, in turn, is followed by a warning that if Israel forsakes God, "He will turn and deal harshly with you and make an end of you" (v. 20).

Another Editorial Hand

It is not only the end of the book that reframes the conquest account that is elsewhere so positive and optimistic. Nor is it only the Deuteronomistic historian who had a hand in reworking these earlier traditions into one that would be religiously meaningful for later generations. As noted earlier, the other great stream that provided biblical material is the Priestly Tradition. These are the authors who seem to have had the final hand in editing the Pentateuch, placing their creation story first, so that all that follows might be read through that lens. It is they who provided a significant narrative and legal framework for most of the Pentateuch. While they did not have a major role in structuring the Deuteronomistic History, they are not totally absent from it.

For example, a narrative near the beginning of the book, concerning the circumcision at Gilgal (Josh. 5:2–9), is (largely) Priestly in origin. That is, this passage features a characteristically Priestly concern. Of all the Torah's legislation, the rite of circumcision is mentioned only in Priestly laws; it is absent from the Covenant Collection and the laws of Deuteronomy.[29] Only in P is circumcision of paramount importance, so much so that, according to Genesis 17:

> Such shall be the covenant between Me and you and your offspring to follow which you shall keep: every male among you shall be circumcised . . . and that shall be the sign of the covenant between Me and you. . . . Thus shall My covenant be marked in your flesh as an everlasting pact. And if any male who is uncircumcised fails to circumcise the flesh of his foreskin, that person shall be cut off from his kin; he has broken My covenant (vv. 10–14).

Similarly, the Priestly law in Exodus 12:48 emphasized that only males who are circumcised may eat of the Pascal offering—which, as Joshua 5:10 indicates, is the backdrop for the story found here. A Priestly author has reworked material in order to reinforce one of his key institutions—circumcision—by mentioning it at the beginning of the conquest narrative.[30]

Conclusion

We have seen that the concern in Joshua is not with "real" history, but with the power of traditions about the past to teach and enlighten. In this book, both the Priestly and Deuteronomistic schools wrote new traditions. Both reframed older traditions—thereby revising their meaning. Through etiological tales they made existing places and practices more meaningful.

The historical-critical method allows us to recover these creative steps, so that we may see the traditions both before their reworking and after their revision. This offers a powerful model for understanding later Judaism, which in a similar way has reworked and revised earlier traditions and texts. Such creativity has allowed Judaism to remain a dynamic, living religion.

REED COLLEGE BOOKSTORE
3203 S.E. WOODSTOCK BLVD
PORTLAND, OR 97202
PH: 503-777-7287 FAX: 503-777-7768
URL: HTTP://BOOKSTORE.REED.EDU

ACCOUNT SALE 001 004 0764732
CASHIER: MARIANNA 10/05/05 11:55

01 EAGLETON/LITERARY THEORY
121 10279953 1 N 13.50
02 BRETTIER/HOW TO READ THE
299 10687901 1 N 35.00*
Less 10.0% Sale -3.50
Tax Exempt: 930386908

Subtotal 45.00

Items 2 Total 45.00

A/R CHARGES 45.00
Cust: JUDAIC STUDIES RESEARCH
Acct: DEPARTMENTAL
Bal: -45.00

Change Due 0.00

!!!!!! PLEASE NOTE !!!!!!
FOR TEXTBOOK PURCHASES
CODE "121" MEANS "USED BOOK"
CODE "111" MEANS "NEW BOOK"
THE "N" STANDS FOR "NOT TAXABLE"

12

"May My Lord King David Live Forever"

Royal Ideology in Samuel and Judges

Primary Reading: Samuel (esp. 1 Samuel 8 through 2 Samuel 8; Judges 1–3, 13–21).

Who Killed Goliath?

Everyone knows that David killed Goliath—the story of 1 Samuel 17 is among the best known in the Bible; a variety of famous paintings have depicted in gory detail the scene of David delivering Goliath's head to Saul.[1] Yet in an appendix added to the book of Samuel, we read: "Again there was fighting with the Philistines at Gob; and Elhanan son of Jaare-oregim the Bethlehemite killed Goliath the Gittite, whose spear had a shaft like a weaver's bar" (2 Sam. 21:19). Historians follow a well-known principle in their research: if two sources each attribute the same action—especially a heroic one—to a well-known figure and to one who is otherwise unknown, it probably happened with the unknown figure; and the story was later transferred to the well-known person. Thus, if there really was a giant named Goliath, then Elhanan killed him—not David. Even if we deny that this tradition about a giant-slayer was historical, we would still think it likely that the Israelites told this story first about Elhanan, and only secondarily about David.

Additional evidence bolsters this claim. The David and Goliath story in 1 Samuel 17 is folkloristic. Its structure and plot do not characterize a narrative interested in the past as it actually transpired. The plot concerns a young whippersnapper who can defeat a fearful giant before whom everyone else cowers. The person who eventually defeats the giant has been promised the hand of the king's daughter in marriage. As in much folklore, the tale includes unexpected twists, such as the manner in which David disposes of Goliath. The scene where David tries to walk in Saul's armor is even comical.

In addition, the David and Goliath story conflicts with its context, suggesting that it is a late addition to Samuel. In the previous story (1 Sam. 16:15–23), David was introduced into Saul's court as a lyre player to help ease Saul's melancholy. However, throughout chapter 17, Saul has no idea who David is. In fact, we read:

> (55) When Saul saw David going out to assault the Philistine, he asked his army commander Abner, "Whose son is that boy, Abner?" And Abner replied, "By your life. Your Majesty, I do not know." (56) "Then find out whose son that young fellow is," the king ordered. (57) So when David returned after killing the Philistine, Abner took him and brought him to Saul, with the head of the Philistine still in his hand. (58) Saul said to him, "Whose son are you, my boy?" And David answered, "The son of your servant Jesse the Bethlehemite."

Chapter 17 fits poorly with what follows as well. In the next story, Saul twice suggests to David that he marry one of his daughters in exchange for certain deeds (1 Sam. 18:17, 25). That unit shows no awareness of 17:25, which had promised the king's daughter to the person who could slay Goliath. These tensions all suggest that a later hand inserted the David and Goliath story into the rest of 1 Samuel.

Where did that later story come from? Probably from storytellers who expanded on the traditions found in the appendix to Samuel mentioned above. Both passages share a couple of unusual features. One is the odd simile that Goliath's spear "had a shaft like a weaver's bar" (1 Sam. 17:7; 2 Sam. 21:19); it appears in the Bible only in these two places—and their parallels in Chronicles. Another is the mention of a giant who "taunts" Israel (1 Sam. 17:10, 25, 26, 36, 45; 2 Sam. 21:21); this root (חרף, *ch-r-p*) is found nowhere else in Samuel. These clues suggest that the David and Goliath story grew from 2 Samuel 21:18–22, a short unit describing the exploits of "David and his men," the giant-slayers.

The suggestion that the David and Goliath story is a late, secondary addition to Samuel raises further questions: Why did someone write this episode? Why did someone insert it here? The answer to those questions will help us uncover the main purpose of the Book of Samuel.

The Ideology of Samuel

Some twentieth-century scholars took the Book of Samuel as an accurate historical text. For example, John Bright claimed that:

> Saul was a tragic figure. Of splendid appearance, modest, at his best magnanimous and willing to confess his faults, always fiercely courageous, there was nevertheless in him an emotional instability that was to be his undoing. Always of a volatile temperament capable of frenzies of excitement, it appears that as pressure was put on him he became increasingly disturbed of mind, swinging like a pendulum between moments of lucidity and black moods in which, incapable to intelligent action, he indulged in behavior calculated to alienate even those closest to him. Before the end Saul was probably no longer quite sane.[2]

Bright simply paraphrased the biblical text and removed divine causality. Thus, according to Bright, it was not God who afflicted Saul (1 Sam. 16:14, "an evil spirit from the LORD began to terrify him") but some unspecified mental malady.

Happily, scholars now widely recognize how unsound this type of history writing is. It fails to address the most basic questions about its sources, such as: When was this text written? Who wrote it? What was the purpose in writing it? Obviously, no one can answer these questions definitively and precisely. We will not be able to say that this part of Samuel was drafted by some physician named Joseph who lived in Gilgal and, after having visited King Saul on what we now reckon as May 5, 1003 B.C.E., wrote it up as case notes the next day. However, by listening for internal hints in the text—by exploring rhetorical features and interpreting them, as I demonstrated earlier in this book—we can answer some of our questions, even if the answers must be tentative. Our answers will determine how we read this unit: as an accurate historical record of the past, or as a work composed with some other goal in mind.

The material from 1 Samuel 8 through 2 Samuel 8 forms a literary unit.[3] The character of this material suggests that its main goal is to delegitimate Saul as king and to legitimate David as Saul's proper successor. The text conveys this message in a number of ways. One way is by depicting David as Saul's son, who thus has a "legal" claim to the throne. Portraying David (the Judean) as the actual son of Saul (the Benjaminite) would exceed the creativity that the audience of a narrative about the past can tolerate. But the text points to David's "filial" relationship with Saul by emphasizing that he was the king's son-in-law.

In addition, clothing imagery plays a role in the motif of legitimacy. The wording is even somewhat awkward, so that the point will not be missed: "Jonathan took off the cloak he was wearing and gave it to David, and his tunic, including his sword, including his bow, and including his belt" (1 Sam. 18:4, transl. adapted).[4] Thus, Jonathan symbolically turns David into himself—the eldest son of Saul and crown prince. Indeed, much later Jonathan says as much to David: "You are going to be king over Israel" (1 Sam. 23:17).

Moreover, the text puts the actual words "my father" and "my son" into the mouths of David and Saul, respectively—although in context those words' plain sense is not their literal meaning. In 1 Samuel 24, David addresses Saul, "Please, *avi* (אָבִי) . . ." (24:12). True to its translation approach, the JPS translation renders *avi* contextually as the honorific "sir," while adding a footnote: "Lit. '[my] father.'" In this way, the translators allow that the wording has a double meaning—namely, it further serves to suggest kinship between David and Saul. As the chapter continues, Saul is made to say with apparent tenderness, "Is that your voice, *beni* (בְּנִי, 'my son') David?" (v. 17). Saul asks the same question again in an alternative version of this story (what scholars call a "doublet"; 26:17), reinforcing the pattern of the earlier chapter.

In short, by combining passages that in different ways create what might be called a pseudogenealogical relationship with Saul, an editor has legitimated David, making him into the crown prince rather than a usurper.

Meanwhile, the text portrays David and Saul as opposites—in particular, as contrasting positive and negative figures.[5] This is true in several ways, starting with their physique. Saul is described twice as "a head taller than all the people" (1 Sam. 9:2, 10:23). In contrast, David is twice called *ha-katan* (הַקָּטָן; 16:11, 17:14). In context, the plain sense of this word is "the youngest" (which is how the JPS translation renders it). However, it can also mean "the smallest/shortest," which resonates in this story when juxtaposed with both the giant Goliath and the tall Saul. Descriptions of physical attributes are rare in the Bible; usually when they appear, it is important for the plot. In this case, two purposes are served by the implicit contrast in size. First, it alerts the reader to the subtler contrasts between David and Saul. Second, it casts a shadow over Saul: he is the one who should have confronted Goliath, but instead the king lets some youngster with less stature do so.

Again, clothing imagery conveys a similar message. In 1 Samuel 17, David tries on Saul's clothes, but they do not fit—David will not become a new Saul. However, the main set of contrasts between David and Saul centers on murder. Specifically, Saul is one who kills the innocent, while David spares even the guilty. Thus, Saul tries twice to have David killed by the Philistines (chap. 18). Moreover, the narration continues, "Saul urged his son Jonathan and all his courtiers to kill David" (19:1) and recounts two attempts on David's life (vv. 10–17). Saul even tries to kill his own son Jonathan (14:44, 20:33) and orders the murder of the priests of the city of Nob (chap. 22). Saul personally chases David in attempts to kill him in chapters 23, 24, and 26.

In contrast, David had easy opportunities to take Saul's life in 1 Samuel 24 and 26; but although the king was trying to hunt him down, David refused to kill "the LORD's anointed" (24:7; 26:11). Likewise, David did not want Abner—Saul's relative and former army officer—killed (2 Sam. 3). He punished those who killed Ish-Bosheth, a son of Saul (chap. 4). Thus, David has compassion even for those who threaten his kingship.

Our unit further contrasts the two anointed figures by juxtaposing their treatment of Amalekites. According to legislation in Deuteronomy (25:19), the Amalekites must be exterminated. In 1 Samuel 15:2–3, Samuel commands Saul to carry this law out by killing the Amalekites along with all their cattle. Saul, however, leaves their king and some of their cattle alive. In contrast, the person who finished off Saul on Mt. Gilboa "just happened" to be an Amalekite (2 Sam. 1:13), and David arranges for him to be killed immediately. David follows the law of the ban that Saul had ignored.

One of the strongest contrasts between the two characters is that David receives God's spirit while Saul loses it. At a crucial moment, Saul is incapable of receiving a divine oracle (1 Sam. 28), while all David needs to do is to ask, and the oracle is received (1 Sam. 23:2; 30:7–8; 2 Sam. 2:1). Furthermore, David's oracles are positive, and he defeats his enemies (1 Sam. 23; 27:7–12; 30), whereas after a negative oracle Saul and much of his family fall to the Philistines (1 Samuel 28; 31). This pattern, in conjunction with the others, underscores the narrator's statement that "the spirit of the LORD gripped David . . . [and] departed from Saul" (1 Sam. 16:13–14).

I have asserted that this part of Samuel (1 Samuel 8 through 2 Samuel 8) is a highly ideological text legitimating David as king. Can I prove this interpretation? No, not in the sense that a scientific fact can be proven. The only "evidence" that we have is the biblical text, whose statements and literary features need to be explained. One explanation is that the text is "simply" recording facts and events. I reject that explanation for several reasons. Premodern texts, including the Bible, show little antiquarian interest and rarely record facts for their own sake. In addition, the structure and other literary features of this material suggest that it seeks something other than the actual past.

Different explanations for a given biblical text need to be weighed against each other. I believe that the purpose suggested here makes sense of content and the current of the passage in question better than any other explanation.

Ideology Serves Theology

Although I perceive a conscious and consistent legitimation of David at the expense of Saul, I do not mean to suggest that it is arbitrary or pure political propaganda. It also has a moral dimension. A key element in this unit is 1 Samuel 15, the story about Saul's failure to proscribe things Amalekite. It tells us that God will transfer the kingship from Saul (to David) as a direct result of his disdaining the divine command. In the poetic words of the prophet Samuel: "Because you rejected the LORD's command, / He has rejected you as king" (15:23). The previous verse, which sounds very much like the later classical prophets such as Amos and Isaiah,[6] emphasizes that "Surely, obedience is better than sacrifice, / Compliance than the fat of rams." Thus, this unit of Samuel legitimates David within a theological framework: Saul loses his kingship when he rejects proper religious norms, and, in typical biblical measure-for-measure manner, is rejected as king for rejecting God. This pronouncement applies not only to King Saul, but also to all those who follow him.

Judges as History

Judges, the book that immediately precedes Samuel, presents itself as the history of the period between the conquest of the land by Joshua and the period of the establishment of the monarchy. The people were led by *shofetim* (singular: *shofet*, שֹׁפֵט), often translated as "judges" (thus the name of the book). However, since they had little to do with judicial matters, "judges" is a misnomer. The term is better rendered as "chieftains," local or tribal leaders who responded to crises and led their tribe—or in some cases, several tribes—to battle.

Social scientists have documented this type of leadership by local chieftains in many premonarchical societies. Thus the Bible's portrayal of Israel's progression from chieftain to king is not only logical, but also most likely historically true. This does not mean, however, that the details found in the Book of Judges are accurate.

None of the facts or events in Judges is corroborated by outside evidence. Given the matters that it deals with, this is not at all surprising; these are not the type of significant events that contemporaneous inscriptions would record. Even so, it would be improper to paraphrase the book and to accept its chronology as correct. In the form in which it has come down to us, the book may preserve some accurate historical traditions, but these have been reworked and reorganized for a purpose other than telling the past as it really was. Thus, reconstructing the "period of judges" on the basis of the Book of Judges is perilous.

Chronology is usually seen as the backbone of history, yet this book does not offer a consistent time line. For example, Judges opens "after the death of Joshua" (1:1), yet Joshua dies (again?) in 2:8. Regarding the action narrated meanwhile, we cannot tell when it transpired. Furthermore, the last five chapters of the book seem to take place at the same time as the initial chapters. In 18:30, a man whom the text suggests was Moses' grandson is functioning as a priest, while in 20:28, Phinehas son of Eleazar son of Aaron is the main priest. Both of those figures bring us back to the generation after Joshua. However, according to the central section of Judges, many generations have passed.

In addition, several of the stories contain significant improbabilities. This is most evident in the final story of Judges, concerning the rape of the concubine by the Benjaminites of Gibeah. After a mob rapes this woman nearly to death, her husband "picked up a knife, and took hold of his concubine and cut her up limb by limb into twelve parts. He sent them throughout the territory of Israel" (19:29), in an attempt to muster the tribes against the offending Gibeonites and Benjaminites. Aside from the strangeness of this action, why would he have needed twelve pieces? After all, Benjamin (one of the twelve tribes) was going to be attacked, so he would hardly have called it to battle. Thus, this gruesome and surrealistic story, in its arc and in its details, seems to be something other than a retelling of actual events of the past.

Micro and Macro Structure in Judges

When we are confronted with a story that is set in the past yet seems not to be portraying the "real" past, we always need to ask: Why has this story been shaped in this fashion? Fortunately, the Book of Judges provides ample clues, both in its stories and in how they are combined. Consider another story in Judges that is clearly not historical:

> (3:7) The Israelites did what was offensive to the LORD; they ignored the LORD their God and worshiped the Baalim and the Asheroth. (8) The LORD became incensed at Israel and surrendered them to King Cushan-rishathaim of Aram-naharaim; and the Israelites were subject to Cushan-rishathaim for eight years. (9) The Israelites cried out to the LORD, and the LORD raised a champion for the Israelites to deliver them: Othniel the Kenizzite, a younger kinsman of Caleb. (10) The spirit of the LORD descended upon him and he became Israel's chieftain. He went out to war, and the LORD delivered King Cushan-rishathaim of Aram into his hands. He prevailed over Cushan-rishathaim, (11) and the land had peace for forty years; then Othniel the Kenizzite died. (transl. of v. 11 adapted)

Cushan-rishathaim, the name of the king of Aram-naharaim (often translated as "Aram of the two rivers"—the Tigris and Euphrates) calls attention to itself: it is metrically balanced and rhymes with the name of his realm, a quite unusual feature. More tellingly, the name means "the dark double-wicked one." In ancient Semitic cultures, names were given by parents at the time of birth, often expressing parental feelings upon the child's birth—it is hard to understand why a parent would name a child "the dark double-wicked one." In addition, Aram is to the north of Israel, while the judge, Othniel, is a Kenizzite, and thus from the tribe of Judah, from the south of Israel. It is hard to grasp why he would fight against an Aramean—this is like saying that a Texan was the first to defend the United States after Canada attacked it.

The misplaced geography and the oddness of the name of Cushan-rishathaim would have suggested to ancient readers that this story is something other than straightforward history. In fact, it is best read as a story about an ideal Judean defeating pure evil. As the book's first story about a chieftain, it is appropriately simple and to the point: all starts out well when Judah is in charge.

As many commentators have noted, most of the other chieftains in Judges are quite imperfect heroes. Among other things, they doubt God, sacrifice a daughter, cavort with Philistine women, and break religious vows. In fact, the chieftains form a pattern: as the narrative progresses from Othniel (of Judah, in the south) to Samson (of Dan, which eventually was the northernmost tribe)—the chieftains become worse and worse. This pattern functions to denigrate northern judges. All told, these stories sharpen the message from the Othniel account: only Judean leadership is satisfactory.

The beginning and end of Judges together amplify that message. These sections do not contain stories about chieftains. Rather, the initial chapters recount the conquest of the land, in which Judah plays a crucial role, defeating those in its territories—whereas other tribes fail to do so. Near the end of the book, chapters 17–18 depict in a derogatory fashion the origin of worship in the north. The last three chapters, about the concubine of Gibeah, are a prequel to the set of stories about Saul in 1 Samuel, which we discussed above. Saul would come from Gibeah in Benjamin, where—so Judges tells us—the people behave in a horrendous manner. The concubine husband's act (mustering the troops by chopping up her body and sending its pieces to all the tribes) will surely come to mind when we read of Saul's later act: "He took a yoke of oxen and cut them into pieces, which he sent by messengers throughout the territory of Israel, with the warning, 'Thus shall be done to the cattle of anyone who does not follow Saul and Samuel into battle!'" (1 Sam. 11:7). By denigrating Gibeah (Saul's birthplace), Benjamin (Saul's tribe), and Jabesh Gilead (a city closely associated with Saul), the concubine of Gibeah story is suggesting that there is no chance that Saul will be a good king.

Judges and Samuel as Parallel Stories

Judges does not describe accurately the period between Joshua and Saul. Instead, it parallels the Book of Samuel. Several times it raises the issue of kingship—by discussing the possibility of Gideon becoming king (8:22), by highlighting Abimelech's role as king of Shechem (chap. 9), and by repeating the formula "in those days there was no king in Israel" four times in its final five chapters. In this vein, it makes a clear value judgment about who the proper king is: he must be an Othniel-like figure who hails from Judah. He cannot be northern. He cannot be a Benjaminite—certainly not one from Gibeah like Saul. The people of Israel do not ask for a king to replace Samuel, the last chieftain, until 1 Samuel 8. Yet by that point, the Deuteronomistic Historian has already conditioned readers to think that Judean, Davidic kingship is the only legitimate kind.

My title for the present chapter, "May My Lord King David Live Forever," reflects 1 Kings 1:31, the book that follows Samuel. Yet that statement really is the message of both Judges and Samuel. Reading these two books as factual, rather than as royal propaganda bolstering the Davidic dynasty and state, would be a serious error. It would be like opening a newspaper and reading the editorial pages as factual news.

13

"For Israel Tore Away from the House of David"

Reading Kings

Primary Reading: 1 Kings 1–12, 16; 2 Kings 17–25.

History Is Too Important to Leave to Chance[1]

Thus far I have emphasized that much of what looks like history in the Bible is really mythological. That is, biblical texts are interested in expressing or promoting particular views about issues of collective importance (see "Genesis 1–3 as Myth" in chapter 6). The issues that these texts explore are sometimes political and sometimes theological; often they are a combination of both. At times, these stories incorporate earlier historical traditions, but rarely, if ever, are those traditions present for their own sake—for what is called "antiquarian interest."[2] At first glance, the Book of Kings looks different from the rest of this material.

We will return to Samuel one more time to underline these differences. In one of Samuel's most central texts, Nathan offers David a divine promise concerning his son:

> (2 Sam. 7:14) I will be a father to him, and he shall be a son to Me. When he does wrong, I will chastise him with the rod of men and the affliction of mortals; (15) but I will never withdraw My favor from him as I withdrew it from Saul, whom I removed to make room for you. (16) Your house and your kingship shall ever be secure before you; your throne shall be established forever.

Although Kings shares some of these same ideas, it narrates them in a very different manner. Instead of long, well-styled[3] character studies, most of the accounts in Kings are short. They also contain different types of details than

Samuel—details of chronology, of tribute paid, of royal building projects, etc. In other words, the structure and style of the book are unlike the books of the early prophets that precede it. This raises the question of whether we should give the traditions it contains the benefit of the doubt, and if we should treat Kings as history, in our modern sense. The answer is that Kings is like the other books of the Bible we have examined: it presents historical information for the sake of other agendas. The following sections will explain why.

The Chronology of Kings

In discussing why Judges is not history, I noted that whereas chronology is the "backbone" of history, Judges is out of chronological order (see "Judges as History" in chapter 12). The same critique applies to Kings. Although it supplies chronological notes more often—and in more detail—if we look carefully we will see that Kings too is out of chronological order.

We need look no farther than the first long unit in Kings, which concerns Solomon, a son of David who followed him as king. Near that unit's end we read: "When Hadad heard in Egypt that David had been laid to rest with his fathers and that Joab the army commander was dead, Hadad said to Pharaoh, 'Give me leave to go to my own country'" (1 Kings 11:21). Clearly, this must have transpired very early in Solomon's reign, not at the end of it. This suggests that the text is doing something other than recalling the reign of Solomon as it actually happened in correct chronological order.

Even the detailed chronological notes themselves sometimes provide problems. In the following excerpt from 1 Kings 16, note the years when different reigns begin and end. How well do they fit together?[4]

> (15) During the twenty-seventh year of King Asa of Judah, Zimri reigned in Tirzah for seven days. At the time, the troops were encamped at Gibbethon of the Philistines. (16) When the troops who were encamped there learned that Zimri had committed treason and had struck down the king, that very day, in the camp, all Israel acclaimed the army commander Omri king over Israel. (17) Omri and all Israel then withdrew from Gibbethon and laid siege to Tirzah. (18) When Zimri saw that the town was taken, he went into the citadel of the royal palace and burned down the royal palace over himself. And so he died— (19) because of the sins which he committed and caused Israel to commit, doing what was displeasing to the LORD and following the ways of Jeroboam. (20) The other events of Zimri's reign, and the treason which he committed, are recorded in the Annals of the Kings of

> Israel. (21) Then the people of Israel split into two factions: a part of the people followed Tibni son of Ginath to make him king, and the other part followed Omri. (22) Those who followed Omri proved stronger than those who followed Tibni son of Ginath; Tibni died and Omri became king. (23) In the thirty-first year of King Asa of Judah, Omri became king over Israel—for twelve years. He reigned in Tirzah six years. (24) Then he bought the hill of Samaria from Shemer for two talents of silver; he built a town on the hill and named the town which he built Samaria, after Shemer, the owner of the hill. (25) Omri did what was displeasing to the LORD; he was worse than all who preceded him. (26) He followed all the ways of Jeroboam son of Nebat and the sins which he committed and caused Israel to commit, vexing the LORD, the God of Israel, with their futilities. (27) The other events of Omri's reign, and his actions, and the exploits he performed, are recorded in the Annals of the Kings of Israel. (28) Omri slept with his fathers and was buried in Samaria; and his son Ahab succeeded him as king. (29) Ahab son of Omri became king over Israel in the thirty-eighth year of King Asa of Judah, and Ahab son of Omri reigned over Israel in Samaria for twenty-two years.

If Zimri only reigned for seven days, and began to reign during the twenty-seventh year of King Asa (v. 15), how did his successor, Omri, begin to reign in the thirty-first year of King Asa (v. 23)? If Omri became king in the thirty-first year of Asa and reigned for twelve years (v. 23), how is it possible that his son, Ahab, began to reign in the thirty-eighth year of Asa (v. 29)? There is no obvious way to solve this arithmetic problem. Some scholars speculate that two kings reigned for the same time *and* their regnal years counted for both kings.[5] Unfortunately, the biblical text itself attests only rarely to such "co-regencies" and justifies them when they were necessary (e.g., the first king became seriously ill).

Other Historical Issues in Kings

A closer look at this section reveals other types of problems, that is, issues that modern historians might be curious about, but that the text does not address. For example: Who favored Zimri and who favored Omri? Likewise, who favored Tibni over Omri (1 Kings 16:21)? How and why did Omri's faction win (v. 22)? Why did Omri move his capital, and why did he choose Samaria (v. 24)? The biblical historian shows little interest in these sorts of questions, which would preoccupy the modern historian.

Instead, the DtrH is mostly interested in evaluating each of these kings and noting their negative behavior. This is especially remarkable concerning Zimri, who reigned only for seven days, yet is condemned "because of the sins which he committed and caused Israel to commit, doing what was displeasing to the LORD and following the ways of Jeroboam" (1 Kings 16:19). The sin is King Jeroboam's building of cult sites with golden calves in Bethel and Dan (12:25–33), an action seen as horrific by the DtrH, since these sites competed with Jerusalem, site of the Temple and royal house. But how much worship could Zimri have done in seven days, especially while he was engaged in a civil war? Rather, the comment in 1 Kings 16:19 is part of the stereotyped evaluation of each northern king by the DtrH, a Judean, who will not miss a chance to denigrate the north.

Although we know of only a small number of extrabiblical sources that bear directly on the Bible, a number of these cluster around the reign of Omri. The Mesha Inscription, written in Moabite (a Semitic language very close to Hebrew), notes: "Omri was the king of Israel, and he oppressed Moab for many days, for Chemosh was angry with his land."[6] (Incidentally, the Moabites attributed the oppression of Moab to the anger of Chemosh, their high god. Israel was not alone in the ancient Near East in believing that deities directly participated in history.) In addition, Assyrian records from more than a century after the time of Omri—and even after the end of his dynasty—continue to call Northern Israel "the house of Omri."[7] This suggests that both Omri and the dynasty he established were militarily powerful. Yet, the biblical text barely mentions this. Although the closing notice in 1 Kings 16:27 mentions Omri's "actions" (or, "his mighty deeds"), it offers no details.

In sum, Kings is not fundamentally different from the previous "historical books" we have examined. It may look a bit different, and may preserve a higher percentage of correct traditions, but this is a difference of extent, not of kind. As the following examples will show, Kings is not interested in the past for its own sake, but for much more important reasons—for teaching ideological and theological lessons.

Solomon

The Solomon material in Kings closely fits this description. Even a cursory reading of 1 Kings 1–11 suggests that its perspective differs from that of a modern historian of antiquity. The text tells us almost nothing about Solomon before he accedes to the throne other than the fact that "the LORD favored him" (2 Sam. 12:24). Many passages in Kings deal with his building projects in exacting detail; nevertheless, these passages contain contradictions. For example, 1 Kings 5:27, in discussing Solomon's building projects, says that "King Solomon imposed forced labor on all Israel," while 9:20–22 claims, "All the people that were left of the Amorites, Hittites, Perizzites, Hivites, and Jebusites who were not of the Israelite stock . . . of these Solomon made a slave force, as is still the case. But he did not reduce any Israelites to slavery . . . ." Did Solomon use Israelite forced labor or not?

Other details in the story seem to be extremely unlikely, for example the suggestion that the usurper Adonijah asked for Abishag the Shunammite, who warmed David in his old age (1 Kings 1), as a wife. This would have been tantamount to asking for the late king's wife, or at the very least, to asking to marry a senior member of the former royal court. It would have suggested to Solomon that Adonijah still wanted to be king, in competition with him.[8] Certainly, Adonijah should have known that Solomon would view his request as an attempt to usurp the throne, and that he would be punished with death (see v. 25). It is likely that the reason for this story is that the narrator wanted to get rid of Adonijah without making Solomon responsible, and creating this incident provided the ideal way to do it.

If the material about Solomon was not arranged chronologically, and if it is not interested in a complete, balanced, or objective picture of Solomon's life, how is it arranged, and what is it interested in doing?[9]

In order to answer these questions we will first look at the structure of the text. The following sets of verses parallel each other in content and structure, and will help us to divide the first eleven chapters into sections:

1 Kings 3	*1 Kings 9*
(1) Solomon allied himself by marriage with Pharaoh king of Egypt. He married Pharaoh's daughter and brought her to the City of David to live there until he had finished building his palace, and the House of the LORD, and the walls around Jerusalem. (2) The people, however, continued to offer sacrifices at the open shrines, because up to that time no house had been built for the name of the LORD. (3) And Solomon, though he loved the LORD and followed the practices of his father David, also sacrificed and offered at the shrines.	(24) As soon as Pharaoh's daughter went up from the City of David to the palace that he had built for her, he built the Millo. (25) Solomon used to offer burnt offerings and sacrifices of well-being three times a year on the altar that he had built for the LORD, and he used to offer incense on the one that was before the LORD. And he kept the House in repair.

Using these parallels to divide 1 Kings 1–11 into sections, the following outline comes into view:

Accession of Solomon to the throne (1–2)[10]
Solomon follows God and is blessed (3:1–9:23)
Solomon does not follow God and is cursed (9:26–11:40)
Typical Deuteronomistic conclusion formula (11:41–43)

This organization is theological rather than chronological. Indeed, it mirrors the structure of the material about David in the Book of Samuel. There, David is blessed up until the time that he sins with Bathsheba in 2 Samuel 11, after which point almost nothing seems to go right for David's family.

The Laws of the King

This material from Kings is part of the DtrH, so it is not surprising that Solomon appears to be cursed for violating the laws of Deuteronomy. Deuteronomy 17:16–17, the beginning of what is often called "the laws of the king," notes:

> Moreover, he shall not keep many horses or send people back to Egypt to add to his horses, since the LORD has warned you, "You must not go back that way again." And he shall not have many wives, lest his heart go astray; nor shall he amass silver and gold to excess.

1 Kings 9:26–11:40 outlines how Solomon violated all three of these prohibitions:

- In 9:28–10:25, Solomon accumulates excessive wealth through his contact with the Queen of Sheba and others. Verse 10:14 notes that Solomon annually received 666 talents of gold—over 50,000 lbs. a year.
- In 10:26–29, Solomon procures many horses, and many of them come from Egypt.
- In chapter 11, Solomon marries *many* foreign wives, who (v. 3) "turned his heart away."

Thus, according to the DtrH, God punished Solomon for good reason. (The punishment came after his death; it consisted of his son's losing part of the kingdom when the northern tribes seceded after Rehoboam dismissed their petition to lighten their corvée burden.)

Regarding the third prohibition that Solomon violates, the initial verses on this topic present themselves as a quote: "of which the LORD had said to the Israelites." Indeed, what follows, "None of you shall join them and none of them shall join you, lest they turn your heart away to follow their gods" is a paraphrase of Deuteronomy 7. That text had charged Israel with proscribing the nations of Canaan, holding that "You shall not intermarry with them: do not give your daughters to their sons or take their daughters for your sons. For they will turn your children away from Me to worship other gods, and the LORD's anger will blaze forth against you and He will promptly wipe you out" (7:3–4).

Strikingly, the text in 1 Kings 11:1–2, which seems to be merely citing Deuteronomy, is actually extending the Deuteronomic laws. Deuteronomy 7 prohibited intermarriage only with the seven resident nations of Canaan (including Hittites); 23:4–7 prohibit intermarriage with the neighboring Moabites and Ammonites; 23:8–9 permit intermarriage with Egyptians and Edomites three generations after Moses. However, 1 Kings 11:1 spotlights Solomon's Egyptian, Moabite, Ammonite, Edomite, Phoenician, and Hittite wives. Of these, Deuteronomy outlawed only his Moabite, Ammonite, and Hittite wives. Hence, 1 Kings extends the injunctions of Deuteronomy in their widest sense, to include Egyptian, Edomite, and Phoenician women—perhaps even all non-Israelite women!

This type of stringency or extension of the law is quite common in rabbinic texts, which develop the notion of "making a fence around the Torah" to safeguard it.[11] However, 1 Kings 11 demonstrates that this was not a rabbinic invention, but that it existed already in the biblical period. In fact, it is even possible that 1 Kings 11 represents a type of protorabbinic interpretation. It is as if the author of that text were saying: "Deuteronomy is prohibiting specific foreign wives because 'they will turn your children away from [God] to worship other gods, and the LORD's anger will blaze forth . . .' Is it only wives from the seven Canaanite nations who can lead Israelite men astray? Certainly not—any non-Israelite can, thus marriage with any non-Israelite woman must be prohibited."

Such an evolution in legal interpretation, if my understanding of it is correct, is remarkable in two ways. First, it shows the audacity of the biblical author, who (just like the rabbis) extends the law while insisting that this is what God really said or meant. Second, it shows that rabbinic-type interpretation did not begin in the rabbinic period, but had significant roots in the biblical period.[12] The fact that we find this type of protorabbinic interpretation in biblical "historical" texts is another reason to be cautious about using these texts to reconstruct the real history of Israel.

Archaeological History

Some readers may object to my skepticism about using 1 Kings 1–11 to reconstruct the history of the reign of Solomon. They may point to the excavation of Solomon's stables in Megiddo or the Solomonic royal gates at the cities of Megiddo, Hazor, and Gezer (see 1 Kings 9:15), to corroborate the biblical account.[13] However, more recent scholarship has raised significant questions about the stratigraphy—the study of levels and their dating—at these cities. It is uncertain if the royal gates should be dated to Solomon or later;[14] in any case, most scholars agree that the Solomonic Stables are neither stables (they are storerooms) nor Solomonic.[15] These cases that remind us that archaeology is not objective, and that it is dangerous to use archaeology in a circular fashion to confirm the Bible.

Jerusalem in 701

Even though we need to be cautious about reading the Bible as history, scholars have reached a consensus about key events in the year 701 B.C.E. The Assyrian king Sennacherib came down the Mediterranean coast, vanquished many city-states, and fought against King Hezekiah of Judea, conquering many Judean cities. The Assyrian army besieged but did not conquer Jerusalem. The convergence of evidence from a wide range of sources—texts from the Bible and from Assyria, the Assyrian palace's wall-relief depictions, and other archaeological finds (especially around the conquered Israelite city of Lachish)—allows us to reconstruct the outlines of that campaign with confidence.[16]

In fact, there is remarkable agreement between the account of the siege given in Sennacherib's Annals about his third campaign, and the short account in 2 Kings 18:13–16. The annals, a genre of historical inscriptions updated yearly, were organized chronologically according to (military) campaigns. They read:

> In my third campaign, I marched against Hatti [Upper Syria]. . . . As for Hezekiah,[17] the Judean, I besieged forty-six of his fortified walled cities and surrounding smaller towns, which were without number. Using packed-down ramps and battering rams . . . I conquered [them]. I took out 200,150 people,[18] young and old, male and female, horses, mules, . . . and sheep without number and counted them as spoil. He himself, I locked up within Jerusalem, his royal city, like a bird in a cage. . . . He, Hezekiah, was overwhelmed by the awesome splendor of my lordship,

and he sent me after my departure to Nineveh, my royal city . . . 30 talents of gold, 800 talents of silver . . . elephant hides . . . his male and female singers.[19]

Why do Assyrian inscriptions mention a siege of Jerusalem but not the city's conquest? Such inscriptions tended not to lie, although they did tend to omit unpleasant facts. Thus it appears that the upstart city survived the siege (which Assyria lifted only after Hezekiah agreed to pay a large tribute to Sennacherib).

A small part of the biblical description of these events reads:

(2 Kings 18:13) In the fourteenth year of King Hezekiah, King Sennacherib of Assyria marched against all the fortified towns of Judah and seized them. (14) King Hezekiah sent this message to the king of Assyria at Lachish: "I have done wrong; withdraw from me; and I shall bear whatever you impose on me." So the king of Assyria imposed upon King Hezekiah of Judah a payment of three hundred talents of silver and thirty talents of gold. (15) Hezekiah gave him all the silver that was on hand in the House of the LORD and in the treasuries of the palace. (16) At that time Hezekiah cut down the doors and the doorposts of the Temple of the LORD, which King Hezekiah had overlaid with gold, and gave them to the king of Assyria.

The points of correspondence between these verses and the Assyrian annals are remarkable: cities conquered, Jerusalem saved, and tribute paid, even exact agreement on the number of gold talents.

The Book of Kings, however, goes on to recount this event for another two and half chapters, through chapter 21. It is clear that this passage is from a different source than 18:13–16. Those four verses always spell the name of Hezekiah as *Chizkiyah* (חִזְקִיָּה—six times), while the continuation spells it as *Chizkiyahu* (חִזְקִיָּהוּ—more than twenty times). Such variation was common in names containing God's name (*YHWH*), wherein the latter may be spelled either יָהוּ; or יָה. However, any given author would tend to use one form or the other consistently.[20] The shift in spelling therefore implies that the material following 2 Kings 18:16 is from a different source or sources.[21]

This material is quite different in tone and content. What is most striking is the way in which it emphasizes, even overemphasizes, the salvation of Jerusalem. The first part of Kings contains a prophecy from Isaiah to the king of Assyria:

(19:32) Assuredly, thus said the LORD concerning the king of Assyria: / He shall not enter this city: / He shall not shoot an arrow at it, / Or advance upon it with a shield, / Or pile up a siege mound against it. /

(33) He shall go back / By the way he came; / He shall not enter this city—declares the LORD. / (34) I will protect and save this city for My sake, / And for the sake of My servant David.

The next verse notes, "that night an angel of the LORD went out and struck down one hundred and eighty-five thousand in the Assyrian camp, and the following morning they were all dead corpses." The following chapter, beginning in verse 12, describes a visit by the Babylonian king Berodach-baladan (also called Merodach-baladan) to Hezekiah. That episode is clearly out of order, since the passage is actually describing a Babylonian visit to Judea to help form a coalition to fight against Assyria and thus is earlier than 701.[22]

Modern scholars' analysis of this material about the events of 701 has taught us a great deal about the writing of historical texts and how to read them. The texts employ multiple sources for the same event. They mix fact with fiction or highly embellished history. We see again that chronology was not the most important organizing factor for these historians writing texts about the past. We also witness how theology enters history—the main object of the text in its final form is to emphasize the inviolability of Jerusalem. Perhaps we can make our point typographically, comparing three versions of the campaign. Nowadays a good historian recounting the events would write:

The Assyrian army destroyed many Judean cities and towns but did not capture Jerusalem.

However, what the Assyrian annals wrote amounts to:

The Assyrian army destroyed many Judean cities and towns but did not capture Jerusalem.

In contrast, the account in Kings implies a summary like this:

The Assyrian army destroyed many Judean cities and towns but did not capture Jerusalem.

In short, readers would do well not to underestimate the role of this—or any other—historian in emphasizing one event at the expense of another.

More Why than What

It should now be clear why I opened the present chapter with the subheading "History is too important to leave to chance." While without question Kings contains many facts, they were not of paramount importance to its author. Like other biblical historians, this author cared much more about "why" than about "what." Here was an interpreter of the community's foundational history, not a university professor of history writing for the record. (In that sense, biblical history is like contemporary popular history, or newscasts—as the highly ideological TV news stations report it. These media can give us a model to understand biblical history, and vice versa.) In some cases, the traditions as the biblical author knew them did not make the point he wanted to make clearly enough, and so those traditions became malleable, and were changed; in some cases, traditions were completely made up. (The traditions concerning Solomon's many wives probably belong in this category, since they almost entirely use Deuteronomistic phraseology, and thus they were likely products of this school.)

We will see the results of this editorial process even more clearly in the next chapter, as we explore the late biblical book of Chronicles.

14

Revisionist History

Reading Chronicles

Primary Reading: 1 Chronicles 1, 5, 20; 2 Chronicles 7, 33, 35.

An Unpropitious Beginning

The Book of Chronicles opens with the dullest material imaginable, useful if you are ever having trouble falling asleep: "(1:1) Adam, Seth, Enosh; (2) Kenan, Mahalalel, Jared; (3) Enoch, Methuselah, Lamech; (4) Noah, Shem, Ham, and Japheth."[1] Most of the first nine chapters read similarly, sometimes containing short interesting notes, but mostly just one genealogy after the next. Someone must have found this interesting, or at least important. Indeed, we know that in the period of Chronicles, most likely the fourth century B.C.E., Jews highly valued genealogies. All twenty-one biblical occurrences of the verb *y-ch-s* (יחשׂ, "to be registered by genealogy") appear either in Chronicles or in the contemporaneous book of Ezra-Nehemiah.[2] Ezra 2:62 mentions certain priests who "searched for their genealogical records, but they could not be found, so they were disqualified for the priesthood." Priesthood in ancient Israel at that point in time was considered to be hereditary. Remarkably, priests kept and updated such records in the Babylonian exile and beyond.

Genealogies played a leading role in legitimating various groups or individuals, as may be seen from Chronicles. For example, we saw above (see "The Joseph Story" in chapter 7) that the narrator of Genesis displaces Jacob's first three sons, Reuben, Simeon, and Levi, with two younger sons, Judah (ancestor of David) and Joseph (ancestor of the first line of Northern kings). By the time the Chronicler (the author of Chronicles[3]) was writing, this was important history, especially since the ten northern tribes were almost completely "lost," and it was largely Judeans, eventually called Jews, who returned from the Babylonian exile.[4] Thus, the genealogy of Judah precedes that of any of the other children of Jacob (1 Chron. 2:3–4:25), and it is the longest of such genealogies. As noted earlier, the following introduction to the genealogy of firstborn Reuben makes it quite clear why Reuben follows Judah:

> (1 Chron. 5:1) The sons of Reuben the first-born of Israel. (He was the first-born; but when he defiled his father's bed, his birthright was given to the sons of Joseph son of Israel, so he is not reckoned as first-born in the genealogy; (2) though Judah became more powerful than his brothers and a leader came from him, yet the birthright belonged to Joseph.)

This is a retelling in miniature of the Joseph story in Genesis.

A Made-up Genealogy

The Chronicler also creates genealogies to solve problems in his sources. One problem presented by Samuel and Kings is the claim that the main Judean priest at the time of David was Zadok, yet Zadok's genealogy is never given. Some scholars posit—for the text nowhere states this—that originally, Zadok officiated at a Canaanite shrine in Jerusalem; he was "inherited" by David who, as Israel's king, conquered that city.[5] For the Chronicler, however, the idea that a high priest had no legitimate genealogy was impossible. Given the importance of having proper priests in his period, he had to "find" a proper genealogy for Zadok, connecting him to Aaron, the first priest and brother of Moses. According to most scholars, the Chronicler accomplishes this by making up a genealogy, which asserts that Zadok is directly descended from Aaron:

> (5:29) The children of Amram: Aaron, Moses, and Miriam. The sons of Aaron: Nadab, Abihu, Eleazar, and Ithamar. (30) Eleazar begot Phinehas, Phinehas begot Abishua, (31) Abishua begot Bukki, Bukki begot Uzzi, (32) Uzzi begot Zerahiah, Zerahiah begot Meraioth, (33) Meraioth begot Amariah, Amariah begot Ahitub, (34) Ahitub begot Zadok . . .

This fabricated genealogy "solves" the problem of the earlier books of Samuel and Kings.

The Method of "Historical Probability"

The notion that the Chronicler made up genealogies is paralleled by cases where he fabricated history. To many, this way of looking at Scripture may be offensive, but we must remember that the recollection of historical traditions in this period was different than it is now. There was little or no interest in history for its own sake, that is, for what it taught about the real past. History mattered because of what it taught about the present, including the legitimacy of the main priestly clan.

Moreover, ancient historians may not have realized that they were manipulating "facts." The classicist Elias Bickerman used the term "historical probability" to describe the Chronicler's method.[6] This refers to the way people make sense of data, based on their understanding of how the world functions. For example, those with a certain notion of "historical probability" doubt the findings of the Warren Commission that a lone gunman assassinated John F. Kennedy in 1963, despite the great deal of evidence in support of that theory. Instead, they might say that Kennedy was killed by a communist—or a CIA plot—based on their belief about how events happen. That underlying belief is their notion of "historical probability." The Chronicler as a historian[7] also had certain ideas about how things happen. For him, it was clear that Zadok had to be descended from Aaron—so he supplied the scenario that seemed most likely.

When in Doubt, Leave it Out

Just as the Chronicler adds material when it suits his purposes, he also leaves material out. Sometimes material is left out simply because it is no longer relevant. For example, when (the first edition of) the Book of Kings was written, everyone remembered the Northern Kingdom; while much of its populace had gone into exile in Assyria, some of its refugees had found their way to Judah. Thus, the Book of Kings relates various traditions about the Northern Kingdom, in particular those that make Judah seem superior. By the time the Book of Chronicles was written, the Northern Kingdom was a distant memory. Thus (although Chronicles retells the history from Adam through the Babylonian exile and the beginning of the following restoration) it omits the traditions about the North, except for when that kingdom interacted with Judah.[8] Thus, the confusing shifts back and forth in Kings concerning Omri and Ahab are simply absent. Because the North was irrelevant, illegitimate, or both, its traditions did not bear repeating. Similarly, Chronicles does not mention the reign of Saul, who preceded David, for only the kingship of David and his descendents now mattered.

As a national symbol, David plays a more important role in Chronicles than in the Deuteronomistic History. For this reason the Chronicler omitted negative material concerning David, especially his affair with Bathsheba and the punishments that followed it.[9] In the book of Samuel, the "Bathsheba affair" takes place during a war against the Ammonites. Chronicles retains the first verse of that source with minor changes (2 Sam. 12:1, paralleled in 1 Chron. 20:1), but follows it immediately with the account about the end of the war (2 Sam. 12:30–31, paralleled in 1 Chron. 20:2–3). Chronicles omits entirely David's affair with Bathsheba, the murder of Uriah, the rebuke by the prophet Nathan, and the death of David and Bathsheba's first child (2 Sam. 12:2–29). It simply did not happen.

Chronicles similarly omits the unflattering set of events that happened next in Samuel: the rape of David's daughter Tamar by Amnon, her half-brother; the murder of Amnon by his half-brother Absalom; and the (largely successful) rebellion by Absalom, followed by his death. These events suggest a measure-for-measure punishment of David and his house. They reflect badly on David, so the Chronicler omitted them (perhaps with the hope that his book would displace Samuel as an authoritative version of history). Instead of David spending the end of his life in ignominy, according to Chronicles he spends these years preparing for Solomon to build the Temple. The Chronicler composes a long section (1 Chronicles 22–29) to illustrate this point.

The Chronicler may also have viewed as "unseemly" the transition from David to Solomon in the first two chapters of Kings. There, David is old and impotent (see 1 Kings 1:4), his son Adonijah tries to assume the throne while David is still alive, and the major players are divided about who the next king should be. Ultimately, after some behind-the-scenes activity and overreaching by a rival, Solomon's claim to the throne is assured. Chronicles mentions none of this. In its place, 2 Chronicles 1:1 states: "Solomon son of David took firm hold of his kingdom, for the LORD his God was with him and made him exceedingly great." According to Chronicles, the transition from David to Solomon was smooth and uncomplicated. When in doubt, leave it out!

Rewriting History

Comparison of Chronicles and its sources reveals hundreds of cases where the Chronicler changed his sources in various ways—not only minor updating of language and spelling (e.g., from דָּוִד, as the earlier spelling of "David," to דָּוִיד), but also significant ideological changes. As we discussed above, the notion of "historical probability" is responsible for many of these changes. Two examples will illustrate this in greater detail.

According to the Book of Kings, the Judean King Manasseh was the worst of all kings—he revived idolatry in the Temple (2 Kings 21:4–5) and he "put so many innocent persons to death that he filled Jerusalem with blood from end to end" (2 Kings 21:16). Yet, according to the regnal formula in 1 Kings 21:55, he reigned for 55 years. It seems not to have disturbed the final editor of Kings that the worst king of Judah was also the longest reigning—longer even than David or Solomon, who each reigned forty years! But it did bother the Chronicler, most likely because he had a different idea of personal retribution than the Deuteronomistic historian—an idea more like Ezekiel 18:4: "The person who sins, only he shall die" (see "Refuting Popular Beliefs" in chapter 19).

To the Chronicler, Manasseh could be "explained" in two ways—either he reigned for a much shorter period, or Kings left out material that would account for such a long reign despite a period of wickedness. The Chronicler chose the latter option, depicting Manasseh as a model penitent:

> (2 Chron. 33:11) So the LORD brought against them the officers of the army of the king of Assyria, who took Manasseh captive in manacles, bound him in fetters, and led him off to Babylon. (12) In his distress, he entreated the LORD his God and humbled himself greatly before the God of his fathers. (13) He prayed to Him, and He granted his prayer, heard his plea, and returned him to Jerusalem to his kingdom. Then Manasseh knew that the LORD alone was God. (14) Afterward he built the outer wall of the City of David west of Gihon in the wadi on the way to the Fish Gate, and it encircled Ophel; he raised it very high. He also placed army officers in all the fortified towns of Judah. (15) He removed the foreign gods and the image from the House of the LORD, as well as all the altars that he had built on the Mount of the House of the LORD and in Jerusalem, and dumped them outside the city. (16) He rebuilt the altar of the LORD and offered on it sacrifices of well-being and thanksgiving, and commanded the people of Judah to worship the LORD God of Israel.

Thus Manasseh deserved to be blessed with the longest reign of all.

But these events never happened—in fact, they could not have happened. Manasseh was a vassal not of Babylon but of Assyria (see "Deuteronomy as a Treaty" in chapter 10); thus he would not have been brought to Babylon. Only a writer working centuries later could say this—a writer who wished to teach that even if you are as bad as Manasseh and have been punished for your grievous sins, if you repent, all will be forgiven and restored. This story was made up for such a purpose. Ultimately, stories about the past are more instructive than the past itself; history is too important to leave to chance.

Rewriting Torah

The Chronicler makes a second type of change as well. For the Deuteronomistic Historian who wrote Kings, the book of Deuteronomy was the "canonical" Torah work. The norms or laws we read about in Kings follow Deuteronomy, and on the rare occasion when a source found in the Torah is cited, it is cited from Deuteronomy. The story of King Amaziah (son of King Joash) of Judah illustrates this point:

> (2 Kings 14:5) Once he had the kingdom firmly in his grasp, he put to death the courtiers who had assassinated his father the king. (6) But he did not put to death the children of the assassins, in accordance with what is written in the Book of the Teaching of Moses, where the LORD commanded, "Parents shall not be put to death for children, nor children be put to death for parents; a person shall be put to death only for his own crime."

This quote follows the law in Deuteronomy 24:16: "Parents shall not be put to death for children, nor children be put to death for parents: a person shall be put to death only for his own crime." Relatively speaking, Kings hardly acknowledges the P source. However, by the time that Chronicles was written, both the D and P sources were authoritative. It is likely that the Torah (more or less as we know it) already had authority in the community. This meant that P traditions as well as D traditions needed to be incorporated into Chronicles. Sometimes the Chronicler found this easy to do, but at other times the task proved quite challenging.

A simple case concerns Solomon and his dedication of the Temple on the fall festival of Sukkot (see "From the Goring Ox . . ." in chapter 8). According to Deuteronomy 16:13, "you shall hold the Feast of Booths for seven days." This seven-day festival is indeed fulfilled when the Temple is dedicated in 1 Kings 8:65.[10] However, Leviticus adds an eighth day to this Sukkot festival, during which the people are to hold "a solemn gathering" (23:36, 39). Unlike the Deuteronomistic version, Chronicles knows this law, and so it revises its source (1 Kings 8:65) to say:

> (2 Chron. 7:8) At that time Solomon kept the Feast for seven days—all Israel with him—a great assemblage from Lebo-hamath to the Wadi of Egypt. (9) On the eighth day they held a solemn gathering; they observed the dedication of the altar seven days, and the Feast seven days. (10) On the twenty-third day of the seventh month [counting

from the beginning of seven-day festival on the 15th to the 21st, followed by a solemn assembly on the 22nd] he dismissed the people to their homes.

The editor updated this text to include the norms described in Leviticus.

A more complicated case in which the Chronicler incorporated both D and P is his description of Josiah's Passover offering in 2 Chronicles 35:13, which should be translated as "They boiled[11] the passover sacrifice in fire, as prescribed . . .." This description is quite odd. What does the locution "boiled in fire" mean, and why is it found here?

The answer is provided by the Chronicler's sources.[12] According to Deuteronomy, "You shall boil and eat [the paschal offering] at the place that the LORD your God will choose" (16:7; transl. adapted). According to P's norms, however, "they shall eat it roasted over the fire, with unleavened bread and with bitter herbs. Do not eat any of it raw, or boiled in any way with water, but roasted—head, legs, and entrails—over the fire" (Exod. 12:8–9, transl. adapted).[13] The boiling-roasting distinction reflects regional and /or chronological differences between D and P (see above, chapters 9–10). Given that both of these sources are equally authoritative, what can the Chronicler recommend?

Chronicles conflates these sources—the boiling of D becomes "They boiled the Passover," while the "roasted" of P in Exodus become "in fire" in Chronicles. We can illustrate the grafting typographically:

D: "**You shall boil** and eat it at the place that the LORD your God will choose" (Deut. 16:7).

P: "They shall eat it *roasted over the fire*, with unleavened bread and with bitter herbs. Do not eat any of it raw, or boiled in any way with water, but *roasted*—head, legs, and entrails—over the fire" (Exod. 12:8–9).

Chronicles: "**They boiled** the passover sacrifice *in fire*, as prescribed . . ." (2 Chron. 35:13).

The phrase "as prescribed" may be an attempt to cover up the fact that Chronicles is combining two irreconcilable traditions.[14]

Centuries later, the process just delineated—where two different Torah texts from two different sources are "reconciled"—becomes a key process in rabbinic midrash.[15] The rabbis did not recognize that the Torah is comprised of sources—to them, it is a single holy text, given by God to Moses. Thus, they too need to reconcile what we see as source-critical differences. But this process does not start with the rabbis. It starts as soon as editors combine the Torah's sources and a community canonizes that text. That process has already taken place by the time of the Chronicler.[16]

How Did He Get Away With It?

After hearing about the Chronicler's radical revisionism, many people wonder how his book managed to get canonized. The answer to this question has several parts.

The Chronicler was not living in a vacuum—his norms were the norms of his community, for whom he was writing. The authoritative and "standard" history of DtrH no longer spoke to that community. It did not reflect their theology, nor did it fully accord with their authoritative text, which now included P. Thus, in a sense, the Chronicler's community was "waiting" for such a history to be written, just as J.F.K. conspiracy theorists were waiting nearly thirty years for Oliver Stone's 1991 movie *JFK* to be released.

In addition, the Chronicler did a wonderful job of "footnoting" his history, giving it greater authority. Chronicles refers to fifteen books that supposedly served as sources,[17] as in this example: "The other events of Manasseh's reign, and his prayer to his God, and the words of the seers who spoke to him in the name of the LORD God of Israel are found in the chronicles of the kings of Israel" (2 Chron. 33:18). Some scholars believe that these were real sources of one sort or another.[18] Others suggest, more plausibly to my mind, that these sources never existed, and they are a type of fake footnote, through which the Chronicler asserts the authority and veracity of his composed traditions. In either case, these notices would have helped the alternative version of history in Chronicles gain acceptance, and ultimately, be canonized as scripture.

Is Chronicles Typical?

The picture developed throughout our discussion of biblical history writing may be disturbing to some. I have contended that authoritative writers fabricate history, making up their sources. Further, I have argued, it was more important to the biblical writers to be relevant than to be true. I do not know how typical the Chronicler was of the other biblical authors. I have highlighted Chronicles simply because its sources are extant, so that scholars could develop a good sense of how its author reworked earlier sources, and how radical he was. Even if some of the earlier historians preserved in the Bible were more conservative, we should remember that for all of them, their greatest concern was not getting the past "correct." Rather, it was to collect, revise, and compose traditions in order to produce texts about the past that would be meaningful to their communities.

15

Introduction to Prophecy

Primary Reading: 1 Kings 17 through 2 Kings 9.

Difficulties in Studying Prophecy

By "prophecy" I mean the "transmission of allegedly divine messages by a human intermediary to a third party."[1] As a literary genre, prophecy is extremely difficult to read and to understand. Prophets are quite alien to contemporary culture. When we see someone dressed oddly in public, proclaiming that the end of the world is near, we typically keep our distance—or perhaps listen but laugh. Most people in our society no longer share the view that God communicates messages to us through certain individuals. Indeed, many of us think that anyone who believes that they have received such a divine message is delusional and requires psychiatric treatment.

Ancient Israelites had a fundamentally different view of the world and how God is manifest in it; the historical-critical method helps us to recover their worldview.

Let me highlight some of the differences between the contemporary and biblical worlds by recasting biblical passages in today's idiom. First, imagine that you are hiring someone to fill a position, and the first stage is for candidates to send in a promotional video. In scene two of one individual's video—let's call him Elisha—he is walking along when a few kids run up and to the side of the road and mock him. He curses them; they promptly drop dead. Then Elisha goes on his merry way. A simple question: would you call this person in for an interview? You might hesitate, to say the least. Yet the Bible relates a similar event about the prophet Elisha—and that passage is intended to reflect positively on him:

> (2 Kings 2:23) From there he went up to Bethel. As he was going up the road, some little boys came out of the town and jeered at him, saying, "Go away, baldhead! Go away, baldhead!" (24) He turned around and looked at them and cursed them in the name of the LORD. Thereupon, two she-bears came out of the woods and mangled forty-two of the children. (25) He went on from there to Mount Carmel, and from there he returned to Samaria.

Now, let's imagine a second scenario. One day you happen to be in New York City, in a house of worship, and the preacher gets up and says:

> Thus said the LORD: / For three transgressions of the residents of Manhattan, / For four, I will not revoke it: / Because they shop in expensive shops and neglect the poor, / Eat in five-star restaurants while others starve. / I will send down fire upon Fifth Avenue, / A conflagration on 57th St. / And it shall devour the fancy penthouses, / Destroy the mansions. / And the people of "the city" shall be exiled to California—said the LORD.

You might wonder how it is that this preacher presumes to speak for God. You might also be puzzled about why the preacher suddenly decided to speak in poetry rather than prose. Yet this imagined sermon is a paraphrase of one of the prophet Amos' oracles against the nations—oracles that grabbed his audience's attention—such as:

> (1:3) Thus said the LORD: For three transgressions of Damascus, / For four, I will not revoke it: / Because they threshed Gilead / With threshing boards of iron. (4) I will send down fire upon the palace of Hazael, / And it shall devour the fortresses of Ben-hadad. (5) I will break the gate bars of Damascus, / And wipe out the inhabitants from the Vale of Aven / And the sceptered ruler of Beth-eden; And the people of Aram shall be exiled to Kir—said the LORD.

Finally, imagine that you are traveling on a public bus. In the seat right behind you, two people are conversing. You overhear one of them telling the other about a recent incident:

> (Zech. 5:9) I looked up again and saw two women come soaring with the wind in their wings—they had wings like those of a stork—and carry off the tub between earth and sky. (10) "Where are they taking the tub?" I asked the angel who talked with me. (11) And he answered, "To build a shrine for it in the land of Shinar; a stand shall be erected for it, and it shall be set down there upon the stand."

Would you change your seat?

These three examples give us an idea of how different biblical prophecy is from our everyday experiences. We cannot read the prophetic texts as moderns—they would come across as too weird. Before we look at such texts again, we need more background, so that we can understand them more sympathetically, within their original context.

Prophecy and Omens in the Ancient Near East

The biggest challenge in our understanding biblical prophecy is to appreciate a widespread belief in the ancient Near East: the divine will can be apparent to people—if we know where and how to perceive it. Prophecy, where the divine communicates directly with a human, is just one manifestation of this belief. In Israel, prophecy served as the predominant way in which people discerned the divine will. Meanwhile, that and other forms of "tuning in" to divine messages existed in many areas throughout the ancient Near East.[2]

The Shape of Things to Come

Our most extensive knowledge about divine communication comes from ancient Mesopotamia.[3] Archaeologists have excavated many kinds of omen texts from various periods, showing that the Mesopotamians valued this genre. Those omen texts study a wide variety of phenomena for signs as to what the gods are intending to do. Many omens are based on sacrifices, typically focusing on the hidden meaning of the shape of a given sacrificial animal's liver, which varies greatly from one specimen to the next. Trained specialists even interpreted these shapes by comparing them to clay models of liver forms.

The omen texts are formulated in two parts: a particular observable condition, and the implication of that condition for the future. (Scholars call these parts "protasis" and "apodosis," respectively.) The following four examples give some sense of their variety:[4]

If a man's chest hair curls upwards: he will become a slave.
If a man has a flushed face and his right eye sticks out: he will be devoured by dogs far from his house.
If the gallbladder (of the sacrificial sheep) is stripped of the hepatic duct: the army of the king will suffer a thirst during a military campaign.

If the north wind sweeps the face of heavens until the appearance of the new moon: the harvest will be abundant.

The texts interpret some conditions on the basis of word association; others, on the basis of whether certain signs seemed ominous or propitious. Still others use criteria that we have not been able to decipher.

In any event, both the people and their leaders invested time and effort into interpreting omens. They gleaned those omens from a huge range of phenomena, both celestial and terrestrial, both normal and unusual. The omen texts show that the populace believed that they could discern the divine will—although it might take an expert to do so reliably.

Prophecy, Mesopotamian Style

Archaeologists have excavated more than 130 Mesopotamian texts that bear on prophecy. Strangely, all of them come from just two sites out of the dozens in the region:[5] Mari on the Tigris River (circa the eighteenth century B.C.E.), and in Assyria during the reigns of Esarhaddon (680–669) and Ashurbanipal (668–627). This concentration of evidence for a social institution is unusual. It raises an obvious question: did prophecy exist in Mesopotamia throughout its history (and the relevant texts simply have been lost)? Or was prophecy important only in these two distinct periods and locales? If the latter is the case, then Mesopotamian prophecy probably could not have influenced the development of Israelite prophecy.

Here are two examples of a Mesopotamian prophecy. The first, from Assyria, is an oracle from the woman Ishtar-la-tashiat of Arbela. The second one comes from Mari:

> Esarhaddon, king of lands, fear not! That wind which blows against you—I need only say a word and I can bring it to an end. Your enemies, like a [young] boar in the month of Simanu, will flee even at your approach. I am the great Belet—I am the goddess Ishtar of Arbela, she who has destroyed your enemies at your mere approach. What order have I given you which you did not rely upon? I am Ishtar of Arbela! I lie in wait for your enemies, I shall give them to you. I, Ishtar of Arbela, will go before and behind you fear not! You who are paralyzed [saying], "Only in crying Woe can I either go up or sit down."[6]

> Moreover, the day I sent this tablet of mine to my lord, [an ec]static of Dagan came and addressed me as follows: "The god sent [me]. Hurry,

> write to the ki[ng] that they are to offer the mortuary-sacrifices to the sha[de] of Yahdun-Li[m]." This is what this ecstatic said to me, and I have therefore written to my lord. Let my lord do what pleases him.[7]

The content and phraseology of some of these prophetic texts is mirrored in the Bible. However, it is important to remember that ancient Israel believed in prophecy more than any other type of divination, seeing it as the best way to comprehend the divine will. We are not sure why. As discussed above, we do not know whether Mesopotamian prophecy influenced Israel at an early stage.

Closer to home, we have some evidence that the Phoenicians also believed in prophets. Meanwhile, across the Jordan River, an eighth-century-B.C.E. inscription found in the city of Deir 'Alla even talks about "Balaam the seer," the same prophet mentioned in Numbers 22–24.[8] However, we have so few texts from Israel's immediate neighbors that we cannot accurately evaluate the potential evidence. Was Israel unique in its heavy reliance on the medium of prophecy? It is hard to say.

The Nature of Prophecy in Israel

The main biblical term for a prophet is *navi* (נָבִיא), used 325 times in the Hebrew Bible. It appears even in the Book of Genesis. In the middle wife-sister story (see "The Ancestors as Symbols" in chapter 7), God refers to Abraham as a *navi*, explaining to the king that Abraham "will intercede for you—to save your life" (20:7). This first use is telling: the common view today of a biblical prophet as "someone who tells the future" was not the only—or even the main—function from the Bible's standpoint. Rather, the *navi* was an intercessor,[9] a go-between the people and God.

The biblical prophet may intercede for others, as Abraham does for Abimelech, or as many later prophets do for the people Israel. However, the texts more commonly recount the prophet's function as a messenger from God to the people; in this sense, the prophet functions as a divine messenger. Thus prophets may be explicitly labeled "the LORD's messenger" (e.g., Hag. 1:13), and one prophet is called Malachi, which means "my messenger." The prophets employ the formula *ko amar* (כֹּה אָמַר, "thus says"), called the "messenger formula"[10] because secular messengers also used it. Thus, as a divine messenger, the prophet should be understood as standing somewhere on a direct line between God and the people: On this line, some prophets stand closer to God, while some stand closer to the people. To see how the prophet functions in both directions on this line, consider this example from Amos:

> (7:1) This is what my Lord GOD showed me: He was creating a plague of locusts at the time when the late-sown crops were beginning to sprout—the late-sown crops after the king's reaping. (2) When it had finished devouring the herbage in the land, I said, "O Lord GOD, pray forgive. How will Jacob survive? He is so small." (3) The LORD relented concerning this. "It shall not come to pass," said the LORD.

This passage begins with the prophet's vision from God (vv. 1–2a), followed by the prophet's plea to God in response (v. 2b). It concludes with God's statement to the prophet (v. 3). Hence Amos not only delivers messages from God but also delivers requests on behalf of the people to God. The content of the concluding statement is especially important, since it suggests that God had a change of heart. This teaches us that according to the biblical authors, prophets had great power to transform the divine decree. In short, the Bible does not view prophets primarily as predictors of the future.[11]

The etymology of the term *navi* is uncertain.[12] Most scholars relate it to an Akkadian (Mesopotamian) root *nabû*, "to name, call," either in the sense of "one who calls out," i.e., a speaker, or "one who has been called." Some terms for prophet are much less frequent, yet their origins are clearer: *chozeh* (**חוֹזֶה**) and *ro'eh* (**רוֹאֶה**) both mean "a seer." Likewise, *ish Elohim* (**אִישׁ אֱלֹהִים**) or *ish ha-elohim* (**אִישׁ הָאֱלֹהִים**) means "(the) man of God." The biblical text treats these various terms as somewhat distinct—for example, it employs *ish Elohim* to describe Elijah and Elisha, but not other prophets like Isaiah or Jeremiah.

Two Main Types of Israelite Prophecy

Why did the Bible use more than one term for a prophet? In part, because there were different types of prophets. Biblical scholars typically distinguish between those who talked at length to the general population, and those who talked primarily to the king and whose messages are brief. Usually we refer to the former group—including the prophets Isaiah, Jeremiah, Ezekiel, Hosea, Amos, and Micah, all of whom have their own books—as "classical" prophets. Their writings date from the eighth century B.C.E.

The latter group is comprised of individuals like Nathan and Gad (tenth century B.C.E.), and Elijah and Elisha (ninth century B.C.E.). Some of them remain nameless, and some are female. Many scholars have referred to them as "preclassical" prophets. However, I avoid that term for two reasons. First, we do not know when prophets of the classical type first developed. Perhaps they existed in earlier eras too—but their speeches went unrecorded or were lost. (Nor do we know what factors in the social, religious, or economic life of ancient Israel first prompted classical prophecy and its records.)[13] Second, we do know that prophets of the type like Elijah continued to exist side by side with the classical prophets.

For both reasons, the term "*pre*classical" is misleading. "Nonclassical" is a better term, though it too is somewhat misleading, since the prophets within this group are so different from each other. Indeed, we can subdivide this group of prophets usefully, either by whether they perform magical acts (e.g., Elijah and Elisha), or by whether they critique the monarchy (e.g., Elisha) or support it (e.g., Nathan).[14]

Those who support the king are the earliest Israelite prophets that the Bible writes about. They are much like other ancient Near Eastern prophets. It is easy to locate them within this context, even if we do not know the lines of influence (see above, "Prophecy, Mesopotamian Style"). But we know precious little about how prophecy developed in Israel.

The remainder of this chapter will focus on the main characteristics of the nonclassical prophets. Often it will clarify their role by contrasting it with that of the classical prophets. Each of the next several chapters will then spotlight a leading classical prophet.

The Nonclassical Prophets

Though the nonclassical prophets were not all alike, most of them had—according to the Bible—some combination of the following traits:

- they generally knew what was happening in other places;
- they were consulted on fixed occasions and often paid for their services;
- they banded together;
- their prophecy could be induced;
- they performed miracles;
- they usually prophesied to the king, speaking in prose;
- they performed unusual actions; and
- they predicted the future.

We will now explore these qualities in turn, giving examples from various prophets.

Viewing and Sensing Remotely

The nonclassical prophets were expected to know what was happening in distant places that they could not physically see. The exception that proves this rule is 2 Kings 4:8–37. In this story, the only child of the Shunammite woman dies, and she entreats the prophet Elisha. His assistant, Gehazi, tries to shoo her away, but Elisha says: "Let her alone, for she is in bitter distress; and the LORD has hidden it from me and has not told me" (v. 27). Elisha implies that he normally knew the divine will and could perceive what had happened elsewhere. In a similar vein, in 2 Kings 6:12 a foreign officer says to the Aramean king (who had failed in several attempts to ambush Israel): "Elisha, that prophet in Israel, tells the king of Israel the very words you speak in your bedroom."

Serving as Freelance Consultants

People who needed these prophets visited them at traditional times. When the son of the Shunammite woman dies and she wants to consult Elisha, her husband attempts to stop her, saying: "Why are you going to him today? It is neither new moon nor sabbath" (2 Kings 4:23). His question implies that on fixed occasions the prophets made themselves available for consultation—not unlike a college professor who posts a schedule of regular office hours.

Other texts suggest that the people paid prophets for advice given on such days. Consider the scene in 1 Samuel where Saul and his servant are searching for some stray donkeys. The dialogue begins with Saul's unnamed servant:

> (9:6) . . . "There is a man of God (*ish elohim*) in that town, and the man is highly esteemed; everything that he says comes true. Let us go there; perhaps he will tell us about the errand on which we set out." (7) "But if we go," Saul said to his servant, "what can we bring the man?[15] For the food in our bags is all gone, and there is nothing we can bring to the man of God as a present. What have we got?" (8) The servant answered Saul again, "I happen to have a quarter-shekel of silver. I can give that to the man of God and he will tell us about our errand."

This, then, is really a discussion about the smallest payment that they believe Samuel will accept in order to tell them where the donkeys are!

Forming Prophetic Fellowships

Many of these nonclassical prophets banded together into groups who lived and prophesied together. The stories concerning Elijah mention that he is the head of such a group. It also appears in 1 Samuel, as King Saul becomes a temporary or ad hoc prophet: "he saw a band of prophets coming toward him. Thereupon the spirit of God gripped him, and he spoke in ecstasy among them" (10:10). The term usually used for these groups is *benei ha-nevi'im* (בְּנֵי הַנְּבִיאִים), literally "sons of prophets," better understood as "members of a prophetic group or guild." The material in Kings about Elijah and Elisha refers to such groups more than ten times.

Preparing to Receive Their Message

For these individuals, prophecy can be induced by the right technique. For example, Elisha says, "Now then, get me a musician" (2 Kings 3:15). The result is described thus: "As the musician played, the hand of the LORD [a technical term for prophecy] came upon him." In various places, prophets prophesy at night, sometimes in temples. This may be similar to "incubation dreams," namely going to sleep at a special place with the hope that you will have a prophetic dream—a phenomenon well-attested in many cultures.

Doing Wonders

One striking aspect of the stories about these nonclassical prophets, especially Elijah and Elisha, is the extent to which they are miracle workers. They feed the masses with a small amount of food, revive the dead, find lost objects, make poisoned food safe, heal lepers, etc. The Bible recounts many types of "miracle worker" stories about these figures. The tales are of varied literary types, and they emphasize different aspects of the prophetic experience. Thus they likely originated in various circles for different purposes.[16] Note that, as a kind of literary fulfillment of Elisha's request of Elijah that "a double portion of your spirit pass on to me" (2 Kings 2:9), miracle accounts are transferred between these two prophets, with the number of miracles performed by Elisha equal to approximately double those of Elijah.

Restricting Their Audience

The Bible suggests that a primary role of nonclassical prophets was to prophesy to the king. Thus, the Elijah unit opens with "Elijah the Tishbite, an inhabitant of Gilead" speaking to Ahab, king of the Northern Kingdom (1 Kings 17:1). Even the famous confrontation between Elijah and the priests of Baal opens: "Much later, in the third year, the word of the LORD came to Elijah: 'Go, appear before Ahab; then I will send rain upon the earth'" (chap. 18). The focus on speaking to the king contrasts sharply with classical prophecy, which typically addresses itself to a broad group of people, even though sometimes classical prophets inveigh against the king; they do so as part of their mission to the people.

Both kinds of prophets engage in rebuking the powerful, but the nonclassical prophets typically rebuke the king only using short, prosaic condemnations. For example, Elijah's famous rebuke of Ahab by Elijah, after Ahab has Naboth killed in order to appropriate Naboth's vineyard, reads: "Thus said the LORD: Would you murder and take possession? Thus said the LORD: In the very place where the dogs lapped up Naboth's blood, the dogs will lap up your blood too" (1 Kings 21:19). Classical prophets, on the other hand, speak to all classes, often in long poetic speeches.

Doing Strange Deeds

Nonclassical prophets perform unusual actions. Recall Elisha's deadly response—mentioned at the start of this chapter—to the children who mock him. Elsewhere, in a single passage of forty-four verses, Elisha produces excessive amounts of oil for a needy widow, promises a woman that she will conceive, revives a dead child, provides the antidote to a poisonous stew, and multiplies a limited amount of food to feed the masses (2 Kings 4). The purpose of such acts is to glorify prophetic prestige. In contrast, when classical prophets do strange things, such acts turn out to have their own meaning; they are teaching tools.

Making Predictions

Nonclassical prophets do predict the future. However, they do not dwell on it. Rather, they offer short, final pronouncements, such as Elijah's word to King Ahab: "As the LORD lives, the God of Israel whom I serve, there will be no dew or rain except at my bidding" (1 Kings 17:1). According to Kings, that one-sentence message turned out to be the start of a three-year drought and famine. In contrast, when the classical prophet predicts doom, most often it is conditional, functioning as a call to repent.

Summary of Prophetic Types in the Bible

According to the Bible, the populace believes that both nonclassical and classical prophets can convey the divine will. Both types serve as intermediaries between the people and their God. Yet the differences between the types are enormous—in terms of their audience and communication style, the reason for their odd actions, and their use of predictions. Given such differences, one may reasonably wonder whether the same title of "prophet" should apply to both groups!

The following table compares and contrasts the classical and nonclassical prophets.

Characteristics of Nonclassical Versus Classical Prophets

Characteristic	*Nonclassical*	*Classical*
Knew secret and hidden information	Yes	No
Typically consulted on fixed occasions	Yes	No
Were paid to disclose or intercede	Yes	No
Banded together	Yes	No
Induced prophecy	Yes	No
Worked miracles	Yes	No
Main audience	King	People
Main genre of speech	Prose	Poetry
Reason for strange deeds	Build prestige	Convey a message
Type of predictions	Short verdicts	Long warnings

16

"Let Justice Well Up like Water"

Reading Amos

Primary Reading: Amos.

Amos as a Typical "Classical Prophet"

The writings of Amos provide a good starting point for understanding books attributed to the classical prophets. (Amos is structured as a book, although ultimately a later editor incorporated it into a larger biblical book, The Twelve [Minor] Prophets. See "Name and Structure" in chapter 2.) As a relatively short text, Amos gives us a workable opportunity to outline the structure, function, and style of prophetic books.

This chapter first highlights mistakes commonly made in reading Amos, due to common misunderstandings of classical prophecy. Then it examines the book's persuasive tactics and themes, specifically the five main points found in classical prophecy that Amos exemplifies. It concludes with observations on the formation of Amos into a book.[1]

Common Mistakes Made in Reading Amos

If we lack training in how to read prophetic texts, we usually think about them in terms of the types of texts we are familiar with. Thus, the Book of Amos is often read as a predictive text—a work intended to foretell the future. Further, we read him like a contemporary rabbi who condemns listeners for not following the norms of the Torah. In addition, we assume that the prophet Amos wrote the book that bears his name—just as we find it in our Bible.

Not a Prediction

The main purpose of classical prophecy was *not* to predict the future. Prophets do spend a lot of time talking about the future, but they do so for two reasons. One reason is to convince the people to repent. The second reason is that if Israel suffers, it means that God has judged and punished them for their covenant infractions. Amos 5:6 illustrates the first point unambiguously: "Seek the LORD, and you will live, / Else He will rush like fire upon the House of Joseph / And consume Bethel with none to quench it." Establishing the second point was more complicated. Remember that in a polytheistic society, nearly everyone believed that any of the many gods could punish a person or a group. (That is why Amos' Northern contemporary Hosea had to contend that the God of Israel is responsible for nature—rather than the Canaanite deity Baal. See especially Hosea 2.) In addition, many neighboring peoples believed that nature or the forces of nature were sometimes more powerful than the gods. Amos—like the other classical prophets—wished to challenge both of these basic views about reality. He held that the God of Israel is responsible for *everything* that happens. In the words of 3:6: "Can misfortune come to a town / If the LORD has not caused it?" This is not a prediction; rather, it is an explanation of how the world works.

Not Referring to the Torah

Amos makes his points about the need for repentance and about divine punishment, but not by urging the people to follow the authoritative Torah text. We can be fairly certain that his failure to mention such a text is because in his day, no such Torah existed. This claim may seem surprising. Consider, then, what Amos means when he says: "Did you offer sacrifice and oblation to Me / Those forty years in the wilderness, / O House of Israel?" (5:25). In context, this is a rhetorical question whose answer is clearly "no." When Amos posed this question, he was taking for granted his audience's belief that the Israelites did *not* offer sacrifices during the wilderness period. Yet according to the (Priestly) Torah passages in Leviticus and Numbers, Aaron the high priest presided over countless sacrifices during that period.

Likewise, Amos' words cannot easily be reconciled with Deuteronomy. For example, he says that one of the punishments of Israel will be "tonsures on every head" (8:10). This refers to pulling out or shaving one's hair as a mourning ritual. However, that practice is expressly prohibited in Deuteronomy 14:1.[2] It would be odd for a prophet who knew Deuteronomy to suggest this as a divine punishment. In fact, the major theme of Deuteronomy is the proper worship of God in one central sanctuary, which in his day could only have meant Jerusalem. Yet Amos never condemns worship at northern "high places." Indeed, he lends the shrine of Bethel prestige by prophesying there!

I do not mean to suggest that Amos knew *nothing* of what is now in the Torah. He speaks of the period of wandering in the wilderness (2:10), the destruction of Sodom and Gomorrah (4:11), and Sabbath and New Moon observances (8:5). Rather, Amos did not know *the* Torah as it now exists, complete and authoritative, blending together various sources. He knew traditions that would eventually become part of the Torah, but he did not know the Torah as a unified book.[3]

How could this be? Recall that the Torah has a long and complex history of composition (see chapters 6–10). That is, it and the prophetic books developed during the same period. Thus even though the Torah appears first in the canon, all Torah texts did not precede in time all prophetic texts. Nor did all prophets know all of the Torah.

In the traditional view, the Torah existed first and influenced the prophets. However, we need to consider seriously the converse possibility—that prophetic notions and material influenced some of what became part of the Torah.[4]

Amos the Book Versus Amos the Prophet

"Amos" may mean two things—the person, or the book of that name. They are not identical. Not all that is in the Book of Amos was written by the prophet Amos himself. Many scholars imagine several stages of growth: the words of Amos; additions by a school of Amos; and more additions in another, later setting.[5] Scholars debate how to discern the various stages; nevertheless, we can point to strong evidence that these stages existed. This picture may be strange to us—we live an era in which educated people take care to cite and quote their sources precisely. However, in antiquity, editors were comfortable adding to their predecessors' works. (Thus was the entire D source added to the Torah; see "A Pious Fraud" in chapter 10.) It was more important for such editors to add their verses to a book like Amos and have them be recognized as authoritative, than to claim them as their own compositions. In some sense this process is like that of the jokes or anecdotes that circulate on the Internet. They may attributed to a particular author, but their recipients revise, add to, subtract from, and update the words before sending them along to others. This means, in the case of both

Amos and the Internet, that tracking down the original text is a difficult if not impossible task.

Some biblical scholars expend a great deal of energy trying to find the original words of Amos and other prophets. In recent decades, however, more scholars have recognized that this is impossible.[6] We simply know too little. How did the prophet Amos recite his speeches? That is, did he write them down and read them aloud, word for word? Did he speak from memory, and write the words down later? Did he revise his words after delivering them, perhaps taking into account the difference between oral and written expression? Or did someone in the audience write down the prophet's words, and if so, was it an exact record? Did anyone change or "improve" on the speeches while recopying them? Given this chain of uncertainty, it is easy to understand why we need to distinguish between the book and the words of Amos. Furthermore, we must admit that we can never recover exactly what Amos said. Thus when we seek to reconstruct the historical conditions of Amos' time and place, we cannot treat the book as if it were his direct first-person account.

The Rhetoric of Amos

Few of us like to be told in public that our actions and core beliefs are both wrongheaded and dangerous. So how did the prophets get the people to listen to such condemnations? The communications approach—that is, the rhetoric—used by each prophet must have made a big difference to listeners. Here, too, not all prophets were identical; for example, Isaiah used fancy poetry when he prophesied; but Amos did not.[7] Different prophets used rhetorical devices that probably reflected their own skills and preferences, as well as their different audiences. Since the devices used by Amos are not fancy, we may guess that he was not speaking, by and large, to a highly educated, poetry-loving audience.

Amos induces the Israelites to listen to him when he begins by prophesying against all of their enemies—Damascus, Gaza, Tyre, etc. One can almost hear the Israelites cheering as Amos condemns enemy after enemy for its behavior. His targets alternate between north and south; they get closer and closer to home, until the audience—now listening attentively—hears: "Thus said the LORD: For three transgressions of Israel, / For four, I will not revoke it" (2:6).

In addition, Amos also lures his audience with rhetorical questions, especially in 3:3–6:

> (3) Can two walk together / Without having met? (4) Does a lion roar

> in the forest / When he has no prey? / Does a great beast let out a cry from its den / Without having made a capture? (5) Does a bird drop on the ground—in a trap— / With no snare there? Does a trap spring up from the ground / Unless it has caught something? (6) When a ram's horn is sounded in a town, / Do the people not take alarm? Can misfortune come to a town / If the LORD has not caused it?

These questions capture listeners by making them wonder: What is this prophet Amos talking about? What does "two walking together" mean, and what does that have to do with Amos' message? Amos' listeners would have answered "no" after each question. Thus when the prophet posed the final question ("Can misfortune come to a town / If the LORD has not caused it?"), they probably were ready to answer "no" again—affirming that God is in charge of all.

Irony also attracts listeners. Thus at one point, Amos has noticed that the people think they will not be punished for their moral failures because their sacrificial offerings are keeping God happy. The prophet wishes to teach that this way of thinking is wrong. He makes his point by carrying the people's reasoning to extremes. He suggests that if they believe offerings work so well, they ought to go ahead and sin more—so long as they make sure to bring extra sacrifices:

> (4:4) Come to Bethel and transgress; / To Gilgal, and transgress even more: / Present your sacrifices the next morning / And your tithes on the third day; (5) And burn a thank offering of leavened bread; / And proclaim freewill offerings loudly. For you love that sort of thing, O Israelites—declares my Lord GOD.

This is of course the last thing that an audience would expect a prophet—or God—to tell them.[8] By giving such unexpected advice, Amos gets their attention.

Amos also resorts to puns, which help disarm his audience. At the same time, the wordplay reinforces his message. Three examples will suffice. First, he plays on the name Gilgal, literally "a round or circular place," and juxtaposes it with a similar-sounding root (*g-l-h*) that means "to be exiled": *ki ha-gilgal galoh yigleh* ("for Gilgal shall go into exile"; 5:5). Second, he plays on the meaning of the odd place-name Lo-dabar, which literally means "nothing": "Ah, those who are so happy about Lo-dabar/nothing" (6:13; transl. adapted). Finally, in one of his visions he sees "a basket of *kayitz* (summer fruit)," which represents that "the hour of *ketz* (doom) has come for My people Israel" (8:2). (This pun would have sounded even stronger to his Northern audience if they pronounced those two words identically, as scholars now believe they did. The pronunciation reflected in our current Bibles is a later, Judean Hebrew.[9])

The Five Main Points of Amos and of Classical Prophecy

Most of the classical prophets, including the prophet Amos, make the following five points:

- The God of Israel is also a universal deity.
- Israel and Judah are accountable to this deity—God is not good to them unconditionally, but rather rewards them only for following the covenant.
- This covenant involves both interpersonal (ethical) and religious (ritual) obligations—not one or the other.
- "The Day of the LORD," a day of punishment, will arrive in the future.
- Even when Israel is punished, it will not be destroyed; there will be a remnant.

Let's explore each of these points, in turn.

A Universal God

Most ancient Near Eastern peoples were polytheistic. Typically they worshipped—among other more personal or familial deities—a high god or goddess who was especially responsible for their city-state. Thus, Ashur was the high god of the Assyrians; Marduk, of the Babylonians; Chemosh, of the Moabites; Milcom, of the Ammonites; and in pre-Israelite times, Baal (superceding Il or El) of the Canaanites. Thus the Moabites would have shrugged off Amos' condemnation of Moab—"Because he burned the bones / Of the king of Edom to lime" (2:1)—for they would have seen this as a matter of concern for their deity, Chemosh, or for the Edomite high god, Qaus, but not for the god of their Israelite neighbors.

Amos, however, insists that the God of Israel has jurisdiction over more than just the land of Israel. This deity cares about more than what the people Israel do—or what is done to them. Indeed, God is the sole deity, and is universal, punishing all nations everywhere for infractions of basic human decency.

Accountability

Although this Israelite deity held sway everywhere, the relationship with the people Israel was a special one. They were supposed to be following divine laws that apply to them alone. Thus, after condemning other nations in 1:3–2:3, Amos indicts only Judah because "they have spurned the Teaching of the LORD / And have not observed His laws" (2:4). In 2:6–8, he condemns the Northern Kingdom for violating norms that the Israelites thought of as binding on the people Israel specifically.

At some point in history, Israelites began to understand this relationship as a *berit* (בְּרִית), a covenant or compact.[10] But this metaphor was ambiguous, for political covenants in the ancient Near East were of two types. In a *covenant of grant*, one party unconditionally gave something to another party. In contrast, a *suzerainty treaty* recorded the agreement reached by two unequal parties, a vassal and a suzerain (overlord). Usually the suzerain undertook to protect the vassal, while the vassal had to pay tribute to the suzerain.[11]

A variety of polemical prophetic texts tell us that many people in Israel viewed their covenant with God as a covenant of grant: God would protect them unconditionally. Amos and other classical prophets, however, maintained that God was suzerain, and Israel was a vassal. Thus God will protect Israel only if they observe the treaty stipulations—that is, heed God's word. This is the import of 9:7: "To Me, O Israelites, you are / Just like the Ethiopians[12]—declares the LORD—True, I brought Israel up / From the land of Egypt, / But also the Philistines from Caphtor / And the Arameans from Kir." God has moved many peoples around, not only this one. Israel's wondrous liberation in the past does not imply unconditional divine protection in the future. Furthermore, to the extent that this relationship is special, it is one that makes demands: "You alone have I singled out [literally: known] / Of all the families of the earth— / That is why I will call you to account / For all your iniquities" (3:2).

Both Ethical and Ritual Obligations

Again, prophetic polemic indicates that some Israelites believed that ritual action alone was enough to assure divine presence and blessing. (Recall the ironic words of Amos, "Come to Bethel and transgress . . ..") Amos asserts an additional dimension to the covenant: proper ethical, interpersonal behavior. Religion involves right as well as rite.[13] Amos claims in God's name:

> (5:21) I loathe, I spurn your festivals, / I am not appeased by your solemn assemblies. / (22) If you offer Me burnt offerings—or your meal offerings— / I will not accept them; / I will pay no heed / To your gifts of fatlings. / (23) Spare Me the sound of your hymns, / And let Me not

> hear the music of your lutes. / (24) But let justice well up like water, / Righteousness like an unfailing stream.

These verses (the last of which Rev. Martin Luther King Jr. featured in his famous "I have a dream" speech) are open to two interpretations. If taken literally, they suggest that religious or cultic rites are unimportant; only justice and righteousness matter. This has been a frequent Protestant interpretation of this (and similar) passages; classical Reform Judaism and the Society for Ethical Culture also emphasized this reading.

Another reading understands that the prophet is exaggerating for effect. His point is that ritual *alone* is not efficacious. This is a more typical Jewish reading of the passage. In condemning unethical behavior, Amos dwells on the oppression of the lower class by the upper class, who "lie on ivory beds,[14] / Lolling on their couches, / Feasting on lambs from the flock / And on calves from the stalls" (6:4).

The Day Will Come

Those who deserve punishment will be punished during the "Day of the LORD." The earliest mention of this day appears to be in Amos:

> (5:18) Ah, you who wish / For the day of the LORD! Why should you want / The day of the LORD? / It shall be darkness, not light! (19)—As if a man should run from a lion / And be attacked by a bear; / Or if he got indoors, / Should lean his hand on the wall / And be bitten by a snake! (20) Surely the day of the LORD shall be / Not light, but darkness, / Blackest night without a glimmer.

This passage suggests that the Day of the LORD was already a popular concept before Amos discussed it[15]—the people were wishing for its arrival. Clearly, they believed it would be a good day, most likely a day in which God would appear as a warrior to save Israel from its enemies. The point Amos makes is that the Day of the LORD is destructive.

Much about this "day" is unclear —we do not know its origin, whether people thought of it as a literal day or some longer period of time, or whether its "darkness" is literal or metaphorical.[16] In some texts, as in Amos, this day brings the punishment of Israel, while others mention the punishment of its enemies. Though the description varies, the Day of the LORD is a widespread and longstanding concept, from Amos all the way through the end of classical prophecy.

All Is Not Lost

God will not totally destroy Israel on the Day of the LORD—nor at any other time, since without the subservient partner the Covenant would no longer exist. As the classical prophets frequently put it, the covenant between God and Israel implies a remnant of the people will be saved—no matter what.

A variety of biblical texts predict that ten percent will survive various destructions (see especially Isa. 6:13, "But while a tenth part yet remains in it . . ."), including in Amos: "For thus said my Lord GOD / About the House of Israel: The town that marches out a thousand strong / Shall have a hundred left, / And the one that marches out a hundred strong / Shall have but ten left" (5:3). Or, using more figurative language: "Thus said the LORD: As a shepherd rescues from the lion's jaws / Two shank bones or the tip of an ear, / So shall the Israelites escape / Who dwell in Samaria— / With the leg of a bed or the head of a couch" (3:12).

The five ideas outlined above relate to each other loosely, which explains why they recur so often in classical prophecy. We can restate the cluster of concepts as follows: YHWH—a universal deity—has a special relationship with Israel, which calls for Israel's heeding both cultic and ethical norms. If Israel does not meet these obligations, they will be punished. One of the possible punishments will occur on the Day of the LORD. However, because of the Covenant, Israel will never be totally destroyed—a remnant will always remain.

The Formation of the Book of Amos

All five ideas discussed in the previous section are found in the *Book* of Amos. Yet we cannot be sure how many of them came from the prophet himself. Later revisions and additions played a role (see above, "Amos the Book Versus Amos the Prophet"). I will sketch the formation of the book here, which must remain only a sketch, because much of the history of the text is obscure.

Amos, the eighth-century prophet, believed that he heard the divine voice, as he reports: "Hear this word, O people of Israel, / That the LORD *has spoken*" (3:1; emphasis added). He saw visions that he believed were divine: "This is what my Lord GOD *showed* me" (7:1; emphasis added). He felt compelled to share these with the public, including at the temple at Bethel (see 7:10, 13).[17] At some point, either he or one of his disciples brought these separate oracles together. When this happened, someone had to decide how to order the oracles. Many methods of ordering would have been possible (e.g., chronological, associative, topical), but the Book of Amos seems to keep similar types of oracles together, like the visions now collected in chapter 7. In this way, the first Book of Amos was produced.

Later, to explain and update the material, someone added superscription and narration. This includes the story about Amos and Amaziah the priest, in what is now 7:10–17. Surely an editor inserted that narrative there because it refers directly to the oracle in the previous verse, even though this placement interrupts the flow of the prophetic speech. Thus the book slowly grew, and probably existed in a few copies only.

Two events helped to popularize the book. The first was the earthquake two years after Amos prophesied (see 1:1); Zechariah 14:5 also mentions "the earthquake in the days of King Uzziah of Judah," and archaeological digs confirm its occurrence.[18] As part of his typical language of destruction, Amos had used earthquake imagery: "Shall not the earth shake for this / And all that dwell on it mourn? / Shall it not all rise like the Nile / And surge and subside like the Nile of Egypt?" (8:8); "I saw my LORD standing by the altar, and He said: Strike the capitals so that the thresholds quake, and make an end of the first of them all. And I will slay the last of them with the sword; not one of them shall escape, and not one of them shall survive" (9:1); and "It is my Lord the GOD of Hosts / At whose touch the earth trembles / And all who dwell on it mourn, / And all of it swells like the Nile / And subsides like the Nile of Egypt" (9:5). He had probably meant this as general imagery of destruction—a figurative earthquake; but once the big temblor hit, these verses were understood as true prophecy, authenticating the book as a whole.

After this earthquake came the book's superscription: "The words of Amos, a sheepbreeder from Tekoa, who prophesied concerning Israel in the reigns of Kings Uzziah of Judah and Jeroboam son of Joash of Israel, two years before the earthquake." This superscription tells us more than most: Amos was originally Judean (from Tekoa, a town about ten miles south of Jerusalem); he directed his prophecies at the Northern Kingdom ("Israel"); and he lived in the early to mid-eighth century B.C.E. (for Jeroboam II reigned approximately 786–746). Most significantly, it notes the calamitous earthquake. (This opening verse of Amos is rich in information, but it leaves many background questions unanswered: Why did Amos migrate to the North? In what social circles did he move? Who comprised his family? And so on. Readers should not, however, harp on these uncertainties.) The phrase "two years before the earthquake" serves to legitimate the prophecies that follow.

The book received further authentication decades later, with the destruction and exile of Samaria in 722–720 B.C.E. Events seemed to bear out the dire warnings:

> "Do not seek Bethel, / Nor go to Gilgal, / Nor cross over to Beer-sheba; / For Gilgal shall go into exile, / And Bethel shall become a delusion" (5:5).
> "As I drive you into exile beyond Damascus . . ." (5:27)
> "Assuredly, right soon / They shall head the column of exiles" (6:7).

As Amos (the book and the person) became more prestigious, scribes produced more copies.

Archaeological evidence suggests that after the destruction of the Northern Kingdom, many Israelites or Northerners migrated to Judah in the south.[19] At least one of them brought along the Book of Amos, which went through further adaptations to fit its new milieu. Specifically, someone added references to Zion and the Davidic house at key points to make the book more suitable for its new audience. Before the oracles against the nations (which at an earlier stage had begun the book), a new opening told readers that Amos had proclaimed: "The LORD roars from Zion, / Shouts aloud from Jerusalem; / And the pastures of the shepherds shall languish, / And the summit of Carmel shall wither" (1:2). This verse is a statement that the "real" Amos, who left Tekoa for Bethel, would surely not have said.

Similarly in response to Judean concerns, the book gained a new closing:

> (9:11) In that day, I will set up again the fallen booth of David: I will mend its breaches and set up its ruins anew. I will build it firm as in the days of old, (12) So that they shall possess the rest of Edom / And all the nations once attached to My name—declares the LORD who will bring this to pass. (13) A time is coming—declares the LORD— / When the plowman shall meet the reaper, / And the treader of grapes / Him who holds the bag of seed; / When the mountains shall drip wine / And all the hills shall wave with grain. (14) I will restore My people Israel. They shall rebuild ruined cities and inhabit them; / They shall plant vineyards and drink their wine; / They shall till gardens and eat their fruits. (15) And I will plant them upon their soil, / Nevermore to be uprooted / From the soil I have given them—said the LORD your God.

We can be sure that the prophet Amos of the eighth century could not have said these verses, for two reasons. First, Amos otherwise shows no concern for the Davidic house, yet suddenly verse 11 mentions that dynasty. Second, in contrast to the adjective in that verse ("*the fallen* booth of David"), during Amos' time the

Davidic house was strong. So why is this passage here? Typically the Bible's editors ended its books on a positive note. And that underscores my point: Only someone in the Southern Kingdom—not the Northern Kingdom—would have perceived this closing note as unabashedly "positive"!

Conclusion: What We Have Learned from Amos

Although the language of Amos is not so difficult, reading his book is not easy. Prophecy is a genre that is foreign to us. As the historical-critical method has taught us, a text like Amos is quite different from most books that we encounter. In particular, the text makes more sense when we grant that the words of the real prophet Amos are not necessarily the same as the words in the book that bears his name and that this book grew over time.

In contrast to other prophetic books—including Isaiah, the focus of the next chapter—Amos is simple. In imagining how this little book developed, and how its oracles functioned in various settings over time, we have taken a step toward understanding much longer, more complex prophetic books.

17

"They Shall Beat Their Swords into Plowshares"

Reading (First) Isaiah

Primary Reading: Isaiah 1, 2, 6, 7, 10, 11, 13, 20, 31.

The Challenge of Reading Isaiah

Isaiah is the longest of the prophetic books, comprised of 66 chapters.[1] In some respects it is the most difficult to read of all the biblical books. This section will touch on each of the factors that make Isaiah such a challenge.

Out of Many, One

The book's history is complex: it embodies the work not of a single prophet, but of at least two prophets and more likely three—or more.

The earliest of these poets, prophesying during the eighth century, is Isaiah son of Amoz (not to be confused with the earlier Amos). Scholars sometimes refer to him as First Isaiah; his work comprises much of chapters 1–39.

The second prophet, whom scholars call Deutero-Isaiah (Second Isaiah), prophesied in Babylonia hundreds of years later, during the Babylonian exile. That work has become chapters 40–55 in the book as we now have it.

The third figure, whom some scholars call Trito-Isaiah (Third Isaiah), prophesied in Israel shortly after the return from exile. That prophet's work comprises chapters 56–66.

However, distinguishing between their oracles is not simply a matter of dividing up the chapters. Just as not all of the book of Amos came from the prophet Amos (see "The Formation of the Book of Amos" in chapter 16), so not all of Isaiah 1–39 is by Isaiah son of Amoz. Deutero-Isaiah and other later, anonymous figures apparently inserted some of their own work there.[2] Many scholars also believe that someone copied chapters 36–39 from the Book of Kings.[3]

Words Without Peer

Another factor that makes the first Isaiah hard to understand is its use of many rare words. A large number of those words appear only once in the whole Bible. (Scholars call such words *hapax legomena*, a Greek expression meaning "unique words." We often use the term *hapax* for short, as I will below.) Recall that context is one of our major guides for what words mean (see "The Act of Reading" in chapter 3). Therefore, when words appear only once—so that we have only one example of how they are used—their meaning often remains unclear. This is why the JPS translation has so many footnotes in Isaiah saying "meaning of Hebrew uncertain."

Ambiguous References and Unclear Boundaries

Beyond the problems of understanding hapax words, the poetry of Isaiah is unusually sophisticated, and its figures are often obscure. In addition, the book has run together many separate oracles. (Some other prophets, such as Amos, use formulas—such as "Thus said the Lord"—to indicate the beginning of an oracle, or a messenger formula—such as "declares the Lord"—to indicate its end. These formulas—which scholars call "form-critical markers"—are largely absent in Isaiah.) Due to the lack of a clear break between many of the units, scholars debate where those units begin and end. This debate manifests in the many different layouts that various translations have employed for this book.

Uncertain Historical Context

As in Amos, this book opens with a superscription that states when the prophet was active. From what we are told, Isaiah's prophecies covered a long period, from "the reigns of Uzziah, Jotham, Ahaz, and Hezekiah, kings of Judah" (1:1), namely from the mid- to late-eighth century. Many major events took place during this time: the Syro-Ephraimite war in the 730s (when Damascus and Northern Israel invaded Judah); the end of the Northern Kingdom and the exile of much of its populace in 722–720; the devastation of the Judean countryside and the siege of Jerusalem in 701 (see "Israel's History as Seen from the Inside" in chapter 4; "Jerusalem in 701" in chapter 13); and more. However, Isaiah tends to present its individual oracles without giving dates or other unambiguous clues to the situations that they refer to. As it happens, the same oracle may read very differently depending on which historical context that we imagine for it.

If the book's editors had placed Isaiah's oracles in chronological order, we might have an easier time inferring their contexts. However, the book is not arranged that way. Indeed, what most consider to be Isaiah's dedication as a prophet does not appear until chapter 6.[4] Conversely, some of the material in chapter 1 appears to date from near the end of Isaiah's mission. (See especially verse 8: "Fair Zion is left / Like a booth in a vineyard." This seems to refer to Jerusalem under siege in 701.)

Instead of chronological order, the book often presents its units associatively. The editors have grouped together oracles pertaining to similar topics. At other times they have arranged units by catchwords, where units beginning and ending with similar words are placed adjacently. For example, Isaiah complains,[5] "My people's rulers are babes, / It is governed by women" (3:12). This is followed associatively by a unit that condemns women—namely "the daughters of Zion" (3:16). That unit ends with the phrase "In that day" (4:1), at which point a new unit starts with those same words (4:2).[6]

The Poetry of Isaiah

Reading Isaiah means understanding it as poetry, which means understanding the characteristics of biblical poetry.[7] Earlier, I noted the error of interpreting poetry as if it were prose (see "The Rules of the Game" in chapter 3). We would be equally wrong to treat biblical poetry as if it were *modern* poetry.[8] Even though many cultures have a genre we might call poetry, those works do not all share the same characteristics. Broadly speaking, poetry may be considered a type of elevated language that is not prose. However, the way in which it is "not prose" differs from society to society and from time to time. Classical English poetry is metrical, that is, it has a patterned number of stressed and unstressed syllables. It is often rhymed, figurative (meaning, it uses many metaphors and similes) and uses special vocabulary. Anyone who reads biblical poetry from Isaiah (or elsewhere) will quickly realize that like English poetry, it is highly figurative and often uses elegant words, but unlike English poetry, it is neither metrical[9] nor rhymed.

Instead, the main characteristic of biblical poetry is "binary repetition." By this I mean that we can divide most poetic verses into two lines (binary), where the second line repeats the meaning of the first in some fashion. For example, the beginning of Isaiah 1:2 reads: "Hear, O heavens, and give ear, O earth." This may be divided into "Hear, O heavens" and "and give ear, O earth," where the latter phrase largely repeats the former in two ways. It repeats the syntax (imperative + "O" + noun). In addition, it repeats the meaning ("hear" and "give ear" are related as synonyms, and "heavens" and "earth" are related as opposites). Each phrase in the verse (such as "Hear, O heavens" or "and give ear, O earth") is called a "colon." Thus, the major feature of biblical poetry is that its lines divide into "bicola" (singular "bicolon").[10]

Scholars call the relationship between the phrases "parallelism," since the second colon parallels the first. The nature of the parallelism has been an issue of great debate. Bishop Robert Lowth (1710–1787) in his *Lectures on the Sacred Poetry of the Hebrews* (1753) suggested three main relationships between the two cola: synonymous, antithetical, and synthetic. In *synonymous parallelism,* the second colon repeats the first in different words, as in Psalm 2:4, "He who is enthroned in heaven laughs; the Lord mocks at them." In *antithetical parallelism,* the second colon expresses the opposite idea of the first, as in Proverbs 15:20, "A wise son makes his father happy; A fool of a man humiliates his mother." In *synthetic parallelism,* the second colon completes the first, and together (i.e., through a synthesis of the two) they express a complete thought. This can be seen in Psalm 23:1, "The LORD is my shepherd; I lack nothing."

Biblical scholars accepted Lowth's system for a long time. It remains helpful, although it has rightly come under assault in recent decades. Some observers have noted that the terms are imprecise—for example, "synthetic parallelism" is a vague, catchall term. In addition, because modern archaeologists have uncovered a large corpus of ancient Semitic poetry, we can now look at parallelism more broadly. It must be even older than the Bible, because it is found in the literature of most ancient Semitic-language cultures. We now understand that both the Bible and other Semitic poetry often create this parallelism through a convention known as "word pairs." Words that are semantically related (e.g., good and bad; day and night; ox and ass) appear in standard combinations. That is, the audience who hears one of those words then expects that its mate will be not far behind—typically, in the next colon. Thus these pairs helped to create parallelism.[11]

Finally, many scholars believe that Lowth's three categories are too restrictive. They prefer to explain the structure of the bicolon like this: "A, and what's more, B" (where "A" and "B" stand for the two cola). In their view, "B" heightens

"A" in a wide range of ways.[12] This understanding of biblical poetry encourages us to pay particular attention to the second colon, for it defines the meaning of a line more than the first.

However, in some cases the second colon is merely a formal repetition of the first, where the poet inserts the second word of a word-pair mechanically.[13] We saw this, for example, in Amos, where the oracles against the nations all open with "For three transgressions . . . / For four . . ." There the numerals "three" and "four" follow a common pattern: A is some number, and B is that number plus one; the numerals in these verses are merely fillers, since only one sin is listed in each section. Another example may be seen in Psalm 121, which portrays God as protector. Verse 6 reads: "By day the sun will not strike you, / nor the moon by night." Colon A ("By day the sun will not strike you") makes sense, given the strong Mediterranean sun. But to the best of my knowledge, no one has ever suffered moonburn. Thus colon B ("nor the moon by night") reflects a formal seconding of A, using the word pairs "day-night" and "sun-moon."

The conflicting analyses of the previous two paragraphs create a dilemma: How do we read biblical poetry? Do we read the second colon as more intensive than the first, or do we see it as simply a filler? Or—to complicate matters still further—is it the case (as I believe) that some poets use the second colon to heighten the first, while others use it as filler? Given that these poets are no longer around to inform us, we do not know for sure how to read many of their poems.

Nevertheless, the binary structure of biblical poetry is easily visible throughout Isaiah. For example, we can parse the first chapter of Isaiah according to the three kinds of parallelism:

(1:2) Hear, O heavens, and give ear, O earth,	bicolon—synonymous parallelism
For the LORD has spoken:	monocolon[14]
"I reared children and brought them up— And they have rebelled against Me!	bicolon—synthetic parallelism
(3) An ox knows its owner, An ass its master's crib:	bicolon—synonymous parallelism
Israel does not know, My people takes no thought."	bicolon—synonymous parallelism
(4) Ah, sinful nation! People laden with iniquity!	bicolon—synonymous parallelism
Brood of evildoers! Depraved children!	bicolon—synonymous parallelism

They have forsaken the LORD,
Spurned the Holy One of Israel,
Turned their backs on Him.

tricolon[15]—synonymous parallelism

The historical-critical method has recovered many of the Bible's rhetorical approaches, allowing us read the text as Israelites might have—using their conventions, not ours. To begin with, we look for natural breaks in each verse, guided by the binary structure that undergirds most verses. Instead of understanding the second bicolon as merely repetitive, we may look for ways in which it heightens the first. I cannot overstate the importance of understanding Isaiah as *biblical* poetry.

Isaiah as a Typical Classical Prophet

Although he is highly poetic—and thus quite different in style from Amos—Isaiah shares with Amos the five features of classical prophecy listed in our previous chapter.

1. Through eleven chapters of oracles against the nations, Isaiah emphasizes that God is a *universal* God (13–23). Elsewhere, according to Isaiah, God famously calls Assyria "rod of My anger, / In whose hand, as a staff, is My fury!" (10:5). In other words, God's will alone induces far away Assyria to conquer large sections of Judah.
2. Chapter 1 explains that this punishment is the result of Judah's *special relationship* with its God—the Judeans are God's children (v. 2) and, from God's perspective, "My people" (v. 3).
3. The continuation of the chapter makes it clear that the covenantal relationship includes interpersonal *obligations*, and that fulfilling cultic responsibilities is not sufficient:

   > (1:11) "What need have I of all your sacrifices?" / Says the LORD. "I am sated with burnt offerings of rams, / And suet of fatlings, / And blood of bulls; / And I have no delight / In lambs and he-goats. (12) That you come to appear before Me— / Who asked that of you? / Trample My courts (13) no more; / Bringing oblations is futile, / Incense is offensive to Me. New moon and sabbath, / Proclaiming of solemnities, / Assemblies with iniquity, / I cannot abide. (14) Your new moons and fixed seasons / Fill Me with loathing; / They are become a burden to

> Me, / I cannot endure them. (15) And when you lift up your hands, / I will turn My eyes away from you; / Though you pray at length, / I will not listen. / Your hands are stained with crime—(16) Wash yourselves clean; / Put your evil doings / Away from My sight. / Cease to do evil; (17) Learn to do good. / Devote yourselves to justice; / Aid the wronged. / Uphold the rights of the orphan; / Defend the cause of the widow."

4. Isaiah describes an ultimate punishment that will come through the *Day of the Lord*. Isaiah's image shares the "darkness" that we saw in Amos 5:18–20, but, not surprisingly—given that Isaiah lived after Amos did—the image is more developed:

   > (13:6) Howl! For the day of the LORD is near; / It shall come like havoc from Shaddai. / (7) Therefore all hands shall grow limp,/ And all men's hearts shall sink; / (8) And, overcome by terror,/ They shall be seized by pangs and throes, / Writhe like a woman in travail. / They shall gaze at each other in horror, / Their faces livid with fright. / (9) Lo! The day of the LORD is coming / With pitiless fury and wrath, / To make the earth a desolation, / To wipe out the sinners upon it. / (10) The stars and constellations of heaven / Shall not give off their light; / The sun shall be dark when it rises, / And the moon shall diffuse no glow. / (11) "And I will requite to the world its evil, / And to the wicked their iniquity; / I will put an end to the pride of the arrogant / And humble the haughtiness of tyrants . . ."

5. Isaiah emphasizes the idea of a *remnant*—not all of Israel will be destroyed. He expresses this idea most clearly in chapter 6 (which many scholars believe recounts his dedication as a prophet, as mentioned above). The coming destruction is inevitable, but "while a tenth part yet remains in it, it shall repent. It shall be ravaged like the terebinth and the oak, of which stumps are left even when they are felled: its stump shall be a holy seed" (v. 13).[16]

How Isaiah Differs

The differences between Isaiah and Amos are more than stylistic, more than the fact that Isaiah uses more difficult vocabulary and poetry. No two prophets' style and concerns are identical; each one is unique to his particular time period and audience, and each has unique mannerisms.

As noted, classical prophets often performed odd symbolic actions (see "Doing Strange Deeds" in chapter 15). This is quite clear from Isaiah, who, for example, is told: "Go, untie the sackcloth from your loins and take your sandals off your feet" (20:2). However, in contrast to nonclassical prophets, this is not a magical activity meant to cause a miraculous outcome, but rather is an unusual act meant to symbolize something. In this case, the passage proceeds to clarify the action's symbolism:

> It is a sign and a portent for Egypt and Nubia. Just as My servant Isaiah has gone naked and barefoot for three years, so shall the king of Assyria drive off the captives of Egypt and the exiles of Nubia, young and old, naked and barefoot and with bared buttocks—to the shame of Egypt! (vv. 3–4).

Of course, the most famous of Isaiah's symbolic acts is found in 7:14: "Assuredly, my Lord will give you a sign of His own accord! Look, the young woman is with child and about to give birth to a son. Let her name him Immanuel." This JPS translation follows the Hebrew closely and presumes that this "sign" is about to take place in the near future. It differs strikingly from the famous (but less accurate) King James rendering: "Behold, a virgin shall conceive, and bear a son, and shall call his name Immanuel," which accords with Matthew 1:23 in the New Testament.

In comparison with Amos, who depicted a total exile of the Northern kingdom, Isaiah (also a Judean) claims that although much of Judah might be decimated, Jerusalem shall never fall. This theme, which scholars call "the inviolability of Jerusalem," distinguishes Isaiah's message from that of other classical prophets. Given the events that Isaiah witnessed in 701—when Sennacherib conquered the countryside but not Jerusalem (see "Jerusalem in 701" in chapter 13)—it is not surprising that he dwells on this theme. Here is one example:

> (31:5) Like the birds that fly, even so will the LORD of Hosts shield Jerusalem, shielding and saving, protecting and rescuing. . . . (8) Then Assyria shall fall, / Not by the sword of man; / A sword not of humans shall devour him. / He shall shrivel before the sword, / And his young men pine away. (9) His rock shall melt with terror, / And his officers shall collapse from weakness—Declares the LORD, who has a fire in Zion, / Who has an oven in Jerusalem.

Was this Isaiah predicting the future, or were these words written later, after

Sennacherib had left Jerusalem alone? Surely, biblical authors sometimes composed an oracle after the event that it refers to, in order to interpret for the audience what had occurred. (Scholars call this *vaticinium ex eventu*, "prophecy after the event.") Today, however, we have no way to distinguish pronouncements written in that situation.

Furthermore, the eschatology depicted in Isaiah—his view of the ideal future—is highly developed compared with Amos (see 9:11–15). Isaiah 1–39 presents no single picture of the ultimate future, either because Isaiah's views evolved during the apparently long period that he prophesied, or because some of that material postdates Isaiah son of Amoz. The most famous of these visions is:

> (2:1) The word that Isaiah son of Amoz prophesied concerning Judah and Jerusalem. / (2) In the days to come,[17] / The Mount of the LORD's House / Shall stand firm above the mountains / And tower above the hills; / And all the nations / Shall gaze on it with joy. / (3) And the many peoples shall go and say: / "Come, / Let us go up to the Mount of the LORD, / To the House of the God of Jacob; / That He may instruct us in His ways, / And that we may walk in His paths." / For instruction shall come forth from Zion, / The word of the LORD from Jerusalem. / (4) Thus He will judge among the nations / And arbitrate for the many peoples, / And they shall beat their swords into plowshares / And their spears into pruning hooks: / Nation shall not take up / Sword against nation; / They shall never again know war.

This vision of the eschaton spotlights the Jerusalem Temple; its central image is God as the just judge, ushering in universal peace. As is typical of the Bible, Isaiah assumes that the nations of the world will recognize as paramount Israel's God—and consequently, His land and Temple.

We cannot be sure who first conceived of the eschaton in this particular way. Micah includes some of the same lines:

> (4:1) In the days to come, / The Mount of the Lord's House shall stand / Firm above the mountains; / And it shall tower above the hills. / The peoples shall gaze on it with joy, / (2) And the many nations shall go and shall say: / "Come, / Let us go up to the Mount of the Lord, / To the House of the God of Jacob; / That He may instruct us in His ways, / And that we may walk in His paths." / For instruction shall come forth from Zion, / The word of the Lord from Jerusalem. / (3) Thus He will judge among the many peoples, / And arbitrate for the multitude of nations, / However distant; / And they shall beat their swords into plowshares /

> And their spears into pruning hooks. / Nation shall not take up / Sword against nation; / They shall never again know war.

These two passages are so similar that either one author copied from the other, or both copied from the same source. (This is a good illustration of one difference between modern and ancient books. In antiquity, editors copied words from one book to another with ease, believing perhaps that "this should have been what Isaiah said.")

Another well-known text in Isaiah ascribes an important role to a Davidic descendant in this new world order:

> (11:1) But a shoot shall grow out of the stump of Jesse [David's father], / A twig shall sprout from his stock. / (2) The spirit of the LORD shall alight upon him: / A spirit of wisdom and insight, / A spirit of counsel and valor, / A spirit of devotion and reverence for the LORD. / (3) He shall sense the truth by his reverence for the LORD: / He shall not judge by what his eyes behold, / Nor decide by what his ears perceive. / (4) Thus he shall judge the poor with equity / And decide with justice for the lowly of the land. / He shall strike down a land with the rod of his mouth / And slay the wicked with the breath of his lips. / (5) Justice shall be the girdle of his loins, / And faithfulness the girdle of his waist. / (6) The wolf shall dwell with the lamb, / The leopard lie down with the kid; / The calf, the beast of prey, and the fatling together, / With a little boy to herd them. / (7) The cow and the bear shall graze, / Their young shall lie down together; / And the lion, like the ox, shall eat straw. / (8) A babe shall play / Over a viper's hole, / And an infant pass his hand / Over an adder's den. / (9) In all of My sacred mount / Nothing evil or vile shall be done; / For the land shall be filled with devotion to the LORD / As water covers the sea.

This passage depicts a new order in the animal world. It suggests that this Davidic king will be the ideal judge, in contrast with chapter 2, where God has that role. Many would call this passage "messianic," in the sense that it describes the ideal future king. The English word "messiah" comes from *mashiach* (מָשִׁיחַ, "anointed"); anointing was the rite that made a person into a king. However, the Hebrew Bible never uses the term *mashiach* to describe such future kings; stated differently, in the Bible, the messiah is never called "messiah."[18] To be precise, I refer to this figure as the "future ideal Davidic king," although that is more cumbersome.

A final difference between Isaiah and Amos concerns the fundamental role of the prophet. Amos often calls upon the people to repent; this is almost totally absent in Isaiah. In fact, God gives Isaiah a most unusual mission: "Dull that people's mind, / Stop its ears, / And seal its eyes— / Lest, seeing with its eyes / And hearing with its ears, / It also grasp with its mind, / And repent and save itself" (6:10). In other words, Isaiah is supposed to make sure the people do *not* repent—and indeed the remainder of the First Isaiah does not contain a single call to repentance, in contrast to Amos.

Bringing It All Together

Of all the prophetic works, that of First Isaiah is the most beautiful yet also the most abstruse. Given its difficulty, I find it remarkable that this book was preserved at all. Clearly, some group with a fine sense of poetry and sympathy to Isaiah's message took responsibility for this.

The fact that the book proclaimed the inviolability of Jerusalem, and that Sennacherib did not conquer the city, certainly helped its prestige at first. In that sense, chapters 36–39, which describe these events, had the same impact as the verses in Amos about the quaking ground (see "The Formation of the Book of Amos" in chapter 16). Such notices vindicated the prophet as a true prophet—namely a prophet whose words came true (see Deut.18:21–22). Yet a main theme of Isaiah, the inviolability of Jerusalem, was disproved with the destruction of the Temple and the exile of 586. One might have thought that after this turn of events the book would have been treated as false prophecy—and consigned to oblivion. However, by that point, Isaiah had probably been authoritative for more than a century. Presumably its sublime style and evocative message about a better future maintained the interest of readers and scribes—and ultimately assured its place in the canon.

18

"I Will Make This House like Shiloh"

Reading Jeremiah

Primary Reading: Jeremiah 1, 3, 15, 17, 20, 21, 25, 26, 28, 31, 36, 52.

Background

The Book of Jeremiah opens with the longest superscription of any prophetic book:

> (1:1) The words of Jeremiah son of Hilkiah, one of the priests at Anathoth in the territory of Benjamin. (2) The word of the LORD came to him in the days of King Josiah son of Amon of Judah, in the thirteenth year of his reign, (3) and throughout the days of King Jehoiakim son of Josiah of Judah, and until the end of the eleventh year of King Zedekiah son of Josiah of Judah, when Jerusalem went into exile in the fifth month.

Translated into modern terms, it says that Jeremiah began to prophesy in 627 B.C.E. and finished around the time of the destruction of the Temple in 586—a period of more than forty years. (According to the Bible and other sources as well, this was an eventful time. King Josiah reformed religious practice in Judah. Babylon defeated Assyria and came into its own as a world power. Egypt briefly imposed vassal status on Judah—more than once. Babylon defeated Egypt at the Battle of Carchemish in 605. The Babylonians exiled Judah's king, Jehoiachin, in 597. Finally, they returned to destroy Jerusalem and exile much of its populace in 586.) We also learn that Jeremiah was a priest and that he hailed from Anathoth, a town about three miles (five km.) north of Jerusalem.

The book is filled with other biographical information—so much so that many scholars identify in the book a separate strand or source devoted to biography.[1] This is unique among prophetic books. As usual, we cannot be certain that any of this information is historically accurate.[2] Yet we possess an unusually rich amount of background that gives us a head start in understanding the oracles attributed to this prophet.

Reading Jeremiah after Isaiah

From the superscription, we learn that Jeremiah prophesied almost a century after Isaiah, during a very different historical period. In particular, in Isaiah's time, the Assyrians were the enemies whom Judah would overcome; for Jeremiah, the Babylonians were the enemies who would destroy the Jerusalem Temple. Thus it is not surprising that the Book of Jeremiah is quite different from those we have already seen.

Compared to the Book of Isaiah, Jeremiah is much easier to read. It contains more prose, and its poetic sections are less complex. It has fewer unique (*hapax*) words. It also gives date formulas and other clues about where one oracle begins and another ends. For example, the phrase "The word which came to Jeremiah from the LORD" appears ten times, always introducing an oracle.

Organizing Principles

Correlation of the date formulas shows that the Book of Jeremiah is not in chronological order. Like Isaiah, much of it is arranged associatively. For example, Jeremiah 20 and 21 are adjacent because they each concern a man named Pashhur (an Egyptian name), although two different Pashhurs are involved. Other passages are ordered by catchphrases. Some of the prophecies an editor has grouped topically; thus 23:9 contains a title—"Concerning the prophets"—and what follows concerns Jeremiah's prophetic adversaries (whom we would call "false prophets," though that term never appears in the Hebrew text).[3] Similarly, a collection of prophecies against the Judean kings appears under the title "To the House of the king of Judah" (21:11). A set of oracles against other peoples follows the title "The word of the LORD to the prophet Jeremiah concerning the nations" (46:1).

The books of earlier prophets—including Isaiah—do not display topical organization. An editor of the Book of Jeremiah appears to have experimented with new ways of assembling prophetic oracles into a book.

Content

The content of Jeremiah's book differs from that of Isaiah's. Scholars attribute some of these differences to the distinct historical contexts noted earlier. We can also point to the impact of each figure's own personality and style. Disparate editorial processes may account for still other differences in content.

The biggest factor, however, is that the two books wish to convey different messages. A major theme of Isaiah is the inviolability of Jerusalem: "the LORD of Hosts [will] shield Jerusalem, shielding and saving, protecting and rescuing" (Isa. 31:5). In contrast, Jeremiah's major theme is the pending destruction of Jerusalem—and of its Temple. The words of 26:6 refer to both disasters: "then I will make this House like Shiloh [the sanctuary site that the Philistines had destroyed centuries earlier], and I will make this city a curse for all the nations of earth." Furthermore, as the previous chapter noted, Isaiah focused more on explaining devastating events than on convincing the people to repent. In contrast, in much of Jeremiah, the prophet calls for repentance, as in 3:14: "turn back, rebellious children—declares the LORD."[4]

Reworking Isaiah

In some cases, Jeremiah may be basing his oracles on earlier prophecies of Isaiah, but if so, then he transforms them in a radical fashion. For example, as we saw earlier, Isaiah had viewed Assyria as God's servant, chosen to punish Israel:

> (10:5) Ha! Assyria, rod of My anger, / In whose hand, as a staff, is My fury! / (6) I send him against an ungodly nation [= Judah], / I charge him against a people that provokes Me, / To take its spoil and to seize its booty / And to make it a thing trampled / Like the mire of the streets.

(Recall that classical prophecy saw the God of Israel as a universal deity.) God, however, would "punish the majestic pride and overbearing arrogance of the king of Assyria" (v. 12); the passage had gone on to describe this punishment in great detail.

That prophesy of Isaiah's may serve as the basis of Jeremiah 25, which describes the destruction of Judah through the agency of Babylon, which has since succeeded Assyria as a great power. Jeremiah views Babylon as a new Assyria, as God's new instrument. However, Babylon's impact will be much greater than Assyria's; it will not only punish Judah, it will also destroy the Temple and exile much of the populace.

Remarkable Words for Remarkable Times

Whether or not Jeremiah 25 was based on Isaiah, it is a turning point in the book—and in Jeremiah's career. After twenty-three years of attempts to convince the people to repent, he abandons his call for repentance (vv. 1–7). Why now? The date formula gives us a clue: "the first year of King Nebuchadrezzar of Babylon" (v. 1). That was the year in which Nebuchadnezzar (the more common biblical form of the name "Nebuchadrezzar") defeated Egypt at the Battle of Carchemish (605 B.C.E.). That victory asserted Babylon's dominance of the ancient Near East.[5] The text thus connects the radical shifts in this chapter to the sudden, regionwide political transformation.

Repeatedly in earlier chapters, Jeremiah included vague threats about an enemy from the north (e.g., "Thus said the LORD: See, a people comes from the northland, / A great nation is roused / From the remotest parts of the earth"; 6:22). The historic rise of Babylon now prompts our text to clarify that this empire is that "northern" power (25:9).[6] (Prior to Babylon's hegemony, Jeremiah's audience would have found it hard to tell which foreign power he meant.)

Furthermore, the text assigns the Babylonians absolute world domination for seventy years (vv. 11–13); neither Judean repentance nor any deeds by Babylon will change this. (The number seventy may be a round number indicating the life span of a healthy person, as in Ps. 90:10, "The span of our life is seventy years." Alternatively, the author of this text perhaps knew an inscription from the earlier Assyrian king Esarhaddon, which claims that the Babylonian deity Marduk decreed seventy years of desolation for Babylon, and reapplied it here in an Israelite context.[7])

Code Words

The passage in Jeremiah 25 continues with a recurring biblical image: the "cup of wrath,"[8] filled with potent—and ultimately poisonous—drink. All the nations will drink from this cup, representing their subservience to Babylon (vv. 15–26). This section ends with a very difficult sentence: "And last of all, the king of Sheshach shall drink" (v. 26). Despite our vast knowledge of ancient Near

Eastern place-names, we cannot point to a likely candidate for "Sheshach." Adding to the puzzle is the fact that this section of verse 26 is missing from the Septuagint of Jeremiah.[9]

We can solve the puzzle with the help of another ancient version, the Aramaic translation (Targum).[10] It renders Sheshach as "Babylon." The medieval Jewish commentator Rashi (1040–1105) elaborates: "Sheshach: this is Babylon using *atbash*." *Atbash* is a system of ciphers, in which we substitute the first letter of the alphabet (*alef,* **א**) for the last (*tav,* **ת**), the second (*bet,* **ב**) for the second to last (*shin,* **ש**), etc. In English, this would be like substituting A for Z; B for Y; C for X, etc. The result of this cipher in Hebrew is that **שֵׁשַׁךְ** (Sheshach) = **בָּבֶל**; (Babylon).

Rashi's explanation fits the evidence. Thus we learn that writers used codes already in antiquity. However, their use in the Bible is extremely rare.[11] (Certainly the entire text should not be read as a code.) What circumstances prompted the code here?

Later Changes to the Book

During the Babylonian exile, some members of the defeated people reserved harsh judgments for the victors. (Compare the *postexilic* Ps. 137:8, in reference to Babylon: "a blessing on him who seizes your babies and dashes them against the rocks!") Probably at that time, a copyist of Jeremiah added 25:26b as a way to "vent" against the Babylonian masters: they too were not exempt from drinking from the prophet's poisonous "cup." Perhaps to avoid the eyes of a Babylonian censor, the copyist made the point only in code. Because this addition came relatively late in the book's development, it did not find its way into all versions of Jeremiah.

Nowadays it may seem astonishing to us that someone would add to Jeremiah's divine prophecies ("thus said the LORD, the God of Israel, to me"; 25:15). But again, such alterations clearly were the norm in the transmission of texts throughout the ancient Near East.

Indeed, 25:26b is not the only piece of the book that stands out from the rest of it. Most of the prose portions of Jeremiah show clear linguistic and theological affinities to Deuteronomy.[12] This suggests that Jeremiah went through a wholesale editing by one or more editors affiliated with the Deuteronomistic school. (Whether those editors were seventh-century Deuteronomists, or later exilic ones, or both, is unclear.[13]) In the process of making this book fit their theology, those editors added much to the "authentic" words of Jeremiah. Again, these editors believed that such is what Jeremiah should have (or must have) said, so they inserted it into his mouth.

Relationship to the Torah

Another difference between the work of (First) Isaiah and the Book of Jeremiah is the latter's greater use of what we recognize as Torah material. (As discussed in the previous chapter, although we might tend to assume that the classical prophets insisted that the people follow the Torah, in fact in their day the Torah as a book did not yet exist.)

Points of Similarity

We can point to close correlations between passages in Jeremiah and what we now know as the Torah. For example, Jeremiah poses a rhetorical question, "Will you steal and murder and commit adultery and swear falsely, and sacrifice to Baal, and follow other gods whom you have not experienced?" (7:9). Here he is accusing the people of violating the Decalogue, which he alludes to via adducing it—by and large—in reverse order. (In the Bible, such reversal indicates that a later source is citing an earlier one—it functions like quotation marks in English.[14])

In addition, Jeremiah includes several passages that insist on punctilious ritual observance. For example, one long prophecy urges strict Sabbath observance (17:19–27). Indeed, it blames the destruction of the Temple on Judah's lack of regard for the Sabbath. Thus the book strikes a different balance between ethical and "religious" concerns from that found in Isaiah (or Amos).

Other correlations with Torah traditions relate to the Book of Deuteronomy specifically. Thus Jeremiah 3:1–3 uses as a parable for Israel's behavior the legal case of a woman who divorced, married another man, divorced him, and then wants to return to her first husband. The Torah mentions this (rather obscure) legal case only in Deuteronomy 24:1–4. Similarly, Jeremiah 28 concerns Hananiah, who from the perspective of Jeremiah is a false prophet. The story quotes Jeremiah as accusing Hananiah of having "urged disloyalty" (v. 16), which matches a key term in Deuteronomy 13:6 (*dibber sarah*, דִבֶּר־סָרָה). Furthermore, the false prophet dies soon thereafter (Jer. 28:17), in accord with Deuteronomy 13:6 and 18:20.

Accounting for the Similarities

With respect to Torah traditions and literature, Jeremiah differs from earlier prophets in three ways: (1) Jeremiah himself was a priest; (2) Jeremiah lived later; (3) significant parts of "his" book postdate the life of Jeremiah.

As a prophet, Jeremiah believed he had access to divine oracles. But as a priest, he knew "instruction," that is, Torah traditions. The book underscores the priestly role as religious teacher when it recounts words of conspiracy:

> Come let us devise a plot against Jeremiah—for *torah*[תּוֹרָה, "instruction"] shall not fail from the priest, nor counsel from the wise, nor oracle from the prophet. Come, let us strike him with the tongue, and we shall no longer have to listen to all those words of his (18:18; transl. adapted).

Jeremiah's adversaries associate *torah* with priests—rather than with sages or prophets. If so, then Jeremiah the priest would naturally be more concerned with Torah traditions than the classical prophets who preceded him.

Recall critical scholars' theory that over time, Torah traditions developed slowly into an authoritative book—one that individuals could quote, cite, and interpret. Jeremiah lived in a time close to the exile; by then it is likely that J and E traditions were well known and authoritative, and many D (but not P) traditions were becoming authoritative. In addition, for the Deuteronomistic editors of the book who lived after Jeremiah, D traditions were certainly authoritative. These factors further explain why Jeremiah cites more "Torah material" than did prior prophets such as (the first) Isaiah.[15]

A New Heart and a New Covenant

Another way in which Jeremiah departs from Isaiah is in his depiction of humankind in the future. Prior biblical eschatological visions typically imagined changes only in the natural world. For example, Amos had painted a verbal picture of great agricultural abundance. The produce will be so bountiful that its harvest will still be underway when the time comes to plant again:

> A time is coming—declares the LORD— / When the plowman shall meet the reaper, / And the treader of grapes / Him who holds the bag of seed; / When the mountains shall drip wine / And all the hills shall wave with grain (9:13).

In turn, Isaiah envisioned dramatic changes in the animal kingdom:

> The wolf shall dwell with the lamb. . . . / The cow and the bear shall graze, / Their young shall lie down together; / And the lion, like the ox, shall eat straw. . . . / A babe shall play over a viper's hole . . . (11:6–8).

Jeremiah's conception, however, is even more extreme. The book foresees basic changes not only in the natural world, but also in human nature:

> (31:31) See, a time is coming—declares the LORD—when I will make a new covenant with the House of Israel and the House of Judah. (32) It will not be like the covenant I made with their fathers, when I took them by the hand to lead them out of the land of Egypt, a covenant which they broke, though I espoused them—declares the LORD. (33) But such is the covenant I will make with the House of Israel after these days—declares the LORD: I will put My Teaching into their inmost being and inscribe it upon their hearts. Then I will be their God, and they shall be My people. (34) No longer will they need to teach one another and say to one another, "Heed the LORD"; for all of them, from the least of them to the greatest, shall heed Me—declares the LORD. For I will forgive their iniquities, And remember their sins no more.

As is typical of eschatological prophecies during that period, this one does not specify the starting date of the eschaton—it is an amorphous "coming" time (v. 31). It defines that time only with respect to the covenant made in the wilderness (a bilateral suzerain-vassal treaty that promised God's protection of Israel if it observed a set of divine regulations; see "Accountability" in chapter 16). This text says that "they broke" that covenant (v. 32), referring to the people Israel. It further presumes that even if God renewed or reinstated it, the nation would break it again.

This prophecy offers a radical solution to this dilemma: "a new covenant" (v. 31). The text gives no sign that this covenant will be new in *content*. Rather, God will now "put" and "inscribe" it inside the people themselves (v. 33). In other words, they will be preprogrammed with the covenant (as firmware, in the parlance of computers), unable to break it.[16] As a result, there will be no more need for prophets to harangue the people (v. 34).

Stated differently, God will take away free choice from Israel. They will automatically abide by God's wishes, assuring divine blessing. The exile will not recur because Israel will not sin again—it cannot. Only in this way will the people's special relationship with God be established as a lasting fact: "Then I will be their God, and they shall be My people" (v. 33).[17]

An Inside Look at Being a Prophet

As noted earlier, the editing of Jeremiah has uniquely preserved a large number of biographical traditions relating to Jeremiah the person. These traditions include sections often called "confessions,"[18] first-person pieces where this prophet speaks directly to God. (These passages remind us that prophets served as intermediaries between God and the people; see "The Nature of Prophecy in Israel" in chapter 15. Although prophets usually conveyed the divine message to the nation, they did also speak *to* God.) There, Jeremiah expresses his emotions—especially concerning the difficulties of the prophetic experience—with intensity. Thus he laments, "I have become a constant laughingstock" (20:7). Sometimes the poetry used is rather flat: "Accursed be the day / That I was born! Let not the day be blessed / When my mother bore me!" (20:14). That outburst compares unfavorably to a similar speech in Job 3. Elsewhere, however, he relates one of the most powerful images of prophecy's impact on a prophet:

> I thought, "I will not mention Him, / No more will I speak in His name"— / But His word was like a raging fire in my heart, / Shut up in my bones; / I could not hold it in, I was helpless (20:9).

This is a highly poetic restatement of the idea found in Amos 3:8: "My Lord GOD has spoken, / Who can but prophesy?"

Often Jeremiah identifies with the people whom he is supposed to rebuke. For example:

> (4:19) Oh, my suffering, my suffering![19] / How I writhe! / Oh, the walls of my heart! / My heart moans within me, / I cannot be silent; / For I hear the blare of horns, / Alarms of war. / (20) Disaster overtakes disaster, / For all the land has been ravaged. / Suddenly my tents have been ravaged, / In a moment, my tent cloths. / (21) How long must I see standards / And hear the blare of horns?

The identification is even clearer in 8:21: "Because my people is shattered I am shattered; / I am dejected, seized by desolation."

Typically, Jeremiah's attitude is one of great sympathy toward the people he is condemning.[20] Quite likely, this attitude compromised his ability to function as a prophet. Perhaps this is the import when God tells him: "Assuredly, thus said the LORD: / If you turn back, I shall take you back / And you shall stand before Me; / If you produce what is noble / Out of the worthless, / You shall be My spokesman" (15:19). This verse suggests that Jeremiah has been (temporarily) "decommissioned" as prophet as a result of (unspecified) conduct. However, God is offering him a second chance to "stand before me"—namely, to hear God's word—and then to act as "spokesman."[21]

In short, these first-person narratives offer an amazing sense of how the prophetic experience affected Jeremiah. Yet we must bear in mind that these recorded "confessions" are unique. Why did those who composed prophetic books not present similar insights into the inner experience of Isaiah—or of Amos, or of other classical prophets? We do not know. Therefore we must be very careful about generalizing from Jeremiah to the other prophets.[22] We have no evidence that they felt the same way as he did.

The Preservation of Jeremiah

Jeremiah's central prediction—the impending destruction of the Temple by Nebuchadnezzar, and the exile of much of the population to Babylon—came to pass. Presumably it was for this reason that successive generations preserved the prophet's words. In fact, the book ends with a narrative probably copied from 2 Kings, about the last days of the kingdom of Judah (chap. 52). This passage, which is an appendix (see the end of chap. 51), serves to punctuate Jeremiah's core message of doom and to underscore his status as a "true" prophet.

With regard to the mechanism of transmission, the book itself describes the copying of an early form of the work. Chapter 36 opens in the fourth year of King Jehoiakim (605 B.C.E.; v. 1) with God's request that Jeremiah prepare a written record: "Get a scroll and write upon it all the words that I have spoken to you . . . to this day" (v. 2). To fulfill this request, Jeremiah called the scribe Baruch son of Neriah: "Baruch wrote down in the scroll, at Jeremiah's dictation, all the words which the LORD had spoken to him" (v. 4).

This account is remarkable on several grounds. First, another person besides the prophet transcribed the oracles.[23] Second, Jeremiah reportedly had the ability to recite or recreate all his earlier oracles from memory. Third—and most extraordinarily—he did this not once but twice. After the king had destroyed that scroll (Jehoiakim himself had burned it upon hearing it read aloud; vv. 21–25): "Jeremiah got another scroll and gave it to the scribe Baruch son of

Neriah. And at Jeremiah's dictation, he wrote in it the whole text of the scroll that King Jehoiakim of Judah had burned" (v. 32a).

Finally, the account concludes by noting that "more of the like was added." Here is direct evidence that prophetic texts existed in a variety of versions. Even after a text was complete, more could be added later.[24]

Reading Jeremiah

I have contrasted Jeremiah with Isaiah, emphasizing the many differences between the two. In so doing, I have been able to survey the variety of experiences of the classical prophet, and the range of forms of their books.

In reading each classical prophet, keep in mind the five aspects that make them a classical prophet and thus similar to the others. Both Isaiah and Jeremiah championed the views that Israel's God is a universal deity with a special focus on the people Israel; that this nation is being held accountable in regard to both cultic and ethical norms; and so forth (see chapter 16).

At the same time, remember that—due to a variety of factors—each prophet is different. Thus, Jeremiah's book is unique in its including a vast amount of biography. It stands out also by having been preserved only in a highly redacted Deuteronomistic edition. In addition, no other preserved prophet so embodies the paradox of the messenger "caught" between the two covenant partners. His mission was to view God's words "as fire, / And this people shall be firewood" (5:14). Ultimately, however, the flames consumed not only the nation, but also Jeremiah himself: "But His word was like a raging fire in my heart" (20:9).

19

"I Will Be for Them a Mini-Temple"

Reading Ezekiel

Primary Reading: Ezekiel 1–11, 16, 23, 33–40, 48.

Location, Location, Location

Ezekiel opens with a superscription that tells us exactly where and when he received his prophecy:

> (1) In the thirtieth year, on the fifth day of the fourth month, when I was in the community of exiles by the Chebar Canal, the heavens opened and I saw visions of God. (2) On the fifth day of the month—it was the fifth year of the exile of King Jehoiachin—(3) the word of the LORD came to the priest Ezekiel son of Buzi, by the Chebar Canal, in the land of the Chaldeans. And the hand of the LORD came upon him there.

This superscription sets Ezekiel apart from the other prophets we have explored in two ways: he begins to prophesy *after* the exile of 597 B.C.E., and he is prophesying outside of Israel in Babylon. As the JPS translation's note at verse 1 observes, we are unsure which year "the thirtieth year" there refers to, but verse 2 places this dedication oracle in the summer of 593. Like Jeremiah, Ezekiel is a priest,[1] but unlike his older contemporary, he begins to prophesy only "by the Chebar Canal, in the land of the Chaldeans."

In other words, Ezekiel was standing near the Babylonian city of Nippur. Some of Ezekiel's contemporaries may have had problems with this setting. After all, they probably conceived of prophecy—communications with the God of Israel—as being bound to the land of Israel. This would explain why the book of Jonah tells us that when that prophet wished to avoid heeding the divine will, he fled *mi-lifnei* YHWH (מִלִּפְנֵי יְהוָה), literally, "from before the LORD" (1:3). Similarly, many Israelites thought that God could only be worshipped within the land of Israel ("How can we sing a song of the LORD on alien soil?"; Ps. 137:4). A belief that prophecy could not occur in foreign lands continued in later times; an early rabbinic midrash, the *Mekhilta*, states: "Before the land of Israel had been especially chosen, all lands were suitable for divine revelations; after the land of Israel had been chosen, all other lands were eliminated."[2] Though not everyone in Ezekiel's community may have believed this, enough did that he felt the need to prove his legitimacy as an "off-site" prophet.

Authentication is the main function of Ezekiel's inaugural vision. That prophecy is long (more than 53 verses; 1:3b–3:16a) and detailed, because Ezekiel needs to prove that his mission is real. In the baroque quality of its detail it resembles the beginning of Deuteronomy (see "A Pious Fraud" in chapter 10), though it is even longer and stranger. Both books, for different reasons, needed to overcome obstacles to their being seen as legitimate.

Ezekiel's inaugural prophecy, like Isaiah 6 and Jeremiah 1, follows the typical form of a prophetic initiation or dedication.[3] As with Isaiah and Jeremiah, Ezekiel's call to prophecy contains the root *sh-l-ch* (שלח, "to send"), reflecting the view that the prophet is a messenger of the divine (Isa. 6:8; Jer. 1:7; Ezek. 2:3). Like them, Ezekiel performs a symbolic action with his mouth (Isa. 6:7: Jer. 1:9; Ezek. 3:2). Just like Jeremiah, Ezekiel is told, "Do not fear" (Jer. 1:8; Ezek. 2:6 [three times], 3:9). By following the same script, Ezekiel is claiming to be a true prophet like Isaiah and Jeremiah.

Yet Ezekiel exceeds the script when he sees "visions of God" (1:1). Jeremiah's inauguration had been aural only (1:4–10), though it had been followed by a set of visions. Isaiah's had been both aural and visual; he had seen "my Lord seated on a high and lofty throne; and the skirts of His robe filled the Temple" (6:1). Yet, Isaiah had described little about God's appearance other than large size[4] and being clothed. Isaiah had gone on to tersely describe seraphim—angels of sorts—and their function. In contrast, Ezekiel 1 describes God's heavenly court in great detail—of the type that only someone "who was really there" might offer. More than that, he describes what God looks like. Ezekiel the priest, using priestly language, sees "the Presence of the LORD":

> (1:26) Above the expanse over their heads was the semblance of a throne, in appearance like sapphire; and on top, upon this semblance of a throne, there was the semblance of a human form. (27) From what appeared as his loins up, I saw a gleam as of amber—what looked like a fire encased in a frame; and from what appeared as his loins down, I saw what looked like fire. There was a radiance all about him. (28) Like the appearance of the bow which shines in the clouds on a day of rain,

> such was the appearance of the surrounding radiance. That was the appearance of the semblance of the Presence of the LORD.

God is depicted indirectly: unlike the elders whom Exodus 24:10 portrays as seeing "the God of Israel" (see "In the Image of God" in chapter 6), Ezekiel sees only the "appearance of the semblance of the Presence of the LORD," which in turn takes "the semblance of a human form." Clearly, Ezekiel accepts the common biblical idea that seeing God directly is deadly (see, e.g., Judg. 13:22; contra Exodus 24). At the same time, he does not seem to accept what is implied in Deuteronomy 4:12, 15, and elsewhere, that God is incorporeal. (The latter view would become standard in medieval Judaism,[5] but it was not standard yet in Ezekiel's time.) By seeing God, Ezekiel proves that he has "stood in [God's] council" (Jer. 23:22)—and is a true prophet.

In the Shadow of Exile

We have explained the strangeness of the book's opening passage by the unusual, exilic setting of Ezekiel himself: he needed to convince the people of his legitimacy as a prophet in exile.[6] Another passage—a frequently misunderstood text—supports this interpretation. In the JPS translation, we read:

> (11:15) O mortal, I will save your brothers, your brothers, the men of your kindred, all of that very House of Israel to whom the inhabitants of Jerusalem say, "Keep far from the LORD; the land has been given as a heritage to us." (16) Say then: Thus said the Lord GOD: I have indeed removed them far among the nations and have scattered them among the countries, and I have become to them a diminished sanctity in the countries whither they have gone.

This section's style is typical of Ezekiel. It begins with "O mortal," *ben adam* (בֶּן־אָדָם), literally "son of man" but better understood as "member of humankind," and thus "mortal."[7] The text continues by quoting a popular proverb that the people are fond of saying—this is also typical for Ezekiel. However, the end of verse 16 is quite odd: "I have become to them a diminished sanctity in the countries whither they have gone."

The phrase "a diminished sanctity" renders *mikdash me'at* (מִקְדָּשׁ מְעַט). Given that the Bible frequently uses the term *mikdash* for the Temple in Jerusalem, many scholars once thought that this verse referred to the origins of the synagogue as an institution. Instead of worshipping at the full-scale Temple in Jerusalem, they suggested that in Babylon, Ezekiel instituted the synagogue as a kind of mini-Temple.[8] The verse, however, is better translated: "I [God] will be for them a mini-Temple in the countries whither they have gone." The sentiment is striking: we do not need a physical building—a Temple—because the divine presence is with us, even if that presence is not housed in a building. (This sentiment contrasts strongly with Exod. 25:8, "And let them make Me a sanctuary that I may dwell among them.") Similarly, God said to Jacob when he left Israel for Egypt, "I Myself will go down with you to Egypt, and I Myself will also bring you back" (Gen. 46:4).

The historical and geographical setting of Ezekiel also explains a great deal about the chapters that follow Ezekiel's initiation. Most classical prophets went out to the people, but in Ezekiel's case it seems that the people came to him: "Certain elders of Israel came to me and sat down before me" (14:1; cf. 20:1). Consider too his habit of making odd symbolic gestures (see especially chapters 4–5): such actions would have conveyed their message only if people were coming to his house—so as to hear his new oracles and to watch his latest weird activity.

Because Ezekiel began his career after the exile of 597 in Babylon, much of his audience believed in the truth of the prophecies of retribution by Jeremiah and others (that the Temple was about to be destroyed and that another exile was inevitable). Thus, Ezekiel had a certain cachet as a post–597 prophet-in-exile, something that Jeremiah lacked in Israel—where the population seemed more blithe (see, e.g., Jeremiah 28). In addition, the exiles probably were feeling cut off from God. Thus they would go visit Ezekiel to hear the latest divine news. This "news" he typically communicated in a straightforward, mostly prosaic fashion. Ezekiel's communication style again suggests that he did not face the challenge of the earlier prophets, who had to go out to the people and win them over with clever rhetoric.

In sum, many unique features of Ezekiel's prophecies make sense if we read them with the proper historical and geographical background. Thus, the opening passage is not a model of an alien spacecraft, as some have suggested.[9] Nor does it point to the lingering affect of childhood psychological trauma.[10] Rather, it reflects Ezekiel's successful campaign to show that he was a true prophet even though he was outside the land of Israel.

Refuting Popular Beliefs

One way that Ezekiel would get the Judeans in exile to listen was by being a careful listener himself, repeating what they said but then correcting it. Earlier I cited an instance where Ezekiel quotes a popular saying in order to show that it is false (11:15–16). Ezekiel offered Judeans something hopeful to replace their pessimistic beliefs. The famous dry bones unit (chap. 37) features the same tactic, quoting the people as saying: "Our bones are dried up, our hope is gone; we are doomed" (v. 11).[11] In another passage he gives a slightly longer rebuttal of a proverb:

> (12:22) O mortal, what is this proverb that you have in the land of Israel, that you say, "The days grow many and every vision comes to naught?" (23) Assuredly, say to them, Thus said the Lord GOD: I will put an end to this proverb; it shall not be used in Israel any more. Speak rather to them: The days draw near, and the fulfillment of every vision. (24) For there shall no longer be any false vision or soothing divination in the House of Israel. (25) But whenever I the LORD speak what I speak, that word shall be fulfilled without any delay; in your days, O rebellious breed, I will fulfill every word I speak—declares the Lord GOD.

The same pattern we saw in chapter 11 appears here: "O mortal," followed by the proverb, and then by the rebuttal. This unit likewise ends with the common prophetic formula "declares the Lord GOD," which typically concludes an oracle.

Much more significant is the proverb that he rebuts in chapter 18. There we read:

> (18:1) The word of the LORD came to me: (2) What do you mean by quoting this proverb upon the soil of Israel, "Parents eat sour grapes and their children's teeth are blunted"? (3) As I live—declares the Lord GOD—this proverb shall no longer be current among you in Israel. (4) Consider, all lives are Mine; the life of the parent and the life of the child are both Mine. The person who sins, only he shall die.

The proverb "Parents eat sour grapes and their children's teeth are blunted" might be rendered into modern English as "The parents eat Snickers® and the children get cavities." It must have been popular, since it appears also in Jeremiah 31:29: "In those days, they shall no longer say, 'Parents have eaten sour grapes and children's teeth are blunted.'" The two prophetic books, however, give a different meaning to this proverb's disuse. In Jeremiah, the proverb will only become false in the future—in the idealized time of the eschaton. But according to Ezekiel, the proverb is already false; he understood God to say that now, in his own time, "all lives are Mine [and will be judged so individually]; the life of the parent and the life of the child are both Mine [as individuals]. The person who sins, only he shall die" (v. 4).

Ezekiel therefore refutes the proverb at length. First, he treats the case of a righteous man who begets a wicked son, who in turn begets a righteous man (18:5–20). From this case he concludes: "The person who sins, he alone shall die. A child shall not share the burden of a parent's guilt, nor shall a parent share the burden of a child's guilt; the righteousness of the righteous shall be accounted to him alone, and the wickedness of the wicked shall be accounted to him alone" (18:20). Then, he proceeds to telescope these three generations into one, teaching that when wicked people repent, or righteous people become wicked, God will judge them according to their later behavior. This is another way of saying: Even though you have been exiled for your sins, all is not lost. Indeed, "it is not My desire that anyone shall die—declares the Lord GOD" (v. 32). This leads to the unit's grand conclusion: "Repent, therefore, and live!" (ibid.).

We can imagine that the exile community was feeling a huge burden of guilt. If so, this unit (chap. 18) must have meant a lot to them.

Ezekiel's address is so long, detailed, and repetitive because he is refuting not only a popular proverb, but also an authoritative set of beliefs.[12] We saw earlier that the Decalogue presumes intergenerational punishment, describing God as "an impassioned God, visiting the guilt of the parents upon the children, upon the third and upon the fourth generations of those who reject Me" (Exod. 20:5; see "The Decalogue" in chapter 8). Other biblical texts suggest that retribution functions on a corporate level, so that the community as a whole receives rewards and punishments (e.g., Deut. 11:13–21; see "Deuteronomy as a Treaty" in chapter 10). Genesis adopts such a view concerning Sodom, where the issue is *not* whether the righteous people will be saved, but how many are needed to save the city (18:22–33). According to these views, individuals cannot change their destiny in the face of family or community evil. Thus, Ezekiel is arguing against two beliefs found in a variety of biblical texts—intergenerational punishment, and corporate (communal) responsibility and retribution. That is why he needs to make his point so forcefully.

Likewise, an oracle in Ezekiel 14:12–23 makes this point repeatedly, stating that if a city were wicked, "should Noah, Daniel, and Job be in it, as I live—declares the Lord GOD—they would save neither son nor daughter; they would save themselves alone by their righteousness" (v. 20; cf. vv. 14, 18). The Daniel mentioned here is not the same as the one in the biblical book of that name—the names are spelled differently; the Daniel there is later than the Daniel of Ezekiel. Here the reference is to Danel, a righteous Canaanite who features in an Ugaritic epic.[13] Thus, "Noah, Dan[i]el, and Job" represent three righteous non-Israelites who lived long before Ezekiel. Following the principle expressed in chapter 18, "they would save themselves alone by their righteousness." Because retribution is personal and not corporate, their meritorious deeds would not benefit the community as a whole.

A Good Listener and a Crude Speaker

Ezekiel did not need to use lofty poetry or rhetoric, because (as noted earlier) people wanted to hear him: he was their primary connection with God in a society without a Temple. He listened to people's belief that God had abandoned them; then he replied so as to contradict their despair. Yet to suggest that it was his theological message alone that attracted people would be an exaggeration. In 33:32, God is portrayed as saying to Ezekiel: "To them you are just a singer of bawdy songs, who has a sweet voice and plays skillfully." This suggests that Ezekiel attracted listeners as much because of his style as because of his message.

Calling Ezekiel a "bawdy" (or "erotic") poet is striking, but it does fit the content of Ezekiel 16 and 23.[14] Many scholars actually consider these chapters to be pornographic—although this term is difficult enough to define in modern times, let alone for ancient texts from different cultures. In any case, these two chapters are sexually explicit. Chapter 16 uses the root *z-n-h* (**זנה**), "to whore, fornicate," thirteen times; chapter 23, seven times. One passage claims, "At every crossroad you built your height and you made your beauty abominable by opening your legs to anyone who passed by. Increasing your harlotry, you harloted with the Egyptians, your big-membered neighbors . . ." (16:25–26)[15] while another describes the Judeans' behavior in this manner: "They harloted in Egypt, in their youth they harloted; there their breasts were squeezed, there they pressed their virgin nipples" (23:3). Such "bawdy" talk probably attracted some of Ezekiel's audience.

The Structure of Ezekiel

The Book of Ezekiel is much more orderly than the two other large prophetic books. Its chronological setting during the Babylonian exile may have contributed to this. In addition, its editor may have been better, or that person redacted more lightly, so that it contains fewer insertions that disrupt earlier literary units. Two ordering principles are evident in the book: a chronological structure, and a collation of material into large thematic units that fit the chronology.

The oracles of Ezekiel are arranged chronologically (with one exception) and can be dated in this way:[16]

Chariot Vision	1:1	June 593 B.C.E.
Call to Be a Watchman	3:16b	June 593
Temple Vision	8:1	August/September 592
Discourse with Elders	20:1	August 591
Second Siege of Jerusalem	24:1	January 588
Judgment on Tyre	26:1	March/April 587/586
Judgment on Egypt	29:1	January 587
Judgment on Egypt	29:17	April 571
Judgment on Egypt	30:20	April 587
Judgment on Egypt	31:1	June 587
Lament over Pharaoh	32:1	March 585
Lament over Egypt	32:17	April 586
Fall of Jerusalem	33:21	December/January 586/585
New Temple Vision	40:1	April 573

A second pattern overlaps with this first one: two "watchman" oracles frame a large section of the book between them. Both of them charge Ezekiel with forewarning both the wicked and the righteous among the people. The first oracle reads:

> (3:17) O mortal, I appoint you watchman for the House of Israel; and when you hear a word from My mouth, you must warn them for Me. (18) If I say to a wicked man, "You shall die," and you do not warn him—you do not speak to warn the wicked man of his wicked course in order to save his life—he, the wicked man, shall die for his iniquity, but I will require a reckoning for his blood from you. (19) But if you do warn the wicked man, and he does not turn back from his wickedness and his wicked course, he shall die for his iniquity, but you will have saved your own life. (20) Again, if a righteous man abandons his righteousness and does wrong, when I put a stumbling block before him, he shall die. He shall die for his sins; the righteous deeds that he did shall not be remembered; but because you did not warn him, I will require a reckoning for his blood from you. (21) If, however, you warn the righteous man not to sin, and he, the righteous, does not sin, he shall live because he took warning, and you will have saved your own life.

The second such oracle reads:

> (33:7) Now, O mortal, I have appointed you a watchman for the House of Israel; and whenever you hear a message from My mouth, you must transmit My warning to them. (8) When I say to the wicked, "Wicked man, you shall die," but you have not spoken to warn the wicked man against his way, he, that wicked man, shall die for his sins, but I will demand a reckoning for his blood from you. (9) But if you have warned the wicked man to turn back from his way, and he has not turned from his way, he shall die for his own sins, but you will have saved your life.

These same two chapters also deal with Ezekiel's silence—an issue that biblical scholars do not fully understand, since the voluble Ezekiel is nowhere directly depicted as being silent![17] Yet God suggests as much in telling him: "And I will make your tongue cleave to your palate, and you shall be dumb; you shall not be a reprover to them, for they are a rebellious breed" (3:26), while the other passage notes:

> (33:21) In the twelfth year of our exile, on the fifth day of the tenth month, a fugitive came to me from Jerusalem and reported, "The city has fallen." (22) Now the hand of the LORD had come upon me the evening before the fugitive arrived, and He opened my mouth before he came to me in the morning; thus my mouth was opened and I was no longer speechless.

Thus, Ezekiel's hearing of the destruction of the city and the Temple in 586 represents a turning point in the book.

Taking into account these factors—the "watchman" frame and the trope of silence—we can outline the book's structure as follows:

I.	1:1–3:15	Dedication as prophet
II.	3:16–24:27	Oracles of retribution against Israel
III.	25–32	Oracles against the nations
IV.	33–48	Oracles of consolation (after the fall of Jerusalem in 586)

This outline captures the ironic arc of the book: until the Temple was destroyed, Ezekiel was a prophet of retribution, explaining to the exiles why the destruction was about to transpire, even though he stressed the opportunity to repent (in contrast with Jeremiah 25). Once the news of the destruction arrived, Ezekiel changed course; indeed, he shifted his tack by 180 degrees. He became a prophet of consolation.

Next we will examine Ezekiel's transformation, highlighting the contrasting themes between sections II–III and section IV. Although 3:16–24:27 and 33–48 are distinct parts of the book, they are best read and understood juxtaposed to one another.

From Divine Abandonment to "The LORD Is There"

According to ancient Near Eastern conceptions, deities resided in their temples, protecting their people and their temples while present at these holy sites. The biblical verse quoted earlier exemplifies this view: "Let them make Me a sanctuary that I may dwell among them" (Exod. 25:8). As we observed earlier in discussing Leviticus (chapter 9), some Israelites concentrated on ensuring that God remained at the Temple—protecting it and the people of the covenant. Various actions that gave offense could conceivably cause the deity to depart.

Some scholars have called this motif of a god leaving a temple "divine abandonment." It may be seen in the following inscription of the Assyrian king Esarhaddon (681–669): "The lord of the gods, Marduk, was angry. He planned evil; to wipe out the land, to destroy its inhabitants . . . an evil curse was on his lips." The gods and goddesses who dwell in it (i.e., the temple Esagila) fled like birds and went up to heaven. The protective gods [. . . ran] off and withdrew.[18] Ezekiel, living in Babylon, knew and adopted this motif. He described the gradual departure of the Presence in several sections throughout the first eleven chapters:

> (8:3) He stretched out the form of a hand, and took me by the hair of my head. A spirit lifted me up between heaven and earth and brought me in visions of God to Jerusalem, to the entrance of the Penimith Gate that faces north; that was the site of the infuriating image that provokes fury. (4) And the Presence of the God of Israel appeared there, like the vision that I had seen in the valley.
>
> (10:4) But when the Presence of the LORD moved from the cherubs to the platform of the House, the House was filled with the cloud, and the court was filled with the radiance of the Presence of the LORD.
>
> (11:22) Then the cherubs, with the wheels beside them, lifted their wings, while the Presence of the God of Israel rested above them.

> (23) The Presence of the LORD ascended from the midst of the city and stood on the hill east of the city.

Once the Presence had left the Temple, the Babylonians could destroy it.

These chapters, however, not only describe "divine abandonment, " but also justify in detail why God is leaving. God is furious, although the focus of divine anger—unlike in Amos and Isaiah—is not ethical concerns. True, some moral considerations are highlighted: "The iniquity of the Houses of Judah and Israel is very very great, the land is full of crime and the city is full of corruption" (9:9; see also chap. 22). More typical, however, are texts such as this one:

> (8:6) And He said to me, "Mortal, do you see what they are doing, the terrible abominations that the House of Israel is practicing here, to drive Me far from My Sanctuary? You shall yet see even greater abominations!" (7) Then He brought me to the entrance of the court; and I looked, and there was a hole in the wall. (8) He said to me, "Mortal, break through the wall"; so I broke through the wall and found an entrance. (9) And He said to me, "Enter and see the vile abominations that they are practicing here." (10) I entered and looked, and there all detestable forms of creeping things and beasts and all the fetishes of the House of Israel were depicted over the entire wall. (11) Before them stood seventy men, elders of the House of Israel, with Jaazaniah son of Shaphan standing in their midst. Everyone had a censer in his hand, and a thick cloud of incense smoke ascended.

We do not know whether the activities described here really happened.[19] Either way, the point here is that Ezekiel imagines that God is letting the Temple be destroyed for cultic infractions, not for ethical violations. Ironically, while committing these cultic sins, the people of Israel think: "The LORD does not see us; the LORD has abandoned the country" (8:12). They are dead wrong: God does see them and has not yet abandoned the country, but—as a result of their "abominations"—is about to do so.

If a main theme of the retribution section is divine abandonment, it should not surprise us that the main theme of the consolation section is the return of the divine Presence. Chapters 40–48 describe Israel after its future restoration and return from exile. These chapters focus on the new Temple to be built in Jerusalem.[20] This unit ends by declaring that the city will eventually be renamed "The LORD Is There" (48:35). Jerusalem's new name will be a reversal of the divine abandonment described earlier in the book.

The last section reverses other earlier motifs as well. Instead of Israel's being victim of the Day of the LORD, chapters 38–39 famously recount the war of Gog[21] and Magog, where Israel's enemies will fall. In 36:2, Ezekiel prophesies "to the mountains of Israel," overturning his earlier prophecy of rebuke of 6:2, also addressed "to the mountains of Israel." Chapter 34 is especially clever in its reversal. It begins like a prophecy of retribution: "O mortal, prophesy against the shepherds [i.e., kings] of Israel. . . . Thus said the Lord GOD: I am going to deal with the shepherds!" (vv. 2–10). However, it moves from retribution to consolation, noting that these derelict kings will be replaced by God as king *and* by an ideal Davidic king: "Then I will appoint a single shepherd over them to tend them—My servant David. He shall tend them, he shall be a shepherd to them. I the LORD will be their God, and My servant David shall be a ruler among them—I the LORD have spoken" (vv. 23–24).[22]

One can imagine the Judeans in exile, feeling their own guilt (and the guilt of their ancestors, despite his reassurances in chapters 14 and 18). They must have wondered: "Do we really deserve to be forgiven and restored?" A phrase appearing in the book fifty-eight times (out of seventy-two times in the Bible) relates why Israel will be redeemed: it is not because of their merit, but so that "they shall know that I am the LORD."[23] The following section from the prophecies of consolation makes clear what this ubiquitous phrase means:

> (36:21) Therefore I am concerned for My holy name, which the House of Israel have caused to be profaned among the nations to which they have come. (22) Say to the House of Israel: Thus said the Lord GOD: Not for your sake will I act, O House of Israel, but for My holy name, which you have caused to be profaned among the nations to which you have come. (23) I will sanctify My great name which has been profaned among the nations—among whom you have caused it to be profaned. And the nations shall know that I am the LORD—declares the Lord GOD—when I manifest My holiness before their eyes through you. . . . (32) Not for your sake will I act—declares the Lord GOD—take good note! Be ashamed and humiliated because of your ways, O House of Israel! . . . (36) And the nations that are left around you shall know that I the LORD have rebuilt the ravaged places and replanted the desolate land. I the LORD have spoken and will act.

In other words, Israel is God's people; and now that God has punished Israel because it broke the covenant, that punishment—their downtrodden state—could be mistaken as a sign of His weakness. Thus, God will restore Israel not because they are deserving, but because their continued punishment is liable to reflect poorly on Him.

The various prophecies of consolation fit together quite tightly, and address the same themes as the rest of the book. Since God is with this people in exile, functioning as a mini-Temple, Israel need not feel hopeless. Likewise, since God will not place the sins of the parents on the children, Israel need not feel guilty. God will overturn earlier prophecies of doom. God will forgive Israel, not for their sake, but for the sake of God's "holy name." Thus, like contemporary books written by a single author, the parts of the Book of Ezekiel fit together. This coherence, however, is most evident when the book is read as a product of its time and place: an ancient Babylonian text, written in response to the tribulations of the Babylonian Jewish community.

20

"Comfort, Oh Comfort My People"

The Exile and Beyond

Primary Reading: Isaiah 40, 41, 44, 45, 49, 51, 53, 55, 63; Haggai 2; Ezra 9–10; Nehemiah 8, 13.

Historical Background

Nabunaid, or Nabonidus, the last king of Babylon, reigned from 556–539 B.C.E.; he directed that the moon god, Sin, be elevated over Marduk, the traditional high god of the Babylonians. Probably this action struck many of his subjects as odd; surely it offended the priests of Marduk. When the Persian king, Cyrus the Great, attacked Babylon in October 539, he was able to conquer the city bloodlessly with the help of the populace, especially the displaced priests of Marduk. Thus Cyrus, who reigned until 530, established the Achaemenid Persian empire that would last for two centuries, until Alexander the Great's victory over Persia. His administration divided the empire into provinces; the territory of the erstwhile kingdom of Judah was now known as the province of Yehud.

The prophecies of Isaiah 40–66 and other literature of the late exilic and early postexilic periods connect deeply to this background. The Persians tolerated other religions, and they allowed various peoples exiled by the Babylonians to return to their homelands. The new rulers even returned the statues and other religious items that the Babylonians had captured and put in storage. In 538, the Judeans received their Temple vessels and were encouraged to return to Yehud. At first, most Judeans must have viewed this dramatic turnaround as fulfillment of the prophecy of Jeremiah 25, which promised restoration of the kingdom after a period of seventy years of domination by Babylon.

At this time, Yehud was an underdeveloped, backwater province. Rather than "return" there, many Judeans preferred to stay in the cosmopolitan cities where they had become established. These people—called *yehudim* ("Jews"; see

n. 4 in chapter 14)—created a voluntary diaspora community in Babylon. Such communities also formed in other cities throughout the empire.

Meanwhile, back in Jerusalem, the Jews who did resettle there did not succeed in rebuilding the Temple immediately. They did not begin work until 520, completing it four years later. This Second Temple was smaller and much less magnificent than the First Temple. In general, the tiny province of Yehud, centered on Jerusalem, remained impoverished and weak throughout the Persian period, both politically and militarily.[1]

Who Saved Babylon?

A document called the Cyrus Cylinder sheds a great deal of light on the rise of Cyrus.[2] It is written in Akkadian, the language of the Babylonians. It describes the failing of King Nabunaid (Nabonidus), "[an] incompetent person" who "did away with the worship of Marduk, the king of gods; he continually did evil against his [Marduk's] city." The cylinder goes on to describe how Marduk responded to the situation:

> Upon [hearing] their cries, the lord of the gods [Marduk] became furiously angry [and he left] their borders. . . . Marduk [ ] turned [?] toward all the habitations that were abandoned and all the people of Sumer and Akkad who had become corpses; [he was recon]ciled and had mercy [upon them]. He surveyed and looked throughout all the lands, searching for a righteous king whom he could support. He called out his name: Cyrus, king of Anshan; he proclaimed his name to be king over all [the world]. . . . He [Marduk] ordered him to march to his city Babylon. . . . He made him enter his city Babylon without fighting or battle; he saved Babylon from hardship. He delivered Nabonidus, the king who did not revere him, into his hands.

This is a remarkable piece of propaganda from the priests of Marduk, who were extremely powerful. This context gives us a way to understand some of Deutero-Isaiah's prophecies. It also shows how useful it is to read biblical works against their ancient Near Eastern background, which modern archaeology and biblical studies have made possible.

For Babylonian Jews who remained steadfast to their religion, the concept that Marduk chose Cyrus was unthinkable, so they developed a counter-theology. Several units in Isaiah from chapter 40 on read as if they respond directly to (that is, are polemics against) the ideas found in the Cyrus cylinder. Here are two examples:

(41:1) Stand silent before Me, coastlands, / And let nations renew their strength. / Let them approach to state their case; / Let us come forward together for argument. / (2) Who has roused a victor from the East, / Summoned him to His service? / Has delivered up nations to him, / And trodden sovereigns down? / Has rendered their swords like dust, / Their bows like wind-blown straw? / (3) He pursues them, he goes on unscathed; / No shackle is placed on his feet. / (4) Who has wrought and achieved this? / He who announced the generations from the start— / I, the LORD, who was first / And will be with the last as well.

(45:1) Thus said the LORD to Cyrus, / His anointed one ["messiah"]— / Whose right hand He has grasped, / Treading down nations before him, / Ungirding the loins of kings, / Opening doors before him / And letting no gate stay shut: / (2) I will march before you / And level the hills that loom up; / I will shatter doors of bronze / And cut down iron bars. / (3) I will give you treasures concealed in the dark / And secret hoards— / So that you may know that it is I the LORD, / The God of Israel, who call you by name. / (4) For the sake of My servant Jacob, / Israel My chosen one, / I call you by name, / I hail you by title, though you have not known Me. / (5) I am the LORD and there is none else; / Beside Me, there is no god. / I engird you, though you have not known Me, / (6) So that they may know, from east to west, / That there is none but Me. / I am the LORD and there is none else.

The phrase "I call you by name" (v. 4) is especially evocative, matching exactly the statement in the Cyrus Cylinder: "He [Marduk] called out his name: Cyrus, king of Anshan; he proclaimed his name." As we shall see, the polemic between those backing Marduk the high-god of the Babylonians, and those backing the God of the Jews, extended far beyond these two passages.

The two prophecies cited above derive from an anonymous prophet whose oracles have been appended to Isaiah 1–39. We do not know if Isaiah 40–66 represents the work of a single prophet or of more than one. Most scholars suppose that two authors composed this section; they call the author of chapters 40–55 "Deutero-Isaiah," and the author of chapters 56–66 "Trito-Isaiah."[3] (See "Out of Many, One" in chapter 17.) Scholars have reached this conclusion in part because 40–55 is almost entirely consolation, and does not reflect the return to Israel, whereas 56–66 does reflect this return and includes substantial rebuke. Exactly how and why someone attached these oracles to those of an earlier prophet is unknown;[4] scholars are certain, however, that 40–66 does not reflect the work of the eighth-century Isaiah son of Amoz.

The following sections will treat Isaiah 40–66 as one unit, even though the same hand may not have written all of that section.

The Message of Deutero-Isaiah

Compared to previous prophets, Isaiah 40–66 presents many new themes. Some of the differences may be due to the unique historical setting of the prophecies, while other aspects reflect the ongoing evolution of Israelite religion. These passages place tremendous emphasis on "radical monotheism" (see n. 30 in chapter 10), which likely belongs to the latter category. Whereas the sentiments of Deuteronomy 4:35 ("It has been clearly demonstrated to you that the LORD alone is God; there is none beside Him") are rare in preexilic texts,[5] they suffuse this part of Isaiah. For example, Isaiah 45:6 similarly notes: "I am the LORD and there is none else." The prophet again and again equates polytheistic gods with their idols, depicting both as powerless fetishes.[6] The following sarcastic passage is typical:

> (44:9) The makers of idols / All work to no purpose; / And the things they treasure / Can do no good, / As they themselves can testify. / They neither look nor think, / And so they shall be shamed. / (10) Who would fashion a god / Or cast a statue / That can do no good? / (11) Lo, all its adherents shall be shamed; / They are craftsmen, are merely human. / Let them all assemble and stand up! / They shall be cowed, and they shall be shamed. / (12) The craftsman in iron, with his tools, / Works it over charcoal / And fashions it by hammering, / Working with the strength of his arm. / Should he go hungry, his strength would ebb; / Should he drink no water, he would grow faint. / 13) The craftsman in wood measures with a line / And marks out a shape with a stylus; / He forms it with scraping tools, / Marking it out with a compass. / He gives it a human form, / The beauty of a man, to dwell in a shrine. / (14) For his use he cuts down cedars; / He chooses plane trees and oaks. / He sets aside trees of the forest; / Or plants firs, and the rain makes them grow. / (15) All this serves man for fuel: / He takes some to warm himself, / And he builds a fire and bakes bread. / He also makes a god of it and worships it, / Fashions an idol and bows down to it! / (16) Part of it he burns in a fire: / On that part he roasts meat, / He eats the roast and is sated; / He also warms himself and cries, "Ah, / I am warm! I can feel the heat!" / (17) Of the rest he makes a god—his own carving! / He bows down to it, worships it; / He prays to it and cries, / "Save me, for you are my god!" / (18) They have no wit or judgment: / Their eyes are

> besmeared, and they see not; / Their minds, and they cannot think. / (19) They do not give thought, / They lack the wit and judgment to say: / "Part of it I burned in a fire; / I also baked bread on the coals, / I roasted meat and ate it— / Should I make the rest an abhorrence? / Should I bow to a block of wood?" / (20) He pursues ashes! / A deluded mind has led him astray, / And he cannot save himself; / He never says to himself, / "The thing in my hand is a fraud!"

This passage, like others in the book, is unfair—it confuses the deity with the representation of the deity. The Mesopotamians who worshipped the statue of Marduk did not believe it was really Marduk. In their eyes, the statue stood for Marduk, and Marduk might have been especially present in it, but the god was not confined to the statue, and the statue was not the god.[7] Nonetheless, Deutero-Isaiah depicts other gods in this polemical fashion in order to argue against the existence of all other deities.

Deutero-Isaiah also emphasized that the God of Israel—the only God—is extremely powerful. One oracle uses the complex image of God the warrior, who tramples enemies as farmers trample grapes to make wine:

> (63:3) I trod out a vintage alone; / Of the peoples no man was with Me. / I trod them down in My anger, / Trampled them in My rage; / Their lifeblood bespattered My garments, / And all My clothing was stained. / (4) For I had planned a day of vengeance, / And My year of redemption arrived. / (5) Then I looked, but there was none to help; / I stared, but there was none to aid— / So My own arm wrought the triumph, / And My own rage was My aid. / (6) I trampled peoples in My anger, / I made them drunk with My rage, / And I hurled their glory to the ground.

Time and again the prophet repeats the theme of YHWH's power, in order to convince the people that God does have the ability to return them to the land of Israel. Other texts recall God's past accomplishments, as a prelude to their repetition in the near future:

> (51:9) Awake, awake, clothe yourself with splendor. / O arm of the LORD! / Awake as in days of old, / As in former ages! / It was you that hacked Rahab in pieces, / That pierced the Dragon. / (10) It was you that dried up the Sea, / The waters of the great deep; / That made the abysses of the Sea / A road the redeemed might walk. / (11) So let the ransomed of the LORD return, / And come with shouting to Zion, / Crowned with joy everlasting. / Let them attain joy and gladness, / While sorrow and sighing flee.

This passage recalls an ancient Israelite myth, in which God creates the world and becomes king by quelling the water deities.[8] After stating that God will soon reenact this act of prowess, the prophet alludes to the Exodus (vv. 10–11). Indeed, the portrayal of the return to Zion as a new Exodus runs like a thread through the fabric of Deutero-Isaiah.[9] The God who has shown unmatched power in these two moments—in forming the world and in forming Israel—can surely do it again.

Not only God, but also Israel has a major role to play in the people's redemption. God is strong enough to fulfill the part of redeemer, but is Israel deserving? Like Ezekiel (see chapter 19), this prophet deals with the guilt that the exiles must have felt. This prophet, too, assuages their guilt, convincing them that they are worthy to return. Already in the initial prophecy, Deutero-Isaiah suggests that Israel's "term of service is over . . . / her iniquity is expiated; / For she has received at the hand of the LORD / Double for all her sins" (40:2). Theologically, this is an audacious and even disturbing notion—Judah has been "over-punished"! Surely, however, it could help a group wracked by guilt.

Another way that Deutero-Isaiah bolsters the confidence of the Judeans in exile is by writing them into the eternal, unconditional covenant granted to David: "Incline your ear and come to Me; / Hearken, and you shall be revived. / And I will make with you [plural, meaning, Israel as a whole] an everlasting covenant, / The enduring loyalty promised to David" (55:3). Israel—rather than only David's descendants—becomes the beneficiary of David's covenant.[10] The prophet revalues the Davidic covenant by democratizing it to all Israel. Not surprisingly, therefore, Deutero-Isaiah—in contrast to most earlier classical prophets—nowhere depicts a Davidic descendant as the future ideal king.

In some places, Isaiah 40–66 depicts a "kinder, gentler" deity by depicting God as female.[11] This new imagery helped convince the Judeans that God, like a mother, would aid them, by restoring them to their homeland. The prophet accomplishes the change not by using feminine verbs or pronouns of God (which the Bible never employs) but by using feminine metaphors and similes as images of God. For example:

> (49:14) Zion says, / "The LORD has forsaken me, / My Lord has forgotten me." / (15) Can a woman forget her baby, / Or disown the child of her womb? / Though she might forget, / I never could forget you. / (16) See, I have engraved you / On the palms of My hands, / Your walls are ever before Me.

Here God is "The Excellent Mother" who cares for her children so much that their picture is engraved or tattooed on her palms. Certainly, such a devoted mother deserves great trust!

Some of the most remarkable passages in Deutero-Isaiah help Israel to understand why it deserves to be redeemed, especially passages concerning a "suffering servant." That servant's identity may not be consistent in all of the passages that invoke this image. The longest such passage would later play a significant role in early Christianity and has been a part of Jewish-Christian polemics throughout the ages. It reads:

> (53:1) "Who can believe what we have heard? / Upon whom has the arm of the LORD been revealed? / (2) For he has grown, by His favor, like a tree crown, / Like a tree trunk out of arid ground. / He had no form or beauty, that we should look at him: / No charm, that we should find him pleasing. / (3) He was despised, shunned by men, / A man of suffering, familiar with disease. / As one who hid his face from us, / He was despised, we held him of no account. / (4) Yet it was our sickness that he was bearing, / Our suffering that he endured. / We accounted him plagued, / Smitten and afflicted by God; / (5) But he was wounded because of our sins, / Crushed because of our iniquities. / He bore the chastisement that made us whole, / And by his bruises we were healed. / (6) We all went astray like sheep, / Each going his own way; / And the LORD visited upon him / The guilt of all of us." / (7) He was maltreated, yet he was submissive, / He did not open his mouth; / Like a sheep being led to slaughter, / Like a ewe, dumb before those who shear her, / He did not open his mouth. / (8) By oppressive judgment he was taken away, / Who could describe his abode? / For he was cut off from the land of the living / Through the sin of my people, who deserved the punishment. / (9) And his grave was set among the wicked, / And with the rich, in his death— / Though he had done no injustice / And had spoken no falsehood. / (10) But the LORD chose to crush him by disease, / That, if he made himself an offering for guilt, / He might see offspring and have long life, / And that through him the LORD's purpose might prosper. / (11) Out of his anguish he shall see it; / He shall enjoy it to the full through his devotion. / "My righteous servant makes the many righteous, / It is their punishment that he bears; / (12) Assuredly, I will give him the many as his portion, / He shall receive the multitude as his spoil. / For he exposed himself to death / And was numbered among the sinners, / Whereas he bore the guilt of the many / And made intercession for sinners."

Here the prophet does not specify the identity of the servant. Given that Deutero-Isaiah often calls Israel "my servant" (e.g., "But hear, now, O Jacob My servant, / Israel whom I have chosen!" in 44:1), the servant might be Israel as a whole.[12] But other readings are also plausible. Is the prophet referring to a past, present, or future figure? Is an individual meant, or a collective? These questions have been the subject of heated debate for centuries. Definitive answers seem to be beyond our reach.

In any case, the text newly emphasizes a type of vicarious punishment. That the unnamed servant suffered for the sake of others (53:4) and was injured (v. 5) in punishment for their guilt (vv. 6, 11–12) is an extreme version of the concept that Ezekiel so firmly rejected (see "Refuting Popular Beliefs" in chapter 19). From a historical perspective, it is likely that the exiles' excessive guilt is what evoked this theological idea. As with the annual scapegoat ritual in the now-vanished Temple (see Leviticus 16), they could understand their guilt as having been transferred onto another party.

Cognitive Dissonance

As we have seen, some of the prophecies in Isaiah 40–66 did come true, especially those concerning Cyrus, the conqueror of Babylon who redeemed the exiled Judeans. However, many oracles did not come true. For example, most of the Judeans did not return to their ancestral land. Those who did often did not enjoy the easy journey that the prophet predicted:

> (40:3) A voice rings out: "Clear in the desert / A road for the LORD! / Level in the wilderness / A highway for our God! / (4) Let every valley be raised, / Every hill and mount made low. / Let the rugged ground become level / And the ridges become a plain. / (5) The Presence of the LORD shall appear, / And all flesh, as one, shall behold— / For the LORD Himself has spoken." . . . / (9) Ascend a lofty mountain, / O herald of joy to Zion; / Raise your voice with power, / O herald of joy to Jerusalem— / Raise it, have no fear; / Announce to the cities of Judah: / Behold your God! / (10) Behold, the Lord GOD comes in might, / And His arm wins triumph for Him; / See, His reward is with Him, / His recompense before Him. / (11) Like a shepherd He pastures His flock: / He gathers the lambs in His arms / And carries them in His bosom; / Gently He drives the mother sheep.

For the hard-pressed returnees, the gap between that prophecy and their reality must have been unsettling, prompting not only disappointment but cognitive dissonance.[13]

The prophetic texts we will now consider use several approaches to combat the perceived dissonance. One approach is to reinterpret the prophecies of consolation so that they remain true. A simple instance of this appears in the second chapter of Haggai, one of the "minor" (that is, short) prophetic texts (see n. 18 in chapter 2). He explicitly recognizes the failures of the restoration: "Who is there left among you who saw this House in its former splendor? How does it look to you now? It must seem like nothing to you" (2:3). Yet, he continues by giving a promise:

> (2:6) For thus said the LORD of Hosts: In just a little while longer I will shake the heavens and the earth, the sea and the dry land; (7) I will shake all the nations. And the precious things of all the nations shall come here, and I will fill this House with glory, said the LORD of Hosts. (8) Silver is Mine and gold is Mine—says the LORD of Hosts. (9) The glory of this latter House shall be greater than that of the former one, said the LORD of Hosts; and in this place I will grant prosperity—declares the LORD of Hosts.

The key phrase here is "In just a little while longer"—the ideal future has clearly not arrived, but it is around the corner.[14] Haggai's early prophecies seem to have been instrumental in spurring the rebuilding the Second Temple. (We will examine more examples of the reinterpretation of earlier oracles in the next chapter on Daniel and apocalyptic literature.)

A second approach to relieve cognitive dissonance is to ignore the discrepancies, focusing instead on the theme of retribution. This is especially obvious in Ezra-Nehemiah.[15] For example, when Nehemiah saw that the Jews were not properly observing the Sabbath, he "censured the nobles of Judah, saying to them, 'What evil thing is this that you are doing, profaning the sabbath day! This is just what your ancestors did, and for it God brought all this misfortune on this city; and now you give cause for further wrath against Israel by profaning the sabbath!'" (Neh. 13:17–18). These verses most likely allude to Jeremiah 17:27: "But if you do not obey My command to hallow the sabbath day and to carry in no burdens through the gates of Jerusalem on the sabbath day, then I will set fire to its gates; it shall consume the fortresses of Jerusalem and it shall not be extinguished." Ezra-Nehemiah's emphasis is not on the consolations but on the prophecies of retribution of previous prophets, and its main concern is making sure that already fulfilled prophecies will not have a reason to be fulfilled again.

In their concern with retribution, the authors of Ezra-Nehemiah were sometimes stringent, "making a fence around the Torah" (see "Solomon" in chapter 13). Ezra's blanket proscription of intermarriage is a strong example of this. Earlier sources had forbidden various specific groups as marriage partners (ibid.); no such text had advocated expelling the children of an intermarried couple from the community. But Ezra 9:2 notes: "They have taken their daughters as wives for themselves and for their sons, so that the holy seed has become intermingled with the peoples of the land."[16] According to that book, the Jews made a covenant to expel not only these foreign wives, but also "those who have been born to them" (Ezra 10:3). This decision grew out of a close study of Torah and prophetic texts,[17] combined with a great concern by some that the exile and the destruction of the Temple not be repeated.

One Important Implication

This survey of postexilic literature suggests that the people in that period studied Torah and other texts closely. This image is corroborated by the description in Nehemiah of the great covenant made in Jerusalem, where

> (8:1) the entire people assembled as one man in the square before the Water Gate, and they asked Ezra the scribe to bring the scroll of the Teaching of Moses with which the LORD had charged Israel. . . . (5) Ezra opened the scroll in the sight of all the people, for he was above all the people; as he opened it, all the people stood up. . . . (8) They read from the scroll of the Teaching of God, translating it and giving the sense; so they understood the reading.

As the passage continues, we learn that specific sections were read and listened to carefully, and then implemented. For example, the people celebrated dwelling in booths during Sukkot, after the scribes read aloud the section about the relevant rites: "They found written in the Teaching that the LORD had commanded Moses that the Israelites must dwell in booths during the festival of the seventh month" (v. 14).

To understand the divine will, such texts suggest, prophecy was no longer necessary. Old, authoritative texts—the Torah and the prophetic books, which became so important in the exilic period—retained their importance and could be studied to determine the divine will as it applied to the contemporary situation. The prophetic impulse did not stop at that point,[18] but, as we will see in the next chapter, prophecy went through remarkable changes.

21

"Those That Sleep in the Dust . . . Will Awake"

Zechariah, Apocalyptic Literature, and Daniel

Primary Reading: Zechariah 1, 2, 5, 7, 8; Daniel 1–6, 8, 9, 12.

Zechariah Stands on a Cusp

Zechariah and the Classical Prophets

The first part of Zechariah (chaps. 1–8) forms a literary unit composed a little more than 2500 years ago, in the late sixth century B.C.E. The rest of the book seems unrelated to this first part; on those grounds, it seems that a later editor added the latter part (just as someone affixed Isaiah 40–66 to oracles by the earlier prophet Isaiah son of Amoz; see "Out of Many, One" in chapter 17).[1] In this chapter, I will focus only on the first portion of the book.

Zechariah 1–8 share many features with the classical prophetic books (see above, chapters 15–19, esp. chapter 16). Zechariah employs many of classical prophecy's typical formulas, such as *ne'um* YHWH ("—declares the LORD") and *ko amar* YHWH ("Thus said the LORD:"). Like the classical prophets, Zechariah depicts God as universal ("The many peoples and the multitude of nations shall come to seek the LORD of Hosts in Jerusalem and to entreat the favor of the LORD"; 8:22). These prophecies presume a special relationship between Israel and its God that entails obligations on the part of each party ("Turn back to me—says the LORD of Hosts—and I will turn back to you"; 1:3). Israel's obligations include ethical as well as cultic responsibilities ("These are the things you are to do: Speak the truth to one another, render true and perfect justice in your gates. And do not contrive evil against one another, and do not love perjury, because all those are things that I hate—declares the LORD"; 8:16–17). Although

Zechariah never uses the classical prophet's phrase "Day of the LORD," he seems to have that notion in mind ("In that day many nations will attach themselves to the LORD and become His people, and He will dwell in your midst. Then you will know that I was sent to you by the LORD of Hosts"; 2:15). According to Zechariah, this day will be a rather peaceful, pro-Israel occasion.

Thus Zechariah subscribes to four of the five main ideas of classical prophecy. At the same time, he significantly alters the fifth characteristic idea—about a "remnant." Earlier prophets had predicted the return of a remnant, but Zechariah never does so. Why not? Because he believes that his generation, which has experienced both exile and return, *is the remnant*. This idea appears several times:

> (8:6) Thus said the LORD of Hosts: Though it will seem impossible to the remnant of this people in those days, shall it also be impossible to Me?—declares the LORD of Hosts.

> (8:11) But now I will not treat the remnant of this people as before—declares the LORD of Hosts—(12) but what it sows shall prosper: The vine shall produce its fruit, the ground shall produce its yield, and the skies shall provide their moisture. I will bestow all these things upon the remnant of this people.

For Zechariah, there is no future remnant because he believes that he is already living in that future.

Because Zechariah has identified himself as part of the remnant that others prophesied about, he uses phrases that set him apart from earlier prophets. Key among these is the idea of "the earlier prophets"—found only in this book—which Zechariah uses three times:

> (1:4) Do not be like your fathers! For when the earlier prophets called to them, "Thus said the LORD of Hosts: Come, turn back from your evil ways and your evil deeds," they did not obey or give heed to Me—declares the LORD.

> (7:7) Look, this is the message that the LORD proclaimed through the earlier prophets, when Jerusalem and the towns about her were peopled and tranquil, when the Negeb and the Shephelah were peopled.

> (7:12) They hardened their hearts like adamant against heeding the instruction and admonition that the LORD of Hosts sent to them by His spirit through the earlier prophets; and a terrible wrath issued from the LORD of Hosts.

Given that classical, preexilic prophecy lasted a long while—at least two hundred years—it is surprising that none of the prophets prior to Zechariah ever referred to his predecessors as a group. He is the first prophet we see looking back and studying earlier oracles, and viewing these oracles as an authoritative body of work coming from a collective source.

Another significant difference between Zechariah and earlier prophets is that an angel mediates his visions. Visions typify classical prophecy, but these usually originate with God, as in Amos ("This is what my Lord GOD showed me"; 7:1) and Jeremiah ("The word of the LORD came to me: What do you see, Jeremiah? I replied: I see a branch of an almond tree"; 1:11). Zechariah's visions are quite different; the prophet recounts that "the angel who talked with me" (5:5 and elsewhere) who explained what he was seeing and conveyed divine words to him.[2] Perhaps such mediation expresses a more distant sense of God. Moreover, unlike the visions of the classical prophets, which had tended to involve everyday items whose symbolism is fairly transparent, Zechariah's visions are often strange: "I looked up again and saw two women come soaring with the wind in their wings—they had wings like those of a stork—and carry off the tub between earth and sky" (5:9).

Zechariah and the Beginnings of Apocalyptic Literature

Some of these features that distinguish Zechariah from classical prophecy typify apocalyptic literature, a genre that probably developed soon after Zechariah's lifetime—that is, in the early Second Temple period. (The adjective "apocalyptic" and the noun "apocalypse" derive from the Greek *apokalypsis*, "to uncover or reveal.") Since the early nineteenth century, scholars have used "apocalyptic" as a genre label in various overlapping ways. I prefer the following definition:

> A genre of revelatory literature with a narrative framework, in which a revelation is mediated by an otherworldly being to a human recipient, disclosing a transcendent reality which is both temporal, insofar as it envisages eschatological salvation, and spatial, insofar as it involves another, supernatural world.[3]

Many parts of Zechariah 1–8 fit this definition:[4] these prophecies are revelatory; they tell a story; they feature an anonymous angel as mediator; and they divulge their revelations to the very human Zechariah. Their "transcendent reality envisages eschatological salvation," especially in chapter 8, which imagines a new Jerusalem ("Jerusalem will be called the City of Faithfulness, and the mount of the LORD of Hosts the Holy Mount"; v. 3). However, Zechariah does not clearly imagine "another, supernatural world" in the same manner as other apocalyptic texts like Enoch, Daniel, 4 Ezra, and 2 Baruch.[5]

The origins of this genre, along with its authors' place in society, are obscure. Apocalypse may have its roots in earlier Canaanite and Israelite mythical traditions, and in preexilic prophecy. Persian motifs probably also influenced the genre.[6] At any rate, apocalyptic ideas went on to play a leading role in Judaism during the Persian and Hellenistic periods. They also had a major impact on early Christianity.[7]

Daniel

Daniel is a short book that boasts some unusual features. Although much of it is in Hebrew, the middle portion (2:4b though end of chap. 8) is in the related language of Aramaic—the lingua franca of the ancient Near East—which was widely spoken in Israel during this time period. (We do not know why the book is written in two languages.) Moreover, it is composed of two fundamentally different genres that overlap the language transitions: stories (chaps. 1–6) and apocalypses (chaps. 7–12).

The Historical Setting

Some of the book's claims are at odds with historical fact:

- Daniel depicts the Babylonians, Medes, Persians, and Greeks as four consecutive empires (chap. 2); however, some of those states existed concurrently.
- It talks about Nebuchadnezzar's being exiled from his kingdom (chap. 4); this probably reflects events involving the last king of Babylon, Nabonidus, who took a "leave of absence" from being king and lived in an oasis on the Arabian peninsula.
- It depicts Belshazzar as the last king of Babylon (chap. 5); this is an error.

Someone living in the Babylonian exile would not have made these kind of mistakes. In other words, Daniel's purported setting during the Babylonian exile (see chap. 4) is not plausible; the book must be from a later era. In fact, it employs Greek loanwords (e.g., *sumfoniah* or "bagpipes," related to the English word "symphony," appears in 3:5), which establishes that someone wrote it during the Greek period.[8]

What the Visions Address

Thus far we have seen that Daniel is a composite text of dubious historicity from different genres.

As noted above, the second half of Daniel comprises apocalyptic visions. Chapter 8 is a typical example of that genre: "revelatory literature . . . in which a revelation is mediated by an otherworldly being."[9] Here, in contrast to the apocalypse in Zechariah, the intermediary is actually named: the angel Gabriel (v. 16). This passage reveals a "transcendent reality" that is both "temporal" and "spatially" different from our world. We can easily interpret some parts of the vision—for example, scholars agree on the meaning of verse 8, "Then the he-goat grew very great, but at the peak of his power his big horn was broken. In its place, four conspicuous horns sprouted toward the four winds of heaven": the "he-goat" is Alexander the Great, and the "four conspicuous horns" represent the four generals who succeeded him.[10]

The continuation of the passage deals, in not-so-veiled language, with Antiochus IV Epiphanes, the Greek king who in 167 B.C.E. took the unprecedented step of converting the Jerusalem Temple into a temple for Zeus, while prohibiting central Jewish practices. (We know little about why he did so. Most Greek kings, like their Persian predecessors, were quite tolerant of local religions.) Other sources tell us that he suspended the regular Temple offerings; this is reflected when Daniel hears mention of a current crisis, "the regular offering . . . forsaken because of transgression" (v. 13). Thus, someone wrote down this vision after 167 (when Antiochus took control of the Temple) but before 164 (when the Hasmoneans restored the Temple following the Maccabean victory). Probably much—if not all—of the apocalyptic material in Daniel was written around that time.

In verse 19 of that chapter, an angelic figure tells Daniel: "I am going to inform you of what will happen when wrath is at an end," continuing: *ki le-mo'ed ketz* (כִּי לְמוֹעֵד קֵץ, "for [it refers] to the time appointed for the end"). This verse is picking up on the vocabulary of Habakkuk 2:3: "For there is yet a prophecy *la-mo'ed* (לַמּוֹעֵד, 'for a set term'), / A truthful witness for *ketz* (קֵץ, 'a time') that will come." Thus, even though the Book of Daniel presents this passage as a new prophecy, it relates to an older prophecy.

Reinterpretation and Creative Philology

Referring to much earlier oracles represents a shift in the evolution of ideas about prophecy. As the Jews who inherited old prophecies came to believe that they could be studied in order to understand the divine will in the present, new prophecies seemed to be less and less necessary.

The apocalypse of Daniel 9 records an important stage in this development. There, Daniel "consulted the books concerning the number of years that, according to the word of the LORD that had come to Jeremiah the prophet, were to be the term of Jerusalem's desolation—*shiv'im* (שִׁבְעִים, 'seventy') years" (9:2). This is quite a strange verse, especially since the initial verb ("consulted") really means "looked at and investigated carefully." Few prophetic texts are more straightforward than Jeremiah's seventy-year oracle, which promised seventy years of Babylonian world domination beginning in 605, followed by punishment of the Babylonians and a restoration of Israel (Jer. 25; see above, chapter 18). At first glance, this would seem like the last prophecy that one who lived centuries later would "consult" for contemporary insights.

However, an author who was writing between 167 and 164 would have had good reason to study that passage carefully. For Jeremiah had promised an ultimate, permanent restoration of Israel after seventy years; yet people were now—under Antiochus IV—unable to worship in Jerusalem, and under pain of death for observing basic Jewish practices. Thus, either Jeremiah's prophecy was false, or else what he said must have a hidden meaning—one that only close study could reveal. The author of Daniel chose the latter approach, revealing this esoteric meaning later in the chapter:

> (21) While I was uttering my prayer, the man Gabriel, whom I had previously seen in the vision, was sent forth in flight and reached me about the time of the evening offering. (22) He made me understand by speaking to me and saying, "Daniel, I have just come forth to give you understanding. . . . (24) Seventy weeks have been decreed for your people and your holy city until the measure of transgression is filled and that of sin complete, until iniquity is expiated, and eternal righteousness ushered in; and prophetic vision ratified, and the Holy of Holies anointed . . ."

The author here reinterprets the prophecy of Jeremiah as if the word *shiv'im* (שִׁבְעִים) in the phrase "seventy years" were tacitly repeated and revocalized: *shavu'im shiv'im* (שָׁבֻעִים שִׁבְעִים), "seventy weeks" of years, namely 70 × 7 = 490 years.[11] Thus, the author grants this central prophecy of Jeremiah a 420-year extension! This reading enables Jeremiah's oracle to remain a true prophecy, and Jeremiah a prophet of truth.

Certainly, the reading in Daniel is not what Jeremiah meant. Several factors that would typify later postbiblical interpretation are already visible here, particularly "creative philology,"[12] where words need not have their usual meaning, especially if they are divine words, which are treated as special.[13] Thus, no clear line divides rabbinic types of interpretation from those found in the biblical period itself.[14] Stated differently, in some ways, we should view the late biblical period as proto-rabbinic.

Continuity holds across the periods not only for interpretation of earlier prophecy, but also for evolving theological ideas. For example, the notion of resurrection of the dead is hardly a central biblical notion, though a few biblical texts may hint at it.[15] In the Bible, resurrection is unambiguously mentioned only in Daniel: "Many of those that sleep in the dust of the earth will awake, some to eternal life, others to reproaches, to everlasting abhorrence" (12:2).[16] For the rabbis, however, the future resurrection becomes a central doctrine.

Themes in the Stories of Daniel

If the reader understands how the genre of apocalypse functions, then the apocalyptic sections of Daniel are not so difficult to grasp. Once one finds the allusions to specific historical events (and apocalyptic authors typically give many clues), the meaning and function of these prophecies become clear. But how are we to understand the fanciful stories in Daniel 1–6? These stories are at least as bizarre as the apocalyptic images that conclude the book.[17]

Daniel's first chapter breaks us in slowly, showing how Daniel and his three friends prosper in the royal court while avoiding the king's ritually impure food and wine.[18] They performed "ten times better than all the magicians and exorcists throughout his realm" (v. 20). In chapter 2, Daniel outdoes the deed of Joseph in Genesis 41: not only can Daniel interpret dreams, but he can divine their content. This reflects positively not only on Daniel, but also on his deity. Thus Nebuchadnezzar concludes, "Truly your God must be the God of gods and Lord of kings and the revealer of mysteries to have enabled you to reveal this mystery" (Dan. 2:47). Of course, it is impossible to imagine the historical Nebuchadnezzar—a worshipper of Marduk who destroyed the Temple in Jerusalem—as saying this.

The following chapter shifts its focus to Daniel's three friends: Shadrach, Meshach, and Abed-nego. When they abrogate Nebuchadnezzar's command by refusing to bow down to a statue, the king's response is immediate and brutal:

> (3:19) Nebuchadnezzar was so filled with rage at Shadrach, Meshach, and Abed-nego that his visage was distorted, and he gave an order to heat up the furnace to seven times its usual heat. . . . (2) Because the king's order was urgent, and the furnace was heated to excess, a tongue of flame killed the men who carried up Shadrach, Meshach, and Abed-nego . . .

The three friends, however, were saved:

> (27) The satraps, the prefects, the governors, and the royal companions gathered around to look at those men, on whose bodies the fire had had no effect, the hair of whose heads had not been singed, whose shirts looked no different, to whom not even the odor of fire clung. (28) Nebuchadnezzar spoke up and said, "Blessed be the God of Shadrach, Meshach, and Abed-nego, who sent His angel to save His servants who, trusting in Him, flouted the king's decree at the risk of their lives rather than serve or worship any god but their own God. (29) I hereby give an order that anyone of any people or nation of whatever language who blasphemes the God of Shadrach, Meshach, and Abed-nego shall be torn limb from limb, and his house confiscated, for there is no other God who is able to save in this way."

This story, full of well-placed details such as the odor of the fire not clinging to these three, repeats the themes of the previous chapter—the miraculous deliverance of the Jewish court hero, and the acknowledgement of God's greatness.

The above themes continue in the following chapters. In Daniel 4, Nebuchadnezzar acknowledges God yet again, while shifting into poetry:

> (31) I blessed the Most High, and praised and glorified the Ever-Living One, / Whose dominion is an everlasting dominion / And whose kingdom endures throughout the generations. / (32) All the inhabitants of the earth are of no account. / He does as He wishes with the host of heaven, / And with the inhabitants of the earth. / There is none to stay His hand / Or say to Him, "What have You done?"

Chapter 5 again features Daniel's ability to interpret: he alone can decipher the "writing on the wall" (MENE MENE TEKEL UPHARSIN).

The last of these narrative chapters is about Daniel and the lion. This story parallels that of the three friends and the fiery furnace (chap. 3). It begins with a bizarre royal decree (in this case, that people may pray only to the king). Pious Daniel, who violates the decree, is caught and punished by being thrown into the lion's den. Again, the text relishes details: "A rock was brought and placed over the mouth of the den; the king sealed it with his signet and with the signet of his nobles, so that nothing might be altered concerning Daniel" (6:18). Daniel of course is saved, and his adversaries are killed. The last few lines summarize the lesson of this chapter as well the initial six chapters.

> (6:26) Then King Darius wrote to all peoples and nations of every language that inhabit the earth, "May your well-being abound! (27) I have hereby given an order that throughout my royal domain men must tremble in fear before the God of Daniel, for He is the living God who endures forever; His kingdom is indestructible, and His dominion is to the end of time; (28) He delivers and saves, and performs signs and wonders in heaven and on earth, for He delivered Daniel from the power of the lions." (29) Thus Daniel prospered during the reign of Darius and during the reign of Cyrus the Persian.

In sum, these stories are not really about specific historical individuals. Rather, they "prove" that God is great and will save any pious Jew, especially those persecuted for religious beliefs. Obviously these stories belong in the literary genre of "royal tales."[19] In addition, they all feature competition between Jew and non-Jew, in which the underdog—who is the Jew—always wins.

The Significance of the Stories

As a scholar, I am curious whether the ancient Jews took these stories as "real history" or recognized them instead as legends. Neither possibility can be ruled out. Other biblical books, such as Jonah[20] and Ruth (see chapter 26 below) drop hints that they are not accurately depicting the past. Because those books are primarily didactic (see "Concluding on a Different Note" in chapter 11), they lack specific historical references. In contrast, Daniel creates the illusion of history with notes such as "the second year of the reign of Nebuchadnezzar" (2:1) and "Darius the Mede received the kingdom, being about sixty-two years old" (6:1). Nevertheless, the stories of Daniel are so exaggerated and implausible that we must wonder whether readers in antiquity believed them.

Ultimately, it may not matter whether the editors and copyists of the stories in Daniel believed that they were true. For the stories exist mainly to illustrate an attitude about living as a Jew: be pious, and even if threatened you will ultimately be saved—to enjoy a better fate than your non-Jewish adversaries.[21] In the words of Daniel 6:29: "Thus Daniel prospered . . ." But this is only half the story—the other half concerns glorification of the God of Israel, who is a great and saving God. Thus Jews are Jews for good reason.

Did these stories originate in the Diaspora, and thus illustrate that God saves even outside of the land of Israel? Or did they originate in Israel during the persecutions of Antiochus, and thus illustrate reasons for hope during a dark time? The historical-critical method has not answered this question decisively. No matter how we resolve such issues, the message of the stories in Daniel is what is important. What we notice most is how the stories in this book reinforce each other, and how effectively they convey their belief that God would reward and protect piety.

22

Prayer of Many Hearts

Reading Psalms

Primary Reading: 1 Samuel 1–2; Psalms 1, 3, 6, 14, 15, 24, 53, 118.

What Is Psalms?

The English title "Psalms" comes to us from the Septuagint, the venerable Jewish translation of the Bible into Greek. It rendered the word *mizmor* (מִזְמוֹר), which features in many superscriptions (chapter titles) in this book, as *psalmos*. Both the Hebrew and Greek words mean "a song sung to the accompaniment of a stringed instrument." In other words, this book consists of song lyrics—about 150 separate songs (largely, but not exactly, identical with the chapter headings). Many of them strike us as familiar, either because of their important role in contemporary religious life, or because we have encountered them as classics of world literature (e.g., "The LORD is my shepherd . . ."; Ps. 23). A "psalm" is a poetic prayer composition that is not necessarily in the Book of Psalms, although that book contains most of the known psalms.

Psalms is an unusually intimidating book. Weighing in at 150 chapters, it is easily the longest book of the Bible. The poetry of its lyrics is rarely straightforward. Its superscriptions are usually obscure or ambiguous. Time and again, upon even a cursory reading, we encounter sudden shifts in tone and focus—often within the same psalm—which compounds the challenge that this book poses.

How are we to read the individual psalms? How are we to understand the book as a whole? Here I do not mean "read" as an act of contemporary personal devotion; that may be important to many of us, but it is not the task at hand. Rather, the historian's role is to view this book and its elements in terms of the ancient milieu in which they arose.

The present chapter will show that Psalms is an ordered collection of collections, comprising different genres from various places and times. To establish this claim, the best place to begin is outside of Psalms—specifically, at the beginning of 1 Samuel, which contains two prayers: one in prose, the other in poetry. The poem is one of those psalms that the Book of Psalms did not incorporate.[1]

Prayer in the Bible: What Samuel Teaches Us

The first prayer found in Samuel is that of Hannah, who had been desperately wanting a (male) child. She prayed:

> O LORD of Hosts, if You will look upon the suffering of Your maidservant and will remember me and not forget Your maidservant, and if You will grant Your maidservant a male child, I will dedicate him to the LORD for all the days of his life; and no razor shall ever touch his head (1 Sam. 1:11).

Like almost one hundred other biblical prayers, this one is prose.[2] (It lacks parallelism and figuration, and it employs plain language.) Its three-part structure is clear: an invocation of God, a long request, and a motivation—why God should heed this request). The following table shows these elements:[3]

Invocation	"O LORD of Hosts"
Request	"if You will look upon the suffering of Your maidservant and will remember me and not forget Your maidservant, and if You will grant Your maidservant a male child"
Motivation	"I will dedicate him to the LORD for all the days of his life; and no razor shall ever touch his head."

Stated differently, after calling upon God (perhaps getting His attention), this prayer offers a deal. Hannah says that if God gives her a child, she will return it to God. The reason why Hannah would want this deal is quite clear from biblical conceptions of biology: if she has one child, then her womb has been opened by God (Gen. 29:31; 30:22), and she will be able to have more children (see 1 Sam. 2:21). One could imagine someone in Hannah's situation coming to the local temple and spontaneously composing such a prayer.

Altogether different is Hannah's second prayer. After she gives birth to a son, weans him, and brings him to the sanctuary,[4] she prays:

> (1 Sam. 2:1) My heart exults in the LORD; / I have triumphed through the LORD. / I gloat over my enemies; / I rejoice in Your deliverance. / (2) There is no holy one like the LORD, / Truly, there is none beside You; /

> There is no rock like our God. / (3) Talk no more with lofty pride, / Let no arrogance cross your lips! / For the LORD is an all-knowing God; / By Him actions are measured. / (4) The bows of the mighty are broken, / And the faltering are girded with strength. / (5) Men once sated must hire out for bread; / Men once hungry hunger no more. / While the barren woman bears seven, / The mother of many is forlorn. / (6) The LORD deals death and gives life, / Casts down into Sheol and raises up. / (7) The LORD makes poor and makes rich; / He casts down, He also lifts high. / (8) He raises the poor from the dust, / Lifts up the needy from the dunghill, / Setting them with nobles, / Granting them seats of honor. / For the pillars of the earth are the LORD's; / He has set the world upon them. / (9) He guards the steps of His faithful, / But the wicked perish in darkness— / For not by strength shall man prevail. / (10) The foes of the LORD shall be shattered; / He will thunder against them in the heavens. / The LORD will judge the ends of the earth. / He will give power to His king, / And triumph to His anointed one.

This prayer of thanksgiving is clearly in poetry. It has the characteristic features of biblical poetry that we discussed in chapter 17: binary lines, parallel structure, and figurative language.[5] If we lifted this text from its context in the narrative, we would read it as a royal psalm of thanksgiving after a military victory. Not only is it full of war language (see esp. vv. 4 and 10), but also it refers outright to the king (v. 10). This is quite strange, since at this point in Israel's history, the monarchy has not yet been established.

Stated differently, the Hannah portrayed in Samuel could not have recited this psalm, which dates from the monarchic period. But the biblical editors were not stupid. So how could one of them have thought to insert this psalm into Hannah's mouth?

Our psalm's presence in its current location shows us that the editor expected the Israelite audience to find it plausible that a woman whose deepest wish had come true would respond by reciting such a psalm. In other words, the Israelites customarily prayed using ready-made psalms. Why did they do so? Probably because they believed such poems to be both movingly beautiful and traditional—that is, proven to be efficacious.

As an Israelite woman visiting the sanctuary, how would Hannah have come to recite this particular psalm? As the person who had come to pray, she would have asked an official (such as a priest) for the most relevant psalm available. Perhaps because the Israelites did not have "off-the-rack" prayers for special occasions in women's lives, the official would have chosen this psalm because it contains a reference to a barren woman who gives birth (v. 5). Furthermore, it celebrates victory over an enemy—a reversal of fortune—which Hannah could relate to her rivalry with Peninnah, her husband's other wife. One can imagine Hannah then reciting this off-the-rack prayer, repeating each phrase after the priest, resonating with the parts concerning children and rivalries—reciting these verses with verve, while mumbling through the rest.

Thus I have accounted for how a royal psalm of victory ended up in Hannah's mouth. That explanation, in turn, sheds light on the nature of the Book of Psalms: That book comprised poetic selections from which worshippers could find something relevant when they felt the need for formal, poetic, traditional language.

When, Where, and Why

As we have seen in earlier chapters, we must first identify a work's literary genre and social setting (what scholars call the *Sitz im Leben*) before we can read it correctly. This is quite difficult for psalms, most of which contain only obscure hints at their background. For example, Psalm 118:27 contains the ritual instruction "bind the festal offering to the horns of the altar with cords," so we know that worshippers (or perhaps Levites) recited this psalm during the sacrifice of a festival offering. But most psalms are silent about which particular rituals, if any, they are associated. Most ritual texts, in turn, are silent about their connections to particular psalms.[6] Consequently, discerning the social setting of psalms involves a lot of guessing. Such speculation is useful, however, if it helps guide us toward the ancient meaning of psalms.

Psalm 6 reads:

> (1) For the leader; with instrumental music on the *sheminith*. A psalm of David. (2) O LORD, do not punish me in anger, / do not chastise me in fury. / (3) Have mercy on me, O LORD, for I languish; / heal me, O LORD, for my bones shake with terror. / (4) My whole being is stricken with terror, / while You, LORD—O, how long! / (5) O LORD, turn! Rescue me! / Deliver me as befits Your faithfulness. / (6) For there is no praise of You among the dead; / in Sheol, who can acclaim You? / (7) I am weary with groaning; / every night I drench my bed, / I melt my couch in tears. / (8) My eyes are wasted by vexation, / worn out because of all my foes. / (9) Away from me, all you evildoers, / for the LORD has heeded the sound of my weeping. / (10) The LORD has heeded my plea, / the LORD will accept my prayer. / (11) All my enemies will be frustrated and

> stricken with terror; / they will turn back in an instant, frustrated (transl. adapted).

In terms of its structure and elements, this psalm resembles Hannah's prose prayer in 1 Samuel 1: invocation of God, requests, and motivations (why God should heed this prayer).

Invocation	"O LORD" (v. 2)
Requests	"do not punish me . . . do not chastise me. . . . Have mercy on me . . . ; heal me . . . rescue me . . . deliver me" (vv. 2–5)
Motivations	"as befits Your faithfulness. For there is no praise of You among the dead; in Sheol, who can acclaim You? I am weary with groaning; every night I drench my bed, I melt my couch in tears. My eyes are wasted by vexation, worn out because of all my foes" (vv. 5–8)

The psalms' expressed motivations give us insight into how the ancient Israelites understood what would move or satisfy God. In this case, for example, the poet assumes that God enjoys praise. Indeed, the speaker almost threatens God by pointing out that (to paraphrase v. 6) "if You let my enemies kill me, there will be one less person around to praise You!"

Assigning a Genre

Many psalms share the triad of elements found here—invocation, requests, and motivation. Biblical scholars have classed such psalms under the genre of "petitions." Because those psalms often begin with complaints or laments, some scholars refer to them as "complaints" or "laments."[7] Sometimes their grammar suggests that individuals recited them, while other psalms couch their language in the plural. Thus scholars subdivide the class of laments into "individual" and "communal" types.

Each genre of psalm follows a convention—a script or form that was engrained in the culture. (In our culture, too, we have certain conventions for writing a personal letter versus a business letter; each type of composition has its own conventions.) For example, Psalm 22, featured in Christian tradition, opens with "My God, my God," which immediately leads into "why have You abandoned me; / why so far from delivering me / and from my anguished roaring?" (v. 2). The psalm proceeds to present many motivations for why God should listen, including "I became Your charge at birth; / from my mother's womb You have been my God" (v. 11), and "Then will I proclaim Your fame to my brethren, / praise You in the congregation" (v. 23).[8]

Accounting for Mood Swings

Thus far, our analysis of Psalm 6 has ignored the end: "for the LORD has heeded the sound of my weeping. / The LORD has heeded my plea, / the LORD will accept my prayer. / All my enemies will be frustrated and stricken with terror; / they will turn back in an instant, frustrated" (vv. 9b–11; transl. adapted). These verses are puzzling partly because their grammatical tense does not seem to fit the context.[9] Some of the verbs seem to depict actions that are completed or are in the past ("has heeded . . . has heeded"). But how can the speaker say this, given the dire straits just described? Furthermore, the mood has shifted sharply and inexplicably.

Such a dramatic change in the mood of a psalm is actually frequent—which of course only heightens the problem. It is found, for example, in the lament of Psalm 3, where there is movement from "O LORD, my foes are so many! / Many are those who attack me" (v. 2) to "I have no fear of the myriad forces / arrayed against me on every side. . . . For You Have slapped all my enemies in the face; / You have broken the teeth of the wicked" (vv. 7–8; transl. adapted). Seeing both a change of tense and the sudden sprouting of confidence in many laments raises the question that form-criticism addresses: What social setting (*Sitz im Leben*) can explain this mood swing?

Form-criticism often asks great questions that it cannot answer decisively. Thus, we cannot identify with certainty the social setting of petitions that contain the confidence motif that we have just described. Many form-critics suggest that worshippers used to recite these psalms in a temple, where an individual (whom the scholars often call a "cultic prophet"[10]) heard each complaint and then let the petitioner know whether God was sympathetic. After having been told that God heeded the lament, the petitioner would recite the lines expressing confidence (such as "for the LORD has heeded the sound of my weeping. / The LORD has heeded my plea, / the LORD will accept my prayer"; 6:9b–10).[11] That reconstruction of certain psalms' ritual setting finds some support from biblical passages that describe a dialogue with God. One verse that may allude to such a ritual exchange is "You have ever drawn nigh when I called You; / You have said, 'Do not fear!'" (Lam. 3:57).

Several Genres in Psalms

We have looked carefully at a few psalms so as to posit their genres. This has helped us to understand the psalm within the larger genre of which it seems to partake. So far we have discussed two genres: the hymn (Hannah's song) and the petition (Pss. 3, 6, and 22). Another genre is the "entrance liturgy," apparently recited by the worshipper who is about to enter the Temple precincts. For example, Psalm 15 begins "LORD, who may sojourn in Your tent, / who may dwell on Your holy mountain? / He who lives without blame . . . " Part of Psalm 24 shares the same genre: "Who may ascend the mountain of the LORD? / Who may stand in His holy place?— / He who has clean hands and a pure heart . . ." (vv. 3–4).[12]

Again, no explicit ritual text in Leviticus or Kings mentions such a liturgy. Rather, our attempt to explain these psalms and their structure is what motivates the reconstruction. The reconstruction, in turn, helps us read and understand the psalm better. Certainly, this is somewhat circular. We must always remember that we are following textual clues, and we must always ask: Is there a different social setting that would better explain the psalm within its ancient context?

Time and Place

Reconstructing the social setting answers the question of "why" someone composed the psalms. In the same way—based on textual clues—we can often reconstruct when and where they were written. In so doing, we cannot take literally the tradition that ascribes the book's authorship to King David. The book itself does not make this claim; the superscriptions seem to attribute less than half of the psalms to David. Many psalms attribute their origin to other figures, such as the two attributed to Solomon (72, 127), and the twelve each to Asaph (50, 73–83) and to the sons of Korah (42–49, 84, 85, 87, 88). Even the superscriptions that do say "Of David. A psalm" or "A Psalm of David" may not mean to attribute authorship to him. Rather, such formulas may mean "a psalm in the style of David."[13]

Looking beyond the superscriptions gives us further clues for dating the psalms. The language of the "Davidic psalms" makes clear that they are not all from the same period, and none of them reflects the early-tenth-century Hebrew that he would have spoken. In fact, the opening of Psalm 137, "By the rivers of Babylon, / *there* we sat," indicates that the psalm comes from the postexilic period—four hundred years after David's time. Other psalms contain postexilic phrases or words. Thus the tradition that developed in the Synagogue and the Church that attributed (much of) the book to David is incorrect.[14] The Psalter clearly has a long history, from the First through the (early) Second Temple period.

Scholars agree that most psalms are connected to the Jerusalem Temple. Even so, some of these poems clearly originated elsewhere. For example, Psalm 80 contains internal hints that its origin lay in the Northern Kingdom: "Give ear, O shepherd of Israel / who leads Joseph like a flock! / Appear, You who are enthroned on the cherubim, / at the head of Ephraim, Benjamin, and Manasseh! / Rouse Your might and come to our help!" (vv. 2–3). This passage invokes God as the leader of the *northern* tribes. Some scholars have defined several psalms as Northern on the basis of their dialect, since we know from archaeological evidence that Northern Hebrew was different than Judean Hebrew.[15] In sum, the psalms preserved in Psalms reflect a wide variety of settings, dates, and places of origin.

A Collection of Collections

We have established that the Book of Psalms came together over a long period of time. Further evidence comes from the notation about halfway through the book, "End of the prayers of David son of Jesse" (72:20), which must mark the conclusion of an earlier edition of the Psalter. The book's development over time has left traces in its present structure. Compare Psalms 14 and 53:

Psalm 14	*Psalm 53*
(1) For the leader. Of David. The benighted man thinks, "God does not care." Man's deeds are corrupt and loathsome; no one does good.	(1) For the leader; on *mahalath*. A *maskil* of David. (2) The benighted man thinks, "God does not care." Man's wrongdoing is corrupt and loathsome; no one does good.
(2) The LORD looks down from heaven on mankind to find a man of understanding, a man mindful of God.	(3) God looks down from heaven on mankind to find a man of understanding, a man mindful of God.
(3) All have turned bad, altogether foul; there is none who does good, not even one.	(4) Everyone is dross, altogether foul; there is none who does good, not even one.
(4) Are they so witless, all those	

evildoers, who devour my people as they devour food, and do not invoke the LORD?
(5) There they will be seized with fright, for God is present in the circle of the righteous.
(6) You may set at naught the counsel of the lowly, but the LORD is his refuge.
(7) O that the deliverance of Israel might come from Zion! When the LORD restores the fortunes of His people, Jacob will exult, Israel will rejoice.

(5) Are they so witless, those evildoers, who devour my people as they devour food, and do not invoke God?
(6) There they will be seized with fright—never was there such a fright—for God has scattered the bones of your besiegers; you have put them to shame, for God has rejected them.
(7) O that the deliverance of Israel might come from Zion! When God restores the fortunes of His people, Jacob will exult, Israel will rejoice.

Clearly this is a single psalm, preserved in two slightly different versions. The discrepancies result from changes and errors during textual transmission. A single editor probably would not have included both versions. More likely, each psalm already existed in two different collections. Later, an editor of the Psalter apparently incorporated both collections. In other words, Psalms is *a collection of collections*.

Further evidence that Psalms 14 and 53 came from two separate collections is the language employed to refer to the Deity. The last two verses of Psalm 14 consistently use *YHWH* ("the LORD"), whereas the same verses in Psalm 53 use *Elohim* ("God"). If we step back from these two psalms, we can see a larger pattern: Psalms 48–83 form a collection that, compared to the rest of the Psalter, prefers to employ *Elohim*. The difference in the relative use of these names is striking:

Psalms 48–83:	*Elohim,* 210 times; *YHWH,* 45 times
Rest of the Psalter:	*Elohim,* 94 times; *YHWH,* 584 times

On the basis of this comparison, scholars consider chapters 48–83 to be a collection in its own right, which they call the "Elohistic Psalter," since it relies upon the name *Elohim*.

We can spot other collections as well. For example, Psalms 120–134 all begin with "A Song of Ascents" or a similar formula. (We are no longer sure what a Song of Ascent is.[16]) Psalms 73–83, whose superscriptions attribute them to

Asaph, once formed a separate collection. (Psalm 50 has a similar attribution, but it is now in a different part of the book.) The final five psalms begin with "Hallelujah!" In sum, we can be quite certain that the Psalter comprises a collection of collections.

Psalms as an Orderly Book

Given the evidence surveyed in the previous section, perhaps Psalms is not really a book at all; it would seem to be a hodge-podge. We can no longer determine why each psalm is in its place. Even so, we can discern some general principles of ordering for Psalms. That order is sufficient to consider Psalms a true book.[17]

On the simplest level of organization, we see that the laments predominate at the beginning of the Psalter, whereas the hymns appear mostly at its end. Thus, Psalms moves from complaint to thanksgiving, from being troubled to being joyful. That is a common biblical structure, as in prophetic books that begin with rebuke and end with consolation (see esp. Ezekiel).

The structure of Psalms is more complex as well. A formula that praises God (what scholars call a "doxology") occurs four times, with only slight variation:

> Blessed is the LORD, God of Israel, / from eternity to eternity. / Amen and Amen. (41:14)

> Blessed is His glorious name forever; / His glory fills the whole world. / Amen and Amen. / End of the prayers of David son of Jesse. (72:19–20)

> Blessed is the LORD forever; / Amen and Amen. (89:53)

> Blessed is the LORD, God of Israel, / From eternity to eternity. / Let all the people say, "Amen." / Hallelujah. (106:48)

Functionally speaking, these formulas divide the book into five parts. Linguistic and contextual evidence suggests that these formulas are not an original part of the book. In other words, a later editor inserted them so as to create a five-part composition.

The book's conclusion reinforces that five-part structure, for it exuberantly underscores the earlier praise formulas (we might call it a "megadoxology"):

> (150:1) Hallelujah. Praise God in His sanctuary; praise Him in the sky, His stronghold. (2) Praise Him for His mighty acts; praise Him for His exceeding greatness. (3) Praise Him with blasts of the horn; praise Him

> with harp and lyre. (4) Praise Him with timbrel and dance; praise Him with lute and pipe. (5) Praise Him with resounding cymbals; praise Him with loud-clashing cymbals. (6) Let all that breathes praise the LORD. Hallelujah.

What is the purpose of this five-part division? Psalms tells us at its very beginning. Possibly the same editor who added the five doxologies also placed Psalm 1 as an introduction to the Psalter. It speaks of the righteous person for whom "the Torah of the LORD is his delight, and he studies that Torah day and night" (v. 2).

As an orientation to the book, that verse accomplishes two things. First, here—at the start of Kethuvim—the third major portion of the Hebrew Bible—it asserts the primacy of the Torah. Of the three parts of the Bible, the Torah is the first among equals (scholars use the Latin expression *primus inter pares*). It is the only portion that gets mentioned at the beginning of the other two.[18]

In addition, the approbation for studying "Torah" in v. 2 is actually double-voiced. That is, the righteous person is supposed to study not only the Five Books of Moses but also this second "Torah," the five-part Book of Psalms. If so, then the editor who created the five-part structure headed by Psalm 1 offered us an amazing rereading of the Book of Psalms. It is not merely a compilation of old poems for worshippers to recite as prayers. Rather, it is now a book—something to be studied.

23

"Acquire Wisdom"

Reading Proverbs and Ecclesiastes

Primary Reading: Proverbs 1, 3, 6, 7, 10, 22, 23, 30, 31; Ecclesiastes 1–3, 7–8, 10, 12.

Outside the Bible's Theological Triangle

Even a cursory glance at the books of Proverbs and of Ecclesiastes suggests that they are unlike anything we have encountered so far. They are not instruction in the same way that Torah is—Proverbs, for example, is largely composed of pithy sayings that are not marked as having divine origin. Nor are they Israelite historical texts—while Proverbs and Ecclesiastes do mention King Solomon, they record little in the way of actual events. Nor are the two books prophetic—the profound sentiments of Ecclesiastes, for example, are words of that preacher; they are not understood to be divine. The messenger formula "thus said the LORD" is lacking in both books.

The same is true of a third biblical book, Job, which is the focus of the next chapter yet treated in this chapter insofar as it is similar to Proverbs and to Ecclesiastes. God communicates directly with a human being only at the very end, and even there provides no real guidance on how to live. The story of Job is set in the land of Uz—not in Israel, and it does not involve Israelites. The book shows no interest in the Israelite past. It bears no prophetic message.

These three books share certain other features, too. They all contain a preponderance of aphorisms and proverbs.[1] Together they account for most of the Bible's usages of the abstract noun *chokhmah* (חָכְמָה, "wisdom"; 88 out of a total of 161) and of verbs formed from the root *ch-kh-m*, (חכם, "to be wise"; 96 out of 166). This, combined with other factors, suggests to many that the three books emanate from a wisdom school—although exactly what that school was still eludes us.[2] They also all engage in exploring the proper cosmic order.[3]

A certain lack binds these books strongly together: they all lack expressions of concern for the covenant that unites Israel and God. In fact, concern with Israel *as a nation* is absent—as noted, Job does not even mention Israel. Furthermore, these books concern themselves more with the individual than with "corporate Israel."

Stated differently, these three books lie outside of the Bible's theological triangle. That is, most of the Bible is interested in the relationships between God, the people Israel, and the land of Israel. I can portray those three concerns as the corners of a triangle (see diagram). At the center of the triangle lies the covenant, because its goal is to unite the three entities: if the people of Israel uphold the covenant of the God of Israel, they will possess the land of Israel.

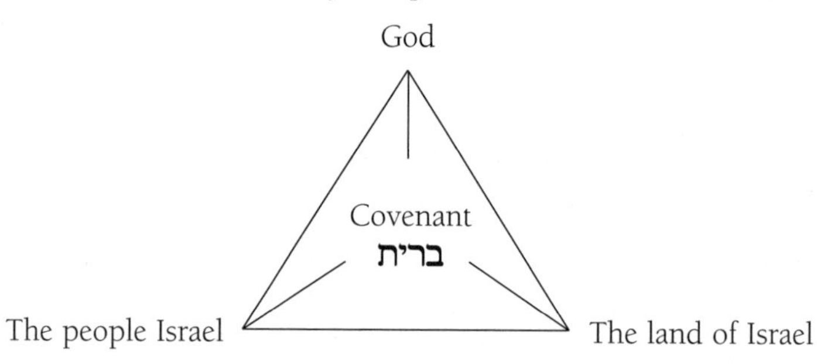

This thesis is a main theme of the Torah, which evokes it often in its land promises, and in the great rebukes in Leviticus 26 and Deuteronomy 28. Meanwhile, the historical books of Nevi'im narrate the connection between Israel's observance of the law and its land tenure. The prophetic books offer warnings to Israel, telling them how to remain on the land—or how to repossess it.

Such a cluster of themes is absent in the three books of Proverbs, Ecclesiastes, and Job. Furthermore, in places, their perspective on "covenantal" concerns is at odds with the other biblical books. For example, both Torah and prophetic texts emphasize the importance of supporting the poor, as may be seen when Deuteronomy discusses the remission of debts every seventh year:

> (15:9) Beware lest you harbor the base thought, "The seventh year, the year of remission, is approaching," so that you are mean to your needy kinsman and give him nothing. He will cry out to the LORD against you, and you will incur guilt. (10) Give to him readily and have no regrets when you do so, for in return the LORD your God will bless you in all your efforts and in all your undertakings. (11) For there will never cease to be needy ones in your land, which is why I command you: open your hand to the poor and needy kinsman in your land.

Likewise, Amos, a prophetic text, shows a strong concern for the poor:

> (2:6) Thus said the LORD: For three transgressions of Israel, / For four, I will not revoke it: / Because they have sold for silver / Those whose cause was just, / And the needy for a pair of sandals. / (7) Ah, you who trample the heads of the poor / Into the dust of the ground . . .

In contrast, Proverbs chides one who has bothered to help out a poor person by cosigning a loan:

> (6:1) My son, if you have stood surety for your fellow, / Given your hand for another, / (2) You have been trapped by the words of your mouth, / Snared by the words of your mouth. / (3) Do this, then, my son, to extricate yourself, / For you have come into the power of your fellow: / Go grovel—and badger your fellow; / (4) Give your eyes no sleep, / Your pupils no slumber. / (5) Save yourself like a deer out of the hand of a hunter, / Like a bird out of the hand of a fowler.

It is hard to believe that Proverbs—with its practical yet less compassionate attitude toward the poor—appears in the same Bible as Deuteronomy and Amos!

Even in cases where all biblical books agree that something is bad or good, Proverbs presents the issue in a distinctive manner. For example, the entire Bible is anti-adultery. (The Bible defines adultery as a man's having sexual intercourse with a woman who is married to another man.) In the Torah, adultery is a capital offense: "If a man is found lying with another man's wife, both of them . . . shall die. Thus you will sweep away evil from Israel" (Deut. 22:22). In the Torah's narrative, Joseph recognizes the seriousness of adultery when he says to Mrs. Potiphar: "How then could I do this most wicked thing, and sin before God?" (Gen. 39:9). In contrast, Proverbs condemns adultery as an offense not against God but rather against the woman's husband:

> (6:32) He who commits adultery is devoid of sense; / Only one who would destroy himself does such a thing. / (33) He will meet with disease and disgrace; / His reproach will never be expunged. / (34) The fury of the husband will be passionate; / He will show no pity on his day of vengeance. / (35) He will not have regard for any ransom; / He will refuse your bribe, however great.

In this respect, Proverbs' view of adultery is like that in the rest of the Near Eastern world.

Indeed, Proverbs, Ecclesiastes, and Job are more international in their purview than other books in the Bible. This is most obvious in the sections of

Proverbs that echo an earlier Egyptian text called *The Instruction of Amenemope*, as we shall see below. But all three books show many more similarities—in style and in specific phrases and lines—to pre-Israelite literature. Apparently the authors of these biblical books had access to this non-Israelite material—and saw fit to make use of it.

Given the similarities among these three books, and their differences from the rest of the Bible, scholars customarily refer to them together as "Wisdom Literature."[4] Not all scholars agree that this is the best term.[5] At the same time, many scholars believe that the scope of this literature extends beyond these three books.[6] Yet in the same way that Leviticus and Deuteronomy may be studied together usefully as Torah, or that Isaiah and Ezekiel may be studied together effectively as classical prophecy, the three books of Proverbs, Ecclesiastes, and Job can be examined productively with regard to each other. Also, given their international flavor, it is often helpful to read them against other ancient Near Eastern texts, rather than in light of the Torah or Israelite prophetic texts.

What Is Proverbs?

Proverbs is a collection of smaller collections of diverse proverbs and other didactic material from diverse settings, some of which reflect international influence. As our discussion will show, the attribution to King Solomon in 1:1 is not historically accurate. Many of its adages address the pursuit of wisdom or righteousness.

Patterns That Reveal the Book's Nature

The same types of evidence that led us to conclude that Psalms is a collection of collections (see chapter 22) apply to Proverbs as well. Partway through this book, a notice reads: "These too are proverbs of Solomon, which the men of King Hezekiah of Judah copied" (25:1), indicating that Proverbs once concluded just before that point. In addition, the book repeats many of its proverbs. For example, both Proverbs 14:12 and 16:25 read: "A road may seem right to a man, / But in the end it is a road to death."[7] Other proverbs are told in nearly identical forms, for example: "Ill-gotten wealth is of no avail, / But righteousness saves from death" (10:2) and "Wealth is of no avail on the day of wrath, / But righteousness saves from death" (11:4).[8] Both phenomena suggest that a proverb (sometimes altered during transmission) found its way into more than one collection, which a later editor compiled into the larger book.

Occasionally, two separate verses share only half of a proverb while their respective other halves each reflect a distinct viewpoint. For example, the following verses give two different answers to the question of how to live long and well:

> The instruction of a wise man is a fountain of life, / Enabling one to avoid deadly snares. (13:14)

> Fear of the LORD is a fountain of life, / Enabling one to avoid deadly snares. (14:27)

The difference in perspective is significant. The first proverb is secular—it advocates following the words of a wise sage, who is not necessarily righteous in terms of following divine law. To recast its message in modern terms: go gain the type of practical wisdom taught in secular schools, for those skills will keep you out of trouble. In contrast, the second proverb is religious. In modern terms, it recommends going to synagogue or church.

To give another example, the following pair offers the same contrast in perspective:

> The horse is readied for the day of battle, / But victory comes from the LORD (21:31).

> For by stratagems you wage war, / And victory comes with much planning (24:6).

The first proverb holds that God causes all ("theonomy"), whereas the second one suggests that humans control their own fate ("autonomy").

Thus, proverbs in Proverbs seem to have two very different perspectives: God is either the major player or else ignored altogether. The first type emphasizes "fear of God," "righteousness," and "wickedness," while the second type highlights "wisdom," "being wise," and "being foolish." Words that characterize one type rarely appear together with words that typify the other type.[9] Some scholars believe that these two types reflect different worldviews:[10] in one, God micromanages; in the other, things just happen.[11] Alternately, the same person may have upheld each of these views at different times. But at any rate, each proverb presents only one point of view.

The Central Section

The bulk of Proverbs (10:1–22:16) is comprised of two-part sayings in which the second part opposes the first part (a poetic form called "antithetical parallelism"; see chapter 17). These sayings seem to have no connection one to the next. Here is a typical three-verse-long passage from this section of the book:

> (10:4) Negligent hands cause poverty, / But diligent hands enrich.
> (5) He who lays in stores during the summer is a capable son, / But he who sleeps during the harvest is an incompetent.
> (6) Blessings light upon the head of the righteous, / But lawlessness covers the mouth of the wicked.

For some reason, the editors of Proverbs prefer sayings of this type, which is often redundant. Such a preference is odd; surely the ancient Israelites did not compose all their proverbs in this form. Indeed, most popular proverbs quoted elsewhere in the Bible and the ancient Near East appear in a wide range of other forms, such as "How can straw be compared to grain?" (Jer. 23:28), or "Let not him who girds on his sword boast like him who ungirds it!" (1 Kings 20:11).[12]

The First Section

Very different from the book's center section is its opening (chaps. 1–9). It contains none of those independent, pithy, two-part sayings. Instead, this section presents a paean to wisdom as an ideal. It develops this theme through several speeches addressed to a young adult male, which contrast two women: an archetypal (yet real) woman, depicted as a foreign[13] seductress; and *chokhmah* (חָכְמָה, "wisdom"), personified as female in vivid terms.[14] In addition to glorifying wisdom, this section drives home the point that the real woman—the smooth-talking temptress—is deadly: "a highway to Sheol / Leading down to Death's inner chambers" (7:27). Obviously this section is xenophobic and misogynistic; we do not know why such opinions figure so prominently in Proverbs' introduction.[15]

The Third Section

The book's third section is also quite distinct from the first two sections described above. It begins with a new introduction of its own (22:17–21). Then it presents a number of sayings that are several verses long; for example: "When you sit down to dine with a ruler, / Consider well who is before you. / Thrust a knife into your gullet / If you have a large appetite. / Do not crave for his dainties, / For they are counterfeit food" (23:1–3). Following that subsection is the superscription mentioned earlier, which introduces another subsection with more of the same: "These too are proverbs of Solomon, which the men of King Hezekiah of Judah copied" (25:1).

The main portion of this section (22:17–24:34) is where we find many similarities—as mentioned above—to an Egyptian work, *The Instruction of Amenemope.*[16] The similarities include the following pairings:

> Do not rob the wretched because he is wretched; / Do not crush the poor man in the gate. (Proverbs 22:22)
> Beware of robbing a wretch, / Of attacking a cripple. (Amenemope 2)

> Do not remove the ancient boundary stone / That your ancestors set up. (Proverbs 22:28)
> Do not remove ancient boundary stones; / Do not encroach upon the field of orphans, / For they have a mighty Kinsman, / And He will surely take up their cause with you. (Proverbs 23:10–11)
> Do not move the markers on the borders of fields, / Nor shift the position of the measuring-cord. / Do not be greedy for a cubit of land, / Nor encroach on the boundaries of a widow. (Amenemope 6)

The two books share too much wording to be independent works. But which borrowed from which? Consider that one verse in Proverbs makes sense only when we assume that its editor borrowed material from some form of *Amenemope*. That verse reads: "Indeed, I wrote down for you a threefold lore" (22:20). This is obscure—there is nothing "threefold" in the context. We can resolve the problem if we assume that the vowels of one word became corrupted in transmission. (The Masoretic tradition already acts as if one of the letters suffered from a scribal error at some point.) If instead of the Masoretic reading of the consonants שליש׳ם as *shalishim* ("threefold") we read *sheloshim* ("thirty"), we can understand this verse as a reference to the thirty sections of *Amenemope*.

We cannot know exactly how and when an Israelite editor employed a version of that earlier work, in part because the history of composition of Proverbs is complex (as the structure discussed so far indicates). Yet it appears that an editor of Proverbs changed the name of the deity mentioned in the Egyptian book, while leaving much of the rest alone.

The Final Section

The continuation of Proverbs contains a variety of material. Some of it resembles what we have seen earlier. Other passages are quite different. This includes a collection of numerical sayings, such as: "The earth shudders at three things, / At four which it cannot bear: / A slave who becomes king; / A scoundrel sated with food; / A loathsome woman who gets married; / A slave-girl who supplants her mistress" (30:21–23). Also unique is the acrostic paean to the "capable wife" (31:10–31), which concludes the book. In other words, passages on the topic of women frame the Book of Proverbs at its beginning and end.[17]

Reading Proverbs

Each section of Proverbs presents particular challenges. The first nine chapters, with their caricature of a "foreign woman," is by today's egalitarian standards offensive. In the second, central section, many proverbs are too obvious to excite, such as: "A wise son brings joy to his father; / A dull son is his mother's sorrow" (10:1). They prompt unanswerable questions, such as: For whom were these words intended? Were they meant for educating children?[18] Other sayings, however, are colorful and surprising; like the best of modern proverbs, they provoke the reader to think about the associations that they make. For example: "A gold ring in the snout of a pig. / A beautiful woman bereft of sense" (11:22; transl. adapted).[19]

Perhaps the most challenging part of reading Proverbs is taking it on its own terms, removed from other biblical literature. Most interpreters have failed to do so. Thus, Yeshua (Joshua) Ben-Sirach, a sage living in the second century B.C.E., identified "wisdom" with "fear of the LORD," conflating what in Proverbs had been two distinct ideas (see above, "Patterns That Reveal the Book's Nature"). For example, Ben-Sirach opens his book with the observation that "all wisdom is from the LORD," and elsewhere it notes that "the whole of wisdom is fear of the Lord" (19:20).[20] This identification of wisdom and righteousness became standard in later Judaism—so much so that later generations took the word "wisdom" in Proverbs to mean "Torah." Thus Jewish tradition has long understood Torah, and not simply wisdom, to be the subject of the famous verse, "She is a tree of life to those who grasp her, / And whoever holds on to her is happy" (Prov. 3:18; compare v. 13). Historical-critical study encourages us to strip away such later identifications, and to understand such texts on their own terms—that is, in reference to secular wisdom.

Ecclesiastes: Utter Futility!

Ecclesiastes, also known by its Hebrew title *Kohelet* (or Koheleth, Qohelet, or Qoheleth), is one of the Bible's most challenging books. Part of the problem derives from our lack of a clear understanding the history of its composition. Most scholars suggest that the book ends with a secondary set of appendices in 12:9–14, which attempt to make a rather radical book more acceptable.[21] Indeed, if we set aside these verses to look at the "original" work, we see a book that is neatly bracketed by an inclusio: 1:2 reads "Utter futility!—said Koheleth—Utter futility! All is futile!"; 12:8 seconds that view by nearly repeating it, "Utter futility—said Koheleth—All is futile!"

But even apart from the dramatic shift of direction in the last six verses, the book is very difficult. It contains a large number of genres, including monologue (chaps. 1–2), poetry (chaps. 3, 12), and proverbial sayings (chaps. 7, 10). How these compositions combine to create meaning is often not clear. Further, the protagonist quotes not only proverbs that he agrees with, but also popular proverbs that he wishes to show are wrong,[22] yet often we cannot tell which are which.

Despite the barriers that we face, we do hold several keys to reading Ecclesiastes.[23] First, we know based on its vocabulary and style that it is a wisdom book, and as such it is full of observations. The protagonist, Koheleth (whom the book seems to identify with King Solomon;[24] 1:1, 12, 16), is constantly finding, looking, and observing. Indeed, the word *ra'iti* (רָאִיתִי;, "I saw, I found, I observed") appears eighteen times in this short book. As in Proverbs, students learn not through Torah study, nor through prophetic oracles, but through observation.

Ecclesiastes, however, differs from Proverbs in one remarkable facet: Proverbs treats wisdom as positive, whereas Ecclesiastes—having experimented with both wisdom and foolishness—finds that wisdom too has limitations:

> (2:15) "The fate of the fool is also destined for me; to what advantage, then, have I been wise?" And I came to the conclusion that that too was futile, (16) because the wise man, just like the fool, is not remembered forever; for, as the succeeding days roll by, both are forgotten. Alas, the wise man dies, just like the fool!

In other words, wisdom is fleeting, because the wise man does not get credit for his perspicacity; thus, later generations do not remember him. An anecdote in 9:13–15 confirms this view: a poor wise man who saves a city is forgotten. Koheleth then concludes, using the form of point and counterpoint: "So I observed: Wisdom is better than valor; but: A poor man's wisdom is scorned, / And his words are not heeded" (v. 16).

A second key to the book is that it assumes a vast gap between God and people: God controls everything in the world, but people cannot understand how He does this. As a result of that chasm, it views people's vaunted wisdom as actually worthless. Koheleth states this quite clearly: "and I have observed all that God brings to pass. Indeed, man cannot guess the events that occur under the sun. For man tries strenuously, but fails to guess them; and even if a sage should think to discover them he would not be able to guess them" (8:17). Thus a major theme of the book is God's control of the world—a domination that is both complete and inscrutable. Indeed, this is the point of the book's famous poem:

> (3:1) A season is set for everything, a time for every experience under heaven: / (2) A time for being born and a time for dying, / A time for planting and a time for uprooting the planted. . . . / (8) A time for loving and a time for hating; / A time for war and a time for peace.

The point is that God has determined what these "seasons" should be; nothing that humans do can change them.[25] People are powerless to change what God has determined. Moreover, they cannot even know when those seasons occur. As the same passage puts it: "I have observed the business that God gave man to be concerned with: He brings everything to pass precisely at its time; He also puts eternity [= the desire to know the future] in their mind, but without man ever guessing, from first to last, all the things that God brings to pass" (vv. 10–11). Such extreme determinism distinguishes Ecclesiastes from the rest of the Bible.[26]

One might think that people's reaction to a world in which they are pawns, in which God "holds all the cards," would cause suicidal pessimism. However, this same passage tells us that "the only worthwhile thing there is for them is to enjoy themselves and do what is good in their lifetime; also, . . . whenever a man does eat and drink and get enjoyment out of all his wealth, it is a gift of God" (vv. 12–13). Irony of ironies: try to be happy, but it is God who will decide if you will be happy or not.

This leads us to the book's third key: happiness is one of its major themes.[27] Koheleth concludes that "the only good a man can have under the sun is to eat and drink and enjoy himself. That much can accompany him . . . through the days of life that God has granted him under the sun" (8:15). Elsewhere the Bible has no problems with happiness. What makes Ecclesiastes exceptional is its giving a central role to happiness, "the gift of God" (3:13; 5:18).

More Wisdom

The theme of wisdom will continue in the next chapter, as we explore Job. Like Proverbs and Koheleth, Job emphasizes the importance of experience in understanding how the world functions. Yet the experience of the author of Job seems to have differed remarkably from that of the authors of the other two works, yielding a much more enigmatic and profound work.

24

"Being But Dust and Ashes"

Reading Job

Primary Reading: Job.

(*Note:* This is a beautiful but complicated book; it is difficult to read in one sitting.)

Beyond Difficult

In chapter 23, I treated Job as one of three exemplars of biblical "wisdom literature." I highlighted how challenging are the other two books, Proverbs and Ecclesiastes: their history of composition is obscure, and their diverse parts do not fit neatly into a meaningful whole. Yet Job is more difficult than both of those books combined.[1]

First of all, the language in this book is extremely hard to understand. Job employs a large number of *hapax* words (see "Words Without Peer"; see chapter 17) and unusual grammatical forms—so much so that some scholars have wondered if it is a bad translation from another language![2] Moreover, that difficult vocabulary pops up at crucial junctures in the text, leaving us unsure how to interpret not only the word, but also the verse—or even an entire section.

The historical-critical method reveals other problems on top of these, connected to the composition of Job. Looking at them can help us understand *why* the book is so difficult, which can make reading Job less frustrating. Some of these problems are obvious from the outline of the book's structure, as follows:

1. Narrative introduction
2. Speeches by Job, Eliphaz, Bildad, Zophar
3. Speeches by Job, Eliphaz, Bildad, Zophar
4. Speeches by Job, Eliphaz, Bildad

5. Speeches by Elihu
6. God's speeches
7. Narrative conclusion

Certain asymmetries here are puzzling. Why, for example, is there no speech by Zophar in the third set of speeches (section 4)? If Zophar's third speech is missing, what does this mean? Perhaps it is not really missing—perhaps the words "Zophar the Naamathite said in reply" simply fell out somewhere, skipped by a distracted scribe; but if so, at what point should we reinsert them? Whether we read a particular section as said by Job, or by Zophar, makes a big difference.

Aside from the strange structure, none of the friends has a distinct personality, as might be expected.[3] More unsettling is the unfulfilled promise when each speech cycle is repeatedly punctuated by the phrase "X said in reply." This suggests that we are reading a true dialogue, yet we never get one. Indeed, the characters not only talk past each other (as we shall see below), they also attempt to define the other's position. For example, Eliphaz says: "You [Job] say, 'What can God know? / Can He govern through the dense cloud? / The clouds screen Him so He cannot see / As He moves about the circuit of heaven'" (22:13–14). These words Eliphaz puts into Job's mouth—and they misconstrue Job's argument!

The threefold cycle of speeches is followed by Elihu's lone speeches in chapters 32–37. His presence is a surprise. He is mentioned neither in the book's prologue (2:11) nor its epilogue (42:7, 9), where Job has only three other friends. What is Elihu doing here? Why does he offer four speeches in a row? Even stranger than this, he depicts himself as a bumbler who talks a lot but says little: "For I am full of words; / The wind in my belly presses me. / My belly is like wine not yet opened, / Like jugs of new wine ready to burst. / Let me speak, then, and get relief; / Let me open my lips and reply" (32:18–20). To make matters more confusing, what God says later on is much like what Elihu says here. What does this tell us about God? If Elihu is a bumbling idiot, then his speeches may foreshadow God's speeches, hinting that even God's answers are not satisfactory.[4]

God's speeches to Job have their own difficulties, as we shall see below. For now we can ask: Why does God need to speak twice? What is the difference between Job's two answers to God, and why is this difference so important that God is satisfied with Job's second response, but not with his first? Most significantly, does God really answer Job's challenge?

These problems are easily multiplied, for the Book of Job is an enigma.[5] This great work of literature is not open to a simple, authoritative explanation.

A Partial Resolution

Despite the extreme challenges, we can make several definitive statements about parts of Job. Once these are considered, we can make some sense out of the book as a whole.

The Book of Job is comprised of two main parts: a prose frame around a poetic center.[6] The prose is now marked as chapters 1–2 and 42:7–17. The rest of the book (3:1–42:6) is poetry. Each part also prefers different divine names. Yet the difference between the two parts is more than a matter of linguistic style. Each of the two sections tells a fundamentally different story. In the prose part, Job's misfortunes arise from a discussion between God and the Adversary, a character who is absent from the poetic part. The afflictions of Job in the prose and poetry are also different. In the prose, all his children are killed, but in the poetry they are alive: "My odor is repulsive to my wife; / I am loathsome to my children" (19:17). Finally, it is the prose that depicts what scholars have called "Job the patient." The poetry portrays a distinct temperament, "Job the impatient."[7]

However, in contrast to what we found through source-analysis of the Torah, when we contrast the two parts of Job, we must conclude that they do *not* represent two separate sources. For neither section is complete without the other. For example, the prose epilogue assumes that some sort of dialogue had occurred between the friends and Job: "After the LORD had spoken these words to Job, the LORD said to Eliphaz the Temanite, 'I am incensed at you and your two friends'" (42:7). Nor could a poetic composition have stood on its own. "Afterward, Job began to speak and cursed the day of his birth" (3:1)—as a beginning, this statement assumes too much.

Although the two parts belong together, they are each distinct enough that it is worth examining each one in turn, to grasp their internal coherence. Then we will be better able to perceive what each part contributes to the overall story.

Job the Patient: Happily Ever After

The opening and closing passages in the book—the two prose sections (chaps. 1–2 and 42:7–17)—fit together quite neatly.[8] Consider the following verses near the end: "Thus the LORD blessed the latter years of Job's life more than the former. He had fourteen thousand sheep, six thousand camels, one thousand yoke of oxen, and one thousand she-asses. He also had seven sons and three daughters" (42:12–13). That is, Job receives double the property that he owned at the start of the book, and his children are "replaced" by the same number as he originally had. (Perhaps doubling property is a blessing, while having twenty children would not be!) According to some scholars, the style of these passages resembles that of an epic, perhaps even of a fairy tale. Thus the narrator treats us to a measured account, featuring patterns of repeating phrases and events. We find many groups of fours—for example, four attributes of Job ("blameless," "upright," "feared God," and "shunned evil") and four catastrophic sets of deaths (those tending the cattle, then the sheep, then the camels, and finally Job's children).

The structure of the opening itself is highly symmetrical, narrating first what happens on the earth, then in heaven, then on earth, then in heaven, then again on earth (as scholars would denote it: ABABA). Meanwhile, the descriptions of the heavenly scene in chapters one and two are very similar. The exact repetition of the phrases "I alone have escaped to tell you" (vv. 15, 16, 17, 19) and "This one was still speaking when another one came and said . . ." (vv. 16, 17, 18) creates an eerie, breathless narrative. It is especially telling that *three* columns of Chaldeans strike in the third catastrophe (1:17), while in the fourth, "a mighty wind . . . struck the *four* corners of the house" (1:19)—this is the structure of imaginative literature, such as fairy tales.

Running like a thematic thread through this introduction is the verb *b-r-kh* (ברך; 1:5, 10, 11, 21; 2:5, 9). Typically in biblical Hebrew, it means "to bless," yet this passage employs it euphemistically—referring to its opposite: "to curse." With reference to God, cursing means "to blaspheme," a locution that the author seems to want to avoid stating outright.[9] In both senses taken together, this word unifies the opening prose section, leaving us to wonder: after being struck with such horrible afflictions, what will Job do—bless God, or "bless" (curse) God?

The book's final prose passage makes it clear that Job does not curse God. It begins: "After the LORD had spoken these words to Job, the LORD said to Eliphaz the Temanite, 'I am incensed at you and your two friends, for you have not spoken the truth about Me as did My servant Job'" (42:7). Here the imaginary quality of the work continues. In verse 11, each of Job's friends give him "one *kesitah*," an old unit of weight mentioned in the Bible only in Genesis 33:19 and Joshua 24:32; its use here suggests a distant, "long, long ago" setting. The end of this narrative section is remarkable: "Afterward, Job lived one hundred and forty years to see four generations of sons and grandsons. So Job died old and contented" (vv. 16–17). In other words, "he lived happily ever after."

This ending, along with the surrealistic patterns in chapters 1–2, suggests that rather than viewing the prose portion as an epic,[10] we should characterize it as being like a fairy tale. That is to say, the storyteller gives us ample clues to convey that we should not take the story as historically true, yet prompts us by those same finely crafted features to listen for a message of truth. This opinion is among those in the Babylonian Talmud, where one unnamed rabbi states that "Job never existed, but is a parable." The contemporary translator Stephen Mitchell adopts this view when he opens his translation with "Once upon a time in the land of Uz."[11]

The Adversary

The heavenly scene described in the book's introduction disturbs many readers. It portrays heaven differently from how we usually imagine the divine world functioning. The image of an angelic court itself is not unique to Job.[12] However, from the perspective of other biblical texts, the presence in this court of *ha-satan* (הַשָּׂטָן, "the Adversary") is odd.

Some translators have rendered *ha-satan* as "Satan." However, for grammatical reasons, this word cannot be a proper name.[13] (True, the figure that this term denotes is a bad guy or troublemaker, who in later thought did develop into a full-fledged Satan.[14]) Given the linguistic evidence that places this prose section's origin in the Persian period,[15] the author may have modeled the role of "the Adversary" after the royal spy who traveled throughout the Persian empire, testing individuals' loyalty in the far-flung provinces.[16] As depicted in Job 1–2, this Adversary can push God to do what God was not intending to do, but he has no independent power.

The theology behind this prose narrative is remarkable: When God is under the Adversary's influence, someone may suffer despite being blameless. Such misfortune may upset the righteous yet they will ideally remain pious like Job, who utters "Naked came I out of my mother's womb, and naked shall I return there;[17] the LORD has given, and the LORD has taken away; blessed be the name of the LORD" (1:21). Even after further afflictions strike their body, such people will say "nothing sinful" (2:10) and merely perform the normal mourning rituals, as needed. Ultimately, God will reward such piety.[18]

Job the Impatient

Polarization of the Debate

As noted, the book's middle portion tells a very different story. No Adversary is causing trouble, but neither is Job taking his afflictions with equanimity.

Structurally, this section is a long dialogue between Job and his "friends." By the end, the two parties seem to need a good mediator or therapist—they do not "hear" each other, and they allow the situation to escalate out of hand.

The book conveys the escalating tension in several ways. At the beginning, Eliphaz approaches Job with respect, noting: "If one ventures a word with you, will it be too much?" (4:2). After he accuses Job merely of speaking improperly, he adds generously, "See, you have encouraged many; / You have strengthened failing hands" (4:3). By the final round, however, Eliphaz is accusing Job of serious crimes:

> (22:5) You know that your wickedness is great, / And that your iniquities have no limit. / (6) You exact pledges from your fellows without reason, / And leave them naked, stripped of their clothes; / (7) You do not give the thirsty water to drink; / You deny bread to the hungry.

Job's speeches point to the escalation even more clearly. After rebutting his friends time and time again, after demanding a hearing from God and getting no meaningful response, Job seems ready to give up. He says, "I cry out to You, but You do not answer me; / I wait, but You do not consider me" (30:20). Ultimately Job does the one thing left to him—he calls down a curse upon himself if he is guilty (chap. 31). In this powerful passage he invokes measure-for-measure retribution: "If I raised my hand against the fatherless, / Looking to my supporters in the gate, / May my arm drop off my shoulder; / My forearm break off at the elbow" (vv. 21–22). The ancients took such imprecations very seriously. For this reason, they serve as a fitting end to Job's speech. After he has taken these multiple curses upon himself in protestation of innocence, what more can be said? Thus his friends are unwilling to challenge him further.[19]

Is Experience the Best Teacher?

The reason that this "dialogue" must end without resolution is that no resolution is possible. Both Job and his friends ground their main arguments in experience, but their own experiences lead them in very different directions. Thus, to explain suffering, the friends argue: "Only the wicked suffer; you are suffering; therefore you are wicked," while Job counters: "I am not wicked, yet I am suffering; therefore God is indifferent to the wicked." Similarly, regarding divine power, the friends argue: "God is powerful, therefore good," whereas Job argues: "God is powerful, therefore destructive." Only God knows which position (if any) is correct. This is why Job calls out so often for God to appear, and why we readers might wish that God's speeches—when they do come—were less obscure.

The reasoning of Job and his friends is not easy to follow. Only rarely do Job and his friends formulate their arguments in a straightforward manner, as one might expect in a work so devoted to debate. But this is not a Platonic dialogue. Rather, the author casts all the discourse as poetry. Elsewhere even the Bible uses prose to state (much like Job's friends) that whereas the righteous do not suffer, the wicked do. Here are three such formulations in Proverbs:

> (10:3) The Lord will not let the righteous go hungry, / But He denies the wicked what they crave.
>
> (12:21) No harm befalls the righteous, / But the wicked have their fill of misfortune.
>
> (13:25) The righteous man eats to his heart's content, / But the belly of the wicked is empty.

This is a traditional perspective. Eliphaz in his last speech makes his similar point in a more complex fashion:

> (22:4) Is it because of your piety that He arraigns you, / And enters into judgment with you? / (5) You know that your wickedness is great, / And that your iniquities have no limit. . . . / (10) Therefore snares are all around you, / And sudden terrors frighten you, / (11) Or darkness, so you cannot see. . . . / (23) If you return to Shaddai you will be restored . . .

Job counters by claiming that God is indifferent to the wicked, as in this poignant speech:

> (24:1) Why are times for judgment not reserved by Shaddai? / Even those close to Him cannot foresee His actions. / (2) People remove boundary-stones; / They carry off flocks and pasture them; / (3) They lead away the donkeys of the fatherless, / And seize the widow's bull as a pledge; / (4) They chase the needy off the roads; / All the poor of the land are forced into hiding. . . . / (9) They snatch the fatherless infant from the breast, / And seize the child of the poor as a pledge. / (10) They go about naked for lack of clothing, / And, hungry, carry sheaves . . . / (12) Men groan in the city; / The souls of the dying cry out; / Yet God does not regard it as a reproach.

In the end, neither side moves the other.

The two parties' positions become similarly entrenched with regard to God's power. For example, Eliphaz sees God's power as only good:

> (5:8) But I would resort to God; / I would lay my case before God, / (9) Who performs great deeds which cannot be fathomed, / Wondrous things without number; / (10) Who gives rain to the earth, / And sends water over the fields; / (11) Who raises the lowly up high, / So that the dejected are secure in victory; / (12) Who thwarts the designs of the crafty, / So that their hands cannot gain success; / (13) Who traps the clever in their own wiles; / The plans of the crafty go awry. / (14) By day they encounter darkness, / At noon they grope as in the night. / (15) But He saves the needy from the sword of their mouth, / From the clutches of the strong.

Job, in contrast, suggests that this powerful God "abuses" power, wielding it recklessly against Job and others:

> (12:13) With Him are wisdom and courage; / His are counsel and understanding. / (14) Whatever He tears down cannot be rebuilt; / Whomever He imprisons cannot be set free. / (15) When He holds back the waters, they dry up; / When He lets them loose, they tear up the land. / (16) With Him are strength and resourcefulness; / Erring and causing to err are from Him. / (17) He makes counselors go about naked / And causes judges to go mad. / (18) He undoes the belts of kings, / And fastens loincloths on them. / (19) He makes priests go about naked, / And leads temple-servants astray. / (20) He deprives trusty men of speech, / And takes away the reason of elders. . . . / (24) He deranges the leaders of the people, / And makes them wander in a trackless waste. / (25) They grope without light in the darkness; / He makes them wander as if drunk.

With regard to other issues as well, Job and his friends come to stand on different sides. Each side sees different implications from the same premise. For example, the friends believe that people are ungodly—so much so that they cannot be guiltless, as Bildad claims in his magnificent last speech:

> (25:2) Dominion and dread are His; / He imposes peace in His heights. / (3) Can His troops be numbered? / On whom does His light not shine? / (4) How can man be in the right before God? / How can one born of woman be cleared of guilt? / (5) Even the moon is not bright, / And the

> stars are not pure in His sight. / (6) How much less man, a worm, / The son-of-man, a maggot.

Job too acknowledges the creaturehood of people, and that they are ungodly. However, he believes that this should prompt God to be lax in judgment—people should not be held to divine standards: "What is man, that You make much of him, / That You fix Your attention upon him? / You inspect him every morning, / Examine him every minute" (7:17–18). The Book of Job presents many more such arguments in which the speakers talk past each other.

What Does Experience Teach?

As stated earlier, the friends and Job disagree on the basis of their experiences. Experience, both personal and as related by others, plays a crucial role in wisdom literature. But everyone has different experiences. This fact explains why each "side" in Job tries to establish that its experience is superior. For example, Eliphaz claims: "See, we have inquired into this and it is so; / Hear it and accept it" (5:27); and Bildad notes: "Ask the generation past, / Study what their fathers have searched out" (8:8). To this, Job counters that his wisdom is at least as good as theirs: "You must have consulted the wayfarers; / You cannot deny their evidence" (21:29), and even, "But ask the beasts, and they will teach you; / The birds of the sky, they will tell you, / Or speak to the earth, it will teach you; / The fish of the sea, they will inform you" (12:7–8).

In sum, although the friends and Job share some premises, they reach different conclusions from them, because their base of experience is different. But as readers, we must wonder after the arguments conclude and the dust has settled: Who is right?

"The LORD Replied to Job" (38:1)

After Elihu's speeches, God finally answers Job. But the only thing that is clear about these speeches is their structure:

I.	38:1–40:2	God's first speech
II.	40:3–5	Job's first response
III.	40:6–41:26	God's second speech
IV.	42:1–6	Job's second response

The relationship between these speeches accords with the power relationship between the two figures; God, who speaks much more, is much more powerful. Emphasizing that differential is the divine appearance "out of the tempest"[20] and by God's two initial statements. The first speech begins, "Who is this who darkens counsel, / Speaking without knowledge? / Gird your loins like a man; / I will ask and you will inform Me" (38:2–3). The start of the second speech repeats part of this verbatim (40:7). God also tells Job to prepare for war[21] and suggests that he is not yet "a man."

A Nonanswer

God's first response (38:1–40:2) does not answer Job's questions—at least not in any direct fashion. Job had wanted to know the charges against him, to understand why he was being punished;[22] he had also insisted on understanding how God practices retribution. God does not address these issues. Instead, God treats us to the longest list of rhetorical questions in the Bible: "Where were you," "Have you," "Which," "Can you," "Do you," "Is it?" and so on. The examples all involve the world of nature, not of human society or behavior.

Some scholars infer from the extravagance of God's list of questions that its purpose is to overwhelm Job.[23] Others suggest that God mediates between the position of the friends (who said that God is powerful and good) and Job (who said that God is powerful and abusive) by answering simply: "God is powerful."[24] A third perspective observes that the depiction of nature here is negative and chaotic—concluding tellingly with the hawk, whose "young gulp blood; / Where the slain are, there is he" (39:30). Human concepts of justice are not part of this picture.

Job's reply to this first speech (40:3–5) amounts to "Well, what can I say?"

An Obscure Answer

Not satisfied with Job's response, God delivers a second speech, which we might expect to be more clear. Indeed, this speech, in both structure and content, is quite different from the first. The structure is best understood as follows:

I.	40:7–14	Justice
II.	40:15–24	Behemoth
III.	40:25–41:26	Leviathan

The paragraphing and layout in the JPS translation do not reflect this structure, and therefore they obscure the meaning of this speech. Even so, we cannot be sure what these sections mean and how they fit together. Most likely this Behemoth is a mythological figure based on a hippopotamus, while Leviathan resembles various sea-creatures known from Ugaritic mythology.[25] But how are they germane? How do they relate to what God was saying about justice?

We may apply here the same interpretations that we applied to God's first speech. For example, we may understand these sections as a continuation of God's overwhelming Job. God may be displaying power by pointing to the ability to control these mythological beasts.

Limits to Divine Power?

Alternatively, God may be saying something quite different. This speech may be conceding that even God cannot control these two creations. By this reading, the verse "See, any hope of capturing [Leviathan] must be disappointed; / One is prostrated by the very sight of him" (41:1) includes God as one of the prostrated. Similarly, "Divine beings are in dread as he rears up; / As he crashes down, they cringe" (41:17) would apply also to God.

If so, we can go back and apply this interpretation to God's introductory speech. Rather than being sarcastic (as many take it), God may actually be admitting weakness:

> (40:10) Deck yourself now with grandeur and eminence; / Clothe yourself in glory and majesty. / (11) Scatter wide your raging anger; / See every proud man and bring him low. / (12) See every proud man and humble him, / And bring them down where they stand. / (13) Bury them all in the earth; / Hide their faces in obscurity. / (14) Then even I would praise you / For the triumph your right hand won you.

That is, God is really saying to Job: "I'm not perfect. But can you do any better? Then stop criticizing!"

Job Responds Again

The book spotlights Job's second reply to God. These are the last words of poetry. Unlike his first reply, God does not respond back afterward—indicating satisfaction that Job has now understood. The JPS translation takes Job's words to mean:

> (42:2) I know that You can do everything, / That nothing you propose is impossible for You. / (3) Who is this who obscures counsel without knowledge? / Indeed, I spoke without understanding / Of things beyond me, which I did not know. / (4) Hear now, and I will speak; / I will ask, and You will inform me. / (5) I had heard You with my ears, / But now I see You with my eyes; / (6) Therefore, I recant and relent, / Being but dust and ashes.

This translation obscures the fact that in part, Job is quoting God's earlier speeches. (In chapter 23, I noted that unmarked quotations feature in another book of wisdom literature, Ecclesiastes.) Clarifying the quotations would make the whole passage much clearer:

> (42:1) Job said in reply to the LORD: (2) I know that You can do everything, / That nothing you propose is impossible for You. (3) Who is this who obscures *counsel without knowledge?* [38:2; 42:3]— / Indeed, I spoke without understanding / Of things beyond me, which I did not know. / (4) *Hear now, and I will speak; I will ask, and You will inform me* [38:3; 42:4]— / (5) I had heard You with my ears, / But now I see You with my eyes; / (6) Therefore, I recant and relent, / Being but dust and ashes.

This reply is longer and more developed than Job's first answer. Yet, even as I have translated the passage here, its meaning is still uncertain. Is Job emphasizing his acknowledgement that as a human, God is beyond his understanding (v. 3b)? Or does he focus on acknowledging God's omnipotence (v. 2)—and if so, how is this a response? Is Job satisfied because he has experienced a visual revelation of God ("now I see You with my eyes"; v. 5)? If so, how does this answer Job's concerns?

To complicate things further, we cannot say for sure what the final verse of poetry—the most important one—means.[26] As we have said, the JPS translation renders verse 6 as "Therefore, I recant and relent, / Being but dust and ashes." In contrast, the New Revised Standard Version (NRSV) translates it, "Therefore I despise myself, / and repent in dust and ashes," whereas Mitchell translates it as "Therefore I will be quiet, comforted that I am dust."[27] So, what is Job doing: recanting, engaging in self-loathing, or attaining enlightenment? All three views—and others as well—are plausible. We may wish to understand the meaning of the poetry in the same way that we can understand prose, yet in all honesty we cannot pin down the meaning of this verse.

Putting Job Back Together Again

By this point, my earlier statement about Job being the most difficult book of the Bible should make sense. With the profound issues that this book addresses, and its potent rhetoric, it prompts us to ask: What does it all mean? In particular, who is right—God? The friends? Job? In particular, how might we read the book as a whole, considering both the poetry and the prose?

At least one thing is clear: according to the way the book has been put together, the friends—with their "traditional" wisdom answers—are wrong. The epilogue begins: "After the LORD had spoken these words to Job, the LORD said to Eliphaz the Temanite, 'I am incensed at you and your two friends, for you have not spoken the truth about Me as did My servant Job'" (42:7). However, the ambiguity of 42:6 still leaves open the possibility that Job's earlier arguments were right. (That possibility looks more likely if we take seriously the idea that Elihu's speeches undermine God's position.) Thus, the book may be saying that the way God runs the world, the innocent do indeed suffer.

Alternatively, its editor may have structured the book so that no single answer wins the debate; instead, this work offers a variety of plausible answers, each of which has some basis in experience.[28] Perhaps it is appropriate that we cannot find a clear answer to our questions, given the very serious and personal issues that the Book of Job confronts.

25

"Drink Deep of Love!"

Reading Song of Songs

Primary Reading: Song of Songs.

The Song of Songs (sometimes called "the Song" for short) is the most exquisite book of the Bible.[1] In trying to guide readers, I do not want to paraphrase it—it is simply too beautiful and too multilayered. No paraphrase can do it justice. The Song of Songs deserves to be read and reread; it cannot be confined to a single meaning.[2] What I can best offer are some signposts that will help readers discover the richness of the text.

Solomon and the Song

In English, in addition to "Song of Songs," this composition is often called the "Song of Solomon," based on the first verse: "The Song of Songs, by Solomon." In previous chapters, I discussed similar attributions, which rarely seem to be historically accurate. (This includes the attribution of much of Psalms to David, and of Proverbs and Ecclesiastes to Solomon.) Here, too, comparison with dated Hebrew inscriptions has shown scholars that many phrases and forms in the Song do not match the language of King Solomon's time. In places, the text is clearly postexilic; for example, 4:13 uses *pardes* (פַּרְדֵּס), a Persian word meaning "orchard." (Hebrew writers would not have borrowed from the Persian language until after the exile to Babylon; see above, chapter 4.) In short, someone wrote it down well after Solomon. Indeed, if Solomon really wrote the book, why would he refer to himself in the third person, as in "King Solomon made him a palanquin . . ." (3:9)?

Critical scholars broadly agree that the first verse is not integral to the book. Everywhere else in the book (thirty-two times), the relative pronoun—translated as "that," "which," or "who"—is expressed using the particle prefix *she-* (שֶׁ).

Only in this first verse do we find the longer form *asher* (אֲשֶׁר; the JPS translation renders it as "by"—or in its footnote, "concerning"). A single author would not have used both forms. This anomaly has prompted scholars to conclude that a later editor added 1:1.

That editor most likely wanted us to think of this book as written by Solomon. Given the description in 1 Kings 11:3 of Solomon's "seven hundred royal wives and three hundred concubines," Solomon would naturally have been a candidate for the love-song business. The Song's own repeated mention of a king may have also motivated the attribution.[3]

While readers may still use the royal Solomonic court as an imagined setting for the book, the historical-critical method suggests that we also try to imagine reading the Song as independent of the initial attribution.

A Collection

Although the Song looks like a unified composition, it is not. It conveys a sense of unity by being a collection of poems of similar genres.

A number of indications argue against its being a composition by a single author. First, the Song contains a refrain, yet the refrain does not appear in exactly the same Hebrew words, as we would expect from a book written by one author:

> (2:7) I adjure you, O maidens of Jerusalem, / By gazelles or by hinds of the field: / *Im* [אִם, "Do not"] wake or rouse / Love until it please!
>
> (3:5) I adjure you, O maidens of Jerusalem, / By gazelles or by hinds of the field: / *Im* [אִם, "Do not"] wake or rouse / Love until it please!
>
> (8:4) I adjure you, O maidens of Jerusalem: / *Mah* [מַה, "Do not"] wake or rouse / Love until it please!

A second sign of the book's multiple authorship is that it uses variant forms of the same words—variants that linguists understand to arise from different Hebrew dialects. For example, the style of the direct object suffix differs between chapters 3 and 5: *bikashtiv* (בִּקַּשְׁתִּיו) versus *bikashtihu* (בִּקַּשְׁתִּיהוּ); both words mean "I sought him."

Perhaps the strongest proof of more than one author is the near repetition of one particular passage, an elaborate description of features of the lover's body, which is called a *waṣf*. (Such descriptions have a long-standing place in Arabic poetry, which is why scholars refer to them by this Arabic term, pronounced "watzf."[4]). The Song repeats one of its *waṣfs*, but does so with variations:

(4:1) Ah, you are fair, my darling,
Ah, you are fair.
Your eyes are like doves
Behind your veil.
Your hair is like a flock of goats
Streaming down Mount Gilead.
(2) Your teeth are like a flock of ewes
Climbing up from the washing pool;
All of them bear twins,
And not one loses her young.
(3) Your lips are like a crimson thread,
Your mouth is lovely.
Your brow behind your veil
Gleams like a pomegranate split open.
(4) Your neck is like the Tower of David,
Built to hold weapons,
Hung with a thousand shields —
All the quivers of warriors.
(5) Your breasts are like two fawns,
Twins of a gazelle,
Browsing among the lilies.
(6) When the day blows gently
And the shadows flee,
I will betake me to the mount of myrrh,
To the hill of frankincense.
(7) Every part of you is fair, my darling,
There is no blemish in you.

(6:4) You are beautiful, my darling, as Tirzah,
Comely as Jerusalem,
Awesome as bannered hosts.
(5) Turn your eyes away from me,
For they overwhelm me!
Your hair is like a flock of goats
Streaming down from Gilead.
(6) Your teeth are like a flock of ewes
Climbing up from the washing pool;
All of them bear twins,
And not one loses her young.
(7) Your brow behind your veil
Gleams like a pomegranate split open.
(8) There are sixty queens,
And eighty concubines,
And damsels without number.
(9) Only one is my dove,
My perfect one,
The only one of her mother,
The delight of her who bore her.
Maidens see and acclaim her;
Queens and concubines, and praise her.

Why would a single author repeat the same description? If he[5] were to repeat it, why do so with these particular variations? The best answer to these questions is that more than one version of these poetic passages circulated in ancient Israel; someone then collated them together in a larger work that eventually became the Song of Songs as we have it.

Saying that this book is a collection leaves many questions open. What type of a collection is it? Is its organization haphazard, or is its collection of poems organized to tell a story? Evidence points in both directions. The historical-critical method justifies reading the book either as a loose anthology or as a unified work.

What Genre of Poetry Is It?

Most often, the Song is described as love poetry, sensual poetry, or erotic poetry. What is meant by these terms is rarely discussed; perhaps the reticence is based on the awareness that we have too little evidence to define these genres for ancient Israel. Some units in the Song can safely be categorized as "love poetry" based on the use of the root *'-h-v* (אהב, "to love")—found, surprisingly, only seven times in the whole book.

Similarly, the label "sensual" is appropriate for passages in which the senses are evoked, both directly and indirectly: "I have come to my garden, / My own, my bride; / I have plucked my myrrh and spice, / Eaten my honey and honeycomb, / Drunk my wine and my milk. / Eat, lovers, and drink: Drink deep of love!" (5:1).

The term "erotic poetry," however, is more slippery: if we understand this term to mean words intended to sexually arouse, all we know is that certain sections of the Song have this effect on some contemporary readers. However, we have no way to tell whether its poetry had the effect of sexual arousal in its setting in antiquity. Without knowing more about its original setting and intended purpose, we cannot determine which of these genres applied to the Song of Songs in ancient times.

Ancient Near Eastern Love Poetry

In reading the Song, we must be careful not to impose Victorian notions of sexuality, nor any notion about what many presume is a "negative" attitude toward sexuality in Judaism or Christianity.[6] The Song may seem odd as a biblical book, yet when viewed in the broader context of the ancient Near East, especially Egyptian literature,[7] it is quite normal. (Gaining such perspective illustrates the utility of the historical-critical method: it can correct our own cultural biases.) In terms of style, the *waṣf*s in the Song are quite similar to the following poem written in the period of the Egyptian New Kingdom (mid-sixteenth to early eleventh centuries B.C.E.):

> The *One*, the sister without peer, / The handsomest of all! / She looks like the rising morning star / At the start of a happy year. / Shining bright, fair of skin, / Lovely the look of her eyes, / Sweet the speech of her lips, / She has not a word too much. / Upright neck, shining breast, / Hair true lapis lazuli; / Arms surpassing gold, / Fingers like lotus buds. / Heavy thighs, narrow waist, / Her legs parade her beauty; / With graceful steps she treads the ground, / Captures my heart by her movements. / She causes all men's neck / To turn about to see her; / Joy has he whom she embraces, / He is like the first of men! / When she steps outside she seems / Like that other *One* [the Sun].[8]

Like the Song, but unlike the rest of biblical literature, this poem refers to the female lover as "sister." Like all but one of the *waṣfs* in the Song, the Egyptian author describes the body from top to bottom, describing many of the same body parts mentioned in the biblical book. The comparisons are equally odd (by modern Western sensibilities)—the Egyptians extol blue hair ("Hair true lapis lazuli") while the Israelites desire elongated noses ("Your nose like the Lebanon tower / That faces toward Damascus"; 7:5). The *waṣfs* in both cultures move from describing the body to drawing implications from that description. Thus the Egyptian text states: "With graceful steps she treads the ground, / Captures my heart by her movements. / She causes all men's necks / To turn about to see her." Similarly, the Israelite poem continues: "I say: Let me climb the palm, / Let me take hold of its branches; / Let your breasts be like clusters of grapes, / Your breath like the fragrance of apples" (7:9). One could argue that some of the authors of the *waṣfs* in the Song were aware of the Egyptian traditions.

Mesopotamian sources, meanwhile, preserve a significant collection of potency incantations; they, too, can help us draw a picture of ancient Near Eastern sexuality. One of the more tame incantations goes like this:

> At the head of my bed a ram is tied. At the foot of my bed a weaned sheep is tied. Around my waist their wool is tied. Like a ram eleven times, like a weaned sheep twelve times, like a partridge thirteen times, make love to me, and like a pig fourteen times, like a wild bull fifty times, like a stag fifty times! Etc.[9]

This incantation shows that some ancient Mesopotamians addressed their concerns with sexual potency in a rather open and creative fashion.

The theme of competition among rivals, so prominent in the Song (see, e.g., 1:8), appears in Mesopotamiam literature as well:

> I sense my beauty spots, / My upper lip becomes moist / While the

> lower one trembles. / I shall embrace him, I shall kiss him, / I shall look at him; / I shall attain victory. . . / Over my gossipy women, / And I shall return happily to my lover.[10]

These literatures clearly are concerned with real lovers, they are secular, and they are avidly sexual. Their similarity to the Song suggests that we should read it in the same manner.

The Taming of the Song

Despite this, tradition has tamed the Song by allegorizing it in a variety of ways. Thus, the Targum, the ancient Aramaic translation of the Bible, views the Song as a historical allegory about the "marriage" between God and Israel. Consider the provocative exclamation, "I have taken off my robe— / Should I don it again? / I have bathed my feet— / Should I soil them again?" (5:3; transl. adapted). The woman is announcing to the man outside that she is naked in bed. The Targum renders this verse as an expression of national guilt and moral judgment:

> The assembly of Israel answered before the prophets: "Lo, already, I have removed the yoke of His commandments from me and have worshipped the idols of the nations. How can I have the face to return to Him?" The Lord of the World replied to them through the prophets: "Moreover, I Myself have already lifted My Presence from among you, how then can I return since you have done evil? I have cleansed my feet from your filth, and how can I soil them among you with your evil deeds?"[11]

Even Abraham ibn Ezra, considered one of the more liberal medieval interpreters (because of Spinoza's advocacy of his work), who himself authored secular love poetry, was adamant that the Song must be interpreted allegorically. In his introduction to the Song, he states: "The Song of Songs is certainly not a poem about desire," adding, "do not be surprised that the bride is a parable for Israel, and her groom is God, for such is the habit of the prophets." Ibn Ezra then brings a set of five prophetic examples and one example from Psalms that use parables of lovers to represent Israel and God (including Ezekiel 16; see "Refuting Popular Beliefs" in chapter 19). However, all of the passages that Ibn Ezra cites clearly indicate that the units are parables. For example, while Isaiah 5 begins, "Let me sing for my beloved / A song of my lover about his vineyard," verse 7 spells out who the players are: "For the vineyard of the LORD of Hosts / Is the House of Israel, / And the seedlings he lovingly tended / Are the men of

Judah." In contrast, no similar statement in the Song suggests that it is allegorical, nor that the male lover is God, and the female lover Israel. In fact, the Song contains no references to God at all.[12]

As I have argued, the *secular* Near Eastern love poems to which it is so similar suggest that the Song was originally a secular work, dealing with two unmarried lovers.[13] The Song itself gives no indication that it intends its words differently.

Sex in the Song Versus the Rest of the Bible

The Song depicts premarital sex positively; this attitude differs dramatically from what is found elsewhere in the Bible. But the Bible is a highly complex book reflecting the outlook of different groups, so such a difference is not surprising. It certainly does not justify reading the book allegorically.

Moreover, in the legal collections, the core objection to a young woman engaging in premarital activity is not a moral one. Instead, the problem is that according to biblical law, a woman did not always have the full right to decide how she might use her sexuality.[14] Thus, for example, according to the Covenant Collection:

> (Exod. 22:15) If a man seduces a virgin for whom the bride-price has not been paid, and lies with her, he must make her his wife by payment of a bride-price. (16) If her father refuses to give her to him, he must still weigh out silver in accordance with the bride-price for virgins.

The law's only concern is with the father's compensation, called the bride-price,[15] and not with any morally improper behavior by the daughter.

Ambiguities

The ambiguity of the Song is one of the features that make it so remarkable. Poetry is ambiguous, but this book seems to revel in that quality.

Double Entendre

Much of the book's ambiguity is sexual in nature. For example, in the second dream sequence from chapter 5, we read:

> (2) I was asleep, / But my heart was wakeful. / Hark, my beloved knocks! / "Let me in, my own, / My darling, my faultless dove! / For my head is drenched with dew, / My locks with the damp of night." / (3) I had taken off my robe— / Was I to don it again? / I had bathed my feet— / Was I to soil them again? / (4) My beloved took his hand off the latch, / And my heart was stirred for him. / (5) I rose to let in my beloved; / My hands dripped myrrh— / My fingers, flowing myrrh— / Upon the handles of the bolt. / (6) I opened the door for my beloved, / But my beloved had turned and gone. / I was faint because of what he said. / I sought, but found him not; / I called, but he did not answer.

This passage turns on the ambiguity of whether the woman's "house" is really her dwelling, or her body. Is the male lover standing outside trying to get inside; or is he next to her, trying to enter her? In what sense is he "knocking"? In verses 4–5, are the "hand" and the "latch" euphemisms for genitalia? In verse 3, when the woman describes herself as clean and naked, is she saying that the man should go away because she is already half-asleep, or is she teasing him to come nearer?[16] Representing the body as a house is a frequent metaphor in many cultures; this allows the poet of this unit to introduce numerous double meanings.

Such sexual ambiguities fill the Song. For example, the vineyard in the Song is an image that often alludes to the woman's ripe and sweet sexuality. Most likely this symbol plays on the visual similarity between a cluster of dark grapes and the pubic triangle.[17] Thus, the woman can say: "My mother's sons . . . made me guard the vineyards; / My own vineyard I did not guard" (1:6)—this means that her brothers tried to keep her chaste by making her work out in the field, but she fooled them. While guarding the literal vineyards, she was free with her own figurative one. Another case where vineyard is used symbolically is 1:13, where the woman says of her male lover: "My beloved to me is a spray of henna blooms / In the vineyards of En-gedi" (transl. adapted). However, En-gedi housed the ancient Judean perfume industry,[18] not a wine vineyard. Thus, "vineyards" is not meant literally; this verse is really a veiled reference to the woman enjoying the man's body.

The Song's Conclusion

A different type of ambiguity appears at the conclusion of the Song. It affects how we read the book as a whole—if we choose to read it as a meaningfully arranged collection. The JPS translation renders the last verse (in which the female lover is speaking) as follows: "Hurry, my beloved, / Swift as a gazelle or a young stag, / To the hills of spices!" (8:14). The initial word is *berach* (בְּרַח), which actually means, "Flee away!" Taken on its own, this verse would seem to be an unhappy ending to the Song, where the woman tells the man (poetically), "Scram!"

However, "the hills of spices" may refer to the woman's body! The similarity in shape between breasts and mountains suggests this interpretation,[19] as does the following verse: "My beloved to me is a bag of myrrh / Lodged between my breasts" (1:14), which more directly depicts the image evoked by "hills of spices." Thus, even the conclusion to the Song is uncertain. Is it about love and desire fulfilled, or about unrequited love and desire?

Canonization of the Song

In chapter 27, I will deal more generally with the issue of how various books became part of the Bible, what is often referred to as the canonization of the Bible. Suffice it to say here that the traditional allegorical interpretation of the Song (see above) raises a question: Was the Song viewed as allegory after it became canonical, or did it become canonical only after it was viewed as allegory?

The way we answer this question determines our basic approach to the question of how books became part of the Bible. We can define biblical books as only those that the people already treated as sacred and religious. Alternatively, we can broaden the notion of books included within the Bible to all books that were central to Israel for a variety of reasons. If the latter is the case, then Jews might have held the Song as a central work—a cultural treasure—on aesthetic grounds. Maybe they even used it for entertainment in settings like wedding receptions.[20] Perhaps only later, once it was in the same "book" alongside prophetic parables that used the image of God as husband and Israel as wife, did the allegorical interpretation take precedence over the literal one.

Conclusions

Although we know little about who wrote the Song of Songs, we can venture a few points of orientation. Secondarily attributed to Solomon, the book is a collection of poems of uncertain genre—probably love poems and sensual poetry that its original audience may have considered erotic. The Song's attitudes and wording resemble other ancient Near Eastern poetry of those genres. It was not written as an allegory, although rabbinic tradition has treated it that way. Its hearty approach to sexuality does not fit most depictions of love and sex elsewhere in the Bible; but given the nature of the Bible as a diverse collection itself, this should not be surprising. The ambiguity of the imagery in this book contributes to its beauty. Finally, the Song may have become part of the Bible even while the ancient Israelites cherished it as a secular work that celebrates human love.

26

"Why Are You So Kind . . . When I Am a Foreigner?"

Ruth vs. Esther

Primary Reading: Ruth and Esther.

Surface Similarities

Ruth and Esther are two of the best-known books of the Hebrew Bible. At first glance they seem quite similar. Both are short stories named for female figures. In each one, women and foreigners play a prominent role. This chapter will compare these two similar works. This comparison will raise explicitly a central issue that has until now been largely implicit: how the Bible functions as a *collection* that expresses a diversity of views.

Beyond History: The Genre of Ruth and Esther

As we have seen, identifying a work's genre can help us understand how to read or interpret that book.[1] Both Ruth and Esther are historical in the sense of "narratives that depict a past" (see "The Bible's Limits as a Source for History" in chapter 4), but neither is history in the sense of depicting an actual past. In fact, both works signal that they are *not* to be read historically.

The Book of Ruth

Ruth, at least in its final form, dates from much later than "the days of the chieftains [judges]," the period mentioned in its opening verse. This is certain because it introduces the ceremony in 4:7 with the words "Now this was formerly done in Israel in cases of redemption or exchange." In other words, the narrator needed to explain a ceremony that had long since become defunct.[2]

Although a work that has literary merit may also be historical,[3] Ruth is more easily labeled as literature than history. It is remarkably well formed from a literary or rhetorical perspective (though such features do not always come through clearly in the translation). In this story, a *gibbor chayil* (גִּבּוֹר חַיִל, "a valiant warrior or gentleman"; translated as "prominent rich man," 2:1) meets an *eshet chayil* (אֵשֶׁת חַיִל, "valiant woman"; translated as "worthy woman," 3:11), and they live happily ever after. The story also highlights Ruth's movement from being under God's general protection to being espoused by Boaz, by playing on two senses of the word *kanaf* (כָּנָף, "extremity"): *lachasot tachat kenafav* (לַחֲסוֹת תַּחַת־כְּנָפָיו, "under whose wings you have sought refuge," 2:12) and *u-farasta khenafekha* (וּפָרַשְׂתָּ כְנָפֶךָ, "spread your robe," 3:9). In other words, Boaz resolves the difficulties facing Naomi and Ruth by acting as a surrogate for God. Such verbal links suggest that good storytelling is the goal of the book, rather than history.

The book gives additional hints that it is not historical. It begins with an image that ancient readers would have found ironic—a famine in Bethlehem (בֵּית לֶחֶם), literally "house of bread." More significantly, with the exception of the name Ruth, the personal names at the start of the book do not fit patterns we find elsewhere in the Bible. Instead, they are clearly symbolic: Naomi means "sweetness"; her sons who die young are named Mahlon ("Illness") and Chilion ("Cessation"); and the daughter-in-law who follows Naomi only partway to Israel is named Orpah—literally "back of the neck," meaning "back-turner." In ancient Israel, no parents would have named their children Mahlon and Chilion. Surely the author employs those names so as to signal that the book should be read symbolically and not as straightforward history.

The Book of Esther

In addition to being substantially longer than Ruth, Esther employs a very different style. It combines real historical circumstances with fancy or fantasy, much like modern historical fiction. Its description of the Persian royal gardens, the extent of the empire, and its division into "satraps" (bureaucratic divisions) are all accurate. Even some of the names, such as Esther and Mordecai (Babylonian names related to the goddess Ishtar and the god Marduk), were real personal names in the Persian period. However, other aspects are at odds with the known historical record: a queen's being chosen though a "Miss Persia contest"[4]; a king's not caring if Haman kills off a portion of his tax base; Haman's offering to give the king ten thousand talents of silver[5]; and the rule that the decrees of Persian kings could not be changed once they were sealed. All of this is fanciful. Indeed, contrary to the picture presented in Esther, the Persian kings typically tolerated minorities; they did not persecute groups because of ethnicity or religion per se.

Like Ruth, the Book of Esther employs markers to indicate that its main interest is not historical. Like Ruth, this book features various literary symmetries. For example, the clause "The text of the document was to the effect that a law . . ." (3:14) is mirrored by "The text of the document was to be issued as a law . . ." (8:13). Some view the book as structured around party scenes in particular.[6]

However, unlike Ruth, the storytelling in Esther is humorous in a variety of places. For example, Haman is eager to know why Esther called him to her party, and the king asks Esther what she wants; after much buildup, rather than discussing any matter of substance, she unexpectedly answers, "If Your Majesty will do me the favor, if it please Your Majesty to grant my wish and accede to my request—let Your Majesty and Haman come to the feast which I will prepare for them; and tomorrow I will do Your Majesty's bidding" (5:8).

All of these pieces of evidence—the factual errors, the literary symmetries, and the lighthearted style—point to the fact that Esther is not a historical account. Rather, it is more like comedy, burlesque, or farce. Probably the original social setting for this book was the annual party in celebration of the already existing holiday of Purim; the book, when read aloud, functioned as a justification for the upside-down festival.[7]

Women in Esther and Ruth

My intention here is not to explain why Ruth and Esther were written. Instead, considering both works to be mainly imaginative rather than factual, I will compare how they each imagine two themes: the role of women, and the Israelite attitude toward foreigners.

Discerning the role of women according to the Book of Esther is not at all straightforward. Partly this derives from the fact that the book is comedy. With comedy, it is normally difficult to untangle what the author really believes from what is meant tongue-in-cheek. On one hand, Esther is a model of bravery when she approaches the king to plead for the Jews because she believes that merely by doing so she risks being put to death (4:11). On the other hand, Esther does not risk her life on her own initiative, so arguably she is an agent[8] rather than a primary character or hero. The book's true stance is likely revealed in its final verse, from which Esther is missing: "For Mordecai the Jew ranked next to King Ahasuerus and was highly regarded by the Jews and popular with the multitude of his brethren; he sought the good of his people and interceded for the welfare of all his kindred." In other words, Esther plays a crucial role at one juncture—a role she is able to play because her beauty moves the king (in 2:17: "she won his grace and favor"; in 5:2: "she won his favor")—but the book could just as well have been named the Book of Mordecai.

In contrast, Ruth depicts a very different world, in which a community of women exists in parallel with that of men. Its protagonists are two women who face a problem largely defined by the society's gender roles: because women may not inherit ancestral land holdings outright, they must find an appropriate man, a "redeemer," who can give them access to the field belonging to Naomi's deceased husband, Elimelech. They do not need a man to tell them how to do this—Naomi advises the younger Ruth, and Ruth follows her mother-in-law's instructions. Ruth also shows her own initiative when she improvises what to do at Boaz's granary.

The Book of Ruth also highlights the larger community of women in which Ruth and Naomi function. After their husbands die, Naomi begs each daughter-in-law, "Turn back, each of you to her *mother's* house" (1:8; emphasis added). In 4:17, it is not the father but rather the women neighbors who name Ruth's child. A few verses earlier, the people bless Ruth in the name of Israel's great Matriarchs:

> May the LORD make the woman who is coming into your house like Rachel and Leah, both of whom built up the House of Israel! Prosper in Ephrathah and perpetuate your name in Bethlehem! And may your house be like the house of Perez whom Tamar bore to Judah—through the offspring which the LORD will give you by this young woman (4:11–12).

Women thus play a much more prominent and positive role in Ruth than in Esther.

Foreigners in Esther and Ruth

It is difficult to characterize the attitude of the Book of Esther toward non-Jews. The book mentions some good foreigners, like Harbonah, who suggests that Haman be impaled on the tree he wanted to use to impale Mordecai (7:9). The predominant non-Jews in the story, however, are Ahasuerus and Haman. The author depicts Ahasuerus as a fool, spending his time partying instead of ruling; he is clueless and easily manipulated. For his part, Haman is a megalomaniac with an irrational fear of Jews who therefore wants them killed. After messengers announce Haman's plan far and wide, nobody either protests on the Jews' behalf or offers to come to their defense. Indeed, the populace includes "enemies" who appear willing to do the killing. In short, this farce generally depicts non-Jews in a negative fashion.

Ruth is quite different. In choosing a Moabite woman as its protagonist, the author picked someone whom the audience would view negatively from the start, for two reasons. First, the Torah portrays the origin of the Moabite people through incest. In Genesis, Lot sleeps with his elder daughter, who names the resulting child Moab, which was understood in Israel to come from *me'av*, "from daddy" (19:30–38). Second, the Torah continues to hold the Moabites at arm's length. When Deuteronomy lists nations with whom intermarriage (being "admitted into the congregation") is questionable, its most extreme strictures apply to the Moabites:

> (23:4) No . . . Moabite shall be admitted into the congregation of the LORD; none of their descendants, even in the tenth generation, shall ever be admitted into the congregation of the LORD. . . . (7) You shall never concern yourself with their welfare or benefit as long as you live.

Contrary to common opinion (based on ancient rabbinic interpretation), I believe that Ruth stays a foreigner throughout the book. She does not "convert to Judaism." There was no such thing as conversion in the biblical period.[9] The famous statement of Ruth in 1:16–17 is rather a declaration of closeness to Naomi:

> Do not urge me to leave you, to turn back and not follow you. For wherever you go, I will go; wherever you lodge, I will lodge; your people shall be my people, and your God my God. Where you die, I will die, and there I will be buried. Thus and more may the LORD do to me if anything but death parts me from you.

Ruth's pronouncement does not make her into an Israelite. Indeed, *after* this declaration the narrator twice uses the phrase "Ruth the Moabite" (2:2, 21), as does Boaz (4:5, 10). Even Ruth calls herself *nochriyyah* ("a foreigner"; 2:10). The attitude of the text seems to have been: "Once a Moabite, always a Moabite."

The author of Ruth, however, does not hold the protagonist's status as a Moabite against her. Even as a foreign woman, Ruth can enter the community. More than that, she becomes the progenitor of King David. Thus the book illustrates that kindness is far more important than ethnicity. It objects to the antipathy toward foreigners that may be present in Esther, an attitude that is found in greater extreme in Ezra. According to Ezra 9:2, intermarriage is forbidden because it allows "the holy seed [to] become intermingled with the peoples of the land." The Book of Ruth presents an opposing perspective.

In the Same Book, in the Same Room

Let's imagine that we could place the authors of Esther and Ruth in the same room together. What might their conversation sound like? In the dialogue that follows, I play up the apparent differences in their perspective. "R" represents the author of Ruth, and "E" that of Esther.

E: How can you stand being married to your Moabite wife? Don't you know that Moabites are the worst—they sin and cause others to sin! And if that isn't enough, they are all the result of incest! You are going to dilute our "holy seed" by having children with her!

R: Moabites, shmoabites! People are what they become, not how they are born. A Moabite woman who performs acts of kindness is better than a Jewish man who doesn't. Don't listen to that fanatic "holy seed" notion—it is just plain wrong. And, while we are at it, your tone makes you sound like you don't like women too much either.

E: That's an overstatement. Some women are wonderful to look at, and when they listen to their husbands and other male relatives, good things happen. But beware the woman who shows independent initiative. She is "the highway to Sheol [hell]" (Prov. 7:27) —stay away from her!

R: That view sounds shortsighted: "Beauty is illusory" (Prov. 31:30). But more important, it's unduly harsh and judgmental. I prefer to judge women as we judge foreigners—by what they do, not by what they are. Don't you know that a Moabite woman was the ancestor of King David?

E: You don't expect me to believe that myth, do you?

You might expect any person who heard such a debate to choose one side over the other. What is most remarkable about the Bible is that, here and in many areas, it takes no sides. Instead, diametrically opposed positions on such fundamental issues as "How do we relate to outsiders?" or "How do we view gender?" are included in one collection of books. This leads us to the overall question of the next chapter: How did the Bible come to be formed out of so many texts filled with conflicting viewpoints?

27

The Creation of the Bible

An Abundance of Ignorance

We know little about the Bible's origin—how so many books comprising so many diverse ideas became "the Bible."[1] Clearly, the process happened in stages, over a long time. Nobody woke up one morning, decided to create the Bible, and arranged the next day for all Jews to adopt it as such.

The process was at least as much "down-up" as "up-down." That is, the wider population helped to determine what the Bible included; it was not primarily an official (rabbinic) decision.[2] Indeed, the Bible likely came into being before the publication of the Mishnah, the first great rabbinic work (ca. 200 C.E.). This is why few rabbinic opinions describe the Bible's development. In any case, the rabbis were not interested in history for its own sake, so we need to interpret all rabbinic evidence with care. Meanwhile, some prerabbinic evidence comes from Josephus and other Jewish Hellenistic authors. Also the Dead Sea Scrolls shed light on the process of "how the Bible became the Bible," but that evidence is indirect and often ambiguous. In short, too much of the picture is obscure to enable me to offer a definite time line of "project milestones."

The Canon

Until recently, scholars addressed the questions raised above in terms of the "canon" of the Bible. Some of us, however, have recently emphasized that this term (related to the Greek work *kanon,* a "reed" or a "measuring stick") may be anachronistic in reference to the Bible; it more properly refers to "a fixed standard (or collection of writings) that defines the faith and identity of a particular religious community."[3] The early Church first used this term with reference to lists of books that are part of the Christian Bible. It is not native to early Jewish literature concerning what is part of—or excluded from—the Bible. Applied to the Jewish Bible, "canon" has been used in many ways, making it an ambiguous and confusing term.[4]

For these reasons, many scholars prefer to speak of "the development of scripture," rather than "the canonization of the Bible."[5] Yet that is not much of an improvement. For me at least, "scripture" is a foreign term. Furthermore, because "scripture" means merely "that which is written," it is historically imprecise. Therefore, I prefer to frame our question as follows: When and how did a central set of books with a particular name (e.g., *mikra* [מִקְרָא, "that which is read or recited"] or *kitvei ha-kodesh* [כִּתְבֵי הַקֹּדֶשׁ, "holy writings"]) come into being within Judaism?[6]

The process evolved gradually, partly because the books that now comprise the Bible were written over a period of more than a thousand years (see "Other Jewish Names: A Historical Review" in chapter 2). Furthermore, the three-part ("tripartite") structure of the Bible most likely reflects historical development: at first, the Torah alone was central. Thus the postexilic books of Ezra-Nehemiah and Chronicles employ phrases such as "the Torah of the LORD," "the Torah of Moses," "My [God's] Torah," and simply "the Torah," referring to a book much like what we now call the Torah.[7] By the Hellenistic period, Jews treated other books as important and worthy of study as well; for example, the Book of Daniel specifically reinterprets the seventy-year oracle of Jeremiah (see "Reinterpretation and Creative Philology" in chapter 21). Daniel 9:2 speaks of "consult[ing] the *sefarim* (סְפָרִים, 'books')," but the word *sefarim*—even used with a definite article as "the" books—is too generic to be a technical term (that is, reflecting texts of communal importance—what Jews would later call the Bible).

The most important datum for a group of sacred books beyond the Torah comes from Josephus—the first-century-C.E. Jewish historian—who notes: "Our books, those of which are just accredited are but two and twenty, and contain the record for all time."[8] He is employing the concept of a set number of authoritative books, which he calls these "holy books."[9] Josephus nowhere enumerates them. However, contemporary scholars widely agree that he means the twenty-four books that we now call the Bible, with Ruth being counted as part of Judges, and Lamentations as part of Jeremiah.[10] One reason to think so is that the roughly contemporaneous IV Ezra (a nonbiblical work) refers to "twenty-four" books (14:44ff.). It seems likely that these two sources had in mind the same collection of central books.

Until several decades ago, many scholars assumed that the rabbis convened a council at Jamnia (modern Jabneh or Yavneh), during which they canonized the Bible.[11] At the end of the nineteenth century, the great Jewish historian Heinrich Graetz had popularized this view, but it is now recognized to be wrong. Rabbinic literature associated with the sages of Jamnia (late first century C.E.) does discuss whether certain biblical books (such as Song of Songs or Esther) "defile the hands." (That is the rabbis' classic technical term for a work that is biblical.[12]) However, as most historians now acknowledge, rabbinic texts from a later period are not reliable for reconstructing an earlier period. In addition, the literary form of these particular texts is suspect: they do not have the give-and-take of "real" rabbinic debates. Most likely, someone composed these "debate" texts to justify why the "problematic" (unsettling) books like Esther and Ecclesiastes were already part of the Bible.

However, even though rabbinic literature often refers to "twenty-four" biblical books (the same number we have),[13] the entire group of sages may not have shared the same Bible.[14] Consider how they cited Ben-Sirach (a nonbiblical second-century-B.C.E. Jewish work composed in the land of Israel; see "Reading Proverbs" in chapter 23). Rabbinic literature sometimes quotes Ben-Sirach using the same citation formulas as for books that we call biblical.[15] As one scholar has observed, it "was sometimes expounded much like any other biblical book,"[16] which suggests that for some rabbis, Ben-Sirach was as authoritative as is the Bible—and most likely for them it was Bible! Thus for the rabbinic period, it might be best to speak of a "*largely* closed" set of texts that comprised the Bible—or several competing conceptions of it, with some sages including Ben-Sirach, and others not.

Quite possibly a "largely closed" set of texts that comprised the Bible, mostly identical to our current Bible, also existed among a Jewish sect that lived in the Judean Desert, whose surviving library is what we now call the Dead Sea Scrolls.[17] This community may not have had a notion of canon; at least, they had no special term for such a thing. However, in their interpretive literature they did tend to cite particular books. Furthermore, certain books are extant in many copies, indicating that they were especially important to the community.

Of the books that are part of the classical rabbis' Bible, only the Book of Esther is missing among the Dead Sea Scrolls that we have today; thus, the community probably did not consider that book authoritative.[18] In contrast, other Dead Sea Scroll texts cite the Temple Scroll and the Book of Jubilees as authoritative. Furthermore, the community kept a large number of manuscripts of both works.[19] Thus, our term "canonical" Bible seems anachronistic for this group in the prerabbinic period. Nevertheless, it is safe to say that its set of authoritative books largely, but not completely, overlapped what would eventually become biblical for the rabbis.

The Order and the Ordering of Biblical Books

For the many centuries before Jewish scribes published books in codex form, they preserved books in the form of separate scrolls.[20] In certain cases, the scribes put several books in a single scroll—and in a particular order. One such book was the Torah, which needed to be ordered because Jews read it ritually in order as part of the lectionary. Similarly, they grouped Joshua, Judges, Samuel, and Kings in sequence, since they tell a more or less continuous story in chronological order. However, for the rest of the Bible, its books fall into no particular order.

Certain people and groups (especially professional scribes!) love order. Mesopotamian scribes often copied series of cuneiform tablets (such as lexical lists) in arbitrary but standard orders. The resulting predictability made it easier for readers to find what they were looking for, no matter which copy they consulted. Similarly, perhaps ancient Israelite librarians may have kept biblical scrolls in ordered cubby holes, so that they could locate the right text easily. This may be the original function of ordering the books of the Bible.[21]

The Bible shows evidence of ordering at both the macro and the micro level. On the microlevel, its text is divided into books—typically, what can fit on a scroll. (Thus, the twelve "Minor" Prophets comprise a single book or scroll, even though it is made up of many books.)[22]

On the macrolevel, this large collection comprises smaller collections. Exactly how and when this was done is the subject of intense current debate: How early is the three-part division of the Bible into Torah, Nevi'im, and Kethuvim? When and why did this tripartite division develop? Rabbinic sources—though not any of the earliest such sources—do attest to a three-part (what scholars call a "tripartite") Bible.[23] Scholars have found allusions to this structure in the New Testament and among the Dead Sea Scrolls. However, these references do not decisively prove that the Bible was organized into three parts as early as the first century C.E.[24] Indeed, Jews clearly employed a variety of orders and ordering schemes in the Second Temple period,[25] and the tripartite ordering was likely one of them.

The tripartite ordering was likely one of the early ordering schemes, for its classifications are not obvious ones. As noted earlier, Daniel properly belongs with the latter prophets; meanwhile, Ezra-Nehemiah, Chronicles, and perhaps some other books belong with the former prophets (see "Name and Structure" in chapter 2). Thus, their present classification seems to reflect an evolution: by the time those later books came along, the set of books known as Prophets had already been determined, so they could not be included in that section. That is, over time the Torah became authoritative first, then Nevi'im, and finally Kethuvim.[26]

This hypothesis for the evolutionary development of the tripartite canon would also explain the stability—and lack of stability—of order within each section. The Torah—authoritative first—is fully stable: all manuscripts have the order as Genesis, Exodus, Leviticus, Numbers, Deuteronomy. (Of course, given the contents of these books, their order is not really flexible.) Within Nevi'im, the same is true for the Former Prophets. Concerning the order of the Latter Prophets, there is more flexibility; most manuscripts do not follow the Talmudic order. Within Kethuvim, manuscripts show a tremendous variation of the order of its books.[27] This accords with its presumed status as the section becoming authoritative latest. Quite surprisingly, the ancient sources do not show even a broad consensus on what the last—culminating—book of the Bible should be!

The Stabilization of the Biblical Text

A book may be authoritative even though it does not have a fixed text. The spelling of its words, certain whole words themselves—even whole verses—such things could and did vary from one written copy to another. Thus, I consider the issues of canonization and textual stabilization separately. Indeed, it is highly likely that the biblical text became stable only in the early rabbinic period. By then, Jews already had a relatively clear idea as to which texts were "in" and which were "out," and they had devised certain methods of midrashic interpretation (namely, methods of interpretation that read the text carefully, and even base their deductions on fine spelling variants). Functionally speaking, the latter development allowed for fluid meaning even as the text became fixed.

As we have seen, the Dead Sea Scrolls community considered authoritative a Bible of sorts, yet they did not have a single stable text for its books.[28] That ancient desert community still proceeded to expound their texts—sometimes in versions that are quite different from those found in (what later crystallized as) the Masoretic text.[29] In fact, in at least one case, they seem to be interpreting two different versions of the same verse. In other words, just because they believed a certain work to be holy and inspired did not imply that it had to exist in a single version.[30] In the words of the contemporary scholar Moshe Greenberg, "Piety is not always accompanied by a critical sense."[31]

Based on the textual witnesses available to us, we can say that the Bible's (consonantal) text largely stabilized by the second century C.E. We do not know exactly how this happened; perhaps someone made a master edition or recension from which other scribes copied.[32] Perhaps the destruction of the Second Temple in 70 C.E. and the failure of the revolt of 132–135 (the Bar Kokhba Rebellion) created a crisis that served as an impetus for creating an authoritative text. The development of a midrashic approach (in the early second century C.E.)[33] that treated the exact spelling of each word as important may have been influential as well in stabilizing the text.

Considering the wider range of ancient versions (and the opportunities meanwhile for scribal errors in transmission), medieval biblical texts show remarkably few variants. However, even that era knew occasional, significant textual variants, including readings in the Babylonian Talmud that differ from most of our biblical manuscripts.[34] The stabilization of the consonantal text continued until well after the advent of printing in the late 1400s. Even so, to this day, a few variant spellings remain. (Of course, printing could—and did!—introduce new errors into the text.)[35]

How the Bible Became the Bible

Today, were we to open two texts of the Hebrew Bible, they would contain the same books, grouped into three major parts, appearing mostly (if not entirely) in the same order, with a well over 99% agreement on the consonants and vocalization (vowels and cantillation). I hope that it is now clear that this consistency was the result of a long and complicated process that took place largely behind the scenes, obscured from our view. At the beginning of the process came the idea of a "Bible" itself. Most likely the Torah (which itself developed over time) became authoritative first. Later, a larger Bible coalesced around the Torah, though different groups at different times viewed the contents of this Bible differently, ordered its books differently, and grouped it variously into major divisions. In the late first or early second century, scribes seemed to stop copying all but one particular consonantal text of this incipient Bible.

More than half a century later, guardians of the biblical text devised various systems of marking the proper vocalization of the consonantal text. By the late first millennium, the vocalization system associated with Aaron Ben-Asher and with the city of Tiberius in the Galilee "won" over competing systems, giving us the Bible as we now have it.[36] This means that in its current form (with vowels), the Bible is only a little more than 1,000 years old!

Afterword

Reading the Bible as a Committed Jew

Thus far I have written this book in my "scholarly" mode, emphasizing what the Bible meant in its time and place. I have emphasized the importance of the historical-critical method, which encourages me to present facts about antiquity as I understand them. In so doing, I have attempted to mask my personal beliefs. These beliefs should not matter—one's own religion (or lack thereof) should not decisively impact how one understands the Hebrew Bible in its original environment.

Many who have just completed this book would guess that I, as its author, lack religious convictions altogether. After all, it is easy to read the previous pages as an acute case of "Bible bashing." I have emphasized the composite nature of the Bible, treating it as a human, rather than a divine, work. I have contextualized it in the ancient Near East, rather than treating it as a timeless book. I have made the following claims: the beginning of Genesis is a "myth"; the Exodus did not happen; and Joshua did not fight the battle of Jericho and make the walls come tumbling down. Further, I have stated that much of the material in the Bible's historical texts is not historical; that not everything found in the work known as Amos (or Isaiah, or Jeremiah, or Ezekiel) was written by Amos (or Isaiah, or Jeremiah, or Ezekiel); and that David composed none of the psalms. I have asserted that not only is the Song of Songs a secular work, but that much of the Bible is also, for it was influenced by (secular) ideology as much as by religion.

I am, in fact, an observant Jew. I take the Bible quite seriously in my personal life. It is not merely a book from which I make a living (as a teacher and author). Rather, it stands at the core of who I am as a person, and as a Jew.

There is no single way to place the Bible at one's core. Indeed, the ways of viewing the Bible as a religious text are at least as numerous as the people who puzzle it out. Thus, I do not intend what follows as *the* way to reconcile the scholars' critical approach with a religious (Jewish) life. Instead, I simply wish to explain how I negotiate not merely what the Bible meant (the subject of the previous chapters), but also what the Bible means *to me*.

From Sourcebook to Textbook

In a nutshell, here is my view of the Bible as a Jew: *The Bible is a sourcebook that I—within my community—make into a textbook. I do so by selecting, revaluing, and interpreting the texts that I call sacred.*

"Sourcebooks" are not the same as "textbooks." A sourcebook, by nature, presents many perspectives, whereas a textbook—in order to be cogent—adopts a particular point of view. An economics textbook that was both Keynesian and Marxist, or an introductory literary textbook that was both new-critical and deconstructivist, would be confusing, as confusing, indeed, as the Bible itself. However, a broad-minded professor teaching "Introduction to Economics" could create a sourcebook showing a variety of approaches, including the Keynesian and the Marxist. Likewise, a good literature professor might compile readings that encouraged students to analyze the same text from competing theoretical perspectives.

The Bible as it presents itself, "off the shelf," is a sourcebook. It comes from many places and times; it conveys the interests of many different groups. Within it, we can find more than one opinion on almost any single item of importance—the nature of God, the corporeality of God, intergenerational punishment, the relationship between men and women, the attitude toward foreigners, retribution, etc. In this sense, the Bible is surely more sourcebook than textbook.[1]

Yet, in order to take the Bible seriously in my religious life—as a guide for various issues—I must make it into something more authoritative. Guidebooks do not say: at the fork in the road, take either a right, a left, or turn around. Rather, they make decisions, they choose between options. Thus, when I confront the Bible as a practicing Jew, I transform it into a more monolithic book.

Selection

As noted, I make the Bible into a textbook in several ways. The simplest is through "selection"—choosing one of the options that the Bible offers. How and why I make those choices is a complicated (and personal) issue. At any rate, in part I do this within my religious community—and in part I choose a community that has already made compatible choices. Such communities might be a synagogue community, a community of like-minded friends, or an extended family. As personal as religion is, it has a very strong social dimension, and thus my finding a religious community is crucial to me. (When people's beliefs change, they may move from one community to another, finding groups that view the Bible and its interpretation in a similar fashion.)

Selecting from among the Bible's sources is nothing new. Already in the biblical period its authors and editors did so. As we saw earlier in this book, the editor of Chronicles knew sources describing more than one way to cook the paschal lamb. By claiming that it should be boiled (2 Chron. 35:13), that author *selected* Deuteronomy 16:7 over Exodus 12:9. True, that author gave a nod to the Exodus text by mentioning fire (see "Rewriting History" in chapter 14). However, the bottom line was a choice: the editor *selected* the ritual practice in Deuteronomy 16:7, setting the other practice aside.

Classical midrash (and medieval Jewish commentary, which followed in its wake) has functioned similarly.[2] As I mentioned in chapter 1, Exodus 21:6 allows a Hebrew to be a "slave for life," whereas Leviticus 25:40 insists that all such slaves "shall serve with you only until the jubilee year"; the editor of the *Mekhilta* resolved the apparent contradiction by reinterpreting "for life" as meaning "until the jubilee year." This was creative philology (see "Reinterpretation and Creative Philology" in chapter 21). Some might speak of this as reconciling these two texts. However, practically speaking, the midrashic editor *selected* Leviticus 25:40 over Exodus 21:6 . (This is ironic given that the *Mekhilta* is a midrash on Exodus.)

So, too, as I engage the Bible: After carefully considering its texts, I use selection to adopt some texts as more meaningful to me than others.

Revaluation

Sometimes, when confronting a particular issue, I find that *all* the biblical texts are problematic for one reason or another. In such cases, I must acknowledge that the Bible is an ancient text; it hails from a society fundamentally different from ours. Perhaps it has not always aged well. Therefore I must actively "translate" the text into terms that fit our society. This is extremely difficult to do with integrity, yet in some areas, especially concerning matters of sex and gender (what "real men" and "real women" do), it is the only workable approach. I then distinguish what the text originally *meant* (in its original historical context) from what it now *means* (taking into consideration certain key differences between ancient Israelite antiquity and modern times).[3] I assign the new meaning by modernizing the text quite carefully.

Interpretation

Interpretation, even radical interpretation, has always played a role in making sense of the Bible. As we saw in a prior chapter, the author of the Book of Daniel wrote that his protagonist "consulted the books concerning the number of years that, according to the word of the LORD that had come to Jeremiah the prophet, were to be the term of Jerusalem's desolation—seventy years" (Dan. 9:2). As a result of this reckoning with Jeremiah's earlier prophecy (and with the help of the angel Gabriel), Daniel realized that "70 years" really meant 490 years (see "Reinterpretation and Creative Philology" in chapter 21).

Examples of similarly radical reinterpretation abound in rabbinic literature. Amos 5:2 reads in part, straightforwardly: **נָפְלָה לֹא תוֹסִיף קוּם** ("Fallen, not to rise again,") / **בְּתוּלַת יִשְׂרָאֵל** ("Is Maiden Israel"). Some rabbinic interpreters found this sentiment unacceptably hopeless. They repunctuated this verse to read: **נָפְלָה לֹא** ("Fallen—no!") / **תֹסִיף קוּם** ("Again to rise") / **בְּתוּלַת יִשְׂרָאֵל** ("Is Maiden Israel").[4] Syntactically, this interpretation is impossible, but it shows how radical interpretation can arise out of necessity. Radical interpretation maintains the place of the biblical text as central within Judaism but allows it to be expounded in a fashion that its original authors would hardly recognize. This method continues to be important today.

Final Words

The approach that I have laid out here allows me to walk something of a tightrope between being a serious historical-critical Bible scholar, emphasizing prerabbinic norms of biblical interpretation and taking the Bible seriously as a Jew, incorporating postbiblical, rabbinic norms. Many feel that these roles are mutually incompatible. Yet, as my supporting examples show, this approach has roots in both biblical and rabbinic texts. Judaism as it has evolved is more than biblical religion, just as Jews are more than only Karaites—and even Karaites have adopted many practices not mentioned in the Bible.[5] Yet we retain some continuity in our approaches to a text that we hold sacred.

The historical-critical method, with its emphasis on the prerabbinic meaning of diverse texts, might seem to be antirabbinic. Not so. Classic rabbinic texts are typically punctuated with the phrase *davar acher* (דָּבָר אַחֵר, "another opinion"), used to separate distinct opinions. Frequently, rabbinic texts offer as many diverse opinions as biblical texts do.[6] In other words, the Bible is really much more like a rabbinic text than people think—it is full of cases of "another opinion." The main difference between the Bible and classic rabbinic texts is that the Bible marks its distinct opinions less forthrightly. Yet in light of the historical-critical method, the Bible appears as a compilation of diverse sources—that is, closer to the structure of much of rabbinic literature.

Indeed, a small number of rabbinic texts seem to recognize the composite nature of the Torah. Certainly, no rabbinic text says that the Torah was written by J, E, D, and P. However, an early medieval midrashic work, *Pesikta de-Rav Kahana*, describes the revelation at Sinai, suggesting that it was not monolithic: "R. Hanina bar Papa said: The Holy One appeared to Israel with a stern face, with an equanimous face, with a friendly face, with a joyous face . . ."—all of which, with the same authority, represented the same God.[7] The midrash proceeds to present another tradition describing God at the moment of revelation as "a statue with faces on every side." In other words, each individual present gained a uniquely personal view of God.

The historical-critical method exemplified in the book assumes that we can no longer recover the single truth of what the Torah describes as Revelation, nor of other religious issues that the ancient Hebrew texts address. The most we can do is to recognize the "faces on every side"—the multiple ancient perceptions of God, preserved in our composite Bible.

Notes

Chapter 1

1. I have borrowed this characterization of traditional biblical interpretation from James L. Kugel, *The Bible as It Was* (Cambridge, MA: Belknap Press, 1997), 18–23. He expands that book in his *Traditions of the Bible: A Guide to the Bible as It Was at the Start of the Common Era* (Cambridge, MA: Harvard Univ. Press, 1998). He makes similar observations about a later period in his *In Potiphar's House: The Interpretive Life of Biblical Texts* (San Francisco: Harper and Row, 1990).
2. For a translation of Pesher Habakkuk, see Geza Vermes, *The Complete Dead Sea Scrolls* (Harmondsworth, UK: Penguin, 1997), 478–85; see esp. 479 (from the middle of column 2): "the priest [in whose heart] God set [understanding] that he might interpret all the words of His servants the prophets, through whom he foretold all that would happen to His people and [His land]" and 481: "the Teacher of Righteousness, to whom God made known all the mysteries of the words of His servants the Prophets." For a discussion of Pesher literature, see Shani L. Berrin, "Pesharim," in *The Encyclopedia of the Dead Sea Scrolls*, ed. Lawrence H. Schiffman and James C. VanderKam, 2.644–47.
3. Classical rabbinic commentary (midrash) explains the Exodus phrase "in perpetuity" with the words "until the jubilee year." See, for example, Jacob Z. Lauterbach, ed. and trans., *Mekhilta de-Rabbi Ishmael* (Philadelphia: Jewish Publication Society, 1935; reissued 2004), 3.17.
4. See esp. Ibn Ezra's commentary to Gen. 36:31.
5. Baruch Spinoza, *Tractatus Theologico-Politicus*, (trans. Samuel Shirley (Leiden: Brill, 1991).

6. Ibid., 141.
7. For a description of the method itself, see John Barton, "Historical-Critical Approaches," in *The Cambridge Companion to Biblical Interpretation*, ed. John Barton (Cambridge: Cambridge Univ. Press, 1998), 9–20. For descriptions of the development of this method, see *The Cambridge History of the Bible*, 3 vols. (Cambridge: Cambridge Univ. Press, 1963–70), and the series *Hebrew Bible/Old Testament: The History of Its Interpretation* (Göttingen: Vandenhoeck & Ruprecht, 1996–). For an outline of the method, see Edgar Krentz, *The Historical-Critical Method* (Philadelphia: Fortress, 1975).
8. The term "historical-critical" may date from the seventeenth century.
9. Julius Wellhausen, *Prolegomena to the History of Ancient Israel* (Gloucester, MA: Peter Smith, 1973). Much of the book brilliantly synthesizes earlier findings. It separates the Bible, especially the Torah, into sources that are dated to particular time periods. Then it puts those sources back together according to a posited historical development of Israelite religion.
10. The works of the German rabbi David Zvi Hoffmann are the most significant of those who decried Wellhausen's approach. Among his contemporaries who defended the historical-critical method was another German-educated rabbi, the American Reform leader Kaufmann Kohler.
11. Solomon Schechter, *Seminary Addresses and Other Papers* (Cincinnati, OH: Ark Publishing Co., 1915), 35–39.
12. Ibid., 38.
13. *Prolegomena*, 227. On Wellhausen's indebtedness to the age he lived in for his understanding of Judaism, see Lou H. Silberman, "Wellhausen and Judaism," *Semeia* 25 (1982), 75–82.
14. Schechter, *Seminary Address*, 37.
15. The *Jewish Study Bible* (New York: Oxford Univ. Press, 2004) is further proof of how far this method has spread; two decades ago it would have been impossible to find enough Jewish scholars committed to the historical-critical method to complete that book.
16. Barry Holtz, ed., *Back to the Sources: Reading the Classic Jewish Texts* (New York: Summit Books, 1984).
17. Richard Elliott Friedman has written several excellent readable works on the Bible. However, his *Who Wrote the Bible* (San Francisco: HarperSan Franciso, 1997) is not Jewishly sensitive, and his more recent *Commentary on the Torah with English Translation and Hebrew Text* (San Francisco: HarperSanFranciso, 1997) does not use source criticism.
18. The classic of this genre is Otto Eissfeldt, *The Old Testament: An Introduction*, (trans. Peter A. Ackroyd (New York: Harper and Row, 1965). For a survey

of the genre, see Brevard S. Childs, *Introduction to the Old Testament As Scripture* (Philadelphia: Fortress, 1979), 27–45.

19. For those interested in more detailed theoretical discussions of methodology, see John Barton, *Reading the Old Testament: Method in Biblical Study* (revised and enlarged edition; Louisville, KY: Westminster John Knox, 1996); Douglass A. Knight, ed., *Methods of Biblical Interpretation* (Nashville, TN: Abingdon, 2004).

Chapter 2

1. The Greek word *biblia*, in turn, likely derives from the Phoenician port city of Byblos, a major exporter of papyrus, from which the ancients made most of their books. Paper reached the West from China only in the late first millennium C.E.
2. See 2 Corinthians 3:14 and Hebrews 8:7.
3. As a technical term for a body of literature, "Old Testament" was first used by Melito of Sardis and the Church Fathers Tertullian and Origen, who lived from the second to the third centuries C.E.
4. Semitic languages (or dialects) in the ancient Near East included Akkadian, Phoenician, Ugaritic, Moabite, Aramaic, and Hebrew. When in this book I refer to "Semitic cultures," I mean the civilizations that produced documents or inscriptions in these languages. From that evidence we know that those cultures shared a great deal in terms of their outlook and way of life.
5. This book uses the dating schema B.C.E. (Before the Common Era) and C.E. (Common Era) for the designations B.C. and A.D., respectively. The dates are equivalent.
6. See Josephus, *Antiquities* 10.210, 13.167, 16.168, 20.264; *Against Apion* 1.54, 127, 228. Another ancient Jew who wrote in Greek, Philo, employed a similar phrase, *hai hierai graphai,* in his *Abraham* 61, *de congressu* 34, 90; *Decalogue* 8, 37; and elsewhere. (See also Josephus in *Against Apion* 2.45.) These references were supplied by Professor Shaye D. Cohen.
7. See *Against Apion* 1.42. This may be found in H. St. J. Thackery, trans., *Josephus I: The Life; Against Apion*, Loeb Classical Library (Cambridge, MA: Harvard Univ. Press, 1926), 178–79.
8. The second term overlaps with the earlier Greek nomenclature. For these and other rabbinic terms for the entire Bible and its sections, see Sid Z. Leiman, *The Canonization of Hebrew Scripture: The Talmudic and Midrashic Evidence* (Hamden, CT: Archon Books, 1976), 57.

9. Ibid., 60–72.
10. Frederick E. Greenspahn, "How Jews Translate the Bible," in *Biblical Translation in Context,* ed. Frederick W. Knobloch (Bethesda: Univ. Press of Maryland, 2002), 52–53.
11. Roland E. Murphy, "Old Testament/*Tanakh*—Canon and Interpretation," in *Hebrew Bible or Old Testament? Studying the Bible in Judaism and Christianity*, ed. Roger Brooks and John J. Collins (Notre Dame, IN: Univ. of Notre Dame, 1990), 11–29.
12. Apart from the Torah, Jews have arranged the biblical books in many other orders. See the discussion in Leiman, *The Canonization of Hebrew Scripture*, 51–53. See also the charts in Christian D. Ginsburg, *Introduction to the Massoretico-Critical Edition of the Hebrew Bible* (1897; repr., Hoboken, NJ: Ktav, 1966), 108. Ginsburg worked without knowledge of the important thousand-year-old Bible manuscript known as the Aleppo Codex (and related codexes such as Leningrad B19a). The order of Kethuvim in Aleppo is: Chronicles, Psalms, Job, Proverbs, Ruth, Song of Songs, Ecclesiastes, Lamentations, Esther, Daniel, Ezra-Nehemiah.
13. This is the first of the "Former Prophets"; three others follow.
14. Although English Bibles list Samuel, Kings, Chronicles, and Ezra-Nehemiah as two books apiece, originally they were each a single book. Because those books were quite long, later editors split each one into two parts for convenience.
15. Many manuscripts placed Job before Proverbs.
16. Jewish scribes and editors have tended to group together five relatively short books (Song of Songs, Ruth, Lamentations, Ecclesiastes, and Esther), placing them usually within Kethuvim or sometimes right after the Torah, at the start of Nevi'im. Within this collection, which is often called the *Chamesh Megillot* ("Five Scrolls"), their order has been highly variable. The order shown reflects the sequence in which Jews read them during the liturgical year. Another common arrangement reflects the chronological order in which they were written according to rabbinic ascription.
17. Three books (Isaiah, Jeremiah, and Ezekiel) form a set called "Major Prophets," where "major" refers to the length of the books. Within this set, Jewish scribes and editors have arranged the books in different sequences.
18. "Minor" in this context means "short." The twelve are Hosea, Joel, Amos, Obadiah, Jonah, Micah, Nahum, Habakkuk, Zephaniah, Haggai, Zechariah, Malachi. In Hebrew manuscripts and printed editions, these twelve texts always appear in the same order.
19. Too much emphasis should not be placed on Chronicles as the "last" book of the Bible—this is not its position in many of the most accurate early manuscripts.

20. As stated, the Septuagint was originally a Jewish translation. For centuries, many Jews spoke Greek as their first language, and they used various Greek translations of the Bible. For example, the Judean Desert community whose library we now call the Dead Sea Scrolls kept Greek translations on hand (see the summary in Eugene Ulrich, "Septuagint," *Encyclopedia of the Dead Sea Scrolls*, 2.863–68). However, the Septuagint was preserved in its entirety only within the Christian community. Scholarly literature on the Septuagint and its origin is immense; see recently Natalio Fernández Marcos, *The Septuagint in Context: Introduction to the Greek Version of the Bible*, trans. Wilfred G. E. Watson (Boston: Brill Academic Publishers, 2001).
21. In antiquity this was the predominant order of these four sections, but not the only arrangement. See the lists and detailed discussion in Henry Barclay Swete, *An Introduction to the Old Testament in Greek* (Cambridge: Cambridge Univ. Press, 1902), 197–230; for less complete, but less technical discussion, see Roger Beckwith, *The Old Testament Canon of the New Testament Church and Its Background in Early Judaism* (Grand Rapids, MI: Eerdmans, 1985), 181–234.
22. The Septuagint placed Ruth after Judges, apparently because the two are recognized as occurring in the same time period (see Ruth 1:1). It also placed Lamentations after the Book of Jeremiah, the prophet who is said to have written those laments.
23. The division into two parts of some of the larger books (Samuel, Kings, Chronicles, Ezra-Nehemiah) is found already in the Septuagint. Greek tradition also assigned different names to some of the biblical books; for example, what we call Chronicles, they called Paralipomena, "that which was omitted [from Samuel and Kings]."
24. In Septuagint manuscripts, the predominant order of the Twelve differs from that found in Hebrew Bibles. However, English Bibles typically order the Twelve according to their Hebrew order.
25. For a chart of these differences, see *JSB*, 2118–19.
26. b. *Bava Batra* 14b–15a.

Chapter 3

1. Much of this chapter, and the title of this book, is based on John Barton, *Reading the Old Testament: Method in Biblical Study*, rev. and enl. ed. (Louisville, KY: Westminster John Knox, 1996).
2. Barton's term for reading the Bible like an ancient Israelite is "literary competence" (see the previous note).

3. James L. Kugel, *The Bible as It Was* (Cambridge, MA: Belknap Press, 1997), 18–23.
4. This poem is quoted in Thomas E. Sanders, *The Discovery of Poetry* (Atlanta: Scott, Foresman and Company, 1967), 33.
5. Our lack of informants may have moved many readers, and some scholars, away from the historical-critical method, which they see as overly conjectural and unverifiable. This is an exaggerated reaction. Many of the results of historical-critical analyses can be trusted with a high degree of confidence.

Chaper 4

1. Based on linguistic evidence, most scholars consider the Song of Deborah in Judges 5 to be the earliest piece of biblical literature. Portions of the Book of Daniel are typically dated to between 167 and 164 B.C.E., based on internal references to historical events.
2. For additional literature on the theoretical issues discussed here, see my book *The Creation of History in Ancient Israel* (London: Routledge, 1995); "The Copenhagen School: The Historiographical Issues," *AJS Review* 27 (2003), 1–21; and V. Philips Long, ed., *Israel's Past in Present Research: Essays on Ancient Israelite Historiography*, Sources for Biblical and Theological Study 7 (Winona Lake, IN: Eisenbrauns, 1999).
3. The most famous of these in America was by John Bright, recently republished in a fourth (posthumous) edition.
4. E. A. Speiser, *Genesis*, Anchor Bible (Garden City, NY: Doubleday, 1964), XL–XLI, 91–93.
5. This tendency pervades the work of William Foxwell Albright, and may be seen especially in his synthesis, *From Stone Age to Christianity: Monotheism and the Historical Process* (Garden City, NY: Anchor, 1957). The book also displays a significant Christian bias. For an important critique of Albright, see Burke O. Long, *Planting and Reaping Albright: Politics, Ideology, and Interpreting the Bible* (University Park: Pennsylvania State Univ. Press, 1997).
6. Thomas L. Thompson, *The Historicity of the Patriarchal Narratives: The Quest for the Historical Abraham*, BZAW 133 (Berlin: de Gruyter, 1974).
7. John Van Seters, *Abraham in History and Tradition* (New Haven, CT: Yale Univ. Press, 1975).
8. See, e.g., Kathleen Kenyon, *Archaeology in the Holy Land*, 3rd ed. (New York: Praeger, 1970), 211.

9. See the summary in Amihai Mazar, *Archaeology of the Land of the Bible 10,000–586 B.C.E.*, Anchor Bible (Garden City, NY: Doubleday, 1990), 328–38. For a recent detailed synthesis, see William G. Dever, *Who Were the Early Israelites and Where Did They Come From?* (Grand Rapids MI: Eerdmans, 2003). For a popular summary, see Amy Dockser Marcus, *The View from Nebo: How Archaeology is Rewriting and Reshaping the Middle East* (Boston: Little, Brown, 2000), 78–104.
10. See the summary and critique in my article "The Copenhagen School: The Historiographical Issues," *AJS Review* 27 (2003), 1–21.
11. The literature on theoretical biases is now immense. See especially the works of Thompson and Lemche from the Copenhagen School, as well as a variety of authors publishing in the *SJOT*. For critiques, see the article cited in n. 10 and various works by Dever. The dispute is reflected in the variety of articles found in Lester L. Grabbe, ed., *Can A 'History of Israel' Be Written?* JSOTSup 245 (Sheffield, UK: Sheffield Academic Press, 1997).
12. Accusations of anti-Zionism have been leveled in particular against Keith W. Whitelam, *The Invention of Ancient Israel: The Silencing of Palestinian History* (London: Routledge, 1996).
13. For more on the methodological issues in using the Bible as a historical source, see my book *The Creation of History* and the various books and articles cited above.
14. For many examples from various cultures, see Bertil Albrektson, *History and the Gods: An Essay on the Idea of Historical Events as Divine Manifestations in the Ancient Near East and in Israel*, CBOT 1 (Lund; Gleerup, 1967).
15. *COS*, 2.137.
16. Assyrian scribes, however, recopied their annals extensively since they were updated annually. Sometimes in this process, they would revise and shorten the events of earlier years; see Louis D. Levine, "Manuscripts, Texts and the Study of the Neo-Assyrian Royal Inscriptions," in F. M. Fales, ed., *Assyrian Royal Inscriptions: New Horizons* (Rome: Instituto per L'Oriente, 1981), 49–70.
17. Detailed discussion of the reliability of textual transmission may be found in Emanuel Tov, *Textual Criticism of the Hebrew Bible*, 2nd rev. ed. (Minneapolis, MN: Augsburg Fortress, 2001).
18. Many books bear titles like "A/The History of (Ancient) Israel," which the following summary draws upon. Two of the more recent such books are Iaian Provan, V. Philips Long, and Tremper Longman III, *A Biblical History of Israel* (Louisville, KY: Westminster John Knox, 2003), and Victor H. Matthews, *A Brief History of Ancient Israel* (Louisville, KY: Westminster John

Knox, 2003—see also his theoretical discussion on 3–97). These lean toward the conservative side in terms of upholding as much of the biblical narrative as possible.

19. See Donald B. Redford, *Egypt, Canaan, and Israel in Ancient Times* (Princeton, NJ: Princeton Univ. Press, 1992), 257–80; note especially 260, where he accuses many biblical scholars of "manhandling of evidence." Contrast the view of James K. Hoffmeier, *Israel in Egypt: The Evidence for the Authenticity of the Exodus Tradition* (New York: Oxford Univ. Press, 1997).
20. Biblical scholars have not reached a consensus on exactly what the Israelite self-understanding was, or even about when the ancestral stories were written. Compare, e.g., E. Theodore Mullen, Jr., *Ethnic Myths and Pentateuchal Foundations: A New Approach to the Formation of the Pentateuch* (Atlanta: Scholars, 1997) to P. Kyle McCarter and Ronald S. Hendel, "The Patriarchal Age: Abraham, Isaac and Jacob," in Hershel Shanks, ed., *Ancient Israel*, rev. and exp. (Washington, DC: Biblical Archaeology Society, 1999), 1–31.
21. *COS*, 2.41.
22. I. Eph'al, "The Western Minorities in Babylonia in the 6th–5th Centuries B.C.: Maintenance and Cohesion," *Orientalia* 47 (1978), 74–90.

Chaper 5

1. See G. F. Moore, "The Vulgate Chapters and Numbered Verses in the Hebrew Bible," in Sid Z. Leiman, ed., *The Canon and Masorah of the Hebrew Bible: An Introductory Reader* (New York: Ktav, 1974), 815–20.
2. See Emanuel Tov, *Textual Criticism of the Hebrew Bible* (Minneapolis, MN: Fortress, 2001), 50–51, 210–11.
3. See Tov, 52–53, and L. Blau, "Massoretic Studies, III.–IV.: The Division into Verses," in *The Canon and Masorah of the Hebrew Bible*, ed. Sid Z. Leiman, 623–64.
4. On the division between words, see Tov, 208–9, 252–53.
5. From comparative linguistic evidence and ancient translations, scholars have determined that in the period of the Bible, the consonant *vav* (ו) represented a "w" sound. That is why scholars often write the unvocalized divine name as "*YHWH*" rather than "*YHVH*."
6. See Jeffrey H. Tigay, *The Evolution of the Gilgamesh Epic* (Philadelphia: Univ. of Pennsylvania Press, 1982). In fact, the most famous part of this composition, the flood story of tablet 11, reflects a reworking of the earlier Atra-Ḫasis epic.

7. See especially 4QpaleoExod^{m}, which has many expansions of the type seen in the Samaritan Pentateuch. See DJD 9, 68–70.
8. For a popular introduction to source criticism, see Richard Elliott Friedman, *Who Wrote the Bible?* (San Francisco: HarperSanFrancisco, 1997); Israel Knohl, *The Divine Symphony: The Bible's Many Voices* (Philadelphia: Jewish Publication Society, 2003), 1–85. For a color-coded delineation of these sources, see Richard Elliott Friedman, *The Bible with Sources Revealed* (San Francisco: HarperSanFrancisco, 2003). For a more technical discussion, see Ernest Nicholson, *The Pentateuch in the Twentieth Century: The Legacy of Julius Wellhausen* (Oxford: Clarendon, 1998).
9. See Michael Fishbane, *Biblical Interpretation in Ancient Israel* (Oxford: Oxford Univ. Press, 1985), who argues for a slowly developing canon, or a canon within a canon. More specifically, on the retention of legal sections of Exodus that were reinterpreted in Deuteronomy, see Bernard M. Levinson, *Deuteronomy and the Hermeneutics of Legal Innovation* (New York: Oxford Univ. Press, 1997).
10. George Foot Moore, "Tatian's Diatessaron and the Analysis of the Pentateuch," in *Empirical Models for Biblical Criticism*, ed. Jeffrey H. Tigay (Philadelphia: Univ. of Pennsylvania Press, 1985), 243–56.
11. For additional models, see *Empirical Models for Biblical Criticism*.

Chaper 6

1. The literature by and about creationism is immense. The following web site offers a good sense of the principles and agendas of creationists: http://www.creationism.org.
2. For a recent discussion of the problem of genre and premodern texts, see Bert Roest and Herman Vanstiphout, eds., *Aspects of Genre and Type in Pre-Modern Literary Cultures* (Groningen: Styx, 1999).
3. Walter Burkert, *Structure and History in Greek Mythology and Ritual* (Berkeley: Univ. of California Press, 1979).
4. Ibid., 28.
5. For more on metaphors, see my *God is King: Understanding an Israelite Metaphor*, JSOTSup 76 (Sheffield, UK: Sheffield Academic Press, 1989).
6. Burkert, *Structure and History in Greek Mythology and Ritual*, 1–34, esp. 23.
7. See, e.g., John Carlos Rowe, "Structure," in Frank Lentricchia and Thomas McLaughlin, eds., *Critical Terms for Literary Study* (Chicago: Univ. of Chicago Press, 1990), 23–38. Among biblical scholars of the late twentieth

century, J. P. Fokkelman emphasized the importance of structure; see e.g. his *Reading Biblical Narrative: An Introductory Guide* (Louisville, KY: Westminster John Knox, 1999), 97–111.

8. The fact that many of these structural elements are not evenly distributed throughout Genesis 1 has led many scholars to suggest that this first creation story has a long prehistory, and has incorporated elements of earlier stories. This is likely correct, yet it does not affect my basic argument about the structure and meaning of this myth.
9. Since the predominant image of God in the Bible is as male, and throughout the Hebrew Bible "God" is always treated as grammatically male, I will employ the masculine pronoun throughout this book in reference to God. Historical-critical methodology is indebted to the norms of the past which it is trying to recapture, rather than the preferences of contemporary religious practice. The use of the masculine pronoun throughout the Bible—and in this book—should have no bearing on modern theological issues, on how we might envision God, nor what pronouns we might use in contemporary discourse.
10. This structure is pointed out in most commentaries; in greater detail see Bernhard W. Anderson, "The Priestly Creation Story: A Stylistic Study," in *From Creation to New Creation*, OBT (Minneapolis, MN: Fortress, 1994), 42–55.
11. As in the Mesopotamian myth Enuma Elish (often incorrectly called The Mesopotamian Creation Story), light exists before the creation of the luminaries.
12. As argued by several scholars, it is likely that this creation story is actually the product of "H," a later representation of the Priestly School, rather than P itself, but this is not important at this point.
13. Thus, the main theme of Rudolf Otto, *The Idea of the Holy: An Inquiry into the Non-rational Factor in the Idea of the Divine and its Relation to the Rational* (London: Oxford Univ. Press, 1925) is correct, but only to a limited degree in the Bible.
14. For early Jewish and Christian interpretations, see James L. Kugel, *The Bible as It Was* (Cambridge, MA: Belknap Press, 1997), 61–63.
15. See Claus Westermann, *Genesis 1–11* (Minneapolis, MN: Augsburg, 1984), 145.
16. See my book *God Is King*, 100–109.
17. See especially James Barr, "The Image of God in the Book of Genesis—A Study of Terminology," *BJRL* 51 (1968–69), 11–26.
18. A different understanding of Genesis 1:27 sees the final third ("male and

female he created them") as a new thought, independent of what precedes; see Phyllis A. Bird, "'Male and Female He Created Them': Genesis 1:27b in the Context of the Priestly Account of Creation," in *Missing Persons and Mistaken Identities: Women and Gender in Ancient Israel,* OBT (Minneapolis, MN: Fortress, 1997), 123–54.

19. Usually creation implies the formation of physical objects. Institutions, however, can also be created. Genesis 2:2–3 deals with the creation of the Sabbath, much like the Mesopotamian myth Enuma Elish narrates the creation of kingship and of the institutions surrounding the worship of the god Marduk.
20. See Louis Ginzberg, *The Legends of the Jews,* trans. Henrietta Szold (Philadelphia: Jewish Publication Society, 1968; reissued, 2002), vol. 5, 97–98.
21. See Phyllis Trible, *God and the Rhetoric of Sexuality* (Philadelphia: Fortress, 1978), 126.
22. For the Fall of Man, see Romans 5; the idea of original sin is not present in the Greek New Testament text here, but already appears in an early Latin translation of the Greek. See Jaroslav Pelikan, *The Christian Tradition: A History of the Development of Doctrine,* vol. 1, *The Emergence of the Catholic Tradition (100–600)* (Chicago: Univ. of Chicago, 1971), 299–300.
23. For a detailed, but different treatment of the story, see James Barr, *The Garden of Eden and the Hope of Immortality* (Minneapolis, MN: Fortress, 1993). I learned many of the ideas that I develop below from I. Tzvi Abusch; some are also found in Susan Niditch, "Genesis," in *The Women's Bible Commentary*, ed. Carol A. Newsom and Sharon H. Ringe (Louisville, KY: Westminster/John Knox, 1992), 12–14. A synthesis of recent feminist readings of the Garden story can be found in Alice Ogden Bellis, *Helpmates, Harlots, Heroes: Women's Stories in the Hebrew Bible* (Louisville, KY: Westminster/John Knox, 1994), 45–66.
24. Concern with overpopulation is not anachronistic; in fact, this is a main theme of the Mesopotamian Atra-Ḫasis epic. (For the text, see Stephanie Dalley, *Myths from Mesopotamia: Creation, the Flood, Gilgamesh, and Others* [Oxford: Oxford Univ. Press, 1991], 1–38.)
25. On merisms, see Luis Alonso Schökel, *A Manual of Hebrew Poetics* (Rome: Pontificio Istituto Biblico, 1988), 83–84.
26. See especially the reading of this verse proposed in Carol Meyers, *Discovering Eve: Ancient Israelite Women in Context* (New York: Oxford Univ. Press, 1988), 95–121.
27. Though some have suggested that the author of his story, the Yahwist, may

be a woman, this is most unlikely. With the exception of the Book of Ruth, which shows particular interest in the women's world and depicts women very positively (see "Women in Esther and Ruth" in chapter 26), biblical authors may be assumed to be male, unless there is strong evidence otherwise.

28. Niditch, "Genesis," 13.
29. In contrast to *bara'* (ברא), the word *yatzar* (יצר) is used in this story, a word often used of human potters (see especially Jer. 18).

Chaper 7

1. On the different types of genealogies and their use, see Robert R. Wilson, *Genealogy and History in the Biblical World*, YNER 7 (New Haven, CT: Yale Univ. Press, 1977), which he summarizes in his article "Genealogy, Genealogies," *ABD*, 2.929–932.
2. See John van Seters, *Prologue to History: The Yahwist as Historian in Genesis* (Louisville, KY: Westminster/John Knox, 1992), 189–191, following Claus Westermann.
3. Gerhard von Rad, *Genesis*, OTL (Philadelphia: Westminster, 1972), 24.
4. The literature on the role of the Matriarchs is now immense. See in particular *A Feminist Companion to Genesis*, ed. Athalya Brenner (Sheffield, UK: Sheffield Academic Press, 1993); idem, *Genesis: A Feminist Companion to the Bible (Second Series)* (Sheffield, UK: Sheffield Academic Press, 1998); Susan Niditch, "Genesis," in *The Women's Bible Commentary*, ed. Carol A. Newsom and Sharon H. Ringe (Louisville, KY: Westminster/John Knox, 1992), 10–25, esp. 15–25; and Alice Ogden Bellis, *Helpmates, Harlots, Heroes: Women's Stories in the Hebrew Bible* (Louisville, KY: Westminster/John Knox, 1994), 67–98 (with extensive bibliography).
5. For a dissenting view, see Carol Meyers, *Discovering Eve: Ancient Israelite Women in Context* (New York: Oxford Univ. Press, 1988), 24–46.
6. See the discussion in my book *The Creation of History in Ancient Israel* (London: Routledge, 1995), 10–12.
7. See above, chapter 4.
8. See Susan Niditch, *Underdogs and Tricksters: A Prelude to Biblical Folklore* (San Francisco: Harper and Row, 1987), 70–125.
9. Quite possibly Genesis 22:15–18 is not an original part of this story, as noted by most commentaries. For the meaning of the binding of Isaac story before these verses were added, see Jon D. Levenson, *The Death and*

Resurrection of the Beloved Son: The Transformation of Child Sacrifice in Judaism and Christianity (New Haven, CT: Yale Univ. Press, 1993). He properly emphasizes that the story may *not* be understood as a polemic against child sacrifice.

10. The following examples are taken from James L. Kugel, *The Bible as It Was*, 144–46.
11. "Pseudepigrapha" are noncanonical works that originated in the Jewish Hellenistic period. Most originated in Hebrew, but they survived because the Church preserved them in Greek, Latin, Syriac, Ethiopic, and other languages. The term means "false writings" because many of the Pseudepigrapha present themselves as authentic words of a well-known sage, such as Moses. James H. Charlesworth has collected them in *The Old Testament Pseudepigrapha*, 2 vols. (Garden City, NY: Doubleday, 1983, 1985).
12. Louis Ginzberg, *The Legends of the Jews,* trans. Henrietta Szold (Philadelphia: Jewish Publication Society, 1968; reissued, 2002), 1.221–222. A version of this book without the valuable footnotes is available under the title *Legends of the Bible*.
13. Ginzberg, *Legends of the Jews*, 1.224; for the sources, see 5.221, n. 75.
14. *Antiquities*, 1.164; for the translation, see H. St. J. Thackery, *Josephus IV: Jewish Antiquities Books I–IV*, Loeb Classical Library (Cambridge, MA: Harvard Univ. Press, 1930), vol. 1, 81. Josephus has here reconciled Genesis 12 with the similar stories in chapters 20 and 26.
15. What follows is a summary of "The Typologies of Genesis" in my book *The Creation of History in Ancient Israel*, 48–61; see there for extensive documentation.
16. See Yohanan Muffs, *Love and Joy: Law, Language and Religion in Ancient Israel* (Cambridge, MA: Harvard Univ. Press, 1992), 67–95.
17. For literature on the wife-sister motif, see my book *The Creation of History*, 176, n. 30, and 177, nn. 35, 36.
18. See my book *The Creation of History*, 48, and more generally my article "Cyclical and Teleological Time in the Hebrew Bible," in *Time and Temporality in the Ancient World*, ed. Ralph M. Rosen (Philadelphia: Univ. of Pennsylvania Museum of Archaeology and Anthropology, 2004), 111–28.
19. See especially the tenuous connection between the Exodus and the Sabbath in Deuteronomy 5:15—it is transparent how the Sabbath is related to creation in the Exodus Decalogue, but it is less clear how it commemorates the Exodus.
20. See, e.g., Robert Alter, *The Art of Biblical Narrative* (NY: Basic, 1981), 5–12.
21. See, e.g., W. Lee Humphreys, *Joseph and His Family: A Literary Study*

(Columbia: Univ. of South Carolina Press, 1988), 15–31; and Van Seters, *Prologue to History*, 311.

22. On the signifance of the firstborn, and generally on the symbolic nature of biblical genealogies, see the works of Wilson cited above, n. 1.
23. See Frederick E. Greenspahn, *When Brothers Dwell Together: The Preeminence of Younger Siblings in the Hebrew Bible* (New York: Oxford Univ. Press, 1994).
24. Peter F. Ellis, *The Yahwist: The Bible's First Theologian* (London: G. Chapman, 1969), 136–38.

Chaper 8

1. For why I prefer the term "Decalogue," see p. 64, "The Decalogue."
2. For Exodus 20, verse numbering varies among Bible editions because there are discrepancies in the numbering of the verses of the Decalogue. The numbers used here follow the JPS translation.
3. On the basic similarities between biblical views and those of Israel's neighbors, see Morton Smith, "The Common Theology of the Ancient Near East," *JBL* 71 (1952), 135–47.
4. For reasons that will become more clear later (see below, "The Covenant Collection"), I am avoiding the term "code." Instead, I am using the terminology found in a recent translation of these and other laws: Martha T. Roth, *Law Collections from Mesopotamia and Asia Minor*, SBL Writings from the Ancient World Series (Atlanta: Scholars, 1995).
5. Roth, *Law Collections*, 80–81.
6. Ibid., 133.
7. Ibid., 135.
8. See my *God Is King*, 113.
9. See Keith Whitelam, *The Just King: Monarchical and Judicial Authority in Ancient Israel*, JSOTSup 12; (Sheffield, UK: JSOT Press, 1979). Note esp. Deuteronomy 17:8–13, which gives the levitical priests a judicial role in a unit that immediately precedes the law of the king (17:14–20). That law emphasizes the king's subservience to the law and the levitical priests (17:18–20). See also the account of 2 Chronicles 19:4–11, concerning King Jehoshaphat, and the comments in Sara Japhet, *I & II Chronicles*, OTL: (Louisville, KY, 1993), 770–79.
10. The reference is to living long in the land of Israel, not to personal longevity.
11. Moshe Greenberg, "Some Postulates of Biblical Criminal Law," in Judah Goldin, ed., *The Jewish Expression* (New Haven, CT: Yale Univ. Press, 1976),

18–37, develops the view that the entire Bible presumes that *all* law was religious, divine law. This has been questioned more recently; see, e.g., Anne Fitzpatrick-McKinley, *The Transformation of Torah from Scribal Advice to Law*, JSOTSup 287 (Sheffield, UK: Sheffield Academic Press, 1999).

12. From law 14 of the Middle Assyrian Laws (Roth, *Law Collections*, 158).
13. Texts such as these are downplayed by Greenberg—see n. 11.
14. This is explored in my paper, "The Many Faces of God in Exodus 19," in *Jews, Christians, and the Theology of the Hebrew Scriptures*, ed. Alice Ogden Bellis and Joel S. Kaminsky, SBL Symposium Series 8 (Atlanta: Society of Biblical Literature, 2000), 353–67.
15. For a contrary opinion—that only the three main sources, J, E, and P are combined here—see Baruch J. Schwartz, "What Really Happened at Mount Sinai? Four Biblical Answers to One Question," *Bible Review* 13:5 (1997): 20–30, 46.
16. Moshe Greenberg, "The Decalogue Tradition Critically Examined," in *The Ten Commandments in History and Tradition*, ed. Ben-Zion Segal (Jerusalem: Magnes, 1990), 96–99; James Kugel, *The Bible as It Was* (Cambridge, MA: Belknap, 1997), 382–84.
17. There is significant difference among the views of various Christian denominations, and among various Jewish traditions, regarding the division of the commandments within the Decalogue. See the chart in Eduard Nielsen, *The Ten Commandments in New Perspective: A Traditio-historical Approach*, SBT^{2}7 (Naperville, IL: Allenson, 1968), 10.
18. See, e.g., Johann Jakob Stamm and Maurice Edward Andrew, *The Ten Commandments in Recent Research*, SBT^{2}2 (Naperville, IL: Allenson, 1967), 18–20; Moshe Weinfeld, "The Uniqueness of the Decalogue and its Place in Jewish Tradition," in *The Ten Commandments in History and Tradition*, ed. Ben-Zion Segal (Jerusalem: Magnes, 1990), 6–8.
19. See the chart in Moshe Greenberg, "The Decalogue Tradition Critically Examined," 92–93.
20. Kugel, *The Bible as It Was*, 383–84.
21. Note how in particular the reason given for Sabbath observance in the Decalogue in Deuteronomy fits with Deuteronomy's broader interest in emphasizing the Exodus from Egypt. On the internal evidence for the development of the Decalogue, see B. Levinson in the *JSB*, 376, on Deuteronomy 5:9.
22. The ancient translations and the Dead Sea Scrolls offer concrete evidence for the fluidity of the biblical text in late antiquity. For a broad discussion of textual transmission of the Bible, see Emanuel Tov, *Textual Criticism of the*

Hebrew Bible (Minneapolis, MN: Fortress, 2001); for essays on the Bible as reflected in the Dead Sea Scrolls, see in addition Eugene Ulrich, *The Dead Sea Scrolls and the Origins of the Bible* (Grand Rapids, MI: Eerdmans, 1999).

23. That the child's death is a punishment of David is clear in the Hebrew text, though the point is obscured by translations (including that of JPS) that incorrectly render *he-evir* (הֶעֱבִיר, "has transferred") as "has remitted"; see S. Bar-Efrat in the *JSB*, 639, on 2 Samuel 12:13.
24. See Michael Fishbane, "Torah and Tradition," in *Tradition and Theology in the Old Testament*, ed. Douglas A. Knight (Philadelphia: Fortress, 1977), 279–80, and various places in Fishbane's *Biblical Interpretation in Ancient Israel* (Oxford: Clarendon, 1985).
25. In addition to the evidence cited in n. 21, it is noteworthy that the Sabbath commandment seems to address women, while the commandment concerning coveting one's neighbor's wife does not, also suggesting that the Decalogue has a complex history of composition.
26. Fishbane, "Torah and Tradition," 275–300; Meir Weiss, "The Decalogue in Prophetic Literature," in *The Ten Commandments in History and Tradition*, 67–81.
27. Much about the law collection in Exodus continues to be debated; see esp. the essays in *Theory and Method in Biblical and Cuneiform Law: Revision, Interpolation, and Development*, ed. Bernard M. Levinson, JSOTSup 181 (Sheffield, UK: Sheffield Academic Press, 1994).
28. Note the title of Roth's book (containing texts and translations), *Law Collections*. All of these collections differ from the later Roman legal codes in size, organization, and use.
29. See Albrecht Alt, "The Origins of Israelite Law," in *Essays on Old Testament History and Religion* (Garden City, NY: Doubleday, 1967), 101–71; W. Malcolm Clark, "Law," in *Old Testament Form Criticism*, ed. John H. Hayes (San Antonio, TX: Trinity Univ. Press, 1974), 99–139.
30. The translation follows Roth, *Law Collections*, 123, although I have rendered *ī*, which she leaves untranslated, as "a member of the upper class."
31. Roth, *Law Collections*, 125.
32. In the Akkadian of Hammurabi—as in the Hebrew of the Bible—there is no separate gender-inclusive pronoun, so "he" is used to include both males and females. In many of the laws that follow, "he" or "him" may be used in a gender-neutral sense.
33. Roth, *Law Collections*, 128.
34. Ibid., 73–76.
35. The following observations are largely taken from Moshe Greenberg, "Some Postulates of Biblical Criminal Law," in *The Jewish Expression*, ed. Judah

Goldin (New Haven, CT: Yale Univ. Press, 1976), 18–37; idem, "More Reflections on Biblical Criminal Law," *ScrHier* 31 (186), 1–17; and J. J. Finkelstein, *The Ox That Gored*, TAPS 71/2 (Philadelphia: American Philosophical Society, 1981). More generally, see David P. Wright, "The Laws of Hammurabi as a Source for the Covenant Collection (Exodus 20:23–23:19)," *Maarav* 10 (2003), 11–87.

36. Some scholars believe that the law here is composite, where an earlier law insisted that the owner be killed, and that this is supplemented by a later law that allowed for this ransoming.
37. See the article of Greenberg cited above (n. 35).
38. It is unclear how the value of the "twenty shekels" of silver in Hammurabi compares to the "thirty shekels" of the Covenant Collection.
39. On Deuteronomy's *cheirem* as "a theory," see Moshe Greenberg, "Ḥerem," *EJ*, 8.349; on the jubilee year as real or ideal, see Christopher J. H. Wright, "Jubilee, Year of," *ABD*, 3.1027–1028.
40. See *Theory and Method in Biblical and Cuneiform Law*, ed. Bernard M. Levinson. For a different opinion, see John van Seters, *A Law Book for the Diaspora: Revision in the Study of the Covenant Code* (New York: Oxford, 2003).
41. See the essays by Greenberg (n. 35).

Chaper 9

1. "Ritual" has been defined in a variety of ways, and no precise understanding of ritual will be presented here. For a discussion, see David P. Wright, *Ritual in Narrative: The Dynamics of Fasting, Mourning, and Retaliation Rites in the Ugaritic Tale of Aqhat* (Winona Lake, IN: Eisenbrauns, 2001), 8–13.
2. Gustavo Benavides, "Modernity," in *Critical Terms for Religious Studies*, ed. Mark C. Taylor (Chicago: Univ. of Chicago Press, 1998), 196.
3. Julius Wellhausen, *Prolegomena to the History of Ancient Israel* (Gloucester, MA: Peter Smith, 1973). For a summary, see the foreward of Douglas A. Knight in the recent reprint by Scholars Press (Atlanta, 1994), v–xvi; specifically on Wellhausen's views on religion, see Patrick D. Miller, Jr., "Wellhausen and the History of Israel's Religion," *Semeia* 25 (1982), 61–73.
4. For a list of ritual texts from Ugarit, see Wright, *Ritual in Narrative*, 2, n. 4.
5. See Wright, *Ritual in Narrative*; G. del Olmo Lete, *Canaanite Religion According to the Liturgical Texts of Ugarit*, trans. W. G. E. Watson (Winona Lake, IN: Eisenbrans, 2004).
6. A small number of ritual texts from Israel's neighbors are collected in *ANET*, 325–61; *COS*, 1.55–57, 160–68, 295–329, 427–44.

7. See J.H. Hertz, *The Authorized Daily Prayer Book of the United Hebrew Congregations of the British Empire* (London: National Council for Jewish Religious Education, 1945), 912–13.
8. I collected much of the etymological information noted below with the help of *HALOT*, vol. 2, 493–94. For a more complete discussion, see Baruch A. Levine, *In the Presence of the Lord: A Study of Cult and Some Cultic Terms in Ancient Israel* (Leiden: Brill, 1974), 123–27. The following discussion concerns the use of the root *k-p-r* specifically in the *Piel* conjugation (and related conjugations).
9. See J. Payne Smith, *A Compendious Syriac Dictionary Founded Upon the Thesaurus Syriacus of R. Payne Smith, D.D.* (Oxford: Clarendon Press, 1976), 223.
10. *CAD*, K 179.
11. Leviticus 16 describes the ritual as it took place in the wilderness sanctuary, though I agree with most scholars that it is retrojecting Temple practice into the (mythic) period of the wandering. For this reason, I will treat it as a Temple ritual throughout this chapter.
12. See also Exodus 30:10.
13. See, e.g., the NRSV.
14. Jacob Milgrom, "Israel's Sanctuary: The Priestly 'Picture of Dorian Gray,'" *RB* 83 (1976), 390–99. I have based much of the following treatment on Milgrom's article, and on his extensive treatment of Leviticus 16 in his *Leviticus 1–16*, AB (Garden City, NY: Doubleday, 1991), 1009–1084. Milgrom calls this biblical chapter "The Day of Purgation." See also the detailed treatment of this chapter by B. Schwartz in the *JSB*, 243–47.
15. On the significant connections between Ezekiel's prophecies and the Priestly corpus, see Walther Zimmerli, *Ezekiel 1*, Hermeneia; (Philadelphia: Fortress, 1979), 52.
16. Morton Cogan, *Imperialism and Religion: Assyria, Judah and Israel in the Eighth and Seventh Centuries B.C.E.*, SBLMS (Missoula, MT: Scholars, 1974), 9–21.
17. The suggested translation accords with the note in the JPS translation at Leviticus 4:3.
18. Milgrom, "Israel's Sanctuary," 391.
19. The typical biblical term for the Temple is *beit* YHWH (בֵּית יהוה, "the house of the LORD"), which should be taken literally.
20. B. Janowski, "Azazel," in *DDD*, 128–31.
21. Milgrom, *Leviticus*, 1020–21.
22. Israel Knohl, *The Sanctuary of Silence: The Priestly Torah and the Holiness School* (Minneapolis, MN: Fortress, 1995).

23. Although later Judaism has conflated these two festivals, here—and in most other places in the Bible—they are separate, contiguous festivals.
24. See Jeffrey H. Tigay, *The JPS Torah Commentary: Deuteronomy* (Philadelphia: Jewish Publication Society, 1996), 472–76.
25. See, e.g., the highly suggestive but controversial proposal concerning permitted and forbidden food in Mary Douglas, "The Abominations of Leviticus," in *Purity and Danger* (London: Routledge & Kegan Paul, 1969), 41–57. Meanwhile, the classic rabbinic notion cannot be upheld that a *chok* (חוק) refers to a class of law that defies rational explanation. In fact, comparative and anthropological evidence make the laws associated with one *chok*—regarding the red heifer (Num. 19)—rather transparent; see, e.g., N. Fox in the *JSB*, 321–23.
26. See Israel Knohl, "Between Voice and Silence: The Relationship between Prayer and Temple Cult," *JBL* 115 (1996), 17–30.
27. For a rich, different type of analysis of many biblical rituals, see Saul M. Olyan, *Rites and Rank: Hierarchy in Biblical Representations of Cult* (Princeton, NJ: Princeton Univ. Press, 2000).

Chaper 10

1. See "The Decalogue" in chapter 8. For a complete list of differences, see chapter 8, n. 19.
2. Moshe Weinfeld, *Deuteronomy and the Deuteronomic School* (Oxford: Clarendon, 1972), 326–30.
3. The best source for characteristics that typify Deuteronomy is Weinfeld, *Deuteronomy and the Deuteronomic School*. Many of these are summarized in Jeffrey H. Tigay, *The JPS Torah Commentary: Deuteronomy* (Philadelphia: Jewish Publication Society, 1996), xii–xix.
4. For the legal material, see Bernard M. Levinson, *Deuteronomy and the Hermeneutics of Legal Innovation* (New York: Oxford Univ. Press, 1997); for a comparable treatment of some narrative material, see my book *The Creation of History in Ancient Israel*, 62–78.
5. See the discussion of this phrase in Levinson, *Deuteronomy and the Hermeneutics of Legal Innovation*, 48; idem, "You Must Not Add Anything to What I Command You: Paradoxes of Canon and Authorship in Ancient Israel," *Numen* 50 (2003), 1–51; and my book *The Creation of History*, 78.
6. The sources and historicity of the account in Kings have been questioned recently. See the discussion in Norbert Lohfink, "Recent Discussion on

2 Kings 22–23: The State of the Question," in *A Song of Power and the Power of Song: Essays on the Book of Deuteronomy*, ed. Duane L. Christensen (Winona Lake, IN: 1993), 36–61.

7. This is often referred to as the *Urtext* (original text). This *Urtext,* as scholars imagine it, has gotten smaller in recent years, as more of Deuteronomy has been ascribed to the exilic period and beyond; see, e.g., Raymond F. Person, Jr., *The Deuteronomic School: History, Social Setting, and Literature* (Atlanta: Society of Biblical Literature, 2002). For a discussion of the critical position, see E. W. Nicholson, *Deuteronomy and Tradition* (Philadelphia: Fortress, 1967), 58–82. For classical Jewish sources, see Louis Ginzberg, *The Legends of the Jews* (Philadelphia: Jewish Publication Society, 1968; reissued, 2002), 4.377, n. 116.
8. See above, n. 5.
9. See the discussion in my book *The Creation of History*, 78.
10. This is defended at length in Levinson, *Deuteronomy and the Hermeneutics of Legal Innovation*; for a different view, see John van Seters, *A Law Book for the Diaspora: Revision in the Study of the Covenant Code* (New York: Oxford, 2003).
11. For this, and a broader discussion of the improvement of the status of women in Deuteronomy, see Carolyn Pressler, *The View of Women Found in the Deuteronomic Family Laws*, BZAW 216 (Berlin: de Gruyter, 1993) and Eckart Otto, "False Weights in the Scales of Biblical Justice? Different Views of Women from Patriarchal Hierarchy to Religious Equality in the Book of Deuteronomy," in *Gender and Law in the Hebrew Bible and the Ancient Near East*, ed. Victor H. Matthews et al., JSOTSup 262 (Sheffield, UK: Sheffield Academic Press, 1998), 128–46.
12. See above, n. 3.
13. This is shown in great detail in Levinson, *Deuteronomy and the Hermeneutics of Legal Innovation*, 23–52.
14. The same idea is reflected in Deuteronomy 12, which not only desacralizes the eating of animals, but also allows meat to be eaten outside of Jerusalem. See Jacob Milgrom, "Profane Slaughter and a Formulaic Key to the Composition of Deuteronomy," *HUCA* 47 (1976), 1–17.
15. See Nahum M. Sarna, *The JPS Torah Commentary: Exodus* (Philadelphia: Jewish Publication Society, 1991), 120.
16. Critical scholars have long believed that not all of the final chapters actually belong to Deuteronomy. Rather, some parts of these represent the conclusion to the Torah from other sources. For details, see my article co-authored with Thomas Römer, "Deuteronomy 34 and the Case for a Persian Hexateuch," *JBL* 119 (2000), 401–19.

17. George E. Mendenhall, "Covenant Forms in Israelite Tradition," *BA* 23/3 (Sept. 1954), 2–22; reprinted in *BAR* 3.25–53.
18. See esp. Weinfeld, *Deuteronomy and the Deuteronomic School*, esp. 59–178, and the earlier article of R. Frankena, "The Vassal-Treaties of Esarhaddon and the Dating of Deuteronomy," *OTS* 14 (1965), 122–54. A more detailed study is found in Dennis J. McCarthy, *Treaty and Covenant*, AnBib 21 (Rome: Biblical Institute Press, 1978). For critiques of Mendenhall, Weinfeld, and McCarthy, see E. W. Nicholson, "Covenant in a Century of Study Since Wellhausen," *OTS* 24 (1986), 54–69, reprinted in *A Song of Power and the Power of Song: Essays on the Book of Deuteronomy*, ed. Duane L. Christensen, 78–93; idem, *God and His People: Covenant and Theology in the Old Testament* (Oxford: Clarendon, 1986), 56–82.
19. Weinfeld, *Deuteronomy and the Deuteronomic School*, 115. For other specific parallels, see 115–29. The text of VTE, quite surprisingly, is not found in *COS* but may be found in *ANET*, 534–41; for the Hittite treaties, see 201–6, 529–30.
20. Weinfeld, *Deuteronomy and the Deuteronomic School*, 244–81; the appropriateness of this wisdom influence has been questioned by C. Brekelmans, "Wisdom Influence in Deuteronomy," in *The Song of Power*, 123–34.
21. Earlier generations of scholars claimed that Assyria imposed its religion on its vassals; this is now believed to be incorrect—see Richard Lowery, *The Reforming Kings*, JSOTSup 120 (Sheffield, UK: JSOT Press, 1990).
22. For a sensitive development of this idea, see Jon D. Levenson, *Sinai and Zion: An Entry into the Jewish Bible* (Minneapolis, MN: Winston, 1985), esp. 80–86.
23. See n. 18, above.
24. It is striking that this paragraph later became so significant—it is not especially important in Deuteronomy or elsewhere in the Bible; and in its original context, it is not even a prayer!
25. *ANET*, 537, paragraph 24, line 266.
26. William L. Moran, "The Ancient Near Eastern Background of the Love of God in Deuteronomy," *CBQ* 25 (1963), 77–87. This is expanded upon in a less technical fashion by S. Dean McBride, Jr., "The Yoke of the Kingdom: An Exposition of Deuteronomy 6:4–5," *INT* 27 (1973), 273–306.
27. In this context, "these words" likely refers to the Decalogue, found in the immediately preceding chapter.
28. In the rabbinic view, the latter actions refer to the injunctions for donning *tefillin* (phylacteries) and affixing a *mezuzah* to each doorpost.
29. See Weinfeld, *Deuteronomy and the Deuteronomic School*, 320–59.
30. This idea is sometimes called "radical monotheism"—a term popularized by

Tikva Frymer-Kensky, *In the Wake of the Goddesses: Women, Culture, and the Biblical Transformation of Pagan Myth* (New York: Free Press, 1992).

31. For example, is Deuteronomy's emphasis on worship in Jerusalem only a *political* move, namely an attempt to bring the cult under royal supervision? Or is it a *theological* idea, namely that the one God should be worshiped in one way in one place only?

Chaper 11

1. Richard D. Nelson, *Joshua*, OTL (Louisville, KY: Westminster, John Knox, 1997), 2–3.
2. On the challenges of reconstructing Israelite history, see chapter 4.
3. Reasonable summaries of the present state of archaeological knowledge may be found in two recent books by William G. Dever, *What Did the Biblical Writers Know and When Did They Know It? What Archaeology Can Tell Us about the Reality of Ancient Israel ?* (Grand Rapids, MI: Eerdmans, 2001); *Who Were the Israelites and Where Did They Come From?* (Grand Rapids, MI: Eerdmans, 2003). For a slightly older popular summary of many of the issues, see Hershel Shanks, ed., *The Rise of Ancient Israel* (Washington, DC: Biblical Archaeological Society, 1992).
4. On toponyms, see Yohanan Aharoni, *The Land of the Bible: A Historical Geography*, trans. A. F. Rainey (London: Burns & Oates, 1979), 105–30.
5. Older studies point to collar-rimmed jars and four-room houses as new Israelite artifacts in this period, but it is now clear that such styles predate Israel and are found elsewhere. The same is true for the supposedly distinctive lack of pig bones in Israelite settlements—this is found outside of Israel as well, and it may reflect climate changes or new animal husbandry practices.
6. On the origins of Israel, see the literature cited above in n. 3. An important early study that developed this idea is George E. Mendenhall, "The Hebrew Conquest of Palestine," *BA* 25/3 (Sept. 1962), 66–87, reprinted in *BAR*, 3.100–120.
7. Some archaeologists and historians believe that the Exodus story may have some basis in history, in that a small group from Egypt joined the hill-country pioneers. However, scant evidence exists to support this claim outside of the biblical text. As noted, early Israelite material culture shows little influence from the material culture of Egypt.
8. In Joshua 11:16 and again in 21:43, the JPS translation does not directly render every occurrence of the word *kol*.

9. Martin Buber and Franz Rosenzweig, *Scripture and Translation*, trans. Lawrence Rosenwald with Everett Fox (Bloomington, IN: Indiana Univ. Press, 1994), xxi-xxii, xxxvi-xlii, 114–28, 143–50; more recently on "key words" see Shimon Bar-Efrat, *Narrative Art in the Bible*, JSOTSup 70 (Sheffield, UK: Almond Press, 1989), 212–15.
10. Everett Fox, *The Five Books of Moses: Genesis, Exodus, Leviticus, Numbers, Deuteronomy*, Schocken Bible (New York: Schocken, 1995), vol. 1., xi–xii.
11. On the ban, see Richard Nelson, "*Ḥerem* and the Deuteronomic Social Conscience," in *Deuteronomy and Deuteronomic Literature: Festschrift for C.H.W. Brekelmans*, ed. M. Vervenne and J. Lust (Leuven: Leuven Univ. Press, 1997), 39–54.
12. This picture could be complicated further by looking at the initial chapters of Judges—see chapter 12, below.
13. See, e.g., Yohanan Aharoni et al., eds., *The Carta Bible Atlas,* 4th ed.; (Jerusalem: Carta, 2002), 59, map 69.
14. On how the first books of the Bible fit together, see my article coauthored with Thomas Römer, "Deuteronomy 34 and the Case for a Persian Hexateuch," *JBL* 119 (2000), 401–419.
15. Martin Noth's book was later translated under the title *The Deuteronomistic History*, JSOTSup 15 (Sheffield, UK: Univ. of Sheffield, 1981). For an evaluation of this book and its impact, see Steven L. McKenzie and M. Patrick Graham, eds., *The History of Israel's Traditions: The Heritage of Martin Noth,* JSOTSup 182 (Sheffield, UK: Sheffield Academic Press, 1994).
16. Noth's theory has been criticized recently, however, and is beginning to fall out of favor; see, e.g., Gary N. Knoppers, "The Deuteronomist and the Deuteronomic Law of the King: A Reexamination of a Relationship," *ZAW* 108 (1996), 329–46, and "Rethinking the Relationship between Deuteronomy and the Deuteronomistic History: The Case of Kings," *CBQ* 63 (2001) 393–415.
17. See, e.g., Richard D. Nelson, *The Double Redaction of the Deuteronomistic History*, JSOTSup 18 (Sheffield, UK: Univ. of Sheffield, 1981).
18. See Raymond F. Person Jr., *The Deuteronomic School: History, Social Setting, and Literature* (Atlanta: Society of Biblical Literature, 2002). The position assuming more than a double redaction is often called "the Göttingen School." One presentation of the text of DtrH according to its sources is found in Antony F. Campbell and Mark A. O'Brien, *Unfolding the Deuteronomistic History: Origins, Upgrades, Present Text* (Minneapolis, MN: Fortress, 2000). There are, however, almost as many reconstructions of DtrH (according to its sources) as scholars working on the DtrH.

19. For example, "the Ark of the LORD" is mentioned ten times in Joshua, twenty times in Samuel, and once in Kings.
20. I discuss in great detail the purpose of ancient storytelling in my book *The Creation of History*.
21. See Nelson, *Joshua*, 34; and in greater detail, Alexander Rofé, "The Piety of the Torah-Disciples at the Winding-Up of the Hebrew Bible: Josh. 1:8; Ps. 1:2; Isa. 59:21," in Helmut Merklein et al., eds., *Bibel in jüdischer und christlicher Tradition: Festschrift für Johann Maier zum 60. Geburtstag* (Frankfurt am Main: Anton Hain, 1993), 78–85.
22. The chutzpah involved in such modifications should not be underestimated.
23. For more on the literary device of resumptive repetition, see my *Book of Judges,* Old Testament Readings (London: Routledge, 2002), 95–96.
24. For a discussion of etiologies with sources, see P. J. van Dyk, "The Function of So-Called Etiological Elements in Narratives," *ZAW* 102 (1990), 19–33.
25. See Robert E. Cooley, "Ai," in *The Oxford Encyclopedia of Archaeology in the Near East*, ed. Eric M. Meyers (New York: Oxford, 1997), 1.33.
26. The phrase "as they still are" is *ad ha-yom ha-zeh* (עַד הַיּוֹם הַזֶּה, literally, "until this day"). Like the expression "that is why" discussed above, it is another major marker of an etiology.
27. Hermann Gunkel, *The Stories of Genesis* (Berkeley, CA: BIBAL, 1994), 18–24.
28. The extent to which this language is Deuteronomistic may be seen by checking Joshua's phrases against the index to Weinfeld's *Deuteronomy and the Deuteronomic School*, 431–32, or by looking at the discussion of Joshua 23 in Nelson, *Deuteronomy*, 255–62.
29. The only non-Priestly narratives that assume the Israelite practice of ritual circumcision are Genesis 34 and the Deuteronomistic History's occasional (and usually disparaging) references to Philistine warriors as uncircumcised, e.g., Judges 14:3, 1 Samuel 18:25, and 2 Samuel 1:20.
30. See the observation of John Gray, *Joshua, Judges, Ruth*, NCBC (Grand Rapids, MI: Eerdmans, 1986), 75, that the extent of P's involvement in the chapter has been underestimated.

Chaper 12

1. This chapter is based on my book *The Creation of History in Ancient Israel* (London: Routledge, 1995), esp. 91–111; and my *Book of Judges*, Old Testament Readings (London: Routledge, 2002). See there for extensive documentation.

2. John Bright, *A History of Israel*, 3rd ed. (Philadelphia: Westminster, 1981), 131.
3. On the integrity of this unit, and on the purposes of the preceding and following units, see my book *The Creation of History in Ancient Israel*, 91–111.
4. This translation reproduces the text's threefold repetition of *ve-ad* (וְעַד, "including"), which highlights the extent to which Jonathan gives David his clothes.
5. Not all of the cases that I adduce below are equally convincing, but together they certainly form a pattern of contrasts.
6. See "The Five Main Points of Amos" in chapter 16.

Chaper 13

1. This is the motto of the European organization CLIOH, which stands for "Creating Links and Innovative Overviews to Enhance Historical Perspective in European Culture."
2. The term "antiquarian interest" is used often by Baruch Halpern, *The First Historians: The Hebrew Bible and History* (San Francisco: Harper & Row, 1988). For a critique, see my book *The Creation of History*, esp. 11–12.
3. Many would state this otherwise, that Samuel is better "literature" than Kings, but I believe that the term "literature" is problematic or misleading when used of biblical texts; see my book *The Creation of History*, 14–17.
4. The example is taken from J. Maxwell Miller, *The Old Testament and the Historian* (Philadelphia: Fortress, 1976), 1–3.
5. Edwin R. Thiele uses this principle extensively in his *The Mysterious Numbers of the Hebrew Kings* (Grand Rapids, MI: Zondervan, 1983). He solves this and other chronological problems by assuming a large number of "co-regencies."
6. *COS*, 2.137; cf. *ANET* 320.
7. See *ANET*, 284–85; *COS* 2.297–98.
8. See Volkmar Fritz, *1 & 2 Kings*, trans. Anselm Hagedorn (Minneapolis, MN: Fortress, 2003), 28.
9. For the analysis that follows, see my article "The Structure of 1 Kings 1–11," *JSOT* 49 (1991), 87–97.
10. There continues to be a debate within biblical studies on whether these chapters complete 2 Samuel, and together comprise a hypothetical source called the succession narrative, dealing with the question "Who will succeed David as king?"

11. M. Avot 1:1; see Jacob Neusner, *The Mishnah: A New Translation* (New Haven, CT: Yale Univ. Press, 1991), 672.
12. See Michael Fishbane, *Biblical Interpretation in Ancient Israel* (Oxford: Clarendon, 1985). A condensed version of this is Michael Fishbane, "Inner Biblical Exegesis: Types and Strategies of Interpretation in Ancient Israel" in *Midrash and Literature*, ed. Geoffrey H. Hartman and Sanford Budick (New Haven, CT: Yale Univ. Press, 1986), 19–37. Specifically on intermarriage, see Fishbane, *Biblical Interpretation in Ancient Israel*, 125–26; and Gary N. Knoppers, "Sex, Religion, and Politics: The Deuteronomist on Intermarriage," *HAR* 14 (1994), 121–41.
13. See, e.g., Kathleen Kenyon, *Royal Cities of the Old Testament* (New York: Schocken, 1971), 53–70.
14. For the traditional view, see Dever, *What Did the Biblical Writers Know?*, 131–38; for the revisionist view, see Israel Finkelstein and Neil Asher Silberman, *The Bible Unearthed: Archaeology's New Vision of Ancient Israel and the Origin of Its Sacred Texts* (New York: Touchstone, 2001), 135–42.
15. See Yohanan Aharoni, *The Archaeology of the Land of Israel from the Prehistoric Beginnings to the End of the First Temple Period*, trans. Anson Rainey (Philadelphia: Westminster, 1982), 201–3.
16. See especially David Ussishkin, *The Conquest of Lachish by Sennacherib* (Tel Aviv: Tel Aviv Univ., The Institute of Archaeology, 1982); Mordechai Cogan and Hayim Tadmor, *II Kings*, AB (New York: Doubleday, 1988), 246–51.
17. The use of Hebrew personal and geographical names (e.g., Jerusalem) in Akkadian inscriptions offer important evidence for how Hebrew was pronounced in the biblical period. Hebrew at that time was written without vowels (which were inserted only in the late first millennium C.E.), while Akkadian was written syllabically, with vowels.
18. Many scholars believe that this number is a scribal error or an exaggeration. It would imply a population of Judea of several million at this time, which is most unlikely based on other evidence.
19. *COS*, 2.302–3.
20. On these suffixes, see Ziony Zevit, "A Chapter in the History of Israelite Personal Names," *BASOR* 250 (1983), 1–16.
21. The analysis of this material is too complex to be detailed here. See Brevard S. Childs, *Isaiah and the Assyrian Crisis*, SBT^{2}3 (London: SCM, 1967); Christopher R. Seitz, *Zion's Final Destiny: The Development of the Book of Isaiah: A Reassessment of the Isaiah 36–39* (Minneapolis, MN: Fortress, 1991).
22. Cogan and Tadmor, *II Kings*, 260–63.

Chaper 14

1. On Chronicles in general, see my book *The Creation of History*, 20–47. Additional excellent material appears in M. Patrick Graham and Steven L. McKenzie, *The Chronicler as Author: Studies in Text and Texture*, JSOTSup 263 (Sheffield, UK: Sheffield Academic Press, 1999); and the commentary of Sara Japhet, *I & II Chronicles*, OTL (Louisville, KY: Westminster/John Knox, 1993).
2. Although English Bibles tend to print Chronicles in two parts and Ezra and Nehemiah as separate books, according to Jewish scribal tradition Chronicles and Ezra-Nehemiah are each single books—see chapter 2, nn. 15 and 23.
3. I use the term "Chronicler" to refer to the author of Chronicles only. For much of the twentieth century, the book of Ezra-Nehemiah was seen as a continuation of Chronicles. Ezra-Nehemiah begins where Chronicles ends. However, in a seminal article, Sara Japhet, "The Supposed Common Authorship of Chronicles and Ezra-Nehemiah Investigated Anew," *VT* 18 (1968), 332–72, argued that the stylistic and theological differences between the two are too great to say that they are written by the same person. Additional evidence (concerning the differing attitude toward intermarriage in Chronicles versus in Ezra-Nehemiah) corroborates that judgment; see Gary N. Knoppers, "Intermarriage, Social Complexity, and Ethnic Diversity in the Genealogy of Judah," *JBL* 120 (2001), 15–30. A majority of scholars have adopted Japhet's conclusions.
4. Judeans so predominated in this period that even non-Judeans could be called Judeans, as in Esther 2:5: "In the fortress Shushan lived a *yehudi* (יְהוּדִי, "Judean" or "Jew") by the name of Mordecai . . . a Benjaminite."
5. For a summary of this theory of Zadok's hidden past, see George W. Ramsey, "Zadok," *ABD*, 6.1035–36.
6. See Elias Bickerman, *From Ezra to the Last of the Maccabees: Foundations of Postbiblical Judaism* (New York: Schocken, 1962), 22. For more discussion on the role of historical probability, see my book *The Creation of History*, esp. 25–26.
7. Scholars debate whether the Chronicler should be called a historian and/or a theologian. I outline why these two concepts are not mutually exclusive in *The Creation of History*, 46–47.
8. On the treatment of the Northern Kingdom in Chronicles, see H.G.M. Williamson, *Israel in the Books of Chronicles* (Cambridge: Cambridge Univ. Press, 1977).

9. The easiest way to see the Chronicler's omissions and changes is to use books such as J. C. Andres et al., *Chronicles and Its Synoptic Parallels in Samuel, Kings, and Related Biblical Texts* (Collegeville, MN: Liturgical Press, 1998), which list the texts of Chronicles and its sources in parallel columns. The large amount of white space in these columns shows how much the Chronicler either adds or subtracts portions of his sources. Seeing such changes brings the Chronicler's ideology into sharper relief.
10. The Hebrew text actually refers to two seven-day festivals, but the second seven-day festival is believed to be a scribal error. It is missing in several important Septuagint manuscripts.
11. In this verse and in the verses discussed in the following paragraphs, I am insisting that the verb *b-sh-l* (בשׁל) be translated as "boil"—its meaning in biblical Hebrew—rather than as the more generic "cook," a meaning often incorrectly assigned to it in harmonizing translations.
12. Fishbane, *Biblical Interpretation*, 135–36.
13. Note how P is repetitive and emphatic, even sounding polemical. Most likely P is polemicizing against D or some similar text or norm.
14. See the discussion of the term *ka-mishpat* (כַּמִּשְׁפָּט, "as prescribed") in Fishbane, *Biblical Interpretation*, 209–13.
15. See "Classical Interpretation" in chapter 1.
16. That the Torah was already a sacred text may be seen in the frequent references to "the Torah," "The Torah of Moses," "The Torah of the LORD" both in Chronicles and the contemporaneous Ezra-Nehemiah. Judson R. Shaver discusses many of these references in his *Torah and the Chronicler's History Work: An Inquiry into the Chronicler's References to Laws, Festivals, and Cultic Institutions in Relationship to Pentateuchal Legislation* (*BJS* 196; Atlanta: Scholars, 1989), though my understanding of many issues differs from his.
17. For a list of the sources that Chronicles claims to draw upon, see Leiman, *Canonization*, 18.
18. Japhet, *I & II Chronicles*, 20–23.

Chaper 15

1. Martti Nissinen, "Preface," in Martti Nissinen, ed., *Prophecy in Its Ancient Near Eastern Context: Mesopotamian, Biblical and Arabian Perspectives*, SBL Symposium 13 (Atlanta: Society of Biblical Literature, 2000), vii. For a more detailed definition, see David L. Petersen, "Defining Prophecy and Prophetic Literature," ibid., 33–44.

2. On the ancient Near Eastern milieu, see the excellent summary in H. B. Huffmon, "Prophecy (ANE)," *ABD*, 5.477–82. For more recent and detailed material, see *Prophecy in Its Ancient Near Eastern Context* (see previous note).
3. Scholars who have uncovered ancient Mesopotamian practices have repeatedly shed light on biblical texts in the process. That is because peoples throughout the ancient Near East shared many cultural institutions and assumptions (something like what we mean when we speak of "Western civilization" today). Also, Mesopotamia's leading city-states were longstanding political—and therefore cultural—centers in the region. On communications from the gods, see the treatments in A. Leo Oppenheim, *Ancient Mesopotamia: Portrait of a Dead Civilization* (Chicago: Univ. of Chicago, 1977), 206–27; Jean Bottéro, *Mesopotamia: Writing, Reasoning, and the Gods*, trans. Z. Bahrani and M. an De Mieroop (Chicago: Univ. of Chicago Press, 1992), 105–37.
4. Bottéro, *Mesopotamia*, 127, 130.
5. On this, see Martti Nissinen, "The Sociological Role of the Neo-Assyrian Prophets," in Nissinen, ed., *Prophecy in Its Ancient Near Eastern Context*, 89–114.
6. *ANET*, 605. More of these prophecies are collected and discussed in Simo Parpola, *Assyrian Prophecies*, State Archives of Assyria 9 (Helsinki: Helsinki Univ. Press, 1997).
7. Ibid., 624. For a detailed discussion of the Mari letters and their bearing on prophecy, see Abraham Malamat, *Mari and the Bible* (Leiden: Brill, 1998), 59–162.
8. For a survey of interpretations of the Deir 'Alla inscription, see Huffmon, "Prophecy (ANE)," *ABD*, 5.477; the text may be found in *COS*, 2.140–45.
9. See Yochanan Muffs, *Love & Joy: Law, Language and Religion in Ancient Israel* (Cambridge, MA: Harvard Univ. Press, 1992), 9–48.
10. See the classic study of Claus Westermann, *Basic Forms of Prophetic Speech*, trans. H. C. White (Louisville, KY: Westminster/John Knox, 1991), 98–128.
11. For an ironic endorsement of the prophets' intercessory role, see Jeremiah 7:16; 11:14; 14:11, where God asks Jeremiah *not* to pray for Israel.
12. On this etymology, see *HALOT*, 2.661–62. The following paragraphs are based on an assortment of critical treatments of biblical prophecy; see esp. Robert R. Wilson, *Prophecy and Society in Ancient Israel* (Philadelphia: Fortress, 1980); Joseph Blenkinsopp, *A History of Prophecy in Israel: From the Settlement in the Land to the Hellenistic Period* (Philadelphia: Westminster, 1983). Two good popular introductions to prophecy are: John F. A. Sawyer, *Prophecy and the Prophets of the Old Testament*, Oxford Bible Series (Oxford:

Oxford Univ. Press, 1987); James Luther Mayes and Paul J. Achtemeier, *Interpreting the Prophets* (Philadelphia: Fortress, 1987).

13. Some scholars have contended that classical prophecy developed as a reaction against the first period of "social disintegration in Israel" and that class differences became especially pronounced at this time (e.g., Bright, *History*, 259–62). That argument is circular—the classical prophets such as Amos first condemn these social conditions, therefore they must have been new in their day. No external evidence exists in support of this idea.
14. Even earlier figures whom the Bible describes as prophets include Moses, Miriam, Deborah, and Samuel.
15. The Hebrew here for "can we bring" is *navi* (נָבִיא), which is pronounced and spelled the same as the word for "prophet." This is a pun, or possibly a popular etymology for *navi*: the one to whom one "brings" payment in exchange for hearing the future.
16. For more on the miracle stories, see Alexander Rofé, *The Prophetical Stories: The Narratives about the Prophets in the Hebrew Bible Their Literary Types and History* (Jerusalem: Magnes, 1988); Robert B. Coote, ed., *Elijah and Elisha in Socioliterary Perspective*, Semeia Studies (Atlanta: Scholars, 1992).

Chaper 16

1. The best English commentaries on Amos are Hans Walter Wolff, *Joel and Amos*, trans. W. Janzen et al., Hermeneia (Philadelphia: Fortress, 1977), and Shalom M. Paul, *Amos* (Hermeneia; Philadelphia: Fortress, 1991). Wolff excels on matters of history of composition, and Paul on the meaning of the book in its final form, especially as elucidated by ancient Near Eastern texts.
2. The same Hebrew word, *korchah* (קָרְחָה), is used in both contexts, though the different JPS translation committees for Torah and Nevi'im translated it differently, obscuring this issue.
3. This distinction is made by Yehezkel Kaufman, *The Religion of Israel* (trans. Moshe Greenberg (New York: Schocken, 1972).
4. This is a major theme of Wellhausen's *Prolegomena*.
5. For one such reconstruction, see Wolff, *Joel and Amos*, 106–13.
6. See Moshe Greenberg, "The Use of the Ancient Versions for Interpreting the Hebrew Text: A Sampling from Ezekiel 2:1–3:11," in Moshe Greenberg, *Studies in the Bible and Jewish Thought*, JPS Scholar of Distinction Series (Philadelphia: Jewish Publication Society, 1995), 209–25. From a different

perspective, Ehud Ben Zvi has emphasized the importance of looking at the prophetic book; see especially Ehud Ben Zvi, "The Prophetic Book: A Key Form of Prophetic Literature," in Marvin A. Sweeney and Ehud Ben Zvi, eds., *The Changing Face of Form Criticism for the Twenty-First Century* (Grand Rapids, MI: Eerdmans, 2003), 276–97.

7. The unpolished rhetoric of many prophets is surprising. On this, see Stephen A. Geller, "Were the Prophets Poets?" *Prooftexts* 3 (1983), 211–21.
8. See the similar sentiment in Micah 6:6–7: "(6) With what shall I approach the LORD, / Do homage to God on high? / Shall I approach Him with burnt offerings, / With calves a year old? (7) Would the LORD be pleased with thousands of rams, / With myriads of streams of oil? Shall I give my first-born for my transgression, / The fruit of my body for my sins?"
9. W. Randall Garr, *Dialect Geography of Syria-Israel, 1000–586* B.C.E. (Philadelphia: Univ. of Pennsylvania Press, 1985), 38–39.
10. Scholars continue to debate when the notion of "covenant" entered Israelite religion, and whether we may assume a covenantal base metaphor even in cases where the word *berit* is absent. On these issues, see Nicholson, *God and His People*.
11. See "Deuteronomy as a Treaty" in chapter 10; George E. Mendenhall and Gary A. Herion, "Covenant," *ABD,* 1.1179–1202.
12. Here the Ethiopians serve as an example of a faraway people.
13. See Shalom Spiegel, "Amos vs. Amaziah," in Judah Goldin, ed., *The Jewish Expression* (New Haven, CT: Yale Univ. Press, 1976), 38–65.
14. Here and in 3:15 the references are to items inlaid with ivory. Such items have been excavated from Samaria—see the survey in Amihai Mazar, ed., *Archaeology of the Land of the Bible 10,000–586 B.C.E.*, AB (Garden City, NY: Doubleday, 1990), 503–5; and King, *Amos, Hosea, Micah*, 139–49.
15. There is almost universal agreement to this point, though Meir Weiss, "The Origin of the 'Day of the Lord'—Reconsidered," *HUCA* 37 (1966), 29–60, in an excellent article surveying the Day of the LORD, dissents.
16. A collection of texts on this topic with some secondary reading is found in Richard H. Hier, "Day of the LORD," *ABD,* 2.82–83. See also the bibliography in Paul, *Amos*, 183, nn. 7–11.
17. We cannot tell clearly whether Amos directly repeated the words that he thought he heard, or whether he embellished them. (See Moshe Greenberg, "Jewish Conceptions on the Human Factor in Biblical Prophecy," in Moshe Greenberg, *Studies in the Bible and Jewish Thought*, 405–19.) Nor do we know over how long a period, and on what separate occasions, Amos uttered his oracles.

18. See Paul, *Amos*, 35, n. 32; Philip J. King, *Amos, Hosea, Micah: An Archaeological Commentary* (Philadelphia: Westminster, 1988), 21–22.
19. See M. Broshi, "The Expansion of Jerusalem in the Reigns of Hezekiah and Manasseh," *IEJ* 24 (1974), 21–26.

Chaper 17

1. While the Book of Isaiah has more chapters, the Book of Jeremiah is slightly longer in terms of verses.
2. See esp. H. G. M. Williamson, *The Book Called Isaiah: Deutero-Isaiah's Role in Composition and Redaction* (Oxford: Clarendon, 1994); Roy F. Melugin and Marvin A. Sweeney, eds., *New Visions of Isaiah*, JSOTSup 214 (Sheffield, UK: Sheffield Academic Press, 1996).
3. See the summary in Brevard S. Childs, *Isaiah*, OTL (Louisville, KY: Westminster John Knox, 2001), 260–66.
4. Scholars continue to debate this issue, however; not all of them agree that this chapter should be read as a prophetic dedication or initiation.
5. When I attribute words to "Isaiah," I do so for convenience. I do not mean to imply that these were the actual words said by Isaiah son of Amoz; see "Amos the Book Versus Amos the Prophet" in chapter 16.
6. Here in 4:1 and 4:2, the phrase "in that day" served as a catchword or catchphrase, leading an editor to combine two units that were originally unrelated. Throughout Isaiah, such catchphrases help us understand the structure of the book, and to realize that the book is not ordered chronologically.
7. For a brief description of biblical poetry, see Adele Berlin, "Reading Biblical Poetry," in *JSB*, 2097–2104. For her longer, more technical discussion with bibliography, see "Parallelism," *ABD*, 5.155–62. The classic work is that of Lowth from 1753, who first used the term "parallelism"; important modifications to his theory are offered in James Kugel, *The Idea of Biblical Poetry: Parallelism and Its History* (New Haven, CT: Yale Univ. Press, 1981); Robert Alter, *The Art of Biblical Poetry* (New York: Basic, 1985). A fundamentally different approach to biblical poetry, which will not be followed here, was developed by Frank M. Cross and D. N. Freedman—see especially David Noel Freedman, *Pottery, Poetry, and Prophecy: Studies in Early Hebrew Poetry* (Winona Lake, IN: Eisenbrauns, 1980).
8. The first-century-C.E. Jewish historian Josephus made this error, when he ascribed various Greek meters to biblical poetry. See Kugel, *The Idea*, 140.
9. There is, however, some debate about whether or not meter exists in biblical poetry. Scholars generally agree that Hebrew poetry (as now vocalized)

has no form of alternating stressed and unstressed syllables. Some believe that an earlier form, which may be reconstructed, had meter. Many parallel phrases in the same biblical composition are of roughly equal length, suggesting to some that an original meter was lost. Others believe that this simply indicates a principle of biblical poetry: lines should be of approximately equal length.

10. There are some tricola, but they are relatively rare.
11. For an exploration of parallelism and word-pairs using modern linguistics, see Adele Berlin, *The Dynamics of Biblical Parallelism* (Bloomington: Indiana Univ. Press, 1985).
12. These scholars follow the lead of Kugel and Alter. See esp. Kugel, *The Idea*, 51–58; the quotation is from 58.
13. See Stanley Gevirtz, *Patterns in the Early Poetry of Israel*, Studies in Ancient Oriental Civilization, 32 (Chicago: Univ. of Chicago Press, 1973); Menahem Haran, "The Graded Numerical Sequence and the Phenomenon of 'Automatism' in Biblical Poetry," *VTS* 22 (1971), 238–67.
14. Framing announcements tend to be separate monocola—simple sentences without a parallel mate or mates.
15. Unlike some other scholars, James Kugel would classify this portion of the verse not as a "tricolon" but as an "unbalanced bicolon"; on classifications of ancient Hebrew poetry, see above, n. 7.
16. Similarly, three out of the four biblical occurrences of *she'ar am* (שְׁאָר עַם), "the remnant of the people," are found in Isaiah (11:11, 16; 28:5). The prophet even believed that God asked him to name one of his children Shear-jashub (שְׁאָר יָשׁוּב), meaning "A-Remnant-Shall-Return" (7:3).
17. Some older translations render this "at the end of days," which is incorrect—see "The Day Will Come" in chapter 16.
18. The classic work on biblical messianism is Sigmund Mowinckel, *He That Cometh: The Messiah Concept in the Old Testament and Later Judaism*, trans. G. W. Anderson (Nashville, TN: Abingdon, 1954); more recently, see John J. Collins, *The Scepter and the Star: The Messiahs of the Dead Sea Scrolls and Other Ancient Literature*, AB (Garden City, NY: Doubleday, 1995), esp. 20–48.

Chaper 18

1. B. Duhm and S. Mowinckel emphasized what they saw as a biographic "strand"; for a summary, see William L. Holladay, *Jeremiah 2* (Minneapolis, MN: Fortress, 1989), 11–12.

2. Even the superscription has not remained beyond suspicion. At least as described elsewhere in the Bible, Josiah's reform turned the nation upside down; therefore, if Jeremiah truly was active during that reform, he presumably would have mentioned it. Yet he never explicitly does. In addition, only one prophecy is dated during Josiah's reign, and the date formula there is unusually vague (3:6). Both facts suggest to some that Jeremiah began to prophesy later than the superscription indicates.
3. It does, however, appear on occasion in the Septuagint's Greek translation of Jeremiah, to render the term *nevi'im* (נְבִיאִים, "prophets").
4. Incidentally, the first clause of 3:14 illustrates my claim (in chap. 16) that the Israelite prophets loved wordplay: *shuvu vanim shovavim* (שׁוּבוּ בָנִים שׁוֹבָבִים). Such alliteration is featured also in 12:11: *samah li-shmamah, avelah alai sh'memah, nashammah kol ha-aretz* (שָׂמָהּ לִשְׁמָמָה אָבְלָה עָלַי שְׁמֵמָה נָשַׁמָּה כָּל־הָאָרֶץ).
5. Joan Oates, *Babylon* (London: Thames and Hudson, 1979), 128.
6. Although Babylon is actually northeast of the land of Israel, the intervening desert was so vast that it prevented direct transit. Historically, armies from the east would skirt the desert and reach the land of Israel via Syria—thus entering from the north.
7. See Weinfeld, *Deuteronomy and the Deuteronomic School*, 143–46.
8. On this "cup of wrath," see Robert P. Carroll, *The Book of Jeremiah*, OTL (Philadelphia: Westminster, 1986), 501–2.
9. Actually, the "missing" verse is not altogether strange with regard to Jeremiah. In general, the Septuagint of Jeremiah reflects a much shorter Hebrew text than the Masoretic Text. Furthermore, its units appear in a different order. Thus this first Greek translation must have been made from a distinct edition (technically, a "recension") of Jeremiah—one that is also attested among some of the Dead Sea Scrolls. See Tov, *Textual Criticism of the Hebrew Bible*, 319–27.
10. This Targum may date from the third century C.E. or earlier; see Holladay, *Jeremiah 2*, 10.
11. The same cipher mechanism is used in the Bible only in one other place, Jeremiah 51:1. There, Leb-kamai [לֵב קָמָי] = the Chaldeans [כַּשְׂדִּים], the name for an Aramean tribe that was important in the neo-Babylonian period, which is often used as a name for the Babylonians. In that verse, however, the identity of the condemned populace is no secret. For a different interpretation of these two ciphers, see Mark Leuchter, "Jeremiah's 70-Year Prophecy and the ששך / לב קמי *Atbash* Codes," *Bib* 85 (2004), 503–22.
12. The alternative position to account for this evidence—that Jeremiah was

influenced by Josiah's reform and the Deuteronomic school—is much less likely. That hypothesis does not explain why only the prose—not the poetry—is so close to Deuteronomy. In addition, as noted earlier, the book offers little evidence that Jeremiah affiliated himself with those associated with Josiah's reform and the "discovery" of Deuteronomy.

13. For one view, see E. W. Nicholson, *Preaching to the Exiles: A Study of the Prose Tradition in the Book of Jeremiah* (New York: Schocken, 1970); more recently, see Louis Stuhlman, *The Prose Sermons of the Book of Jeremiah: A Redescription of the Correspondences with the Deuteronomistic Literature in the Light of Recent Text-critical Research*, SBLDS 83 (Atlanta: Scholars, 1986); and the summary in Carroll, *Jeremiah*, 38–50, especially his concluding remarks that "the problems surrounding the composition and redaction of the book of Jeremiah persist and are unlikely to be resolved in favour of one overarching theory."
14. See Levinson, *Deuteronomy and the Hermeneutics of Legal Innovation*, 18–20.
15. See Holladay, *Jeremiah* 2, 36–40, 53–62.
16. Michael A. Carasik, "Theologies of the Mind in Biblical Israel" (PhD diss., Brandeis Univ., 1997) 85.
17. For a very different early understanding of this "new covenant," see 2 Corinthians 3:1–6 in the New Testament.
18. On the "confessions," see the discussions in the commentaries, as well as Kathleen M. O'Connor, *The Confessions of Jeremiah: Their Interpretation and Role in Chapters 1–25*, SBLDS 94 (Atlanta: Scholars, 1988).
19. A glance at the King James translation of this phrase suggests the value of using modern, idiomatic biblical translations.
20. Occasionally, however, Jeremiah does seek retribution, especially upon his enemies. See, for example, "O LORD of Hosts, O just Judge, / Who test the thoughts and the mind, / Let me see Your retribution upon them, / For I lay my case before You" (11:20).
21. For this interpretation, see esp. William McKane, *Jeremiah*, ICC (Edinburgh: T & T Clark, 1986), 1.357–58.
22. To be more specific, little of such "angst" is visible in Isaiah, who volunteered to become a prophet (see Isaiah 6:8), whereas this "profession" was forced upon Jeremiah (see 1:4–10).
23. Perhaps Jeremiah, like most people in his day, did not know how to write and therefore needed the services of a scribe. The extent of reading and writing abilities in ancient Israel is debated; see the reasonable discussion in James L. Crenshaw, *Education in Ancient Israel: Across the Deadening Silence*, AB (Garden City, NY: Doubleday, 1998), 29–40.

24. Today we have two different Hebrew editions ("recensions") of the Book of Jeremiah; see above, note 9.

Chaper 19

1. On the connection between priests and Torah traditions, see the previous chapter. See also Risa Levitt Kohn, *A New Heart and a New Soul: Ezekiel, the Exile and the Torah*, JSOTSup 358 (Sheffield, UK: Sheffield Academic Press, 2002).
2. Jacob Z. Lauterbach, trans. and ed., *Mekhilta de-Rabbi Ishmael* (Philadelphia: Jewish Publication Society, 1976), 1.4.
3. For more on this form, see esp. Norman Habel, "The Form and Significance of the Call Narratives," ZAW 77 (1965), 297–323; and Klaus Baltzer, "Considerations Regarding the Office and Calling of the Prophet," *HTR* 61 (1968), 567–81.
4. See my book *God is King: Understanding an Israelite Metaphor*, JSOTSup 76 (Sheffield, UK: Sheffield Academic Press, 1989), 83.
5. To Moses Maimonides—who lived some 1700 years after Ezekiel—divine incorporeality was a basic principle (although it was still disputed even in his day). Thus states the version of his Thirteen Principles recited after the morning prayers: "I believe with perfect faith that our creator—blessed be his name—is not a body and no bodily qualities apply to Him, and He has no appearance whatsoever." On this translation, see the discussion in Lawrence A. Hoffman's *My People's Prayer Book: Traditional Prayers, Modern Commentaries*, vol. 6, *Tachanun and Concluding Prayers* (Woodstock, VT: Jewish Lights, 2002), 162. On the continuity between biblical and postbiblical images of the divine, see Michael Fishbane, *Biblical Myth and Rabbinic Mythmaking* (Oxford: Oxford Univ. Press, 2003).
6. For a sharply contrasting view, which psychoanalyzes the prophet, see David J. Halperin, *Seeking Ezekiel: Text and Psychology* (University Park: Pennsylvania State Univ., 1993).
7. This phrase, found 94 times in Ezekiel (out of a total of 139 in the Bible) creates a very human image of Ezekiel as a prophet who felt distant from God, in contrast with some other prophets, especially Isaiah, who in chapter 6 moves quite comfortably among the heavenly court.
8. We now have enough evidence to know that the synagogue did not arise until several centuries after Ezekiel. This should have been obvious from the text of Ezekiel itself, which does not say that the people should build any-

thing. See the excellent summary in Lee I. Levine, *The Ancient Synagogue: The First Thousand Years* (New Haven, CT: Yale Univ. Press, 2000), 1–41; and Birger Olsson and Magnus Zetterholm, *The Ancient Synagogue from Its Origins Until 200 C.E.*, CBNT 39 (Stockholm: Almqvist & Wiksell, 2003).

9. On July 30, 2004, at 6 p.m., a Google search for "Ezekiel spacecraft" yielded 1,700 hits.
10. See Halperin, *Seeking Ezekiel: Text and Psychology*.
11. This chapter is speaking about national resurrection, and has little or no bearing on the issue of personal resurrection, which likely was a later belief.
12. See Joel S. Kaminsky, *Corporate Responsibility in the Hebrew Bible*, JSOTSup 196 (Sheffield, UK: Sheffield Academic Press, 1995).
13. Ugarit was a city in northern Canaan that flourished throughout the Bronze Age, only to be destroyed around 1200 B.C.E. When twentieth-century archaeologists excavated its remains, they discovered a vast Canaanite literature, written in a language close to biblical Hebrew. See Michael David Coogan, *Stories from Ancient Canaan* (Philadelphia: Westminster, 1978), 27–47; or COS, 1.343–56.
14. On these chapters, see S. Tamar Kamionkowski, *Gender Reversal and Cosmic Chaos: A Study on the Book of Ezekiel*, JSOTSup 368 (Sheffield, UK: Sheffield Academic Press, 2003).
15. This translation follows Moshe Greenberg, *Ezekiel 1–20*, AB 22 (Garden City: Doubleday, 1983), 271. The translation that follows is from Moshe Greenberg, *Ezekiel 21–37*, AB 22a (Garden City: Doubleday, 1997), 471. In contrast, the JPS translation has somewhat bowdlerized these passages.
16. See: www.bible.org/docs/ot/books/eze/ezk-intr.htm.
17. For interpretations of his silence, see Ellen F. Davis, *Swallowing the Scroll: Textuality and the Dynamics of Discourse in Ezekiel's Prophecy*, JSOTSup 78: Sheffield, UK: Almond Press, 1989), 48–58.
18. See Morton Cogan, *Imperialism and Religion: Assyria, Judah and Israel in the Eighth and Seventh Centuries B.C.E.*, SBLMS 19 (Missoula, MT: Scholars Press, 1974), 12; see more generally 9–21.
19. What Ezekiel describes is not mentioned in the Book of Kings, which generally did not hesitate to note cultic sins. They look more like activities sponsored by the much earlier King Manasseh than activities performed during the reign of Zedekiah, the last king of Judah. See Moshe Greenberg, "Prolegomenon," in Charles Cutler Torrey, *Pseudo-Ezekiel and the Original Prophecy* (New York: Ktav, 1970), xviii-xxix.
20. There is significant debate on whether this reflects a real Temple, or is imaginary. In addition to the commentaries, see Jon Douglas Levenson, *Theology*

of the Program of Restoration of Ezekiel 40–48, HSM 10 (Missoula, MT.: Scholars, 1976); Steven Shawn Tuell, *The Law of the Temple in Ezekiel 40–48*, HSM 49 (Atalanta: Scholars, 1992); and Kalinda Rose Stevenson, *The Vision of Transformation: The Territorial Rhetoric of Ezekiel 40–48*, SBLDS 154 (Atlanta: Scholars, 1996).

21. Gog is believed to be a reflection of the seventh-century Lydian king Gyges.
22. It is difficult to know how literally to read this passage, which seems to suggest that David himself, rather than a Davidic descendant, will be king!
23. A classic treatment of this formula is Walther Zimmerli, "Knowledge of God According to the Book of Ezekiel," in his *I Am Yahweh*, trans. Douglas W. Stott (Atlanta: John Knox, 1982), 29–98.

Chaper 20

1. For a detailed history of the Persian period, see Lester L. Grabbe, *Judaism from Cyrus to Hadrian* (Minneapolis, MN: Fortress, 1992).
2. See *COS*, 2.314–16.
3. See J. F. A. Sawyer, "Isaiah, Book of," in John H. Hayes, ed., *Dictionary of Biblical Interpretation* (Nashville, TN: Abingdon, 1999), 552–54; and Christopher R. Seitz, "Trito-Isaiah," *ABD*, 3.501–7.
4. A reason often given, that these later sections complement the words of First Isaiah, does not hold up to scrutiny. Isaiah 40–66 shows more continuity with Jeremiah, as Benjamin D. Sommer has observed in his *A Prophet Reads Scripture: Allusion in Isaiah 40–66* (Stanford, CA: Stanford Univ. Press, 1998).
5. In fact, it is likely that this verse in Deuteronomy comes from an exilic Deuteronomist.
6. See Kaufmann, *The Religion of Israel*, 16–17.
7. See the essays in Michael B. Dick, ed., *Born in Heaven, Made on Earth: The Making of the Cult Image in the Ancient Near East* (Winona Lake, IN: Eisenbrauns, 1999).
8. See Fishbane, *Biblical Myth and Rabbinic Mythmaking*, 37–92.
9. A classic discussion is found in Bernard W. Anderson, "Exodus Typology in Second Isaiah," in B. Anderson and W. Harrelson, eds., *Israel's Prophetic Heritage: Essays in Honor of James Muilenburg* (Harper & Brothers, 1962), 177–195.
10. See Otto Eissfeldt, "The Promises of Grace to David in Isaiah 55.1–5," in Anderson and Harrelson, eds., *Israel's Prophetic Heritage*, 196–207.
11. See Mayer I. Gruber, "The Motherhood of God in Second Isaiah," in his *The Motherhood of God and Other Studies* (Atlanta: Scholars, 1992), 3–15.

12. An old, but excellent discussion of the many possibilities for identifying the servant is Christopher R. North, *The Suffering Servant in Deutero-Isaiah: An Historical and Critical Study* (London: Oxford Univ. Press, 1948).
13. One definition of cognitive dissonance is "a psychological phenomenon which refers to the discomfort felt at a discrepancy between what you already know or believe, and new information or interpretation." See J.S. Atherton, *Learning and Teaching: Cognitive Dissonance* (UK, 2003); http://www.learningandteachinginfo/learning/dissonance.htm. Psychologists first used the idea of cognitive dissonance in the late 1950s to help explain the behavior of persons in cults. Biblical scholars later applied the concept to biblical oracles. See Robert P. Carroll, *When Prophecy Failed: Cognitive Dissonance in the Prophetic Traditions of the Old Testament* (New York: Seabury Press, 1979).
14. Carroll, *When Prophecy Failed*, 161.
15. While verses are numbered to according to their location in "Ezra" or "Nehemiah," the two are combined as a single book according to Jewish reckoning—see n. 15 in chapter 2.
16. See the discussion in Christine E. Hayes, *Gentile Impurities and Jewish Identities: Intermarriage and Conversion from the Bible to the Talmud* (New York: Oxford Univ. Press, 2002), 27–33.
17. See Fishbane, *Biblical Interpretation in Ancient Israel*, 115–23.
18. The cessation of prophecy is a complex issue—see Benjamin D. Sommer, "Did Prophecy Cease? Evaluating a Reevaluation," *JBL* 115 (1996), 31–47.

Chaper 21

1. Most scholars agree that the latter part of Zechariah is a later addition. See M. Saebø, "Zechariah, Book of," in John H. Hayes, ed., *Dictionary of Biblical Interpretation*, 666–69.
2. Similar to Zechariah's visions with an angelic guide—and close to them chronologically—is Ezekiel's vision featuring a supernatural guide, "a man who shone like copper" (Ezek. 40:3).
3. This is cited from *Semeia* 14 in the survey of John J. Collins, *The Apocalyptic Imagination: An Introduction to Jewish Apocalyptic Literature*, 2nd ed. (Grand Rapids, MI: Eerdmans, 1998), 5. For a different definition, see Klaus Koch, "What Is Apocalyptic? An Attempt at a Preliminary Definition," in Paul D. Hanson, ed., *Visionaries and Their Apocalypses* (Philadelphia: Fortress, 1983), 16–36.
4. For a more extensive exposition of these chapters as apocalyptic, from a dif-

ferent starting point, see Stephen L. Cook, *Prophecy and Apocalypticism: The Postexilic Social Setting* (Minneapolis, MN: Fortress, 1995), 123–65.

5. These books are examined in detail in Collins, *The Apocalyptic Imagination*.
6. The Persian influence is hard to trace because our earliest extant manuscripts of both literatures tend to date from much later than this period. Therefore we cannot tell the difference between early and late developments. For various suggestions concerning the origin of apocalypticism, see the essays in John J. Collins, *The Encyclopedia of Apocalypticism,* vol. 1, *The Origins of Apocalypticism in Judaism and Christianity* (New York: Continuum, 1998), 3–161.
7. See the essays in Collins, *The Encyclopedia of Apocalypticism,* vol. 1, 267–414.
8. For more details on these and other introductory issues, see John J. Collins, *Daniel*, Hermeneia (Minneapolis, MN: Fortress, 1993), 1–123.
9. For the definition of apocalyptic literature, see our discussion of Zechariah earlier in this chapter.
10. See Collins, *Daniel*, 331.
11. Again, just to be clear: the basis for this reinterpretation is the doubling of the word *sh-v-'-m* (**שבעים**—Hebrew was written without vowels in this period), once as "seventy" (**שִׁבְעִים**—*shiv'im*) and once as "weeks" (**שָׁבֻעִים**—*shavu'im*).
12. This term is borrowed from the Israeli scholar Joseph Heinemann, whose major work has not been translated into English.
13. See Kugel, *The Bible as It Was*, 18: "The first assumption that all ancient interpreters seem to share is that the Bible is a fundamentally cryptic document."
14. See Michael Fishbane, *Biblical Interpretation in Ancient Israel* (Oxford: Clarendon, 1985). A condensed version of this is Michael Fishbane, "Inner Biblical Exegesis: Types and Strategies of Interpretation in Ancient Israel" in *Midrash and Literature*, ed. Geoffrey H. Hartman and Sanford Budick (New Haven, CT: Yale Univ. Press, 1986), 19–37.
15. See Leonard J. Greenspoon, "The Origin of the Idea of Resurrection," in Baruch Halpern and Jon D. Levenson, eds., *Traditions in Transformation: Turning Points in Biblical Faith* (Winona Lake, IN: Eisenbrauns, 1981), 247–321; Klaas Spronk, *Beatific Afterlife in Ancient Israel and in the Ancient Near East*, AOAT 219 (Kevelaer: Butzon & Bercker, 1986).
16. The origins of the doctrine of resurrection are not clear. It might be a reaction to the historical events between 167 and 164, when Jews were first punished for their specific religious beliefs, which may have led to the idea that God was postponing the reward for faithfulness, to a time after death.

Alternatively, it might reflect Greek influence; see my "Is There Martyrdom in the Hebrew Bible?" in Margaret Cormack, ed., *Sacrificing the Self: Perspectives on Martyrdom and Religion* (New York: Oxford Univ. Press, 2002), 3–22, esp. 15.

17. In addition to commentaries on Daniel, the following three books are especially helpful: Danna Nolan Fewell, *Circle of Sovereignty: A Story of Stories in Daniel 1–6*, JSOTSup 72 (Sheffield, UK: Sheffield Academic Press, 1988); Pamela J. Milne, *Vladimir Propp and the Study of Structure in Hebrew Biblical Narrative* (Sheffield, UK: Almond Press, 1988) and Lawrence M. Wills, *The Jew in the Foreign Court*, HDR 26 (Minneapolis, MN: Fortress, 1990).
18. This is the only biblical reference that suggests that God requires members of the Covenant to drink special wine. (It would be anachronistic to use the word "kosher" in reference to the food that Daniel and his four friends eat.)
19. See the discussion of the "royal tale" genre in the works cited in n. 17, above, and in Collins, *Daniel*, 38–52.
20. On the ahistorical character of the Book of Jonah, see Amos Funkenstein, *Perceptions of Jewish History* (Berkeley: Univ. of California Press, 1993), 64–70.
21. See W. Lee Humphreys, "A Life-Style for Diaspora: A Study of the Tales of Esther and Daniel," *JBL* 92 (1973), 211–23. The Septuagint version of Esther, which has many additions relative to the Hebrew text, tells a similar story.

Chaper 22

1. For a survey of general issues concerning Psalms, see Klaus Seybold, *Introducing the Psalms*, trans. R. Graeme Dunphy (Edinburgh: T & T Clark, 1990).
2. On these, see Moshe Greenberg, *Biblical Prose Prayer as a Window to the Popular Religion of Ancient Israel* (Berkeley: Univ. of California Press, 1983), esp. 59–60 (for the enumeration of the ninety-seven prose prayers). Scholars and students often study prose and poetic prayers separately, but this is unfortunate since the two genres may be mutually enlightening.
3. For this type of analysis, see Greenberg, *Biblical Prose Prayer*.
4. For the analysis that follows, see my "Women and Psalms: Toward an Understanding of the Role of Women's Prayer in the Israelite Cult," in Victor H. Matthews et al., eds, *Gender and Law in the Hebrew Bible and the Ancient Near East*, JSOTSup 262 (Sheffield, UK: Sheffield Academic Press, 1998), 25–56, esp. 45–48.

5. Specifically, this psalm features two types of parallelism: synonymous (e.g., "He raises the poor from the dust, / Lifts up the needy from the dunghill"; v. 8), and antithetical (e.g., "The bows of the mighty are broken, / And the faltering are girded with strength"; v. 4). As for figurative language, it refers to God via the metaphor "rock" (v. 2).
6. On why this may be so, see Knohl, "Between Voice and Silence."
7. See the terms used in Erhard S. Gerstenberger, *Psalms Part 1 With an Introduction to Cultic Poetry*, FOTL XIV (Grand Rapids, MI: Eerdmans, 1988), 9–21.
8. For more on this type of analysis see Claus Westerman, *Praise and Lament in the Psalms*, trans. Keith R. Crim and Richard N. Soulen (Atlanta: John Knox, 1981), though he has a slightly different understanding of the lament's structure.
9. Scholars debate whether biblical Hebrew expresses tenses. Some hold that the verbal forms instead indicate whether actions are complete or not. However, that debate is not important for this particular text, since here the Hebrew makes it clear that these are actions completed in the past.
10. For one description of this inferred functionary in Israel's shrines, see Aubrey R. Johnson, *The Cultic Prophet in Ancient Israel* (Cardiff: Univ. of Wales Press, 1962).
11. For an investigation of various types of divine responses to prayers, see Patrick D. Miller, *They Cried to the Lord: The Form and Theology of Biblical Prayer* (Minneapolis, MN: Fortress, 1994), 135–77.
12. On the genre of "entrance liturgy," see Hermann Gunkel, *An Introduction to the Psalms*, trans. James D. Nogalski (Macon, GA: Mercer Univ. Press, 1998), 313.
13. Of the psalms attributed to the "Korahites," Psalm 43 lacks an explicit superscription, but on the grounds of content and style, most scholars assume that it is the second half of Psalm 42. On the meaning of the superscriptions that mention David, see Alan M. Cooper, "The Life and Times of King David According to the Psalter," in *The Poet and The Historian*, ed. R. E. Friedman (Chico, CA: Scholars, 1983), 117–31. Historians do not view King David as the true inventor of psalmody, because psalm genres exist in even older literature from Mesopotamia.
14. See Nahum M. Sarna, *Songs of the Heart: An Introduction to the Book of Psalms* (New York: Schocken, 1993), 19–20.
15. See Gary A. Rendsburg, *Linguistic Evidence for the Northern Origin of Selected Psalms*, SBLMS 43 (Atlanta: Scholars, 1990). He likely overstates the case for Northern psalms.

16. See Loren D. Crow, *The Songs of Ascents (Psalms 120–134): Their Place in Israelite History and Religion*, SBLDS 148 (Atlanta: Scholars, 1996), 1–27.
17. See Gerald Henry Wilson, *The Editing of the Hebrew Psalter*, SBLDS 76 (Chico, CA: Scholars, 1985); and J. Clinton McCann, *The Shape and Shaping of the Psalter*, JSOTSup159 (Sheffield, UK: Sheffield Academic Press, 1993).
18. As we saw in chapter 11, a secondary insertion at the start of Joshua also inserts Torah into the beginning of the second major portion of the Bible, Nevi'im.

Chaper 23

1. A "proverb" is a type of saying, while "Proverbs" is the name of a book.
2. The nature of ancient wisdom schools is explored in John G. Gammie and Leo G. Pedue, eds., *The Sage in Israel and the Ancient Near East* (Winona Lake, IN: Eisenbrauns, 1990).
3. See, for example, Roland E. Murphy, *The Tree of Life: An Exploration of Biblical Wisdom Literature*, AB (Garden City, NY: Doubleday, 1990), 115–18.
4. The two major introductions to the genre of wisdom literature are: James L. Crenshaw, *Old Testament Wisdom: An Introduction* (Atlanta: John Knox, 1981); and Murphy, *The Tree of Life*.
5. Rather than "wisdom literature," R. N. Whybray prefers to speak instead of "the intellectual tradition." See his *The Intellectual Tradition in the Old Testament*, BZAW 135 (Berlin: de Gruyter, 1974).
6. See, for example, the essays in John Day et al., eds., *Wisdom in Ancient Israel* (Cambridge: Cambridge Univ. Press, 1995), 94–169.
7. For other such identical pairs, see Daniel C. Snell, *Twice-Told Proverbs and the Composition of the Book of Proverbs* (Winona Lake, IN: Eisenbrauns, 1993), esp. 35.
8. See Snell, *Twice-Told Proverbs*.
9. See R. B. Y. Scott, "Wise and Foolish, Righteous and Wicked," *VT* 29 (1972): 145–65.
10. See William McKane, *Proverbs*, OTL (Philadelphia: Westminster, 1977), 10–22.
11. See Klaus Koch, "Is There a Doctrine of Retribution in the Old Testament?" in James L. Crenshaw, ed., *Theodicy in the Old Testament* (Philadelphia: Fortress, 1983), 57–87.
12. For additional examples, see R. B. Y. Scott, "Folk Proverbs of the Ancient Near East," in James L. Crenshaw, ed., *Studies in Ancient Israelite Wisdom* (New York: Ktav, 1976), 417–26.

13. It is uncertain whether "foreign" in this context means non-Israelite, or any women outside of one's wife.
14. According to some scholars, wisdom is hypostasized here as a deity. For different views, see Bernhard Lang, *Wisdom and the Book of Proverbs: An Israelite Goddess Redefined* (New York: Pilgrim Press, 1986); Claudia V. Camp, *Wisdom and the Feminine in the Book of Proverbs* (Sheffield, UK: Almond Press, 1985); and Michael V. Fox, *Proverbs 1–9*, AB (Garden City, NY, 2000).
15. For one possible explanation, see Joseph Blenkinsopp, "The Social Context of the 'Outsider Woman' in Proverbs 1–9," *Bib* 72 (1991), 457–73.
16. See COS, 1.115–22.
17. Some scholars believe that a later editor added the closing passage so as to counter the misogynistic introduction. See Richard J. Clifford, *Proverbs*, OTL (Louisville, KY: Westminster John Knox, 1999), 273–74.
18. See James L. Crenshaw, *Education in Ancient Israel*, 62.
19. For a brief description of how proverbs function, see James G. Williams, "The Power of Form: A Study of Biblical Proverbs," *Semeia* 17 (1980), 35–58; for a longer discussion see his *Those Who Ponder Proverbs: Aphoristic Thinking and Biblical Literature* (Sheffield, UK: Almond Press, 1981).
20. See for example, Murphy, *The Tree of Life*, 78–79.
21. For the mainstream view, see, e.g., Michael V. Fox, The *JPS Bible Commentary: Ecclesiastes* (Philadelphia: Jewish Publication Society, 2004), 82–83. Peter Machinist expresses a contrary view in the *JSB*, 1621–22.
22. See Robert Gordis, "Quotations in Wisdom Literature," in Crenshaw, ed., *Studies in Ancient Israelite Wisdom*, 220–44; and R. N. Whybray, "The Identification and Use of Quotations in Ecclesiastes," *SVT* 32 (1981), 435–51.
23. The best introduction to Ecclesiastes, which also contains a detailed commentary, is Michael V. Fox, *A Time to Tear Down and a Time to Build Up: A Rereading of Ecclesiastes* (Grand Rapids., MI; Eerdmans, 1999).
24. Linguistic evidence suggests that Ecclesiastes is a much later book, from the Second Temple period. Apparently its author wanted to lend the protagonist the aura of Solomon's wealth and wisdom. Although the book does not contain any Greek words, many scholars believe that it reflects the influence of Greek thought.
25. Based on this passage in Ecclesiastes, the folksinger Pete Seeger composed a song that the Byrds made famous in 1965:

    To everything—turn, turn, turn
    There is a season—turn, turn, turn
    And a time for ev'ry purpose under heaven
    . . . .

A time to gain, a time to lose
A time to rend, a time to sew
A time to love, a time to hate
A time of peace: I swear it's not too late!

Ironically, these lyrics—which American protesters sang often during the Vietnam War—dramatically altered the original point of Ecclesiastes.

26. The determinism in Ecclesiastes continues in the Dead Sea Scrolls. (This shared feature is one aspect that scholars cite in dating this biblical book to the Hellenistic period.) See Jean Duhaime, "Determinism," in Lawrence H. Schiffman and James C. VanderKam, eds., *Encyclopedia of the Dead Sea Scrolls* (New York: Oxford Univ. Press, 2000), 194–98.
27. See R.N. Whybray, "Qoheleth, Preacher of Joy," *JSOT* 23 (1982), 87–98.

Chaper 24

1. In addition to the various commentaries cited below, see Edwin M. Good, *In Turns of Tempest: A Reading of Job with a Translation* (Stanford, CA: Stanford Univ. Press, 1990).
2. For an overview of the difficulties of the language of Job, see Jonas C. Greenfield, "The Language of the Book" in Moshe Greenberg et al., *The Book of Job: A New Translation According to the Traditional Hebrew Text* (Philadelphia: Jewish Publication Society, 1980), xiv–xvi.
3. For a different view, see David J.A. Clines, "The Arguments of Job's Three Friends," in D. J. A. Clines et al., eds., *Art and Meaning: Rhetoric in Biblical Literature*, JSOTSup 19 (Sheffield, UK: JSOT Press, 1982), 199–214.
4. For the purpose of this exposition, the content of Elihu's speeches will be ignored, following the model of Matitiahu Tsevat, "The Meaning of the Book of Job," in *The Meaning of the Book of Job and Other Biblical Studies: Essays on the Literature and Religion of the Hebrew Bible* (New York: Ktav, 1980), 1–37, along with many others. Some see Elihu's speeches as "retarding" the action, while others note the similarities between them and God's speeches in the following chapter—both deal extensively with God's power in nature.
5. For example, Job 28 raises several questions: Who is speaking, Job or the narrator? Does the chapter reflect the work of one author or several? Is it original or secondary? All of these questions affect the most basic question: what does it really mean?
6. For additional details concerning this and other source-critical distinctions, see the commentaries.

7. For this distinction, see, among others, Robert Gordis, *The Book of God and Man: A Study of Job* (Chicago: Univ. of Chicago Press, 1978), 13.
8. On this unit, see Nahum M. Sarna, "Epic Substratum in the Prose of Job," *Studies in Biblical Interpretation*, 411–24.
9. Some would discuss this in terms of "corrections of the scribes" or "a scribal euphemism" (e.g., Samuel Rolles Driver and George Buchanan Gray, *The Book of Job*, ICC [Edinburgh: T & T Clark, 1971], 8; Marvin H. Pope, *Job*, AB [Garden City, NY: Doubleday, 1973], 8), but this is not correct—see Tov, *Textual Criticism*, 64–67.
10. Sarna, "Epic Substratum in the Prose of Job."
11. Stephen Mitchell, *The Book of Job* (San Francisco, CA: North Point, 1987), 5.
12. Isaiah portrayed God as surrounded by angels (Isa. 6:1–8; see "Location, Location, Location" in chapter 19). Elsewhere the prophet Micaiah expresses the same idea: "I saw the LORD seated upon His throne, with all the host of heaven standing in attendance to the right and to the left of Him" (1 Kings 22:19).
13. See the comment in E. Dhorme, *A Commentary on the Book of Job*, trans. Harold Knight (Nashville, TN: Thomas Nelson, 1984), 5.
14. For the story of this development, see Elaine Pagels, *The Origin of Satan* (New York: Random House, 1995). For more on the Satan in the Hebrew Bible, see Peggy L. Day, *An Adversary in Heaven: Satan in the Hebrew Bible*, HSM 43 (Atlanta: Scholars, 1988).
15. Avi Hurvitz, "The Date of the Prose-tale of Job Linguistically Reconsidered," *HTR* 67 (1974), 17–34.
16. For more on this point, see my book *God Is King*, 105.
17. The reference is to "Mother Earth," see Norman C. Habel, *The Book of Job*, OTL (Philadelphia: Westminster, 1985), 93.
18. For a different, (overly) close reading of this section, see Meir Weiss, *The Story of Job's Beginning: A Literary Analysis* (Jerusalem: Magnes Press, 1983).
19. See Michael Brennen Dick, "The Legal Metaphor in Job 31," *CBQ* 41 (1979), 37–50 and "Job 31, The Oath of Innocence, and the Sage," *ZAW* 95 (1983), 31–53.
20. See Habel, *Job*, 535–36.
21. On girding one's loins, see Habel, *Job*, 536.
22. On the strong forensic background of the book, see Habel, *Job*, 54–57 and passim.
23. For the function of these rhetorical questions, see (in addition to the com-

mentaries) Michael V. Fox, "Job 38 and God's Rhetoric," *Semeia* 19 (1981), 53–61.

24. In addition to the commentaries, the following three very different treatments of these speeches are helpful: R. A. F. MacKenzie, "The Purpose of the Yahweh Speeches in the Book of Job," in *Studia Biblical et Orientalia*, AnOr 10 (Rome: Pontifical Biblical Institute, 1959), 1.301–11; Tsevat, "The Meaning of the Book of Job"; and Athalya Brenner, "God's Answer to Job," *VT* 31 (1981), 129–37.
25. In addition to the commentaries, see B. F. Batto, "Behemoth," *DDD* 165–69 and C. Uehlinger, "Leviathan," *DDD*, 511–15. On Ugarit, see n. 13 in chapter 19.
26. For one attempt to resolve this ambiguity, see John Briggs Curtis, "On Job's Response to Yahweh," *JBL* 98 (1979), 497–511.
27. Mitchell, *The Book of Job*, 88, 128–29.
28. This is the thesis of Carol A. Newsom, *The Book of Job: A Contest of Moral Imagination* (New York: Oxford Univ. Press, 2003); she speaks throughout of Job as a "polyphonic construction."

Chaper 25

1. This chapter is based on my forthcoming article "A Lock Whose Key Is Lost: Unresolved and Unresolvable Problems in Interpreting the Song" in *Scrolls of Love: Reading Ruth and the Song of Songs*, ed. Peter S. Hawkins and Lesleigh Cushing Stahlberg (Bronx, NY: Fordham Univ. Press, forthcoming); see further literature there.
2. Readers in English may find it fruitful to consult more than one translation, such as Marvin H. Pope, *Song of Songs*, AB 7C (Garden City, NY: Doubleday, 1977); Marcia Falk, *Love Lyrics from the Bible: A Translation and Literary Study of The Song of Songs* (Sheffield, UK: Almond Press, 1982); Ariel and Chana Bloch, *The Song of Songs* (New York: Random House, 1995).
3. The text mentions a "king" in 1:4, 12; 3:9, 11; and 7:6. It mentions "Solomon" in 1:5; 3:7, 9, 11; and 8:11.
4. On the *waṣfs*, see the essays in Athalya Brenner, ed., *A Feminist Companion to The Song of Songs* (Sheffield, UK: Sheffield Academic Press, 1993), 214–57.
5. Scholars have investigated the possibility of female authorship of the Song; for a discussion, see A. Brenner and F. van Dijk-Hemmes, *On Gendering*

Texts: Female and Male Voices in the Hebrew Bible (Leiden: Brill, 1986), esp. 71–81. For a critique, see my article "Lock Without a Key."

6. For a broader view of the Jewish attitude, see Jonathan Magonet, ed., *Jewish Explorations of Sexuality* (Providence, RI: Berghahn Books, 1995).
7. See especially Michael V. Fox, *The Song of Songs and the Egyptian Love Songs* (Madison: Univ. of Wisconsin Press, 1985).
8. Miriam Lichtheim, *Ancient Egyptian Literature* (Berkeley: Univ. of California Press, 1976), 2.182.
9. Robert D. Biggs, *Šà.zi.ga: Ancient Mesopotamian Potency Incantations* (Locust Valley, NY: J. J. Augustin, 1967), 30.
10. This is quoted from Marvin H. Pope, *Song of Songs*, 79.
11. Pope, *Song of Songs*, 516.
12. A possible exception to this is in 8:6, where *shalhevetyah* (שַׁלְהֶבֶתְיָה) may be understood as either "the flame of God" or "a great flame"; see Pope, *Song of Songs*, 670–71.
13. Despite some interpreters' claims to the contrary, it is quite clear that (at least in most passages) the lovers are unmarried, and are not bride and groom. For example, in 1:6 the female speaker is under her brothers', not her husband's, control.
14. Women's sexual rights according to biblical law are explained most clearly in Judith Romney Wegner, *Chattel or Person? The Status of Women in the Mishnah* (New York: Oxford Univ. Press, 1988), 40–41. Widows and divorcees were exceptional, in that they controlled their own sexuality.
15. The bride-price must not be confused with the dowry. The bride-price goes from the groom's family to the bride's family, whereas the dowry is brought by the bride into the marriage. Biblical law does not make clear whether the dowry becomes the groom's property or not; in rabbinic law, the groom may enjoy the benefits from or interest on the dowry, but the dowry belongs to the bride.
16. For a more detailed reading of this passage (5:2–6), see my article "Sensual or Sublime: On Teaching the Song of Songs," in *Approaches to Teaching the Hebrew Bible as Literature in Translation*, ed. Barry N. Olshen and Yael S. Feldman (New York: Modern Language Association, 1989), 133–35.
17. See especially Marcia Falk, *Love Lyrics from the Bible*, 100–102.
18. See Victor H. Matthews, "Perfumes and Spices," *ABD*, 5.226–28, esp. 227.
19. See Frank Moore Cross, *Canaanite Myth and Hebrew Epic* (Cambridge, MA: Harvard Univ. Press, 1973), 55–56, n. 44, especially his reference to the "Grand Teton range" as it may relate to the divine name *Shaddai*.
20. See b. Sanhedrin 101a.

Chaper 26

1. The observations below on Ruth and Esther are largely based on Danna Nolan Fewell and David Miller Gunn, *Compromising Redemption: Relating Characters in the Book of Ruth* (Louisville, KY: Westminster/John Knox, 1990); Kirsten Nielson, *Ruth*, OTL (Louisville, KY: Westminster John Knox, 1997); Michael V. Fox, *Character and Ideology in the Book of Esther* (Columbia: Univ. of South Carolina Press, 1991); Jon D. Levenson, *Esther*, OTL (Louisville, KY: Westminster John Knox, 1997); and Adele Berlin, *The JPS Bible Commentary: Esther* (Philadelphia: Jewish Publication Society, 2001).
2. Some consider this single verse (4:7) to be a later gloss added on to a much earlier book. Scholars are continuing a healthy debate concerning Ruth's date.
3. See my *The Creation of History*, 8–19.
4. See André Lacoque, *The Feminine Unconventional: Four Subversive Figures in Israel's Tradition*, OBT (Minneapolis, MN: Fortress, 1990), 51.
5. What Haman offers is a sum larger than any one person could possibly have possessed. Fox, *Character and Ideology*, 52, estimates this amount as "58%–68% of the annual revenue of the empire."
6. See Sandra Beth Berg, *The Book of Esther: Motifs, Themes and Structure*, SBLDS 44 (Missoula, MT: Scholars, 1979), 31–35; for other structures, see 106–13.
7. Kenneth Craig strongly advocates the view that Purim preceded the Book of Esther; see his *Reading Esther: A Case for the Literary Carnivalesque* (Louisville, KY: Westminster John Knox, 1995). See also Adele Berlin, in *Esther*, xxvii, and in the *JSB*, 1623.
8. See Athalya Brenner, *The Israelite Woman: Social Role and Literary Type in Biblical Narrative* (Sheffield, UK: JSOT Press, 1985), 31–32.
9. See Shaye J.D. Cohen, *The Beginnings of Jewishness: Boundaries, Varieties, Uncertainties* (Berkeley: Univ. of California Press, 1999).

Chaper 27

1. A more detailed overview of many of the issues discussed here is John Barton, "The Significance of a Fixed Text and Canon," in Magne Saebø, ed., *The Hebrew Bible/Old Testament: The History of Its Interpretation*, vol. 1 (Göttingen: Vandenhoeck & Ruprecht, 1996), 67–83.
2. Philip R. Davies emphasizes the role of the populace in his *Scribes and*

Schools: the Canonization of the Hebrew Scriptures (Louisville, KY: Westminster John Knox, 1998), which is summarized in his "The Jewish Scriptural Canon in Cultural Perspective," in Lee Martin McDonald and James A. Sanders, eds., *The Canon Debate* (Peabody, MA: Hendrickson, 2002), 36–52.

3. See Lee Martin McDonald and James A. Sanders, "Introduction," in Lee Martin McDonald and James A. Sanders, eds., *The Canon Debate*, 11.
4. See Moshe Halbertal, *People of the Book: Canon, Meaning, and Authority* (Cambridge, MA: Harvard Univ. Press, 1997); Eugene Ulrich, "The Notion and Definition of Canon," in McDonald and Sanders, eds., *The Canon Debate*, 21–35.
5. See James Barr, *Holy Scripture: Canon, Authority, Criticism* (Philadelphia: Westminster, 1983).
6. For the rabbinic terms used for "the Bible," see Sid Z. Leiman, *The Canonization of Hebrew Scripture: The Talmudic and Midrashic Evidence* (Hamden, CT: Archon, 1976), 53–72.
7. See my article coauthored with Thomas Römer, "Deuteronomy 34 and the Case for a Persian Hexateuch," *JBL* 119 (2000), 401–19.
8. See Leiman, *The Canonization of Hebrew Scripture*, 31–33; Steve Mason, "Josephus and His Twenty-two Book Canon," in McDonald and Sanders, eds., *The Canon Debate*, 110–27.
9. Leiman, *Canonization*, 33.
10. For this reconstruction of the canon of Josephus, see Leiman, *Canonization*, 32–33.
11. On determining what did and did not happen at Jamnia, see Jack P. Lewis, "Jamnia Revisited," in McDonald and Sanders, eds., *The Canon Debate*, 146–62.
12. For texts and the meaning of "defiling the hands," see Leiman, *Canonization*, 102–120.
13. Leiman, *Canonization*, 53–56.
14. In addition to Leiman, *Canonization*, see Jack N. Lightstone, "The Rabbis' Bible: The Canon of the Hebrew Bible and the Early Rabbinic Guild," in McDonald and Sanders, eds., *The Canon Debate*, 163–84.
15. Leiman, *Canonization*, 92–102.
16. Leiman, *Canonization*, 97.
17. For the late Second-Temple period, scholars use the term "sect" to refer to one of the many groups of Jews who adhered to distinctive doctrine and their own authorities. For a cogent defense of the identification of the Qumran (Dead Sea Scrolls) community with Josephus' description of the

party that he called Essenes, see James C. VanderKam, *The Dead Sea Scrolls Today* (Grand Rapids, MI: Eerdmanns, 1994), 71–98.

18. However, some of the Dead Sea Scrolls do relate to Esther; see Sidnie White Crawford, "Esther, Book of," in Schiffman and VanderKam, eds., *Encyclopedia of the Dead Sea Scrolls*, 269–70. For a list of the number of manuscripts of each biblical book found at Qumran, see Esther Eshel, "The Bible in the Dead Sea Scrolls," *JSB*, 1922.
19. See James C. VanderKam, "Questions of Canon Viewed through the Dead Sea Scrolls," in McDonald and Sanders, eds., *The Canon Debate* , 91–109.
20. For a history of the place of the codex in Judaism, see Mordechai Glatzer, "The Book of Books—From Scroll to Codex and into Print," in Mordechai Glatzer, ed., *The Jerusalem Crown: Companion Volume* (Jerusalem: N. Ben-Zvi, 2002), 61–101.
21. See Nahum M. Sarna, "Ancient Libraries and the Ordering of the Biblical Books," in his *Studies in Biblical Interpretation*, 53–66.
22. When the scribes of the Dead Sea Scrolls sometimes copied Genesis and Exodus onto a single long scroll, they skipped several lines between the two books, which indicates that those books were viewed as separate.
23. Leiman, *Canonization*, 53–72.
24. The main defender of an alternative reconstruction—an original two-part canon—is John Barton, *Oracles of God: Perceptions of Ancient Prophecy in Israel after the Exile* (Oxford: Oxford Univ. Press, 1986), 35–95. On problems with many of the standard arguments in favor of an original or early tripartite canon, see Julio C. Trebolle Barrera, "Origins of a Tripartite Old Testament Canon," in McDonald and Sanders, eds., *The Canon Debate*, 128–45; Eugene Ulrich, "The Non-Attestation of a Tripartite Canon in 4QMMT," *CBQ* 65 (2003), 202–14.
25. The older characterization of an Alexandrian vs. a Palestinian canon is not viable; see Albert C. Sundberg Jr., "The Septuagint: The Bible of Hellenistic Judaism," in McDonald and Sanders, eds., *The Canon Debate*, 79.
26. See, for example, Leiman, *Canonization*, 131.
27. On variation in the order of the Latter Prophets and in Kethuvim, see Christian C. Ginsburg, *Introduction to the Massoretico-Critical Edition of the Bible* (New York: Ktav, 1966), 1–8.
28. For a summary on the "Bible" of the Dead Sea Scrolls community, see Tov, *Textual Criticism*, 100–117; see also the specific evidence that Eugene Ulrich cites in many of the essays in his *The Dead Sea Scrolls and the Origins of the Bible* (Grand Rapids, MI: Eerdmans, 1999).
29. See, for example, the differences systematically noted in James H.

Charlesworth, ed., *The Dead Sea Scrolls: Hebrew, Aramaic, and Greek Texts with English Translations*. Vol. 6b, *Pesharim, Other Commentaries, and Related Documents* (Louisville, KY, Westminster John Knox, 2002).

30. See Pesher Habakkuk 4:9–16, and the discussion in William H. Brownlee, *The Midrash Pesher of Habakkuk*, SBLMS 24 (Missoula, MT.: Scholars, 1979), 80–83.
31. Moshe Greenberg, "The Stabilization of the Text of the Hebrew Bible, Reviewed in Light of the Biblical Materials from the Judean Desert," reprinted in Sid Z. Leiman, *The Canon and Masorah of the Hebrew Bible: An Introductory Reader* (New York: Ktav, 1974), 314.
32. On the difficult question of how various competing textual versions resolved over time into one "official" version, see the discussion of M. H. Goshen-Gottstein, "Hebrew Biblical Manuscripts: Their History and Their Place in the HUBP Edition," in Frank Moore Cross and Shemaryahu Talmon, eds., *Qumran and the History of the Biblical Text* (Cambridge, MA: Harvard Univ. Press, 1975), 42–89.
33. Rabbinic literature often associates the midrashic move of interpreting variant spellings—*malei* (מָלֵא, "full"; Latin: "plene") versus *chaser* (חָסֵר, "short" or "defective")—with R. Akiva.
34. On the variant Talmudic (and later) readings of biblical texts, see B. Barry Levy, *Fixing God's Torah: The Accuracy of the Hebrew Bible Text in Jewish Law* (New York: Oxford Univ. Press, 2001).
35. For a summary of the evolution of the biblical text, see David E. S. Stein's preface to the *JPS Hebrew-English Tanakh* (Philadelphia: Jewish Publication Society, 1999), ix–xix.
36. The standard reference work on the Masoretes is Israel Yeivin, *Introduction to the Tiberian Masorah*, trans. E. J. Revell, Masoretic Studies 5 (Missoula, MT: Scholars, 1980); on the victory of the Tiberian tradition as represented in the Aleppo Codex, see Yosef Ofer, "The History and Authority of the Aleppo Codex," in Glatzer, ed., *The Jerusalem Crown: Companion Volume*, 25–50.

Afterword

1. On the multiplicity of conceptions in the Bible, see the essays in Jason P. Rosenblatt and Joseph C. Sitterson, Jr., eds., *"Not in Heaven": Coherence and Complexity in Biblical Narrative* (Bloomington: University of Indiana Press, 1991), especially Bernard M. Levinson, "The Right Chorale: From the Poetics to the Hermeneutics of the Hebrew Bible," 129–153.

2. In this book I had originally intended to include chapters on these modes of interpretation, but with the publication of the essays "Classical Rabbinic Interpretation" (Yaakov Elman), "Midrash and Midrashic Interpretation" (David Stern), and "Medieval Jewish Interpretation" (Barry D. Walfish) in *JSB*, 1844–1900, this is no longer necessary.

   I perceive only minimal continuities between these modes of Bible study and contemporary critical studies. Earlier scholars did anticipate important aspects of historical-critical study, including the use of other Semitic languages (some classical rabbis and Spanish exegetes), the idea that some small parts of the Torah are not Mosaic (Abraham ibn Ezra), certain aspects of "lower" textual criticism (various Spanish exegetes), and the idea that similar biblical laws in different books should be studied independently of each other (Rashbam). Yet those rabbis applied such ideas only to a small number of texts. No single premodern scholar ever combined them together. In addition, they never employed other key features of the historical-critical method, such as conducting systematic source analysis or consulting ancient versions such as the Septuagint. Most important, premodern Jewish scholarship focused on the place of the Bible in Jewish life, not on its place as an ancient Near Eastern document. Nevertheless, the interpretations (and modes of interpretation) in these Jewish sources are rich, profound, and varied.
3. The distinction between what the Bible "meant" and what it "means" is central to the program of Krister Stendahl (Swedish bishop, theologian, and Harvard professor emeritus); see esp. "Biblical Theology: A Program," in his *Meanings: The Bible as Document and as Guide* (Philadelphia: Fortress, 1984), 11–44, esp. 14–16. In Jewish circles during the twentieth century, a leading exponent of this approach was Mordecai M. Kaplan (professor of homiletics at the Jewish Theological Seminary and founder of Reconstruc-tionism), who called it "revaluation."
4. This is a primary example used in James L. Kugel, "Two Introductions to Midrash" in Geoffrey H. Hartman and Sanford Budick, eds., *Midrash and Literature* (New Haven, CT: Yale Univ. Press. 1986), 77–103; see esp. 78.
5. On Karaites, a group that does not uphold the sanctity of the "oral law" (rabbinic interpretation), see Meira Polliack, "Medieval Karaism," in Martin Goodman et al., eds., *The Oxford Handbook of Jewish Studies* (Oxford: Oxford Univ. Press, 2002), 295–326.
6. See my earlier discussion on this issue in "Biblical History and Jewish Biblical Theology," *JR* 77 (1997), 563–83, esp. 574–77.
7. *Pesikta de-Rav Kahana*, "In the third month," paragraph 25; p. 223 of

Mandelbaum edition; for the complete texts and a discussion, see my "The Many Faces of God in Exodus 19," in Alice Ogden Bellis and Joel S. Kaminsky, eds., *Jews, Christians, and the Theology of the Hebrew Scriptures*, SBL Symposiums Series 8 (Atlanta: Society of Biblical Literature, 2000), 353–67, esp. 353.

Sources Cited*

Ackroyd, P. R. et al., eds., *The Cambridge History of the Bible*. 3 vols. Cambridge: Cambridge University. Press, 1963–70.

Aharoni, Yohanan. *The Archaeology of the Land of Israel from the Prehistoric Beginnings to the End of the First Temple Period*. Translated by Anson Rainey. Philadelphia: Westminster, 1982.

——.*The Land of the Bible: A Historical Geography*. Translated by A. F. Rainey. London: Burns & Oates, 1979.

Aharoni, Yohanan et al., eds. *The Carta Bible Atlas*. 4th ed. Jerusalem: Carta, 2002.

Albrektson, Bertil. *History and the Gods: An Essay on the Idea of Historical Events as Divine Manifestations in the Ancient Near East and in Israel*. CBOT 1. Lund: Gleerup, 1967.

Albright, William Foxwell. *From Stone Age to Christianity: Monotheism and the Historical Process*. Garden City, NY: Anchor, 1957.

Alt, Albrecht. "The Origins of Israelite Law." In his *Essays on Old Testament History and Religion*, 101–71. Garden City, NY: Doubleday, 1967.

Alter, Robert. *The Art of Biblical Narrative*. New York: Basic, 1981.

——. *The Art of Biblical Poetry*. New York: Basic, 1985.

Anderson, Bernard W. "Exodus Typology in Second Isaiah." In *Israel's Prophetic Heritage: Essays in Honor of James Muilenburg*, edited by B. Anderson and W. Harrelson, 177–95. New York: Harper, 1962.

——. "The Priestly Creation Story: A Stylistic Study." In his *From Creation to New Creation*, 42–55. OBT. Minneapolis, MN: Fortress, 1994.

Andres, J. C. et al., *Chronicles and Its Synoptic Parallels in Samuel, Kings, and Related Biblical Texts*. Collegeville, MN: Liturgical Press, 1998.

*Only works in English have been included.

Atherton, J.S. *Learning and Teaching: Cognitive Dissonance*. http://www.learningandteaching.info/learning/dissonance.htm.

Baltzer, Klaus. "Considerations Regarding the Office and Calling of the Prophet." *HTR* 61 (1968): 567–81.

Bar-Efrat, Shimon. *Narrative Art in the Bible*. JSOTSup 70. Sheffield, UK: Almond Press, 1989.

Barr, James. *The Garden of Eden and the Hope of Immortality*. Minneapolis, MN: Fortress, 1993.

——. *Holy Scripture: Canon, Authority, Criticism*. Philadelphia: Westminster, 1983.

——. "The Image of God in the Book of Genesis—A Study of Terminology." *BJRL* 51 (1968–69): 11–26.

Barton, John. "Historical-Critical Approaches." In *The Cambridge Companion to Biblical Interpretation*, edited by John Barton, 9–20. Cambridge: Cambridge University Press, 1998.

——. *Oracles of God: Perceptions of Ancient Prophecy in Israel after the Exile*. Oxford: Oxford University Press, 1986.

——. *Reading the Old Testament: Method in Biblical Study*. Rev. ed. Louisville, KY: Westminster John Knox, 1996.

——. "The Significance of a Fixed Text and Canon." In *The Hebrew Bible/Old Testament: The History of Its Interpretation*. Edited by Magne Saebø. 1:67–83. Göttingen: Vandenhoeck & Ruprecht, 1996.

Batto, B. F. "Behemoth." In *DDD*, 165–69. Leiden: Brill, 1999.

Beckwith, Roger. *The Old Testament Canon of the New Testament Church and its Background in Early Judaism*. Grand Rapids, MI: Eerdmans, 1985.

Benavides, Gustavo. "Modernity." In *Critical Terms for Religious Studies*, edited by Mark C. Taylor, 186–204. Chicago: University of Chicago Press, 1998.

Ben Zvi, Ehud. "The Prophetic Book: A Key Form of Prophetic Literature." In *The Changing Face of Form Criticism for the Twenty-First Century*, edited by Marvin A. Sweeney and Ehud Ben Zvi, 276–97. Grand Rapids, MI: Eerdmans, 2003.

Berg, Sandra Beth. *The Book of Esther: Motifs, Themes and Structure*. SBLDS 44. Missoula, MT: Scholars, 1979.

Berlin, Adele. *The Dynamics of Biblical Parallelism*. Bloomington: Indiana University Press, 1985.

——. *The JPS Bible Commentary: Esther*. Philadelphia: Jewish Publication Society, 2001.

——. "Parallelism." In *ABD*, 5:155–162.

Berlin, Adele and Marc Zvi Brettler. *The Jewish Study Bible*. New York: Oxford University Press, 2004.

Berrin, Shani L. "Pesharim." In *The Encyclopedia of the Dead Sea Scrolls*, edited by Lawrence H. Schiffman and James C. VanderKam, 2.644–47. New York: Oxford University Press, 2000.

Bickerman, Elias. *From Ezra to the Last of the Maccabees: Foundations of Postbiblical Judaism*. New York: Schocken, 1962.

Biggs, Robert D. *Šà.zi.ga: Ancient Mesopotamian Potency Incantations*. Locust Valley, NY: J. J. Augustin, 1967.

Bird, Phyllis A. "'Male and Female He Created Them': Genesis 1:27b in the Context of the Priestly Account of Creation." In her *Missing Persons and Mistaken Identities: Women and Gender in Ancient Israel*, 123–54. OBT. Minneapolis, MN: Fortress, 1997.

Blenkinsopp, Joseph. *A History of Prophecy in Israel: From the Settlement in the Land to the Hellenistic Period*. Philadelphia: Westminster, 1983.

——. "The Social Context of the 'Outsider Woman' in Proverbs 1–9." *Bib* 72 (1991): 457–73.

Bloch, Ariel, and Chana Bloch. *The Song of Songs*. New York: Random House, 1995.

Bottéro, Jean. *Mesopotamia: Writing, Reasoning, and the Gods*. Translated by Z. Bahrani and M. Van De Mieroop. Chicago: University of Chicago Press, 1992.

Brenner, Athalya, ed. *A Feminist Companion to Genesis*. Sheffield, UK: Sheffield Academic Press, 1993.

——, ed. *A Feminist Companion to The Song of Songs*. Sheffield, UK: Sheffield Academic Press, 1993.

——, ed. *Genesis: A Feminist Companion to the Bible*. 2nd Series. Sheffield, UK: Sheffield Academic Press, 1998.

——. "God's Answer to Job." *VT* 31 (1981): 129–37.

——. *The Israelite Woman: Social Role and Literary Type in Biblical Narrative*. Sheffield, UK: JSOT Press, 1985.

Brenner, A. and F. van Dijk-Hemmes. *On Gendering Texts: Female and Male Voices in the Hebrew Bible*. Leiden: Brill, 1986.

Brettler, Marc Zvi. "Biblical History and Jewish Biblical Theology." *JR* 77 (1997): 563–83.

——. *The Book of Judges*. Old Testament Readings. London: Routledge, 2002.

——. "The Copenhagen School: The Historiographical Issues." *AJS Review* 27 (2003): 1–21.

——. *The Creation of History in Ancient Israel*. London: Routledge, 1995.

——. "Cyclical and Teleological Time in the Hebrew Bible." In *Time and Temporality in the Ancient World*, edited by Ralph M. Rosen, 111–28. Philadelphia: University of Pennsylvania Museum of Archaeology and Anthropology, 2004.

——. *God Is King: Understanding an Israelite Metaphor*. JSOTSup 76. Sheffield, UK: Sheffield Academic Press, 1989.

——. "Is There Martyrdom in the Hebrew Bible?" In *Sacrificing the Self: Perspectives on Martyrdom and Religion*, edited by Margaret Cormack, 3–22. New York: Oxford University Press, 2002.

——. "A Lock Whose Key Is Lost: Unresolved and Unresolvable Problems in Interpreting the Song." In *Scrolls of Love: Reading Ruth and the Song of Songs*, edited by Peter S. Hawkins and Lesleigh Cushing Stahlberg. Bronx, NY: Fordham University Press, forthcoming.

——. "The Many Faces of God in Exodus 19." In *Jews, Christians, and the Theology of the Hebrew Scriptures*, edited by Alice Ogden Bellis and Joel S. Kaminsky, 353–67. SBL Symposium Series 8. Atlanta: Society of Biblical Literature, 2000.

——. "Sensual or Sublime: On Teaching the Song of Songs." In *Approaches to Teaching the Hebrew Bible as Literature in Translation*, edited by Barry N. Olshen and Yael S. Feldman, 133–35. New York: Modern Language Association, 1989.

——. "The Structure of 1 Kings 1–11." *JSOT* 49 (1991): 87–97.

——. "Women and Psalms: Toward an Understanding of the Role of Women's Prayer in the Israelite Cult." In *Gender and Law in the Hebrew Bible and the Ancient Near East*, edited by Victor H. Matthews et al., 25–56. JSOTSup 262. Sheffield, UK: Sheffield Academic Press, 1998.

Brettler, Marc Z., and Thomas Römer. "Deuteronomy 34 and the Case for a Persian Hexateuch." *JBL* 119 (2000): 401–19.

Bright, John. *A History of Israel*. 3rd ed. Philadelphia: Westminster, 1981.

Broshi, M. "The Expansion of Jerusalem in the Reigns of Hezekiah and Manasseh." *IEJ* 24 (1974): 21–26.

Brownlee, William H. *The Midrash Pesher of Habakkuk*. SBLMS 24. Missoula, MT: Scholars, 1979.

Buber, Martin and Franz Rosenzweig. *Scripture and Translation*. Translated by Lawrence Rosenwald with Everett Fox. Bloomington: Indiana University Press, 1994.

Burkert, Walter. *Structure and History in Greek Mythology and Ritual*. Berkeley: University of California Press, 1979.

Camp, Claudia V. *Wisdom and the Feminine in the Book of Proverbs*. Sheffield, UK: Almond Press, 1985.

Campbell, Antony F., and Mark A. O'Brien. *Unfolding the Deuteronomistic History: Origins, Upgrades, Present Text*. Minneapolis, MN: Fortress, 2000.

Carasik, Michael A. "Theologies of the Mind in Biblical Israel." PhD diss., Brandeis University, 1997.

Carroll, Robert P. *The Book of Jeremiah*. OTL. Philadelphia: Westminster, 1986.
———. *When Prophecy Failed: Cognitive Dissonance in the Prophetic Traditions of the Old Testament*. New York: Seabury Press, 1979.
Charlesworth, James H., ed. *The Dead Sea Scrolls: Hebrew, Aramaic, and Greek Texts with English Translations*. Vol. 6b, *Pesharim, Other Commentaries, and Related Documents*. Louisville, KY: Westminster John Knox, 2002.
———. *The Old Testament Pseudepigrapha*. 2 vols. Garden City, NY: Doubleday, 1983, 1985.
Childs, Brevard S. *Introduction to the Old Testament as Scripture*. Philadelphia: Fortress, 1979.
———. *Isaiah*. OTL. Louisville, KY: Westminster John Knox, 2001.
———. *Isaiah and the Assyrian Crisis*. SBT^2 3. London: SCM, 1967.
Christensen, Duane L., ed. *A Song of Power and the Power of Song: Essays on the Book of Deuteronomy*. Winona Lake, IN: Eisenbrauns, 1993
Clark, W. Malcolm. "Law." In *Old Testament Form Criticism*, edited by John H. Hayes, 99–139. San Antonio, TX: Trinity University Press, 1974.
Clifford, Richard J. *Proverbs*. OTL. Louisville, KY: Westminster John Knox, 1999.
Clines, David J. A. "The Arguments of Job's Three Friends." In *Art and Meaning: Rhetoric in Biblical Literature*, edited by D. J. A. Clines et al., 199–214. JSOTSup 19. Sheffield, UK: JSOT Press, 1982.
Cogan, Mordechai, and Hayim Tadmor. *II Kings*. AB. New York: Doubleday, 1988.
Cogan, Morton. *Imperialism and Religion: Assyria, Judah and Israel in the Eighth and Seventh Centuries B.C.E.* SBLMS 19. Missoula, MT: Scholars, 1974.
Cohen, Shaye J. D. *The Beginnings of Jewishness: Boundaries, Varieties, Uncertainties*. Berkeley: University of California Press, 1999.
Collins, John J. *The Apocalyptic Imagination: An Introduction to Jewish Apocalyptic Literature*. 2nd ed. Grand Rapids, MI: Eerdmans, 1998.
———. *Daniel*. Hermeneia. Minneapolis, MN: Fortress, 1993.
———. *The Encyclopedia of Apocalypticism*. Vol. 1, *The Origins of Apocalypticism in Judaism and Christianity*. New York: Continuum, 1998.
———. *The Scepter and the Star: The Messiahs of the Dead Sea Scrolls and Other Ancient Literature*. AB. Garden City, NY: Doubleday, 1995.
Coogan, Michael David. *Stories from Ancient Canaan*. Philadelphia: Westminster, 1978.
Cook, Stephen L. *Prophecy and Apocalypticism: The Postexilic Social Setting*. Minneapolis, MN: Fortress, 1995.
Cooley, Robert E. "Ai." In *The Oxford Encyclopedia of Archaeology in the Near East*, edited by Eric M. Meyers, 1.33. New York: Oxford, 1997.
Cooper, Alan M. "The Life and Times of King David According to the Psalter." In

The Poet and The Historian, edited by R. E. Friedman, 117–31. Chico, CA: Scholars, 1983.

Coote, Robert B., ed. *Elijah and Elisha in Socioliterary Perspective*. Semeia Studies. Atlanta: Scholars, 1992.

Craig, Kenneth. *Reading Esther: A Case for the Literary Carnivalesque*. Louisville, KY: Westminster John Knox, 1995.

Crenshaw, James L. *Education in Ancient Israel: Across the Deadening Silence*. AB. Garden City, NY: Doubleday, 1998.

——. *Old Testament Wisdom: An Introduction*. Atlanta: John Knox, 1981.

Cross, Frank Moore. *Canaanite Myth and Hebrew Epic*. Cambridge, MA: Harvard University Press, 1973.

Cross, Frank M. and D. N. Freedman. *Pottery, Poetry, and Prophecy: Studies in Early Hebrew Poetry*. Winona Lake, IN: Eisenbrauns, 1980.

Crow, Loren D. *The Songs of Ascents (Psalms 120–134): Their Place in Israelite History and Religion*. SBLDS 148. Atlanta: Scholars, 1996.

Curtis, John Briggs. "On Job's Response to Yahweh." *JBL* 98 (1979): 497–511.

Dalley, Stephanie. *Myths from Mesopotamia: Creation, the Flood, Gilgamesh, and Others*. Oxford: Oxford University Press, 1991.

Davies, Philip R. *Scribes and Schools: the Canonization of the Hebrew Scriptures*. Louisville, KY: Westminster John Knox, 1998.

Davis, Ellen F. *Swallowing the Scroll: Textuality and the Dynamics of Discourse in Ezekiel's Prophecy*. JSOTSup 78. Sheffield, UK: Almond Press, 1989.

Day, John et al., eds. *Wisdom in Ancient Israel*. Cambridge: Cambridge University Press, 1995.

Day, Peggy L. *An Adversary in Heaven: Satan in the Hebrew Bible*. HSM 43. Atlanta: Scholars, 1988.

del Olmo Lete, G. *Canaanite Religion According to the Liturgical Texts of Ugarit*. Translated by W. G. E. Watson. Winona Lake, IN: Eisenbrans, 2004.

Dever, William G. *What Did the Biblical Writers Know and When Did They Know It? What Archaeology Can Tell Us about the Reality of Ancient Israel*. Grand Rapids, MI: Eerdmans, 2001.

——. *Who Were the Early Israelites and Where Did They Come From?* Grand Rapids, MI: Eerdmans, 2003.

Dhorme, E. *A Commentary on the Book of Job*. Translated by Harold Knight. Nashville, TN: Thomas Nelson, 1984.

Dick, Michael Brennen, ed. *Born in Heaven, Made on Earth: The Making of the Cult Image in the Ancient Near East*. Winona Lake, IN: Eisenbrauns, 1999.

——. "Job 31, The Oath of Innocence, and the Sage." *ZAW* 95 (1983): 31–53.

——. "The Legal Metaphor in Job 31." *CBQ* 41 (1979): 37–50.

Discoveries in the Judaean Desert. 39 vols. Oxford: Clarendon, 1955–.

Dockser Marcus, Amy. *The View from Nebo: How Archaeology is Rewriting and Reshaping the Middle East*. Boston: Little, Brown, 2000.

Douglas, Mary. "The Abominations of Leviticus." In her *Purity and Danger*, 41–57. London: Routledge & Kegan Paul, 1969.

Driver, Samuel Rolles, and George Buchanan Gray. *The Book of Job*. ICC. Edinburgh: T & T Clark, 1971.

Duhaime, Jean. "Determinism." In *Encyclopedia of the Dead Sea Scrolls*, edited by Lawrence H. Schiffman and James C. VanderKam, 194–98. New York: Oxford University Press, 2000.

Eissfeldt, Otto. *The Old Testament: An Introduction*. Translated by Peter A. Ackroyd. New York: Harper and Row, 1965.

——. "The Promises of Grace to David in Isaiah 55.1–5." In *Israel's Prophetic Heritage: Essays in Honor of James Muilenburg*, edited by Anderson and Harrelson, 196–207. New York: Harper, 1962.

Ellis, Peter F. *The Yahwist: The Bible's First Theologian*. London: G. Chapman, 1969.

Eph'al, I. "The Western Minorities in Babylonia in the 6th–5th Centuries B.C.: Maintenance and Cohesion." *Orientalia* 47 (1978): 74–90.

Falk, Marcia. *Love Lyrics from the Bible: A Translation and Literary Study of The Song of Songs*. Sheffield, UK: Almond Press, 1982.

Fernández Marcos, Natalio. *The Septuagint in Context: Introduction to the Greek Version of the Bible*. Translated by Wilfred G. E. Watson. Boston: Brill Academic Publishers, 2001.

Fewell, Danna Nolan. *Circle of Sovereignty: A Story of Stories in Daniel 1–6*. JSOTSup 72. Sheffield, UK: Sheffield Academic Press, 1988.

Fewell, Danna Nolan, and David Miller Gunn. *Compromising Redemption: Relating Characters in the Book of Ruth*. Louisville, KY: Westminster/John Knox, 1990.

Finkelstein, Israel, and Neil Asher Silberman. *The Bible Unearthed: Archaeology's New Vision of Ancient Israel and the Origin of Its Sacred Texts*. New York: Touchstone, 2001.

Finkelstein, J. J. *The Ox That Gored*. TAPS 71/2. Philadelphia: American Philosophical Society, 1981.

Fishbane, Michael. *Biblical Interpretation in Ancient Israel*. Oxford: Clarendon, 1985.

——. *Biblical Myth and Rabbinic Mythmaking*. Oxford: Oxford University Press, 2003.

——. "Inner Biblical Exegesis: Types and Strategies of Interpretation in Ancient Israel." In *Midrash and Literature*, edited by Geoffrey H. Hartman and Sanford Budick, 19–37. New Haven, CT: Yale University Press, 1986.

——. "Torah and Tradition." In *Tradition and Theology in the Old Testament*, edited by Douglas A. Knight, 279–80. Philadelphia: Fortress, 1977.

Fitzpatrick-McKinley, Anne. *The Transformation of Torah from Scribal Advice to Law*. JSOTSup 287. Sheffield, UK: Sheffield Academic Press, 1999.

Fokkelman, J. P. *Reading Biblical Narrative: An Introductory Guide*. Louisville, KY: Westminster John Knox, 1999.

Fox, Everett. *The Five Books of Moses: Genesis, Exodus, Leviticus, Numbers, Deuteronomy*. Vol. 1. of Schocken Bible. New York: Schocken, 1995.

Fox, Michael V. *Character and Ideology in the Book of Esther*. Columbia: University of South Carolina Press, 1991.

——. "Job 38 and God's Rhetoric." *Semeia* 19 (1981): 53–61.

——. *The JPS Bible Commentary: Ecclesiastes*. Philadelphia: Jewish Publication Society, 2004.

——. *Proverbs 1–9*. AB. Garden City, NY, 2000.

——. *The Song of Songs and the Egyptian Love Songs*. Madison, WI: University of Wisconsin Press, 1985.

——. *A Time to Tear Down and a Time to Build Up: A Rereading of Ecclesiastes*. Grand Rapids, MI: Eerdmans, 1999.

Frankena, R. "The Vassal-Treaties of Esarhaddon and the Dating of Deuteronomy." *OTS* 14 (1965): 122–54.

Friedman, Richard Elliott. *The Bible with Sources Revealed*. San Francisco: HarperSanFrancisco, 2003.

——. *Commentary on the Torah with English Translation and Hebrew Text*. San Francisco: HarperSanFranciso, 1997.

——. *Who Wrote the Bible?* San Francisco: HarperSanFrancisco, 1997.

Fritz, Volkmar. *1 & 2 Kings*. Translated by Anselm Hagedorn. Minneapolis, MN: Fortress, 2003.

Frymer-Kensky, Tikva. *In the Wake of the Goddesses: Women, Culture, and the Biblical Transformation of Pagan Myth*. New York: Free Press, 1992.

Funkenstein, Amos. *Perceptions of Jewish History*. Berkeley: University of California Press, 1993.

Gammie, John G., and Leo G. Pedue, eds. *The Sage in Israel and the Ancient Near East*. Winona Lake, IN: Eisenbrauns, 1990.

Garr, W. Randall. *Dialect Geography of Syria-Israel, 1000–586* B.C.E. Philadelphia: University of Pennsylvania Press, 1985.

Geller, Stephen A. "Were the Prophets Poets?" *Prooftexts* 3 (1983): 211–21.

Gerstenberger, Erhard S. *Psalms Part 1 With an Introduction to Cultic Poetry*. FOTL XIV. Grand Rapids, MI: Eerdmans, 1988.

Gevirtz, Stanley. *Patterns in the Early Poetry of Israel*. Studies in Ancient Oriental Civilization, 32. Chicago: University of Chicago Press, 1973.

Ginsburg, Christian C. *Introduction to the Massoretico-Critical Edition of the Bible*. New York: Ktav, 1966. First published in 1897.

Ginzberg, Louis. *The Legends of the Jews*. Translated by Henrietta Szold. Philadelphia: Jewish Publication Society, 1968. 7 vols. Reissued in 2002.

Glatzer, Mordechai. "The Book of Books—From Scroll to Codex and into Print." In *The Jerusalem Crown: Companion Volume*, edited by Mordechai Glatzer, 61–101. Jerusalem: N. Ben-Zvi, 2002.

Good, Edwin M. *In Turns of Tempest: A Reading of Job with a Translation*. Stanford, CA: Stanford University Press, 1990.

Gordis, Robert. *The Book of God and Man: A Study of Job*. Chicago: University of Chicago Press, 1978.

——. "Quotations in Wisdom Literature." In *Studies in Ancient Israelite Wisdom*, edited by James Crenshaw, 220–44. New York: Ktav, 1976.

Goshen-Gottstein, Moshe H. "Hebrew Biblical Manuscripts: Their History and Their Place in the HUBP Edition." In *Qumran and the History of the Biblical Text*, edited by Frank Moore Cross and Shemaryahu Talmon, 42–89. Cambridge, MA: Harvard University Press, 1975.

Grabbe, Lester L., ed. *Can A 'History of Israel' Be Written?* JSOTSup 245. Sheffield, UK: Sheffield Academic Press, 1997.

——. *Judaism from Cyrus to Hadrian*. Minneapolis, MN: Fortress, 1992.

Graham, M. Patrick, and Steven L. McKenzie. *The Chronicler as Author: Studies in Text and Texture*. JSOTSup 263. Sheffield, UK: Sheffield Academic Press, 1999.

Gray, John. *Joshua, Judges, Ruth*. NCBC. Grand Rapids, MI: Eerdmans, 1986.

Greenberg, Moshe. *Biblical Prose Prayer as a Window to the Popular Religion of Ancient Israel*. Berkeley: University of California Press, 1983.

——. "The Decalogue Tradition Critically Examined." In *The Ten Commandments in History and Tradition*, edited by Ben-Zion Segal, 96–99. Jerusalem: Magnes, 1990.

——. *Ezekiel 1–20*. AB. Garden City, NY: Doubleday, 1983.

——. *Ezekiel 21–37*. AB. Garden City, NY: Doubleday, 1997.

——. "Jewish Conceptions on the Human Factor in Biblical Prophecy." In his *Studies in the Bible and Jewish Thought*, 405–19. JPS Scholar of Distinction Series. Philadelphia: Jewish Publication Society, 1995.

——. "More Reflections on Biblical Criminal Law." *ScrHier* 31 (1986): 1–17.

——. "Prolegomenon." In *Pseudo-Ezekiel and the Original Prophecy*, edited by Charles Cutler Torrey, xviii-xxix. New York: Ktav, 1970.

——. "Some Postulates of Biblical Criminal Law." In *The Jewish Expression*, edited by Judah Goldin, 18–37. New Haven, CT: Yale University Press, 1976.

——. "Ḥerem." *EJ* 8.349.

——. "The Use of the Ancient Versions for Interpreting the Hebrew Text: A Sampling from Ezekiel 2:1–3:11." In his *Studies in the Bible and Jewish Thought*, 209–225. JPS Scholar of Distinction Series. Philadelphia: Jewish Publication Society, 1995.

Greenfield, Jonas C. "The Language of the Book." In *The Book of Job: A New Translation According to the Traditional Hebrew Text*, edited by Moshe Greenberg et al., xiv–xvi. Philadelphia: Jewish Publication Society, 1980.

Greenspahn, Frederick E. "How Jews Translate the Bible." In *Biblical Translation in Context*, edited by Frederick W. Knobloch, 52–53. Bethesda: University Press of Maryland, 2002.

——. *When Brothers Dwell Together: The Preeminence of Younger Siblings in the Hebrew Bible*. New York: Oxford University Press, 1994.

Greenspoon, Leonard J. "The Origin of the Idea of Resurrection." In *Traditions in Transformation: Turning Points in Biblical Faith*, edited by Baruch Halpern and Jon D. Levenson, 247–321. Winona Lake, IN: Eisenbrauns, 1981.

Gruber, Mayer I. "The Motherhood of God in Second Isaiah." In his *The Motherhood of God and Other Studies*, 3-15. Atlanta: Scholars, 1992.

Gunkel, Hermann. *An Introduction to the Psalms*. Translated by James D. Nogalski. Macon, GA: Mercer University Press, 1998.

——. *The Stories of Genesis*. Berkeley, CA: BIBAL, 1994.

Habel, Norman C. *The Book of Job*. OTL. Philadelphia: Westminster, 1985.

——. "The Form and Significance of the Call Narratives." *ZAW* 77 (1965): 297–323.

Halbertal, Moshe. *People of the Book: Canon, Meaning, and Authority*. Cambridge, MA: Harvard University Press, 1997.

Halperin, David J. *Seeking Ezekiel: Text and Psychology*. University Park: Pennsylvania State University, 1993.

Halpern, Baruch. *The First Historians: The Hebrew Bible and History*. San Francisco: Harper & Row, 1988.

Haran, Menahem. "The Graded Numerical Sequence and the Phenomenon of 'Automatism' in Biblical Poetry." *VTS* 22 (1971): 238–67.

Hayes, Christine E. *Gentile Impurities and Jewish Identities: Intermarriage and Conversion from the Bible to the Talmud*. New York: Oxford University Press, 2002.

Hertz, J.H. *The Authorized Daily Prayer Book of the United Hebrew Congregations of the British Empire*. London: National Council for Jewish Religious Education, 1945.

Hier, Richard H. "Day of the LORD." *ABD* 2.82–83.

Hoffman, Lawrence A., ed. *My People's Prayer Book: Traditional Prayers, Modern Commentaries*. Vol. 6, *Tachanun and Concluding Prayers*. Woodstock, VT: Jewish Lights, 2002.

Hoffmeier, James K. *Israel in Egypt: The Evidence for the Authenticity of the Exodus Tradition*. New York: Oxford University Press, 1997.

Holladay, William L. *Jeremiah 2*. Minneapolis, MN: Fortress, 1989.

Hallo, William W., and K. Lawson Younger, eds. *The Context of Scripture*. 3 vols. Leiden: Brill, 1997-2002.

Holtz, Barry, ed. *Back to the Sources: Reading the Classic Jewish Texts*. New York: Summit Books, 1984.

Huffmon, H. B. "Prophecy (ANE)." *ABD*, 5.477–482.

Humphreys, W. Lee. *Joseph and His Family: A Literary Study*. Columbia: University of South Carolina Press, 1988.

——. "A Life-Style for Diaspora: A Study of the Tales of Esther and Daniel." *JBL* 92 (1973): 211–23.

Hurvitz, Avi. "The Date of the Prose-tale of Job Linguistically Reconsidered." *HTR* 67 (1974): 17–34.

Janowski, B. "Azazel." In *DDD*, 128–31. Leiden: Brill, 1999.

Japhet, Sara. *I & II Chronicles*. OTL. Louisville, KY: Westminster/John Knox, 1993.

——. "The Supposed Common Authorship of Chronicles and Ezra-Nehemiah Investigated Anew." *VT* 18 (1968): 332–72.

Johnson, Aubrey R. *The Cultic Prophet in Ancient Israel*. Cardiff: University of Wales Press, 1962.

Kaminsky, Joel S. *Corporate Responsibility in the Hebrew Bible*. JSOTSup 196. Sheffield, UK: Sheffield Academic Press, 1995.

Kamionkowski, S. Tamar. *Gender Reversal and Cosmic Chaos: A Study on the Book of Ezekiel*. JSOTSup 368. Sheffield, UK: Sheffield Academic Press, 2003.

Kaufman, Yehezkel. *The Religion of Israel*. Translated by Moshe Greenberg. New York: Schocken, 1972.

Kenyon, Kathleen. *Archaeology in the Holy Land*. 3rd ed. New York: Praeger, 1970.

——. *Royal Cities of the Old Testament*. New York: Schocken, 1971.

King, Philip J. *Amos, Hosea, Micah: An Archaeological Commentary*. Philadelphia: Westminster, 1988.

Knight, Douglass A., ed. *Methods of Biblical Interpretation*. Nashville, TN: Abingdon, 2004.

——. "Forward." Pp. v–xvi in the reprint of Julius Wellhausen, *Prolegomena to the History of Ancient Israel*. Atlanta: Scholars, 1994.

Knohl, Israel. "Between Voice and Silence: The Relationship between Prayer and Temple Cult." *JBL* 115 (1996): 17–30.

——. *The Divine Symphony: The Bible's Many Voices*. Philadelphia: Jewish Publication Society, 2003.

——. *The Sanctuary of Silence: The Priestly Torah and the Holiness School*. Minneapolis, MN: Fortress, 1995.

Knoppers, Gary N. "The Deuteronomist and the Deuteronomic Law of the King: A Reexamination of a Relationship." *ZAW* 108 (1996): 329–46.

——. "Intermarriage, Social Complexity, and Ethnic Diversity in the Genealogy of Judah." *JBL* 120 (2001): 15–30.

——. "Rethinking the Relationship between Deuteronomy and the Deuteronomistic History: The Case of Kings." *CBQ* 63 (2001): 393–415.

——. "Sex, Religion, and Politics: The Deuteronomist on Intermarriage." *HAR* 14 (1994): 121–41.

Koch, Klaus. "Is There a Doctrine of Retribution in the Old Testament?" In *Theodicy in the Old Testament*, edited by James L. Crenshaw, 57–87. Philadelphia: Fortress, 1983.

—— "What Is Apocalyptic? An Attempt at a Preliminary Definition." In *Visionaries and Their Apocalypses*, edited by Paul D. Hanson, 16–36. Philadelphia: Fortress, 1983.

Kohn, Risa Levitt. *A New Heart and a New Soul: Ezekiel, the Exile and The Torah.* JSOTSup 358. Sheffield, UK: Sheffield Academic Press, 2002.

Krentz, Edgar. *The Historical-Critical Method*. Philadelphia: Fortress, 1975.

Kugel, James L. *The Bible as It Was*. Cambridge, MA: Belknap Press, 1997.

——. *The Idea of Biblical Poetry: Parallelism and Its History*. New Haven, CT: Yale University Press, 1981.

——. *In Potiphar's House: The Interpretive Life of Biblical Texts*. San Francisco, CA: Harper and Row, 1990.

——. *Traditions of the Bible: A Guide to the Bible as It Was at the Start of the Common Era*. Cambridge, MA: Harvard University Press, 1998.

——. "Two Introductions to Midrash." In *Midrash and Literature*, edited by Geoffrey H. Hartman and Sanford Budick, 77–103. New Haven, CT: Yale University Press, 1986.

Lacoque, André. *The Feminine Unconventional: Four Subversive Figures in Israel's Tradition*. OBT. Minneapolis, MN: Fortress, 1990.

Lang, Bernhard. *Wisdom and the Book of Proverbs: An Israelite Goddess Redefined.* New York: Pilgrim Press, 1986.

Lauterbach, Jacob Z., ed. and trans. *Mekhilta de-Rabbi Ishmael*. 3 vols. Philadelphia: Jewish Publication Society, 1976. First published in 1935.
Leiman, Sid Z., ed. *The Canon and Masorah of the Hebrew Bible: An Introductory Reader*. New York: Ktav, 1974.
——. *The Canonization of Hebrew Scripture: The Talmudic and Midrashic Evidence*. Hamden, CT: Archon Books, 1976.
Leuchter, Mark. "Jeremiah's 70-Year Prophecy and the לב קמי / ששך *Atbash* Codes." *Bib* 85 (2004): 503–22.
Levenson, Jon Douglas. *The Death and Resurrection of the Beloved Son: The Transformation of Child Sacrifice in Judaism and Christianity*. New Haven, CT: Yale University Press, 1993.
——. *Esther*. OTL. Louisville, KY: Westminster John Knox, 1997.
——. *Sinai and Zion: An Entry into the Jewish Bible*. Minneapolis, MN: Winston, 1985.
——. *Theology of the Program of Restoration of Ezekiel 40–48*. HSM 10. Missoula, MT: Scholars, 1976.
Levine, Baruch A. *In the Presence of the Lord: A Study of Cult and Some Cultic Terms in Ancient Israel*. Leiden: Brill, 1974.
Levine, Lee I. *The Ancient Synagogue: The First Thousand Years*. New Haven, CT: Yale University Press, 2000.
Levine, Louis D. "Manuscripts, Texts and the Study of the Neo-Assyrian Royal Inscriptions." In *Assyrian Royal Inscriptions: New Horizons*, edited by F. M. Fales, 49–70. Rome: Istituto l'Oriente, 1981.
Levinson, Bernard M. *Deuteronomy and the Hermeneutics of Legal Innovation*. New York: Oxford University Press, 1997.
——, ed. *Theory and Method in Biblical and Cuneiform Law: Revision, Interpolation, and Development*. JSOTSup 181. Sheffield, UK: Sheffield Academic Press, 1994.
——. "'The Right Chorale': From the Poetics of Biblical Narrative to the Hermeneutics of the Hebrew Bible." In *"Not in Heaven": Coherence and Complexity in Biblical Narrative*, edited by Jason P. Rosenblatt and Joseph C. Sitterson, 129-53, 242-47. Indiana Studies in Biblical Literature. Bloomington: Indiana University Press, 1991.
——. "'*You Must Not Add Anything to What I Command You*': Paradoxes of Canon and Authorship in Ancient Israel." *Numen* 50 (2003): 1–51.
Levy, B. Barry. *Fixing God's Torah: The Accuracy of the Hebrew Bible Text in Jewish Law*. New York: Oxford University Press, 2001.
Lichtheim, Miriam. *Ancient Egyptian Literature*. 3 vols. Berkeley: University of California Press, 1976.

Long, Burke O. *Planting and Reaping Albright: Politics, Ideology, and Interpreting the Bible*. University Park: Pennsylvania State University Press, 1997.

Long, V. Phillips., ed. *Israel's Past in Present Research: Essays on Ancient Israelite Historiography*. Sources for Biblical and Theological Study 7. Winona Lake, IN: Eisenbrauns, 1999.

Lowery, Richard. *The Reforming Kings*. JSOTSup 120. Sheffield, UK: JSOT Press, 1990.

MacKenzie, R. A. F. "The Purpose of the Yahweh Speeches in the Book of Job." *Studia Biblical et Orientalia*. AnOr 10. Rome: Pontifical Biblical Institute, 1959. 1.301–11

Magonet, Jonathan, ed. *Jewish Explorations of Sexuality*. Providence, RI: Berghahn Books, 1995.

Malamat, Abraham. *Mari and the Bible*. Leiden: Brill, 1998.

Matthews, Victor H. *A Brief History of Ancient Israel*. Louisville, KY: Westminster John Knox, 2003.

——. "Perfumes and Spices." *ABD*, 5.226–28.

Mayes, James Luther, and Paul J. Achtemeier. *Interpreting the Prophets*. Philadelphia: Fortress, 1987.

Mazar, Amihai. *Archaeology of the Land of the Bible 10,000–586 B.C.E.* AB. Garden City, NY: Doubleday, 1990.

McBride, S. Dean, Jr. "The Yoke of the Kingdom: An Exposition of Deuteronomy 6:4–5." *Int* 27 (1973): 273–306.

McCann, J. Clinton. *The Shape and Shaping of the Psalter*. JSOTSup 159. Sheffield, UK: Sheffield Academic Press, 1993.

McCarter, P. Kyle, and Ronald S. Hendel. "The Patriarchal Age: Abraham, Isaac and Jacob." In *Ancient Israel*, edited by Hershel Shanks, 1–31. Rev. and expanded. Washington, DC: Biblical Archaeology Society, 1999.

McCarthy, Dennis J. *Treaty and Covenant*. AnBib 21. Rome: Biblical Institute Press, 1978.

McDonald, Lee Martin, and James A. Sanders, eds. *The Canon Debate*. Peabody, MA: Hendrickson, 2002.

McKane, William. *Jeremiah*, vol. 1. ICC. Edinburgh: T & T Clark, 1986.

——. *Proverbs*. OTL. Philadelphia: Westminster, 1977.

McKenzie, Steven L., and M. Patrick Graham, eds. *The History of Israel's Traditions: The Heritage of Martin Noth*. JSOTSup 182. Sheffield, UK: Sheffield Academic Press, 1994.

Melugin, Roy F., and Marvin A. Sweeney, eds. *New Visions of Isaiah*. JSOTSup 214. Sheffield, UK: Sheffield Academic Press, 1996.

Mendenhall, George E. "Covenant Forms in Israelite Tradition," *BA* 23/3 (Sept. 1954): 2–22; reprinted in *BAR* 3.25–53.

——. "The Hebrew Conquest of Palestine." *BA* 25/3 (Sept. 1962): 66–87. Reprinted in *BAR* 3.100–120.

Mendenhall, George E., and Gary A. Herion. "Covenant." *ABD*, 1.1179–1202.

Meyers, Carol. *Discovering Eve: Ancient Israelite Women in Context*. New York: Oxford University Press, 1988.

Milgrom, Jacob. "Israel's Sanctuary: The Priestly 'Picture of Dorian Gray.'" *RB* 83 (1976): 390–99.

——. *Leviticus 1–16*. AB. Garden City, NY: Doubleday, 1991.

——. "Profane Slaughter and a Formulaic Key to the Composition of Deuteronomy." *HUCA* 47 (1976): 1–17.

Miller, J. Maxwell. *The Old Testament and the Historian*. Philadelphia: Fortress, 1976.

Miller, Patrick D., Jr. "Wellhausen and the History of Israel's Religion." *Semeia* 25 (1982): 61–73.

——. *They Cried to the LORD: The Form and Theology of Biblical Prayer*. Minneapolis, MN: Fortress, 1994.

Milne, Pamela J. *Vladimir Propp and the Study of Structure in Hebrew Biblical Narrative*. Sheffield, UK: Almond Press, 1988.

Mitchell, Stephen. *The Book of Job*. San Francisco, CA: North Point, 1987.

Moore, George Foot. "Tatian's Diatessaron and the Analysis of the Pentateuch." In *Empirical Models for Biblical Criticism*, edited by Jeffrey H. Tigay, 243–56. Philadelphia: University of Pennsylvania Press, 1985.

Moran, William L. "The Ancient Near Eastern Background of the Love of God in Deuteronomy." *CBQ* 25 (1963): 77–87.

Mowinckel, Sigmund. *He That Cometh: The Messiah Concept in the Old Testament and Later Judaism*. Translated by G. W. Anderson. Nashville, TN: Abingdon, 1954.

Muffs, Yohanan. *Love and Joy: Law, Language and Religion in Ancient Israel*. Cambridge, MA: Harvard University Press, 1992.

Mullen, E. Theodore, Jr. *Ethnic Myths and Pentateuchal Foundations: A New Approach to the Formation of the Pentateuch*. Atlanta, GA: Scholars, 1997.

Murphy, Roland E. "Old Testament/*Tanakh*—Canon and Interpretation." In *Hebrew Bible or Old Testament? Studying the Bible in Judaism and Christianity*, edited by Roger Brooks and John J. Collins, 11–29. Notre Dame, IN: University of Notre Dame, 1990.

——. *The Tree of Life: An Exploration of Biblical Wisdom Literature*. AB. Garden City, NY: Doubleday, 1990.

Nelson, Richard D. *The Double Redaction of the Deuteronomistic History*. JSOTSup 18. Sheffield, UK: University of Sheffield, 1981.

——. *Joshua*. OTL. Louisville, KY: Westminster, John Knox, 1997.

——. "Ḥerem and the Deuteronomic Social Conscience." In *Deuteronomy and Deuteronomic Literature: Festschrift for C.H.W. Brekelmans*, edited by M. Vervenne and J. Lust, 39–54. Leuven: Leuven University Press, 1997.

Neusner, Jacob. *The Mishnah: A New Translation*. New Haven, CT: Yale University Press, 1991.

Newsom, Carol A. *The Book of Job: A Contest of Moral Imagination*. New York: Oxford University Press, 2003.

Nicholson, Ernest W. "Covenant in a Century of Study Since Wellhausen." *OTS* 24 (1986): 54–69. Reprinted in *A Song of Power and the Power of Song: Essays on the Book of Deuteronomy*, edited by Duane L. Christensen, 78–93.

——. *Deuteronomy and Tradition*. Philadelphia: Fortress, 1967.

——. *God and His People: Covenant and Theology in the Old Testament*. Oxford: Clarendon, 1986.

——. *The Pentateuch in the Twentieth Century: The Legacy of Julius Wellhausen*. Oxford: Clarendon, 1998.

——. *Preaching to the Exiles: A Study of the Prose Tradition in the Book of Jeremiah*. New York: Schocken, 1970.

Niditch, Susan. "Genesis." In *The Women's Bible Commentary*, edited by Carol A. Newsom and Sharon H. Ringe, 10–25. Louisville, KY: Westminster/John Knox, 1992.

——. *Underdogs and Tricksters: A Prelude to Biblical Folklore*. San Francisco: Harper and Row, 1987.

Nielsen, Eduard. *The Ten Commandments in New Perspective: A Traditio-historical Approach*. SBT^2 7. Naperville, IL: Allenson, 1968.

Nielson, Kirsten. *Ruth*. OTL. Louisville, KY: Westminster John Knox, 1997.

Nissinen, Martti. Preface to *Prophecy in Its Ancient Near Eastern Context: Mesopotamian, Biblical and Arabian Perspectives*, edited by Martti Nissinen. SBL Symposium 13, vii-vii. Atlanta: Society of Biblical Literature, 2000.

——. "The Sociological Role of the Neo-Assyrian Prophets." In *Prophecy in Its Ancient Near Eastern Context*, edited by Marttti Nissinen, 89–114.

North, Christopher R. *The Suffering Servant in Deutero-Isaiah: An Historical and Critical Study*. London: Oxford University Press, 1948.

Noth, Martin. *The Deuteronomistic History*. JSOTSup 15. Sheffield, UK: University of Sheffield, 1981.

Oates, Joan. *Babylon*. London: Thames and Hudson, 1979.

O'Connor, Kathleen M. *The Confessions of Jeremiah: Their Interpretation and Role in Chapters 1–25*. SBLDS 94. Atlanta: Scholars, 1988.

Ofer, Yosef. "The History and Authority of the Aleppo Codex." In *The Jerusalem Crown: Companion Volume*, edited by Mordechai Glatzer, 25–50. Jerusalem: N. Ben-Zvi, 2002.

Ogden Bellis, Alice. *Helpmates, Harlots, Heroes: Women's Stories in the Hebrew Bible*. Louisville, KY: Westminster/John Knox, 1994.

Olsson, Birger, and Magnus Zetterholm. *The Ancient Synagogue from Its Origins until 200 C.E.* CBNT 39. Stockholm: Almqvist & Wiksell, 2003.

Olyan, Saul M. *Rites and Rank: Hierarchy in Biblical Representations of Cult*. Princeton, NJ: Princeton University Press, 2000.

Oppenheim, A. Leo. *Ancient Mesopotamia: Portrait of a Dead Civilization*. Chicago: University of Chicago, 1977.

Otto, Eckart. "False Weights in the Scales of Biblical Justice? Different Views of Women from Patriarchal Hierarchy to Religious Equality in the Book of Deuteronomy." In *Gender and Law in the Hebrew Bible and the Ancient Near East*, edited by Victor H. Matthews et al., 128–46. JSOTSup 262. Sheffield, UK: Sheffield Academic Press, 1998.

Otto, Rudolf. *The Idea of the Holy: An Inquiry into the Non-rational Factor in the Idea of the Divine and its Relation to the Rational*. London: Oxford University Press, 1925.

Pagels, Elaine. *The Origin of Satan*. New York: Random House, 1995.

Parpola, Simo. *Assyrian Prophecies*. State Archives of Assyria 9. Helsinki: Helsinki University Press, 1997.

Paul, Shalom M. *Amos*. Hermeneia. Philadelphia: Fortress, 1991.

Pelikan, Jaroslav. *The Christian Tradition: A History of the Development of Doctrine*. Vol. 1, *The Emergence of the Catholic Tradition (100–600)*. Chicago: University of Chicago, 1971.

Person, Raymond F., Jr. *The Deuteronomic School: History, Social Setting, and Literature*. Atlanta: Society of Biblical Literature, 2002.

Petersen, David L. "Defining Prophecy and Prophetic Literature." In *Prophecy in Its Ancient Near Eastern Context: Mesopotamian, Biblical and Arabian Perspectives*, edited by Martti Nissinen, 33–44. SBL Symposium 13. Atlanta: Society of Biblical Literature, 2000.

Polliack, Meira. "Medieval Karaism." In *The Oxford Handbook of Jewish Studies*, edited by Martin Goodman et al., 295–326. Oxford: Oxford University Press, 2002.

Pope, Marvin H. *Job*. AB. Garden City, NY: Doubleday, 1973.

——. *Song of Songs*. AB 7C. Garden City, NY: Doubleday, 1977.

Pressler, Carolyn. *The View of Women Found in the Deuteronomic Family Laws*. BZAW 216. Berlin: de Gruyter, 1993.

Pritchard, James B., ed. *Ancient Near Eastern Texts Relating to the Old Testament*. 3rd ed. with supp. Princeton, NJ: Princeton University Press, 1969.

Provan, Iaian, V. Philips Long, and Tremper Longman III. *A Biblical History of Israel*. Louisville, KY: Westminster John Knox, 2003.

Ramsey, George W. "Zadok." *ABD*, 6.1035–36.

Redford, Donald B. *Egypt, Canaan, and Israel in Ancient Times*. Princeton, NJ: Princeton University Press, 1992.

Rendsburg, Gary A. *Linguistic Evidence for the Northern Origin of Selected Psalms*. SBLMS 43. Atlanta: Scholars, 1990.

Roest, Bert, and Herman Vanstiphout, eds. *Aspects of Genre and Type in Pre-Modern Literary Cultures*. Groningen: Styx, 1999.

Rofé, Alexander. "The Piety of the Torah-Disciples at the Winding-Up of the Hebrew Bible: Josh. 1:8; Ps 1:2; Isa. 59:21." In *Bibel in jüdischer und christlicher Tradition: Festschrift für Johann Maier zum 60. Geburtstag*, edited by Helmut Merklein et al., 78–85. Frankfurt am Main: Anton Hain, 1993.

———. *The Prophetical Stories: The Narratives about the Prophets in the Hebrew Bible; Their Literary Types and History*. Jerusalem: Magnes, 1988.

Rosenblatt, Jason P., and Joseph C. Sitterson, Jr., eds. *"Not in Heaven": Coherence and Complexity in Biblical Narrative*. Bloomington: University of Indiana Press, 1991.

Roth, Martha T. *Law Collections from Mesopotamia and Asia Minor*. SBL Writings from the Ancient World Series. Atlanta: Scholars, 1995.

Rowe, John Carlos. "Structure." In *Critical Terms for Literary Study*, edited by Frank Lentricchia and Thomas McLaughlin, 23–38. Chicago: University of Chicago Press, 1990.

Saebø, M. "Zechariah, Book of." *Dictionary of Biblical Interpretation*, edited by John H. Hayes, 666–69. Nashville, TN: Abingdon, 1999.

Sanders, Thomas E. *The Discovery of Poetry*. Atlanta: Scott, Foresman and Company, 1967.

Sarna, Nahum M. "Ancient Libraries and the Ordering of the Biblical Books." In his *Studies in Biblical Interpretation*, 53–66. Philadelphia: Jewish Publication Society, 2000.

——. "Epic Substratum in the Prose of Job." In his *Studies in Biblical Interpretation*, 411–24. Philadelphia: Jewish Publication Society, 2000.

——. *The JPS Torah Commentary: Exodus*. Philadelphia: Jewish Publication Society, 1991.

——. *Songs of the Heart: An Introduction to the Book of Psalms*. New York: Schocken, 1993.

Sawyer, John F. A. "Isaiah, Book of." In *Dictionary of Biblical Interpretation*, edited by John H. Hayes, 552–54. Nashville, TN: Abingdon, 1999.

——. *Prophecy and the Prophets of the Old Testament*. Oxford Bible Series. Oxford: Oxford University Press, 1987.

Schechter, Solomon. *Seminary Addresses and Other Papers*. Cincinnati, OH: Ark Publishing Co., 1915.

Schökel, Luis Alonso. *A Manual of Hebrew Poetics*. Rome: Pontificio Istituto Biblico, 1988.

Schwartz, Baruch J. "What Really Happened at Mount Sinai? Four Biblical Answers to One Question." *Bible Review* 13:5 (1997): 20–30, 46.

Scott, R. B. Y. "Folk Proverbs of the Ancient Near East." In *Studies in Ancient Israelite Wisdom*, edited by James L. Crenshaw, 417–26. New York: Ktav, 1976.

——. "Wise and Foolish, Righteous and Wicked." *VT* 29 (1972): 145–65.

Seitz, Christopher R. "Trito-Isaiah." *ABD*, 3.501–7.

——. *Zion's Final Destiny: The Development of the Book of Isaiah: A Reassessment of the Isaiah 36–39*. Minneapolis, MN: Fortress, 1991.

Seybold, Klaus. *Introducing the Psalms*. Translated by R. Graeme Dunphy. Edinburgh: T & T Clark, 1990.

Shanks, Hershel, ed. *The Rise of Ancient Israel*. Washington, DC: Biblical Archaeological Society, 1992.

Shaver, Judson R. *Torah and the Chronicler's History Work: An Inquiry into the Chronicler's References to Laws, Festivals, and Cultic Institutions in Relationship to Pentateuchal Legislation*. BJS 196. Atlanta: Scholars, 1989.

Silberman, Lou H. "Wellhausen and Judaism." *Semeia* 25 (1982): 75–82.

Smith, J. Payne. *A Compendious Syriac Dictionary Founded Upon the Thesaurus Syriacus of R. Payne Smith, D.D.* Oxford: Clarendon Press, 1976.

Smith, Morton. "The Common Theology of the Ancient Near East." *JBL* 71 (1952): 135–47.

Snell, Daniel C. *Twice-Told Proverbs and the Composition of the Book of Proverbs*. Winona Lake, IN: Eisenbrauns, 1993.

Sommer, Benjamin D. "Did Prophecy Cease? Evaluating a Reevaluation." *JBL* 115 (1996): 31–47.

——. *A Prophet Reads Scripture: Allusion in Isaiah 40–66*. Stanford, CA: Stanford University Press, 1998.

Speiser, E. A. *Genesis*. AB. Garden City, NY: Doubleday, 1964.

Spiegel, Shalom. "Amos vs. Amaziah." In *The Jewish Expression*, edited by Judah Goldin, 38–65. New Haven, CT: Yale University Press, 1976.

Spinoza, Baruch. *Tractatus Theologico-Politicus*. Translated by Samuel Shirley. Leiden: Brill, 1991.

Spronk, Klaas. *Beatific Afterlife in Ancient Israel and in the Ancient Near East*. AOAT 219. Kevelaer: Butzon & Bercker, 1986.

Stamm, Johann Jakob and Maurice Edward Andrew. *The Ten Commandments in Recent Research*. SBT^2 2. Naperville, IL: Allenson, 1967.

Stein, David E. S. Preface to *JPS Hebrew-English Tanakh*, ix–xix. Philadelphia: Jewish Publication Society, 1999.

Stendahl, Krister. "Biblical Theology: A Program." In his *Meanings: The Bible as Document and as Guide*, 11–44. Philadelphia: Fortress, 1984.

Stevenson, Kalinda Rose. *The Vision of Transformation: The Territorial Rhetoric of Ezekiel 40–48*. SBLDS 154. Atlanta: Scholars, 1996.

Stuhlman, Louis. *The Prose Sermons of the Book of Jeremiah: A Redescription of the Correspondences with the Deuteronomistic Literature in the Light of Recent Text-critical Research*. SBLDS 83. Atlanta: Scholars, 1986.

Swete, Henry Barclay. *An Introduction to the Old Testament in Greek*. Cambridge: Cambridge University Press, 1902.

Thackery, H. St. J., trans. *Josephus I: The Life; Against Apion*. Loeb Classical Library. Cambridge, MA: Harvard University Press, 1926.

———., trans. *Josephus IV: Jewish Antiquities Books I–IV*. Loeb Classical Library. Cambridge, MA: Harvard University Press, 1930.

Thiele, Edwin R. *The Mysterious Numbers of the Hebrew Kings*. Grand Rapids, MI: Zondervan, 1983.

Thompson, Thomas L. *The Historicity of the Patriarchal Narratives: The Quest for the Historical Abraham*. BZAW 133. Berlin: de Gruyter, 1974.

Tigay, Jeffrey H. *Deuteronomy*. JPS Torah Commentary. Philadelphia: Jewish Publication Society, 1996.

——. *The Evolution of the Gilgamesh Epic*. Philadelphia: University of Pennsylvania Press, 1982.

Tov, Emanuel. *Textual Criticism of the Hebrew Bible*. 2nd rev. ed. Minneapolis, MN: Fortress, 2001.

Trible, Phyllis. *God and the Rhetoric of Sexuality*. Philadelphia: Fortress, 1978.

Tsevat, Matitiahu. "The Meaning of the Book of Job." In his *The Meaning of the Book of Job and Other Biblical Studies: Essays on the Literature and Religion of the Hebrew Bible*, 1–37. New York: Ktav, 1980.

Tuell, Steven Shawn. *The Law of the Temple in Ezekiel 40–48*. HSM 49. Atlanta: Scholars, 1992.

Uehlinger, C. "Leviathan." *DDD*, 511–15. Leiden: Brill, 1999.

Ulrich, Eugene. *The Dead Sea Scrolls and the Origins of the Bible*. Grand Rapids, MI: Eerdmans, 1999.

——. "The Non-Attestation of a Tripartite Canon in 4QMMT." *CBQ* 65 (2003): 202–14.

——. "Septuagint." In *Encyclopedia of the Dead Sea Scrolls*, edited by Lawrence H. Schiffman and James C. VanderKam, 2.863–68. New York: Oxford University Press, 2000.

Ussishkin, David. *The Conquest of Lachish by Sennacherib*. Tel Aviv: Tel Aviv University, The Institute of Archaeology, 1982.

VanderKam, James C. *The Dead Sea Scrolls Today*. Grand Rapids, MI: Eerdmanns, 1994.

van Dyk, P. J. "The Function of So-Called Etiological Elements in Narratives." *ZAW* 102 (1990): 19–33.

van Seters, John. *Abraham in History and Tradition*. New Haven, CT: Yale University Press, 1975.

——. *A Law Book for the Diaspora: Revision in the Study of the Covenant Code*. New York: Oxford, 2003.

——. *Prologue to History: The Yahwist as Historian in Genesis*. Louisville, KY: Westminster/John Knox, 1992.

Vermes, Geza. *The Complete Dead Sea Scrolls*. Harmondsworth, UK: Penguin, 1997.

von Rad, Gerhard. *Genesis*. OTL. Philadelphia: Westminster, 1972.

Wegner, Judith Romney. *Chattel or Person? The Status of Women in the Mishnah*. New York: Oxford University Press, 1988.

Weinfeld, Moshe. *Deuteronomy and the Deuteronomic School*. Oxford: Clarendon, 1972.

——. "The Uniqueness of the Decalogue and its Place in Jewish Tradition." In *The Ten Commandments in History and Tradition*, edited by Ben-Zion Segal, 6–8. Jerusalem: Magnes, 1990.

Weiss, Meir. "The Decalogue in Prophetic Literature." In *The Ten Commandments in History and Tradition*, 67–81.

——. "The Origin of the 'Day of the Lord'—Reconsidered." *HUCA* 37 (1966): 29–60.

——. *The Story of Job's Beginning: A Literary Analysis*. Jerusalem: Magnes Press, 1983.

Wellhausen, Julius. *Prolegomena to the History of Ancient Israel*. Gloucester, MA: Peter Smith, 1973.

Westermann, Claus. *Basic Forms of Prophetic Speech*. Translated by H. C. White. Louisville, KY: Westminster/John Knox, 1991.

——. *Genesis 1–11*. Minneapolis, MN: Augsburg, 1984.

——. *Praise and Lament in the Psalms*. Translated by Keith R. Crim and Richard N. Soulen. Atlanta: John Knox, 1981.

White Crawford, Sidnie. "Esther, Book of." In *Encyclopedia of the Dead Sea Scrolls*, edited by Schiffman and VanderKam, 269–70. New York: Oxford University Press, 2000.

Whitelam, Keith W. *The Invention of Ancient Israel: The Silencing of Palestinian History*. London: Routledge, 1996.

——. *The Just King: Monarchical and Judicial Authority in Ancient Israel*. JSOTSup 12. Sheffield, UK: JSOT Press, 1979.

Whybray, R. N. "The Identification and Use of Quotations in Ecclesiastes." *SVT* 32 (1981): 435–51.

——. *The Intellectual Tradition in the Old Testament*. BZAW 135. Berlin: de Gruyter, 1974.

——. "Qoheleth, Preacher of Joy." *JSOT* 23 (1982): 87–98.

Williams, James G. "The Power of Form: A Study of Biblical Proverbs." *Semeia* 17 (1980): 35–58.

——. *Those Who Ponder Proverbs: Aphoristic Thinking and Biblical Literature*. Sheffield, UK: Almond Press, 1981.

Williamson, H. G. M. *The Book Called Isaiah: Deutero-Isaiah's Role in Composition and Redaction*. Oxford: Clarendon, 1994.

Wills, Lawrence M. *The Jew in the Foreign Court*. HDR 26. Minneapolis, MN: Fortress, 1990.

Wilson, Gerald Henry. *The Editing of the Hebrew Psalter*. SBLDS 76. Chico, CA: Scholars, 1985.

Wilson, Robert R. *Genealogy and History in the Biblical World*. YNER 7. New Haven, CT: Yale University Press, 1977.

——. "Genealogy, Genealogies." *ABD*, 2.929–32.

——. *Prophecy and Society in Ancient Israel*. Philadelphia: Fortress, 1980.

Williamson, H.G.M. *Israel in the Books of Chronicles*. Cambridge: Cambridge University Press, 1977.

Wolff, Hans Walter. *Joel and Amos*. Translated by W. Janzen et al. Hermeneia. Philadelphia: Fortress, 1977.

Wright, Christopher J. H. "Jubilee, Year of." *ABD*, 3.1027–28.

Wright, David P. "The Laws of Hammurabi as a Source for the Covenant Collection (Exodus 20:23–23:19)." *Maarav* 10 (2003): 11–87.

——. *Ritual in Narrative: The Dynamics of Fasting, Mourning, and Retaliation Rites in the Ugaritic Tale of Aqhat*. Winona Lake, IN: Eisenbrauns, 2001.

Yeivin, Israel. *Introduction to the Tiberian Masorah*. Translated by E. J. Revell. Masoretic Studies 5. Missoula, MT: Scholars, 1980.

Zevit, Ziony. "A Chapter in the History of Israelite Personal Names." *BASOR* 250 (1983): 1–16.

Zimmerli, Walther. *Ezekiel 1*. Hermeneia. Philadelphia: Fortress, 1979.

——. "Knowledge of God According to the Book of Ezekiel." In his *I Am Yahweh*, 29–98. Translated by Douglas W. Stott. Atlanta: John Knox, 1982.

Index of Subjects

Index of Biblical Passages and Other References